JUDAISM AND ENLIGHTENMENT

This study investigates the philosophical and political significance of Judaism in the intellectual life of seventeenth- and eighteenth-century Europe. Adam Sutcliffe shows how the widespread and enthusiastic fascination with Judaism prevalent around 1650 was largely eclipsed a century later by attitudes of dismissal and disdain. He argues that Judaism was uniquely difficult for Enlightenment thinkers to account for, and that their intense responses, both negative and positive, to Jewish topics are central to an understanding of the underlying ambiguities of the Enlightenment itself. Judaism and the Jews were a limit case, a destabilising challenge and a constant test for Enlightenment rationalism. Erudite and highly broad-ranging in its sources, and yet extremely accessible in its argument, *Judaism and Enlightenment* is a major contribution to the history of European ideas, of interest to scholars of Jewish history and to those working on the Enlightenment, toleration and the emergence of modernity itself.

ADAM SUTCLIFFE is Assistant Professor of European Jewish History at the University of Illinois at Urbana-Champaign. This is his first book.

D1557079

IDEAS IN CONTEXT

Edited by Quentin Skinner (*General Editor*) Lorraine Daston,
Dorothy Ross and James Tully

The books in this series will discuss the emergence of intellectual traditions and of related new disciplines. The procedures, aims and vocabularies that were generated will be set in the context of the alternatives available within the contemporary frameworks of ideas and institutions. Through detailed studies of the evolution of such traditions, and their modification by different audiences, it is hoped that a new picture will form of the development of ideas in their concrete contexts. By this means, artificial distinctions between the history of philosophy, of the various sciences, of society and politics, and of literature may be seen to dissolve.
The series is published with the support of the Exxon Foundation.

A list of books in the series will be found at the end of the volume.

JUDAISM AND ENLIGHTENMENT

ADAM SUTCLIFFE

University of Illinois at Urbana-Champaign

CAMBRIDGE
UNIVERSITY PRESS

CAMBRIDGE UNIVERSITY PRESS
Cambridge, New York, Melbourne, Madrid, Cape Town, Singapore,
São Paulo, Delhi, Dubai, Tokyo, Mexico City

Cambridge University Press
The Edinburgh Building, Cambridge CB2 8RU, UK

Published in the United States of America by Cambridge University Press, New York

www.cambridge.org
Information on this title: www.cambridge.org/9780521672320

First published 2003
Reprinted 2004

A catalogue record for this publication is available from the British Library

ISBN 978-0-521-82015-8 Hardback
ISBN 978-0-521-67232-0 Paperback

Contents

List of contents

Illustrations

Acknowledgements

When I embarked on this project more than seven years ago as a graduate student in London my attitudes towards the academic world were, on bad days, highly ambivalent. I remember often reading fulsome academic acknowledgements with extreme scepticism: their paeans to cooperation and scholarly generosity did not seem to match the chilly isolation I at first experienced in the old North Library at the British Museum. This early cynicism has since given way to a sense of delight in the interactivity and mutual aid that characterises the university world at its best. In completing this study I have benefited from the help, advice, criticism, inspiration, encouragement and support of a vast number of people, including many students, librarians, colleagues and friends who I will not be able personally to thank here.

My greatest scholarly debt of gratitude is to Jonathan Israel, who supervised the Ph.D. thesis (University College London, 1998) on which this book is based. His immense erudition guided me swiftly to a huge range of relevant primary and secondary material, and his own extremely high standards of rigour and breadth inspired me to stretch myself linguistically and intellectually in ways I had not imagined when starting my research. Other colleagues and friends in London, particularly Karen Adler, Brenda Assael, Gareth Bish, Stephen Conway, Hera Cook, Penny Corfield, Cathy Crawford, Luke Davidson, Rebecca Flemming, Anne Goldgar, Valerie Mainz, Roger Mettam, Jonathan Price, Robert Rabinowitz, Tessa Rajak, Ada Rapaport-Albert, David Solomon and Rebecca Spang, have helped and supported me immeasurably, both during my graduate student days and since.

For their hospitality in the Netherlands I would like to thank Wiep van Bunge, Wanya Kruyer and Lo Woudstra; in France, Barbara and Jean Marguin; and in Italy, Renata Pozzo. I would also like to thank the many librarians who have assisted me, and the many conference and seminar participants who responded thoughtfully to presentations of my research. I was

extremely fortunate to spend the academic year 1998–9 as a research fellow
of the Center for Judaic Studies at the University of Pennsylvania. I am immensely grateful to the director of the Center, David Ruderman, for making
this possible, and for his hospitality and support throughout the year. The
staff of the Center, my fellow fellows there, and many other friends from
within and without the Penn community made this year an intellectually
formative one for me. I would particularly like to thank Esperanza Alfonso,
Sheila Allen, Allan Arkush, Aviva Astrinsky, Ross Brann, Richard Cohen,
Roslyn Don, Alessandro Guetta, Margaret Jacob, Jonathan Karp, Arthur
Kiron, Alyssa Sepinwall, Adam Shear, Jonathan Skolnik, Katya Tenenbaum,
Liliane Weissberg, Beth Wenger and David Zeeman.

I am extremely grateful to many colleagues and friends at the University
of Illinois at Urbana-Champaign, where I have taught since 1999. The
excellent library resources of the University of Illinois, and its vibrant
and eclectic intellectual community, have made it an excellent institution at which to finish this book. I would particularly like to thank
Matti Bunzl, Clare Crowston, Dara Goldman, Stephen Hartnett, Brett
Kaplan, Suvir Kaul, Craig Koslofsky, Lisa Lampert, Harry Liebersohn, Ania
Loomba, Martin Manalansan, Gary Porton, Michael Shapiro, Larry Schehr
and Billy Vaughn. For their support from elsewhere in North America I
would also like to thank David Churchill, Dick Popkin and Danny
Postel.

I have been financially supported by a Scouloudi research fellowship
at the Institute of Historical Research of the University of London, in
1997–8; a grant for Huguenot research from the Trustees of the French
Protestant Church in London; a travel grant from the Friends of University
College London; a semester of teaching release funded by the Campus
Research Board of the University of Illinois at Urbana-Champaign; and
by the research funds of the Program for the Study of Jewish Culture and
Society at the University of Illinois. I would like to thank all the donors
and trustees of these funds, and also the Koret Foundation of San Francisco
for supporting the publication of this volume.

An earlier version of chapter 6, 'Judaism in Spinoza and his Circle',
has previously been published in *Studia Rosenthaliana* 34 (2000) 7–22.
An extended version of chapter 7 has been published as 'The spirit of
Spinoza and the Enlightenment image of the pure philosopher', in Geoffrey
Cubitt and Allen Warren, eds., *Heroic Reputations and Exemplary Lives*
(Manchester, Manchester University Press, 2000, 40–56). I would like to
thank these publishers for their permission to re-use this material, and also

Richard Fisher and the staff of Cambridge University Press for their work in preparing this volume for publication.

A very special gratitude is owed to my family: my brother, William, and above all my parents, Sue and John, who have unstintingly supported me in every way possible. My final and greatest thanks are to them.

Abbreviations

BL MS   British Library, Department of Manuscripts
BMBGN   *Bijdragen en Mededelingen Betreffende de Geschiedenis der Nederlanden*
BN FF   Bibliothèque Nationale, Paris, Fonds Français
BN NAF   Bibliothèque Nationale, Paris, Nouvelle Acquisitions Françaises
BUH   *Bibliothèque Universelle et Historique* (1686–1718)
HOS   *Histoire des Ouvrages des Savans* (1687–1709)
HS Ros.   Bibliotheca Rosenthaliana, Amsterdam, Manuscripts Collection
JHI   *Journal of the History of Ideas*
LIAS   *LIAS: Sources and Documents relating to the Early Modern History of Ideas*
MS Aix   Bibliothèque Méjanes, Aix-en-Provence, Manuscripts Collection
MS Ars.   Bibiliothèque de l'Arsenal, Paris, Manuscripts Collection
MS Clark   William Andrews Clark Memorial Library, University of California, Los Angeles, Manuscripts Collection
MS Maz.   Bibliothèque Mazarine, Paris, Manuscripts Collection
NRL   *Nouvelles de la République des Lettres* (1684–9)
SVEC   *Studies in Voltaire and the Eighteenth Century*
TTP   Benedict de Spinoza, *Tractatus Theologico-Politicus* (1670), trans. R. H. M. Elwes, *A Theologico-Political Treatise*, New York, Dover Publications, 1951

Most primary texts have been consulted and cited in their original language, wherever possible from first editions. However, in some cases I have used reliable translations into English or other major European languages, both contemporary and modern. Apart from the correction of clear typographical errors and some potentially confusing idiosyncrasies, spelling and capitalisation of all quotations have been left as in the original, and all emphases – whether in the form of italicisation, capitalisation, underlining or bold print – are also from the original sources.

Introduction: disentangling Judaism and Enlightenment

The legacy of the Enlightenment remains deeply mired in political and philosophical controversy. The core Enlightenment values of freedom, toleration and the paramountcy of reason are now securely enshrined as the guiding principles of modern liberal democracy, but this has not produced the transparent, virtuous, ordered and contented society that the *philosophes* of the eighteenth century optimistically envisaged. Is this because we need more Enlightenment, or have we already had a good deal too much? Postmodern critics of the alleged instrumentalism and naivety of Enlightenment reason, such as Jean-François Lyotard, Jacques Derrida and Richard Rorty, have been vigorously and prominently engaged by Jürgen Habermas, for whom there can be no viable alternative to a sustained commitment to the 'Enlightenment project', and to its central vision of the establishment of undistorted communication.[1] Despite the highly historical nature of the questions at stake, the detailed contours of eighteenth-century European thought have been surprisingly little explored in this debate.[2] In order to evaluate the fate of the Enlightenment, however, it is surely vital to understand the context and the contingencies of its emergence.

The history of European Jewry since 1789 sharply highlights the ambiguities of modernity. In the most obvious sense, Jews were seemingly the most dramatic beneficiaries of the Enlightenment. In 1790 and 1791, after much debate, the revolutionaries of the French First Republic swept away the various legal, economic and bureaucratic restrictions that had regulated Jewish life for centuries, initiating the faltering process of Jewish emancipation that was soon exported across Europe by Napoleon.[3] The arguments of those

---

[1] See Jürgen Habermas, *The Philosophical Discourse of Modernity* (1987) esp. 336–67; Józef Niżnik and John T. Sanders, eds., *Debating the State of Philosophy: Habermas, Rorty and Kolakowski* (1996); N. J. Rengger, *Political Theory, Modernity and Postmodernity* (1995) 1–11; John Gray, *Enlightenment's Wake* (1995) 144–84.

[2] For a recent corrective see Daniel Gordon, ed., *Postmodernism and the Enlightenment* (2001).

[3] Arthur Hertzberg, *The French Enlightenment and the Jews* (1968) 314–68; Simon Schwarzfuchs, *Napoleon, the Jews and the Sanhedrin* (1979).

I

who pressed most eagerly for the integration of the Jews into the social and political mainstream were suffused with the language of Enlightenment rationalism and improvement: we need only observe the title of Christian Wilhelm Dohm's highly influential 1781 essay, *On the Civic Improvement of the Jews*, or that of the prize essay title set by the Royal Society of Metz in 1785, won by Henri Grégoire, the leading advocate of the emancipation of the Jews of eastern France – 'How to Make the Jews Happy and Useful'.[4] However, this enthusiastically integrationist attitude was not in every way ameliorative. The denial of the distinctiveness of Jewish identity and community life meant the end of the considerable legal and fiscal autonomy typically enjoyed by Jewish communities in the early modern period. It also fixed Jewish difference as a problem. Jews were now to be accorded respect as citizens, but not necessarily as Jews. Despite the energetic attempts of many nineteenth-century western European Jews, particularly the most successful and prosperous, to assimilate into mainstream, secular society, Jewish difference became an increasingly intense popular preoccupation, leading to the emergence of antisemitism as an explicit political creed in late nineteenth-century Germany.[5]

The eager and intense rush of droves of German Jews from ghetto traditionalism to flourishing prominence in the secular high culture of the *Bildungsbürgertum* was one of the most visible social transformations that accompanied the dawn of the modern age. There was never, however, a comfortable 'German-Jewish symbiosis': German-Jewish identity was inescapably bifurcated, its two components always eluding easy reconciliation.[6] Modernity, and its universalist ideals, enticed Jews in particular; but these same ideals persistently destabilised the significance, and for some even the legitimacy, of Jewishness itself. There was clearly no inexorable highway from the tensions of post-Enlightenment modernity to the genocide of Auschwitz and elsewhere. However, as Zygmunt Bauman has argued, while the Holocaust was in many ways a product of the political, social and technological structures of the modern state, it simultaneously also stands as an extreme anti-modernist assault on the disorienting complexities of modernity, which seemed to crystallise in the cultural indefinability

---

[4] See Robert Liberles, 'From Toleration to *Verbesserung*: German and English Debates on the Jews in the Eighteenth Century', *Central European History* 21:1 (1989) 1–31; David Sorkin, *The Transformation of German Jewry 1780–1840* (1999 (1987)) 23–30; Jacob Katz, *Out of the Ghetto: The Social Background of Jewish Emancipation, 1770–1870* (1973) 57–79.

[5] See Peter Pulzer, *The Rise of Political Anti-Semitism in Germany and Austria* (1988) esp. 47–57.

[6] Paul Mendes-Flohr, *German Jews: A Dual Identity* (1999) esp. 1–24; *Divided Passions: Jewish Intellectuals and the Experience of Modernity* (1991); Gershom Scholem, *On Jews and Judaism in Crisis* (1976) 61–92; George Mosse, *German Jews Beyond Judaism* (1985) esp. 1–20.

of the Jews.[7] The precariousness of the Jewish position in European society of course long predates the eighteenth century. Nonetheless, the struggles, dilemmas and overarching tragedy of the modern European Jewish experience cannot be understood without an awareness of the Enlightenment paradoxes and contradictions that essentially defined the parameters of the barbed embrace of Jewishness and modernity.

Theodor Adorno and Max Horkheimer's seminal *Dialectic of Enlightenment*, written in 1944 in exile from Nazi Germany, bleakly but brilliantly recognised the fraught relationship of eighteenth-century idealism to the authoritarianism of the fascist era. Enlightenment reason, they argued, had become self-destructive: having crushed the remnants of myth, uncertainty and individuality that are essential to the human spirit, it had become an instrument of economic domination and cultural deception, from which the mass delusion of antisemitism served as a convenient decoy.[8] 'Wholly enlightened man', they wrote, 'has lost himself.'[9] Antagonism towards Jews, they realised, was not simply a random outlet for this alienation. The mythic power of Judaism itself attracted ire, because it exposed the limits of Enlightenment rationalism:

The Jews seemed to have succeeded where Christianity failed: they diffused magic by its own power – turned against itself as ritual in the service of God...And so they are thought to lag behind advanced civilization and yet to be too far ahead of it: they are both clever and stupid, similar and dissimilar. They are declared guilty of something that they were the first to overcome: the lure of base instincts, reversion to animality and to the ground, the service of images.[10]

Whereas the Enlightenment sought to eliminate all dependency on myth, Judaism most anciently and thoroughly incorporated mythic structures into its cultural codes of meaning and identity. Its endurance therefore frustrated the aspiration of Enlightenment thought towards absolute rationalist mastery. Elemental desires, forbidden within the logic of Enlightenment, are sublimated into a jealous hostility towards Jews: 'There is no antisemite who does not basically want to imitate his mental image of a Jew.'[11]

Adorno and Horkheimer's Enlightenment is only loosely articulated with the historical Enlightenment of eighteenth-century Europe. They essentially conflated Enlightenment with the exploitative instrumentalism of capitalism, which they detected incipiently even in the individualistic cunning of Homer's Odysseus. Judaism, they argued, was not structurally

---

[7] Zygmunt Bauman, *Modernity and the Holocaust* (1989) esp. 6–12, 39–46.
[8] Theodor Adorno and Max Horkheimer, *Dialectic of Enlightenment* (1989 (1944)) esp. 173–6.
[9] *Ibid.*, 38.   [10] *Ibid.*, 186.   [11] *Ibid.*, 184.

indispensable as the foil of Enlightenment: it could readily be substituted, just as capitalism itself was able to shuffle its units of rationalised production according to expediency.[12] Adorno and Horkheimer's reluctance to place too much weight on the specific significance of Judaism in modern European thought was due not only to their Marxism, but also to the cultural ambivalences inherent in their own position as militantly secular and assimilated German Jews. However, an understanding of the tragic predicament of this final generation of German-Jewish intellectuals itself requires a more sustained examination of the specific entanglement of Jewishness and Enlightenment rationalism.[13]

The Enlightenment was, of course, a diverse and eclectic intellectual movement, incorporating the celebration of passion and sensibility as well as of reason.[14] Much postmodern criticism has underestimated or ignored this complexity, caricaturing the Enlightenment as falsely monolithic and relentlessly absolutist.[15] However, Adorno and Horkheimer's negative dialectic of disillusionment must be balanced against its positive twin, with which they conclude their text, and which has since been forcefully emphasised by Habermas: rational thought contains within itself the possibility of overcoming its own limitations.[16] It is meaningless to place the Enlightenment monolithically in the dock. Not only is modern thought so suffused with Enlightenment concepts that such a trial would entail an unsustainable degree of intellectual schizophrenia, but the wider historical impact of the Enlightenment – as the Jewish experience so powerfully demonstrates – has been profoundly double-edged.

However, precisely because of its complexity and its inescapability, the Enlightenment, and its internal tensions and lacunae, remain of supreme importance. Many of the ideas and modes of thought that crystallised in this period have since been largely absorbed into the realm of the semi-invisible, unchallenged assumptions of the modern age. The history of the early articulation of these ideals of rationality, toleration and independence

---

[12] *Ibid.*, 43–80, 207. See also Ronald Schechter, 'Rationalizing the Enlightenment: Postmodernism and Theories of Anti-Semitism', in Gordon, ed., *Postmodernism and the Enlightenment*, 95–7.

[13] See Martin Jay, *The Dialectical Imagination* (1973) esp. 31–5; John Murray Cuddihy, *The Ordeal of Civility: Freud, Marx, Lévi-Strauss and the Jewish Struggle with Modernity* (1987) esp. 153–4; Mosse, *German Jews*, 61–2.

[14] See Susan James, *Passion and Action: The Emotions in Seventeenth-Century Philosophy* (1997); Mark S. Micale and Robert L. Dietle, eds., *Enlightenment, Passion, Modernity* (2000); David Marshall, *The Surprising Effects of Sympathy: Marivaux, Diderot, Rousseau and Mary Shelley* (1988); Schechter, 'Rationalizing the Enlightenment', 110–13.

[15] See Daniel Gordon, 'On the Supposed Obsolescence of the French Enlightenment', *Postmodernism*, 201–21.

[16] Adorno and Horkheimer, *Dialectic*, 208; Habermas, *Philosophical Discourse*, 84–6.

of thought challenges the transparency of these concepts, and in so doing offers vital insights into the internal structure and defining birthmarks of notions on which an immense political and philosophical burden is now freighted.

The charting of these new philosophical parameters was a tortuous and troubled process. As Ernst Cassirer long ago noted, the Enlightenment, despite its prevalent secularism, was inevitably profoundly indebted to religious thought: 'The more insufficient one finds previous religious answers to basic questions of knowledge and morality, the more intensive and passionate become these questions themselves.'[17] In defining their ideas around and against those of traditional Christianity, the pioneers of the Enlightenment continued to work within a frame of reference that was largely conditioned by theological orthodoxies. Judaism, seen as not only the most venerably orthodox but also as the most inscrutable and most potentially subversive strand of theology, was uniquely difficult for Enlightenment thinkers to negotiate. Their awkward and contradictory articulations of the relationship between Judaism and Reason bring into sharp relief the problematics of Enlightenment highlighted by Adorno and Horkheimer, and enable us to situate these tensions within the historical context that conditioned their emergence.

Throughout the Enlightenment the question of the status of Judaism and of Jews was a key site of intellectual contestation, confusion and debate. Because of the centrality of the Jewish scriptures, adopted in the form of the Old Testament as the foundational document on which the claims to legitimacy of Christianity were based, Judaism was the most obvious target for those who sought to attack the Judaeo-Christian tradition at its roots. In much Enlightenment thought, the vital conceptual space of that which is most deeply antithetical to reason – Enlightenment's defining 'Other' – was occupied above all by the Jew. Rational inquiry opposed Jewish legalism; belief in progress opposed Jewish traditionalism; the scholarly, urbane, cosmopolitan citizen of the Republic of Letters opposed the petty-minded, mumbling ghetto rabbi. But these easy oppositions hovered above much more difficult and threatening imponderables. In exposing the Old Testament as both thoroughly implausible and extremely unedifying as a historical account, Enlightenment critics also faced their inability to offer any conclusive alternative to the Judaic account of the roots of European society. While attacking the tribalism and insularity of Jewish nationhood, the eighteenth century was also a period in which conscious attempts were

---

[17] Ernst Cassirer, *The Philosophy of the Enlightenment* (1951 (1932)) 136.

made to construct loosely equivalent myths and rituals of national pa-triotisms; these identities were inevitably based on national divisions which the transnational Jews awkwardly blurred. Most fundamentally, the Enlightenment vision of universal tolerance and emancipation stood un-easily alongside the identification of Judaism as so atavistically contrary to all emancipatory values and modes of thought.

Judaism was thus profoundly ensnared in the relationship between the Enlightenment and the Christian worldview from and against which it emerged. It is a key argument of this study that the significance of Judaism during the Enlightenment can only be understood in the context of this relationship, and, concomitantly, that the complexities clustered around Judaism are of central importance for a general understanding of the Enlightenment itself. The inevitable inconclusiveness of attempts to recon-ceptualise history, ethics and politics in purely rational and transparent terms was highlighted above all by the persistent anomaly of the Jewish case. The shifts and ambiguities of Enlightenment thought concerning Judaism crucially influenced the shape of Jewish political emancipation, and have undergirded the vicissitudes, triumphs and tragedies of European Jewish life ever since.

The significance of these ambiguities, however, resonate beyond the Jewish case. The limits of Enlightenment are today challenged and strained by all perspectives that question the transcendental authority of techno-cratic rationalism. While the tensions between Judaism and Enlightenment were, as I hope this study will demonstrate, uniquely intense and histori-cally significant, they are closely related to the more general problematics of the relationship of Enlightenment rationality to whatever it cannot readily encompass. The legacy of the Enlightenment is far too omnipresent for any wholesale rejection of its values to be meaningful. However, an aware-ness of its complexity, imperfection and historical contingency can offer an important social and political safeguard against the self-contradictory but seductive pitfalls of Enlightenment fundamentalism.

ANTI-, PHILO- AND ALLOSEMITISMS

Viewed within the broad temporal perspective of Jewish history, the relative civility of the Enlightenment has appeared to some historians as a decep-tive interlude between the religious persecution of the medieval era and the political antisemitism of the nineteenth and twentieth centuries. Arthur Hertzberg, in his *The French Enlightenment and the Jews: The Origins of Modern Anti-Semitism*, unequivocally signals in his subtitle his aspiration to close this apparent historical gap. Although he closely examines the anti-Judaic animus of many of the English Deists and French *philosophes*, the key figure in his narrative is Voltaire, whose notoriously hostile pronouncements on Jews and Judaism repeatedly recur in many of his writings. For Hertzberg, Voltaire is the 'vital link' between medieval and modern antisemitism.[18] Jew-hatred, he argues, was not a deformation of Enlightenment reason, but was deeply ingrained within its spirit, which, in this respect at least, merely coated ancient prejudices with a fresh veneer of secularism.[19]

Scholars of non-Jewish attitudes towards Jews have generally emphasised deep historical continuities in patterns of prejudice and projection. Explanations for these continuities have been rooted in psychology, sociology, anthropology, theology and in hybrids of all these and other causal factors.[20] These multifarious studies have immensely illuminated the multidimensionality and historical persistence of anti-Jewish prejudice. However, synthetic interpretations of this phenomenon stand in inevitable tension with a historical attentiveness to the distinctive nature of anti-Jewish attitudes at different times and places. This problem has been heightened by the question of terminology: should the word 'antisemitism', technically an anachronism when applied to periods prior to the late nineteenth century, be restrictively defined, or avoided altogether, in relation to the premodern era? According to Gavin Langmuir, the chimerical irrationality of European Jew-hatred in the twelfth and thirteenth centuries marks a passage from 'anti-Judaism' to 'antisemitism'. Peter Schäfer, challenging this distinction, has argued that the ancient Egyptian and Greek accusations of Jewish 'misanthropy', although to some extent a response to actual Jewish separatism in certain circumstances, should nonetheless be considered as antisemitic.[21]

---

[18] Hertzberg, *French Enlightenment*, 313.
[19] *Ibid.*, 7. For similar arguments, see Jacob Katz, *From Prejudice to Destruction: Anti-Semitism, 1700–1933* (1980) 27–33; D. Sorkin, 'Jews, the Enlightenment and Religious Toleration: Some Reflections', *Leo Baeck Institute Yearbook* (1992) 3–16.
[20] For essentially psychological interpretations of antisemitism, see Theodor Adorno *et al.*, *The Authoritarian Personality* (1950); Léon Poliakov, *The History of Anti-Semitism*, 4 vols. (1965–85) e.g. vol. III, 91; Jean-Paul Sartre, *Anti-Semite and Jew* (1948) esp. 143ff. For sociological interpretations see Bauman, *Modernity and the Holocaust*, 39–45; Hannah Arendt, *The Burden of Our Time* (1951) 56ff.; and, with a stronger anthropological accent, Hyam Maccoby, *A Pariah People* (1996). On Christian antisemitism see James Parkes, *The Jew and his Neighbour* (1930) esp. 62–81; *The Conflict of the Church and the Synagogue* (1934) esp. 42–45, 81–85; Joshua Trachtenberg, *The Devil and the Jews* (1966); Gavin Langmuir, *History, Religion and Antisemitism* (1990) esp. 295–305; Robert Chazan, *Medieval Stereotypes and Modern Antisemitism* (1997) esp. 125–40; Stephen R. Haynes, *Jews and the Christian Imagination* (1995) esp. 9–24. For a multicausal overview see Robert S. Wistrich, *Antisemitism: The Longest Hatred* (1991); Paul Lawrence Rose, *Revolutionary Antisemitism in Germany from Kant to Wagner* (1990).
[21] Gavin Langmuir, *Toward a Definition of Antisemitism* (1990) 16–17, 311–52; Peter Schäfer, *Judeophobia: Attitudes Toward the Jews in the Ancient World* (1997) 197–211.

While these debates are valuable, the historical extension of the concept of antisemitism is also perilous. The most acute danger of this strategy is that it obscures the embeddedness of 'antisemitic' attitudes within diverse wider structures of thought. The Pauline commitment to a universalist community of faith carries with it an inescapable streak of intolerance towards Jewish difference. This hostility is, however, inextricable from Paul's enunciation of his Christian ethic of inclusive love: it would therefore be extremely simplistic to characterise Paul as antisemitic.[22] A broadly similar knot applies in the case of Enlightenment thinkers such as Voltaire, whose anti-Jewish animus, I argue, was closely woven into the same intellectual structures that energised his political polemics against intolerance, superstition and authoritarianism. The accusation of antisemitism, and the immediate recoil that it induces, short-circuits investigation of the complicated relationship between the violent undercurrents of Voltairean Enlightenment – or Pauline Christianity – and their recuperable, or even indispensable, emancipatory ideals.

Enlightenment attitudes towards Judaism were also far from unremittingly negative. The notion of the Jews as God's chosen people, which inspired intensive Christian study of Jewish texts during the seventeenth century, mutated during the Enlightenment into a widespread fascination with Jewish rituals and themes. Hopes for the economic regeneration of the Jews, which so animated reformists such as Dohm and Grégoire in the 1780s, were inspired not only by disdain for the Jews' current condition but also by a belief in their prodigious economic potential. While rabbinic Judaism was frequently derided, ancient Judaism was commonly believed to encapsulate the essence of the perfect polity. A tradition of 'philosemitism', advanced by some historians in juxtaposition to the more familiar narrative of antisemitism, might appear to offer a suitable rubric for these more positive attitudes.[23] However, use of this category readily leads to the same oversimplifications as its opposite. The same philosophical problems drew many Enlightenment thinkers both to the idealisation and simultaneously to the repudiation of elements of Judaism.

Several scholars have attempted to demarcate between what they have discerned as two distinctly separate traditions of Enlightenment thought concerning Jews: one positive and reformist, the other negative and

---

[22] Daniel Boyarin, *A Radical Jew: Paul and the Politics of Identity* (1994) 136–57.
[23] David Katz, 'The Phenomenon of Philo-Semitism', *Christianity and Judaism* (1992) 327–61; Hilary L. Rubinstein and William D. Rubinstein, *Philosemitism* (1999). For an early use of this term, primarily in relation to seventeenth-century Sweden, see Hans Joachim Schoeps, *Philosemitismus im Barock* (1952).

antisemitic.[24] However, while individuals such as Voltaire might seem relatively easy to categorise, others – most notably Pierre Bayle – evade straightforward classification. In this study I shall eschew the use not only of the terms philo- and antisemitism, but also of any one-dimensional positive-to-negative spectrum along which differing attitudes to Judaism can be ranged. Such schematisation is inappropriate for a period in which the consideration of Judaism took place in very tenuous, if any, relation to encounters with actual Jews. It also cannot encompass the complexity of the issues in which Judaism was ensnared, or the confused ambivalence with which it was widely regarded in the Enlightenment period.

According to Zygmunt Bauman, the overarching characteristic of Western attitudes to Jews is 'allosemitism': the conviction that Jews are in some sense radically different from all others. Allosemitism is fundamentally ambivalent. In the structural logic of Christianity, in medieval society and in the sociological transformations of early modernity, Jews occupied intermediate positions of quintessential incongruity. Never quite fitting into dominant categories, they have persistently stood for 'ambivalence incarnate', and have repeatedly served as lightning conductors for opposition to the intellectual and social complexity highlighted by their existence.[25] This analytical framework accounts for the intricate mix of admiration and repulsion, and of identification and expulsion, that suffuses so much Enlightenment writing on Jewish topics. A similar ambivalence has been identified in very different contexts, such as Ancient Rome, and, despite an effective absence of Jews, modern Japan.[26] The conceptual 'slipperiness' of Jewish difference, while it has been reinforced by the social and economic roles filled by Jews in certain historical contexts, is to some extent the product of the irreducible tension between Judaism and the philosophical drive for integrative tidiness. The Enlightenment negotiation of its ambivalence towards Judaism had its own unique dynamics and consequences. However, it also forms part of the eternal problematic, sustainedly focused on Judaism, of how to situate difference within a philosophical and political totality.

---

[24] Richard H. Popkin, 'Medicine, Racism, Anti-Semitism: A Dimension of Enlightenment Culture', in G. S. Rousseau, ed., *The Languages of Psyche: Mind and Body in Enlightenment Thought* (1990) 413ff.; Miriam Yardeni, *Anti-Jewish Mentalities in Early Modern Europe* (1990) 207; Paul H. Meyer, 'The Attitude of the Enlightenment towards the Jew', *SVEC* 26 (1963) 1161–205; Frank Manuel, *The Broken Staff: Judaism Through Christian Eyes* (1992) 108.

[25] Zygmunt Bauman, 'Allosemitism: Premodern, Modern, Postmodern', in Brian Cheyette and Laura Marcus, eds., *Modernity, Culture and 'the Jew'* (1998) 143–56, esp. 146.

[26] Schäfer, *Judeophobia*, 180–95; David G. Goodman and Masanori Miyazawa, *The Jews in the Japanese Mind* (1995) esp. 220–60.

This conundrum was equally present within Jewish thought. The social and religious boundaries that segregated Jewish from non-Jewish life had been eroding in much of western Europe since the sixteenth century, due to more intensive economic contacts and the influence of prominent 'Court Jews', who increasingly absorbed the values of the non-Jewish elite society they largely inhabited.[27] This led inevitably to the emergence among Jews of a radical questioning of the relationship of Jewish difference to the universalistic scientific and political ideals that were in the ascendant in the non-Jewish world. It is no accident that arguably the single most influential thinker of the Early Enlightenment – Baruch Spinoza – emerged from among the Sephardim of Amsterdam. This small but immensely dynamic community was uniquely caught in the eye of the intellectual storms that accompanied the emergence of modernity. The seventeenth-century Sephardim of north-west Europe, and of Amsterdam above all, deserve to figure far more prominently in the history of the beginnings of the Enlightenment than has generally been acknowledged. Their reincorporation within this wider intellectual history clearly dislocates accounts that see the current between Judaism and the Enlightenment flowing only in one direction.

However, it is nonetheless true that in the eighteenth century Jews essentially responded to the Enlightenment rather than fashioned it. Moses Mendelssohn, the son of a Torah scribe from Dessau, wrestled from the 1750s onwards to reappraise Judaism in accordance with the natural philosophy of Gottfried Leibniz and Christian Wolff.[28] Central and eastern European *maskilim* – proponents of Enlightenment in the Jewish world – soon promoted reforms that ultimately transformed the structures of traditional Jewish life, while Jewish intellectuals in France and England both defended and rethought Judaism in the fast-changing intellectual climate of the late eighteenth century.[29] The implications and consequences of these varying modes of *Haskalah* – Jewish Enlightenment – are of course of immense importance, but they form a later and essentially different story

[27] Jonathan I. Israel, *European Jewry in the Age of Mercantilism* (1989) 41–2, 243–6; Selma Stern, *The Court Jew* (1950): Michael Graetz, 'Court Jews in Economics and Politics', in Vivian B. Mann and Richard I. Cohen, eds., *From Court Jews to the Rothschilds: Art, Patronage and Power 1600–1800* (1996) 27–43; Jacob Katz, *Exclusiveness and Tolerance: Studies in Jewish–Gentile Relations in Medieval and Modern Times* (1961) 156–68.

[28] Allan Arkush, *Moses Mendelssohn and the Enlightenment* (1994) esp. 1–35; David Sorkin, *Moses Mendelssohn and the Religious Enlightenment* (1996) esp. 5–14.

[29] Jacob Katz, *Exclusiveness and Tolerance*, 169–196; *Tradition and Crisis: Jewish Society at the End of the Middle Ages* (2000 (1957)) 214–36; Frances Malino, *A Jew in the French Revolution: The Life of Zalkind Hourwitz* (1996); David B. Ruderman, *Jewish Enlightenment in an English Key: Anglo-Jewry's Construction of Modern Jewish Thought* (2000).

from the one I will explore in this book. However, the prior philosophical and political tensions between Judaism and Enlightenment constitute the fundamental intellectual backdrop against which *Haskalah* was played out. It is in these debates that the key stakes of this movement first came into focus, even before the *Haskalah* itself had begun.

The Enlightenment was both shaped by and itself profoundly reshaped an immense gamut of cultural traditions, extending far beyond the confines of Europe.[30] In the case of Judaism, however, this intercultural engagement was uniquely intense, as was the rapid transformative impact of the Enlightenment's triumphant ideals. It is therefore particularly inappropriate to conceptualise these two intellectual currents as neatly separate from each other. The core values of the Enlightenment – justice, reason, toleration, self-actualisation, freedom of thought and speech – provide the fundamental grounds on which the entitlements of minorities such as Jews are protected in modern societies. However acutely aware we may be of the limits and lacunae of these ideals, as thinkers and political agents within the western tradition we cannot repudiate them. Any philosophically coherent exploration of the persistence of prejudice and violence within this tradition must be deeply self-reflexive, acknowledging both the indispensability and the limits of Enlightenment rationality. The disentanglement of Judaism and Enlightenment can never be complete: it can only enable us to see more clearly the underlying knot that awkwardly holds them together.

WHAT IS (THE) ENLIGHTENMENT?

The debate over the nature of Enlightenment, initiated by a footnoted query in the *Berlinische Monatsschrift* in 1783 and most famously addressed by Immanuel Kant, raged furiously in the Enlightenment's twilight decades, and more than two centuries later shows no sign of abating.[31] Historians, however, have recently tended almost to ignore this conceptual discussion, concentrating instead on the more limited problem of the Enlightenment's accompanying definite article. Was there one Enlightenment, or were there several? Did it radiate outward from Paris, or was it an endlessly diverse and diffuse phenomenon?[32] The differing national contexts of

[30] See Edward Said, *Orientalism* (1978) 113–23.
[31] See Frederick C. Beiser, *The Fate of Reason: German Philosophy from Kant to Fichte* (1987) esp. 1–13; James Schmidt, ed., *What is Enlightenment? Eighteenth-Century Answers and Twentieth-Century Questions* (1996).
[32] For an influential argument for pluralism see J. G. A. Pocock, *Barbarism and Religion 1: The Enlightenments of Edward Gibbon, 1734–1764* (1999) 5–10. The traditional francocentric model, most

Enlightenment have been brought to the fore, while recent historians have made strong claims for the distinctive importance of the Enlightenment in England, which Franco Venturi had influentially judged as uniquely without *philosophes*, and therefore without an Enlightenment.[33] The old view of the Enlightenment as almost a private affair involving only a handful of Parisian intellectuals in the middle decades of the eighteenth century has rightly been radically overhauled. However, relentless historiographical pluralisation and fragmentation risks severing the discipline entirely from Kant's crisp philosophical question. Although the historical trajectories of the Enlightenment were varied, and can be usefully mapped in many ways, a central core of problems, aspirations and concerns connect and transcend all these contexts. An overarching notion of 'Enlightenment', characterised essentially by a commitment to the unity and power of critical reason, is vital in order to grasp the underlying philosophical issues at stake in this sprawling intellectual transformation.

While no historical era marks an absolute break with its past, the acceleration of secularisation and the rise of scientific and rational thought in Europe from around 1650 onwards constitute a uniquely dramatic phase in the emergence of the ideas and modes of thought that are today recognised as 'modern'.[34] Modernity is an even more notoriously slippery concept than Enlightenment, and its origins have been traced through an almost innumerable multiplicity of historical routes. Scholars have variously traced the early impact of the Reformation, Renaissance natural philosophy, civic republicanism and epistemological scepticism on the unravelling of premodern theological and political certainties.[35] However, in almost all of these accounts the Enlightenment period, and its early phase in particular, remains of key importance. The four or five decades approximately centred on 1700, long ago identified by Paul Hazard as the years of the 'crisis of the European mind', most clearly mark the threshold between

cogently advanced in Peter Gay, *The Enlightenment – An Interpretation: The Science of Freedom* (1977), has been reanimated in Robert Darnton, 'George Washington's False Teeth', *New York Review of Books*, 27 March 1997.

[33] Roy Porter and Mikuláš Teich, eds., *The Enlightenment in National Context* (1981); Franco Venturi, *Utopia and Reform in the Enlightenment* (1971) 132–3; J. G. A. Pocock, 'Post-Puritan England and the Problem of the Enlightenment', in Perez Zagorin, ed., *Culture and Politics from Puritanism to the Enlightenment* (1980) 91–112; Roy Porter, *The Creation of the Modern World: The Untold Story of the British Enlightenment* (2000).

[34] See Jonathan I. Israel, *Radical Enlightenment: Philosophy and the Making of Modernity, 1650–1750* (2001) 3–22.

[35] Amos Funkenstein, *Theology and the Scientific Imagination from the Middle Ages to the Seventeenth Century* (1986); J. G. A. Pocock, *The Machiavellian Moment: Florentine Political Thought and the Atlantic Republican Tradition* (1975); Richard H. Popkin, *The History of Scepticism from Erasmus to Spinoza* (1979); Ira O. Wade, *The Intellectual Origins of the French Enlightenment* (1971).

the mental worlds of the premodern and the modern eras.[36] To segregate an 'Early Enlightenment' from a late, high or 'real' Enlightenment, like all other subdivisions, obscures the fundamental philosophical unities of Enlightenment *in toto*. However, inverting the implicit bias of much Enlightenment historiography, this study will pay particularly close attention to these earlier decades. Already by the 1740s most of the key arguments of the Enlightenment had been sketched out, and were even beginning to become commonplaces. It was above all in the immediately preceding period that the parameters, possibilities and pitfalls of secular critical reason were most keenly explored, contested and debated.

Enlightenment ideas were of course absorbed and articulated in very different ways by different groups of European intellectuals. The radical vanguard of the Enlightenment, characterised by its polemical vigour and associated with new and distinctive forms of sociability such as freemasonry, was energised by a powerfully subversive spirit of anticlericalism and republicanism.[37] In contrast, particularly in England but also elsewhere, a more measured 'religious Enlightenment' sought gradually to integrate science and critical scholarship within the frameworks of traditional theologies.[38] However, while the differences between these wings are immense, the key intellectual problems they faced were essentially the same. Many individuals also do not fit comfortably in either category, or in a centrist Enlightenment 'mainstream'. The uncertainty, mobility and experimentalism of much Enlightenment writing by its very nature frustrates attempts to identify neatly distinct currents of opinion. Scholars remain deeply divided on the ultimate inner commitments of most major Enlightenment thinkers, such as Voltaire, Rousseau, Spinoza and Bayle, in large degree because these thinkers themselves were not definitively fixed in their worldviews. It is impossible to give shape to the Enlightenment without some form of sub-categorisation. However, in this study I will focus on the intellectual dynamics of particular ideas as they unfold through time, rather than attempt to classify thinkers according to alignments that were in many cases fluid or overlapping.

[36] Paul Hazard, *The European Mind 1680–1715* (1953 (1935)). See also Margaret C. Jacob, *Scientific Culture and the Making of the Industrial West* (1997) 73–5; 'The Crisis of the European Mind: Hazard Revisited', in Margaret C. Jacob and Phyllis Mack, eds., *Politics and Culture in Early Modern Europe: Essays in Honor of H. G. Koenigsburger* (1987); Shmuel Ettinger, 'The Beginnings of the Change in the Attitude of European Society Towards the Jews', *Scripta Hierosolymitana* 7 (1961) 193–219.

[37] Margaret C. Jacob, *The Radical Enlightenment: Pantheists, Freemasons and Republicans* (1981); Charles Taylor, *Sources of the Self* (1989) 321–54; Israel, *Radical Enlightenment*, 59–81.

[38] Pocock, *Barbarism and Religion 1*, 292–308; B. W. Young, *Religion and Enlightenment in Eighteenth-Century England* (1998); David Sorkin, 'The Case for Comparison: Moses Mendelssohn and the Religious Enlightenment', *Modern Judaism* 14 (2) (1994) 121–38.

The social institutions and practices of the Enlightenment were, however, intimately connected to its ideology. As Jürgen Habermas has influentially argued, it was in the late seventeenth century that a 'bourgeois' public sphere began to emerge, its values of openness, debate and critical reasoning enacted in the new coffee houses and espoused by the new scholarly journals of the period.[39] The eighteenth-century proliferation of libraries, book clubs, salons and Masonic lodges transformed the nature of urban sociability; in particular, the rise of the *salonnière* and of women's reading to an important degree feminised European intellectual life.[40] Even in the more elitist circles of the self-defined Republic of Letters, issues of scholarly form were at least as important as matters of propositional content. Codes of politeness and deference were crucial in defining membership of this community, as they had been in establishing the distinctive authority of English scientific culture centred on the Royal Society.[41] However, a contrastingly raffish tone marked other strands of Enlightenment discourse: pornography and materialist radical philosophy overlapped considerably in eighteenth-century France, and both genres were avidly consumed for their common transgressive spirit.[42] The reinforcement of manners and the fantasy of their overthrow were simultaneous and symbiotically related social faces of the Enlightenment, reflecting a fissure inextricable from the nature of critical reason itself. The emergence of 'rational' modes of intellectual regulation and hierarchy was closely shadowed by an awareness of the perpetual power of independent thought to challenge and subvert all fixities.[43]

Judaic themes were invoked with equal intensity across the entire spectrum of the Enlightenment. For traditionalist theologians the retrenchment of the status of the Old Testament was of fundamental intellectual importance; concomitantly, for many radicals nothing was more satisfyingly

[39] Jürgen Habermas, *The Structural Transformation of the Public Sphere* (1989 (1962)) 14–26.
[40] Thomas Munck, *The Enlightenment: A Comparative Social History 1721–1794* (2000) 46–75; Dena Goodman, *The Republic of Letters* (1994); Reinhard Wittmann, 'Was there a Reading Revolution at the End of the Eighteenth Century?', in Guglielmo Cavallo and Roger Chartier, eds., *A History of Reading in the West* (1999) 295–301. On reading and the Enlightenment see also Henri-Jean Martin, *Print, Power and People in 17th-Century France* (1993); Jack Censer, 'The History of the Book in Early Modern France: Directions and Challenges', *Eighteenth Century Life* 19 (1995) 84–95; Roger Chartier, *Cultural History: Between Practices and Representations* (1988) 151–71; *The Order of Books* (1994).
[41] Ann Goldgar, *Impolite Learning* (1995) esp. 115–73, 211–18; Steven Shapin, *A Social History of Truth: Civility and Science in Seventeenth-Century England* (1994) esp. 65–125.
[42] Robert Darnton, *The Literary Underground of the Old Regime* (1982); *The Forbidden Best-Sellers of Pre-Revolutionary France* (1995) 85–114; Margaret C. Jacob, 'The Materialist World of Pornography', in Lynn Hunt, ed., *The Invention of Pornography* (1993) 157–202.
[43] See Arlette Farge, *Subversive Words: Public Opinion in Eighteenth-Century France* (1994).

disruptive than the mockery of this text. Most intellectuals, however, stood somewhere between these two extremes, attempting to think in both critical and reconstructive terms. The deep historical, theological and political uncertainties associated with Judaism cut to the core of the difficulties inherent in this mediating project. Questions related to Judaism therefore attracted widespread interest, but were also particularly difficult to resolve. These debates were a crucial terrain of contest between the opposing flanks of Enlightenment thought. However, they also highlight the extent to which even extremely contrasting thinkers were vexed by essentially the same philosophical imponderables, to which nobody could provide a conclusive answer.

The various axes of variation within the Enlightenment – geographical, chronological, philosophical and cultural – are all of the utmost importance in understanding the similarly intricate variations in responses to Judaism in this period. In tracing this particular strand of debate through the seventeenth and eighteenth centuries, this study presents a case study that will hopefully elucidate the dynamics of intellectual and cultural change in this period, and the interplay of the major factors determining its rhythm. However, while always attentive to the importance of conjuncture, this study will nonetheless resist the reduction of these Judaic debates to any all-enveloping frame of contextual reference. If there were many historical Enlightenments, there nonetheless also remains the core problem of the nature and limits of Enlightenment. The tensions that unite the topic of this book, reified politically in the nineteenth century as 'The Jewish Question', are central to enduring questions concerning the relationships of identity to nationhood, history to origins and myth to knowledge. If one of the key purposes of intellectual history is, in Quentin Skinner's words, to 'enable us to acquire a self-conscious understanding of a set of concepts that we now employ unselfconsciously',[44] then very few subjects can offer more promising terrain than the exploration of the dense cluster of conceptual problems associated with the status of Judaism in the Enlightenment.

OLD CERTAINTIES, NEW POLEMICS, CONFLICTED POLITICS

The diffusion and development of ideas is an untidy business, which proceeds without heed of geopolitical borders or steady chronological progression. This study therefore eschews the misleading neatness of a structure organised by country or by decade. The volume is instead subdivided into

---

[44] Quentin Skinner, *Liberty Before Liberalism* (1998) 110.

three broad sections. The first section explores the gradual erosion of the traditional, pre-Enlightenment certainties that underpinned early modern Christian attitudes to Judaism. Part II examines the new, more explicitly rationalist perspectives that challenged and eventually eclipsed these older assumptions. The final section turns to the relationship of these new perspectives to the wider social and political concerns of the period. These are very rough-hewn and perhaps even Procrustean categories: many individuals and debates could be positioned in more than one section, and several indeed are. While this book's repeated shifts across time and space may at times seem to disrupt the flow of narrative, I hope that the privileging of the Enlightenment's ideas over its geography or chronology will provide a stronger sense of the conceptual unfolding of its approaches and responses to Judaism.

The opening section focuses on the culmination of Christian theological interest in Judaism in the discipline of Christian Hebraism, which reached its heyday in the early seventeenth century. Already at this moment of grand intellectual confidence, however, the complexities posed by the textual-critical values of humanism were beginning to undermine the foundations of this scholarly enterprise. A seemingly arcane dispute over the status of the Masoretic pointing of the Hebrew Bible highlighted the fragility, under close examination, of the authority of the biblical text. In the later seventeenth century these conceptual uncertainties, in an increasingly impatient and sceptical intellectual climate, combined to weaken the prestige of Hebraist study, which was widely cast by enthusiasts of Enlightenment as the epitome of sterile uselessness.

The decline of Christian Hebraism was closely related to parallel difficulties and doubts that increasingly afflicted other early modern cultural convictions as the paradigm of reason took grip. Among the most striking of these was the shifting rhetoric of Hebraic politics. English Protestant identification with the ancient Hebrews reached a dramatic crescendo in the Interregnum period, and is reflected in the writings of Selden, Hobbes and Harrington. The political invocation of the Old Testament did not disappear in the latter part of the seventeenth century, but it lost its innocent straightforwardness.

Meanwhile, the centrality of the Bible in the overarching shape of global history also became increasingly difficult to sustain. The discipline of biblical chronology, dominated in 1600 by the giant figure of Joseph Scaliger, became increasingly mired in complexity and confusion, and a century later had lost almost all its lustre. Many late seventeenth-century traditionalists tried to reassert the historical supremacy of the Bible, but the coherence of this endeavour was strained by the varied and proliferating attempts to integrate with western history the myths and chronologies both of familiar ancient civilisations, such as Egypt and China, and of other newly encountered societies in the East and in the New World.

Two major texts written around 1700, both by Huguenot refugees to Holland, majestically draw together the compelling uncertainties that clustered around Judaism as intellectuals struggled to explore the relationship of Enlightenment reason to traditional Christian perspectives. In his monumental *History of the Jews* Jacques Basnage attempted to apply the values of critical scholarship to the study of the Jewish past. However, the methodical thoroughness of this monumental work of scholarship occludes but does not conceal its underlying ambiguities of outlook and purpose. In contrast, Pierre Bayle's *Historical and Critical Dictionary* reflects its author's uniquely acute and unflinching awareness of these philosophical stakes. Judaism is central to Bayle's overarching preoccupation with the insoluble incommensurability of reason and faith. The Jews, uniquely standing outside the realm of individual ethics and conscience, are for him the key historical witnesses to this paradox.

The second section begins in the Jewish milieu of seventeenth-century Sephardic Amsterdam. The significance of this Jewish context as an early forerunner of quintessentially modern modes of religious doubt and rebellion has seldom been acknowledged. However, if it is true that the eighteenth-century collapse of the hegemony of religion was largely the consequence of sustained attrition from the clash of competing theologies since the Reformation, then the Sephardim of Amsterdam, reestablishing Judaism in Protestant surroundings after centuries of immersion in Catholicism, were uniquely caught in triangular theological crossfire. It is not surprising, therefore, that this community even before the emergence of Spinoza was a notable hotbed of dispute and dissent.

Spinoza himself was undoubtedly the crucial conduit connecting this Jewish heretical tradition to the wider Enlightenment. The Jewish inflection of Spinoza's thought has been frequently overlooked, but it subtly yet crucially differentiated his arguments from those of his closest non-Jewish radical collaborators. His Jewishness was of similarly semi-invisible but nonetheless profound significance in his rise to iconic status as the philosophical hero *par excellence* of Early Enlightenment philosophical radicals. In a sense, I suggest, Spinoza was cast as the Enlightenment's Messiah: the necessarily originally and then no longer Jewish harbinger of a new philosophical age.

The ambivalence and instability of most rationalist responses to Judaism is highlighted in engagements with the Jewish mystical tradition. Knorr von Rosenroth's immense *Kabbalah Denudata* (1677) for the first time made Kabbalistic texts accessible to non-readers of Hebrew. Whereas Knorr enthusiastically regarded the Kabbalah as an uncontaminated *prisca theologica*, writers of the next generation tended to be more unsure, but often nonetheless highly intrigued by the subject. The dramatic reversal of opinion by Georg Wachter, a German radical, and the fascinated but uncertain writings on the topic by several other thinkers, including Leibniz, reveal the depth of confusion engendered by the Kabbalah in the early eighteenth century.

A particular focus of fascination among radicals of this period were Jewish arguments against Christianity, which had circulated widely in seventeenth-century Sephardic Amsterdam as a fortification of the religious commitment of the community, and which in the early eighteenth century percolated into the clandestine philosophical literature circulating in France. These texts were relished as a piquantly subversive challenge to Christian orthodoxy. However, many of the French translations of these manuscripts were subtly recast in a fashion that undermined and ridiculed their Jewish voice, while at the same time appropriating their core arguments. These contortions reflect the severe intellectual complexities posed by Judaism. Reason itself was an elusive concept, most easily defined negatively: Jewish legalism and textual fetishism were frequently held up as the defining antithesis of 'natural religion'. However, the challenge of providing an alternative reading of the Old Testament, and of its historical status, was both impossible for radicals to evade and equally impossible for them conclusively to put to rest. Like a stubborn shard of intellectual grit, Judaism was an ubiquitous, troubling and often frustrating presence in the minds of early advocates of reason and Enlightenment.

The final section of the book turns to the wider political, social and cultural dimensions of the deployment of Jewish themes in Enlightenment thought. The Hebraic radical politics of earlier writers such as James Harrington was inherited in the Early Enlightenment by John Toland in England and Pietro Giannone in Italy, both of whom invoked elements from the ancient Jewish tradition as a source and model of primitive 'natural religion'. However, the stance of writers of this generation towards Judaism was much more conflicted. At the same time as idealising certain strands of Judaism, Toland denigrated others, in order to heighten his critique of the Anglican establishment. Jews were also idealised as the marquis d'Argens' wise and cosmopolitan observers of European society in his satirical *Lettres juives* (1736–8). This universalisation of Jewishness, however, hollowed it of all traces of its actual cultural difference.

The intellectual agenda of the Enlightenment was in many respects extremely practical. Almost all significant thinkers saw a close connection between the abstract exploration of science and philosophy and the immediate political issues of toleration and freedom of thought. Judaism figured prominently in the extensive toleration debates of the period, because the religion inspired such diverse, intense and often conflicting responses, and also because Jews were potentially the leading beneficiaries of more open settlement and economic policies. Spinoza, Locke and Bayle all advanced theories of toleration that were inclusive of Jews; however, in all three cases the status of Jewish toleration is marked by traces of ambiguity and exceptionalism.

Nowhere are these persistent ambiguities more sharply expressed than in the prodigious output of Voltaire. The most widely revered of all the *philosophes*, Voltaire is remembered above all as an indefatigable fighter for the cause of tolerance. Only one blemish blights his popular reputation: his vociferous and oft-repeated hostility to Jews and Judaism. Many surgical attempts have been made to excise this blemish from Voltaire's philosophical image. No such neat separation, however, is possible: Voltaire's anti-Judaic rhetoric is not incidental to his philosophy, but forms a structurally crucial element of it. In his convoluted attempts to integrate Judaism into his vision of a tolerant society, while simultaneously characterising it as the quintessence of intolerance, Voltaire reveals with unique starkness the paradoxical nature of the Enlightenment notion of toleration itself.

The intricate web of fascination and repulsion that drew Judaism so deeply into Enlightenment thought also formed the intellectual underlay for the transformation of Jewish life in Europe initiated by political emancipation in the wake of the French Revolution. This is essentially another story, but this study concludes with a brief sketch of the connections between the attitudes and uncertainties of the earlier period and those of both non-Jews and assimilated Jews in the post-Enlightenment era. The structural ambivalence towards Judaism of so many eighteenth-century writers is echoed in Hegel, and also, much later, in Sigmund Freud's *Moses and Monotheism*. In recent decades, Jews have generally ceased to be a primary target of rationalist antagonism towards allegedly unassimilable difference. However, similar patterns of exclusionary thought continue to be applied to other groups. The history of the tension between Judaism and Enlightenment, and the continued anomalousness of Jewish identity in today's world, valuably disrupts hasty certainties and offers a potential guard against the seductions of rationalist absolutism.

PART I

The crumbling of old certainties: Judaism, the Bible and the meaning of history

CHAPTER I

The crisis and decline of Christian Hebraism

Despite the suspicion and at times violent hostility with which most medieval Europeans generally treated the Jews in their midst, from a theological perspective medieval Christians understood the existence and survival of this dispersed minority as meaningful and necessary. The key principles of Christian dogma with regard to the Jews were classically formulated in the fifth century by Augustine of Hippo. For Augustine, Jewish disbelief in the Messiah was foretold in Scripture, and thus the Jews' 'blindness' to the meaning of their own sacred writings only confirmed these texts' truth. God's decision, Augustine argued, to disperse rather than exterminate 'our enemies' the Jews both demonstrated divine mercy and marked the Jews with a unique and crucial theological significance, as 'witnesses' to the truth of Christianity.[1] The Augustinian doctrine of Jewish witness, although subject to repeated reinterpretation, remained until the Renaissance the overarching paradigm within which Christian attitudes towards the Jews in their midst were theorised and legitimated. By the twelfth century this notion stood at the core of a more elaborate doctrine of the divine purpose of the preservation of the Jews. Not only did the Jews' dispersion serve to bear witness to the historical truth of the Church, but their misery was also a reminder of the punishment deservedly meted out to the killers of Christ. However, their suffering was not to be permanent – at the end of days, the completion of the mission of the Church would be signalled by the final coming to Christ of even his most hostile and obdurate enemies.

HEBRAISM, CONVERSION, REFORMATION

The doctrine of Jewish witness implicitly – and in its early, Augustinian form explicitly – militated against any engagement by Christians with postbiblical Judaism. All meaningfulness within Judaism was understood abruptly

[1] Augustine of Hippo, *City of God* (1960), §7:32, 18:46.

to have ceased at the historical moment of Jesus' crucifixion, when the old religion was superseded by the new.[2] However, this theological premise was problematised in the twelfth and thirteenth centuries by a dramatic rise in Christian awareness of the texts of rabbinic Judaism. This intellectual development was associated with a general hardening of attitudes towards contemporary Jews, and an increased virulence of anti-Judaic polemic.[3] The primary aim of the conversionist friars of this period was to expose the blasphemy of rabbinic literature. However, a striking tension can be discerned in the friars' attitude towards rabbinical literature. Texts such as Raymund Martin's *Pugio Fidei* (1278), the most sophisticated conversionist text of the thirteenth century, acknowledged the presence within the Talmud and other rabbinic writings of occasional seeds of the divine truth revealed to Moses and the prophets. As 'honey is the spittle of bees' despite their poisonous sting, so Martin argued that Christians should not disregard everything transmitted by the rabbis.[4] In attempting to locate within the Talmud proofs of the truth of Christianity, and to use this strategy to undermine Judaism from within, Martin paradoxically ascribed a new element of value to this text, which he nonetheless intensely reviled and condemned. The universalistic impulse of scholasticism to incorporate all domains of knowledge as buttresses to Christian truth thus inspired a tentative positive interest in postbiblical Jewish writings that was subtly at odds with the dismissal of Judaism that this same universalistic rationalism simultaneously reinforced.

In the late fifteenth century, several Christian Humanist scholars turned with renewed interest to Jewish texts.[5] The Kabbalah was a particular source of fascination for men such as Pico della Mirandola and Johannes Reuchlin, who scoured the Jewish mystical tradition for further proofs of the truth of Christianity. However, there was also a powerful contrary tendency within Humanism, best exemplified by Erasmus, who was equivocal towards Christian Hebraism and repeatedly described Hebrew as a 'barbaric language'.[6] Uncertainty and ambivalence towards Judaism was heightened in the polemically charged Reformation period. In the new, unprecedented

---

[2] Jeremy Cohen, *Living Letters of the Law: Ideas of the Jew in Medieval Christianity* (1999) 65; *The Friars and the Jews* (1982) 19–22.

[3] Amos Funkenstein, *Perceptions of Jewish History* (1993) 172–201; Robert Chazan, 'The Deteriorating Image of the Jews: Twelfth and Thirteenth Centuries' in Scott L. Waugh and Peter D. Diehl, eds., *Christendom and its Discontents* (1996) 220–33; *Daggers of Faith* (1989).

[4] Cohen, *Living Letters*, 342–58, esp. 355. See also Chazan, *Daggers of Faith* 118–36; Aaron Katchen, *Christian Hebraists and Dutch Rabbis* (1984) 3–6.

[5] See Ilana Zinguer, ed., *L'Hébreu au temps de la Renaissance* (1992) esp. 8–27.

[6] Shimon Markish, *Erasmus and the Jews* (1986) 112–41, esp. 119.

environment of interdenominational rivalry, the establishment of authoritative and distinctive scholarly credentials was of vital importance in the
formation of confessional identities. Almost from the beginnings of the
Reformation, and with increased intensity from the 1540s onward, the appropriate status of Hebraic study within Protestantism was a markedly
conflicted issue. The theological authority of study in the original language
of the Old Testament held a powerful allure within the intellectual culture of a nascent and internally riven Protestantism, intellectually driven
by the imperative to underpin its truth claims. However, Hebrew was also
widely perceived as a field of danger. Learning this language effectively almost always required assistance from a Jewish teacher, and led naturally to
an immersion in rabbinic writings. Such contacts and intellectual pursuits
carried with them the fear of contamination, and left scholars open to the
highly charged accusation of 'judaising'.

Luther's enduring hostility towards Judaism is now widely acknowledged. Despite the contrast in tone between the optimism of his early conversionist and eschatological essay *That Jesus Christ Was Born a Jew* (1523)
and the ferocity of his infamous *On The Jews and Their Lies* (1543), throughout his career Luther was wary and contemptuous of Jewish difference.[7]
Although the hope of an imminent Jewish conversion to Christianity was
a powerful animating force in his early rhetoric, this stood as an abstract
ideal rather than as a concrete goal towards which he was actively working. Jews in Luther's thought were remote and largely imaginary figures,
usually invoked in service of the polemical needs of the moment.[8] Luther's
approach to Hebraist scholarship was similarly for the most part instru-
mentalist. The Christian Hebraist tradition developed at Wittenberg, in
isolation from any Jewish teachers, was characterised by the determined
reading of New Testament concepts into Old Testament passages.[9]

Lutheran Hebraism differed significantly from the more intellectual dy-
namic approach developed in the Reformed centres of Basel, Zurich and
Strasbourg. Whereas the Wittenberg approach insistently subordinated the
Old Testament to the Gospels, Reformed scholars were more inclined to

[7] Richard Marius, *Martin Luther* (1999) 372–80. See also Gavin Langmuir, 'The Faith of Christians and
Hostility to Jews', in *Christianity and Judaism* (1992) 77–92; Eric W. Gritsch, 'The Jews in Reformation
Theology', in Marvin Perry and Frederick M. Schweitzer, eds., *Jewish-Christian Encounters Over the
Centuries* (1994) 197–213.
[8] See Marius, *Luther*, 372–3; Betsy Halpern Amaru, 'Martin Luther and Jewish Mirrors', *Jewish Social
Studies* 46 (1984) 95–102; Carl Cohen, 'Martin Luther and his Jewish Contemporaries', *Jewish Social
Studies* 25 (1963) 195–204.
[9] Jerome Friedman, *The Most Ancient Testimony: Sixteenth-Century Christian-Hebraica in the Age of
Renaissance Nostalgia* (1983) esp. 168–9.

view the two covenants as separate, and were therefore less wary of using Jewish sources.[10] However, even in the Calvinist world such scholarship was widely regarded as a perilous endeavour. Hebraism drew the Christian theologian deep into alien territory, raising the fear that the outwardly Jewish activity of reading rabbinic texts could lead to a shift of perspective or even of religious loyalties. The reality of these anxieties is reflected in the scandal of the famous 'circumcision incident' in Basel in 1619, when the esteemed Hebraist Johannes Buxtorf the elder was severely reprimanded and fined for attending the circumcision of the son of one of his Hebrew printers. Despite Buxtorf's unquestionable conviction of the profound falsity of Judaism, his friendships with his Jewish collaborators ran against the grain of the expectations of his fellow citizens, and reinforced their suspicion of his Hebraist activities.[11]

The leading Protestant Hebraists of the mid sixteenth century typically presented their work as conversionist texts. However, the polemical fierceness of such ostensible missionary treatises as Sebastian Münster's *Mashiach* (1539) and Paul Fagius' *Sefer Emunah* (1542) would, it can safely be assumed, swiftly alienate any potential Jewish convert, and strongly suggests that these texts were in fact intended for a Christian rather than a Jewish audience.[12] By the end of the sixteenth century, Hebraist missionising to Jews had in general receded to little more than a rhetorical gesture. The formation of Protestant national and confessional identities, meanwhile, assumed an increasingly overt role in the advance of the discipline. In the decades around 1600 the intellectual commitment to Christian Hebraism was strongest in England and in the Dutch Republic: the two states that were most heavily invested in the formation of new theologico-political identities. Across Europe, though, Calvinists and other Protestant minorities frequently asserted their affinity with the ancient Israelites. A sense of a shared emphasis on the Mosaic commandments and a common experience of persecution and survival in diaspora powerfully fuelled interest in Jewish exegesis among Calvinist scholars.[13] In Elizabethan England, Hebrew scholarship developed rapidly from a very low base, culminating in the publication of the King James Bible in 1611. Most English enthusiasts for Hebrew, such as Hugh Broughton, the leading English Hebraist of this period, were Puritans, for whom promotion of the 'purity' of Hebrew was heavily charged

[10] *Ibid.*, 134, 165–75.
[11] Stephen G. Burnett, 'Johannes Buxtorf I and the Circumcision Incident of 1619', *Basler Zeitschrift für Geschichte und Altertumskunde* 89 (1989) 135–44.
[12] Friedman, *Ancient Testimony*, 215–51.
[13] See Salo Wittmayer Baron, 'John Calvin and the Jews', *Ancient and Medieval Jewish History* (1972) 338–52.

with anti-Catholic rhetoric.[14] In the nascent Dutch Republic, the new universities of Franeker and Leiden soon became important centres for the study of Hebrew.[15] The self-conscious identification of the Dutch nation with the ancient Israelite Kingdom was a recurrent motif in Dutch cultural politics both during the revolt against the Spanish and throughout the seventeenth century.[16] The development of Hebraic studies in Holland was greatly facilitated by the establishment of a community of Portuguese crypto-Jews in Amsterdam in 1595. Amongst the arguments put forward by Grotius in 1614 in favour of allowing Jewish settlement throughout the States of Holland was the claim that it was of great value for Christians to study Hebrew, which could only be learnt effectively from Jews.[17]

By the early seventeenth century Christian Hebraism had developed into a pan-European phenomenon. Catholic participation was hampered by the extremely restrictive policy of the Papacy towards rabbinic literature, particularly after the promulgation of Clement VIII's Sisto-Clementine Index of 1596, which prohibited even editions of the Talmud expurgated of 'calumnies against Christianity', which had been tolerated since the Council of Trent.[18] However, Jesuits such as Robert Bellarmine and Georgius Mayr published brief and successful Hebrew grammars.[19] Basel, home to the Buxtorf dynasty of Hebraists, had the most active Hebrew press in Europe.[20] Increasingly, editions and translations of rabbinic commentaries, portions of Midrash, Talmud and Kabbalistic texts and specialist Hebrew dictionaries and lexicons to facilitate their reading were being printed and circulated across the continent. The surviving correspondence of the Buxtorfs includes letters from scholars all over Europe, including Italians, Poles, Swedes, Englishmen and Hungarians.[21] The self-conscious internationalism of Hebraist scholarship, however, did not displace the centrality of inter-confessional rivalry in establishing Hebraist credentials. Beneath a generally maintained veneer of intellectual *politesse*, all Christian groupings, Catholics included, were competitively engaged in demonstrating

---

[14] See Gareth Lloyd Jones, *The Discovery of Hebrew in Tudor England* (1983) esp. 266–73; Eliane Glaser, 'Hebrew as Myth and Reality in Renaissance England', in Robert Rabinowitz, ed., *New Voices in Jewish Thought* (1998) 4–19.

[15] See Katchen, *Christian Hebraists*, 15–37; Peter van Rooden, *Theology, Biblical Scholarship and Rabbinical Studies* (1989) 1–13, 49–57.

[16] Simon Schama, *The Embarrassment of Riches: An Interpretation of Dutch Culture in the Golden Age* (1997 (1987)) 93–5.

[17] Israel, *European Jewry*, 64.

[18] Salo Wittmayer Baron, 'The Council of Trent and Rabbinic Literature', *Ancient and Medieval Jewish History* (1972) 353–71.

[19] Robert Bellarmine, *Institutiones linguae Hebraicae* (1578), Giorgius Mayr, *Institutiones linguae Hebraicae* (1622).

[20] Raphael Loewe, 'Hebraists, Christian', in *Encyclopaedia Judaica* (1971) VIII, 11.

[21] Manuel, *Broken Staff*, 84.

their scholarly competence in the holy tongue. Up to approximately the middle of the seventeenth century this competitive edge heightened the importance of the discipline, and functioned as an important stimulus to its development.

Nonetheless, beneath this veneer of intellectual confidence and prolific production, Christian Hebraism in the early seventeenth-century heyday was beset with an underlying uncertainty of purpose. Popular and durable works such as Johannes Buxtorf the Elder's *Synagoga Judaica* (1603) were strikingly ambiguous in tone. This text was the first extensive account of Jewish religious beliefs and practices written by a non-Jew for a Christian audience, and was modelled on the earlier ethnography of the sixteenth-century Jewish convert Antonius Margaritha.[22] Buxtorf's study provides a detailed and in general dispassionate description of Jewish rituals and traditions of birth, circumcision, marriage, divorce and death, of the Sabbath, Passover and other festivals, and of Jewish communal treatment of criminals, the poor and the sick. In his introduction, Buxtorf emphasises that his text is not intended to imply any admiration of the Jews, but to reveal the full burdensomeness of their hollow rituals. He states that his text should lead the Christian reader to ponder the 'massive incredulity and hardheartedness' of the Jews, and thus to be all the more aware of God's 'unspeakable mercy and goodness towards us'.[23] However, Buxtorf's stated scorn for the empty rituals of Jewish life is difficult to reconcile with the meticulous and respectful explanation he gives of the theological significance of almost every aspect of Jewish practice. His dismissal of the Talmud as 'a labyrinth of errors'[24] is similarly at odds with his painstaking efforts to translate and interpret this text accurately. Buxtorf legitimated his ethnographic study in the same terms in which he defended his attendance at the 1619 circumcision: as part of an informed and active conversionist mission to the Jews.[25] However, while we have no reason to doubt that his abstract desire to see the Jews convert was sincere, there was no direct sense in which his work furthered this end. The attitude of Buxtorf towards his subject of study was, it seems, profoundly ambivalent, embracing contradictory impulses of fascination and denigration (see figure 1).[26]

In the Dutch Republic, fears of the possible consequences of excessive exposure to Jewish thought gave rise to sustained controversy during the first

---

[22] Stephen G. Burnett, 'Distorted Mirrors: Antonius Margaritha, Johann Buxtorf and Christian Ethnographies of the Jews', *Sixteenth Century Journal* 25 (1994) 275–87.

[23] Johannes Buxtorf, *The Jewish Synagogue* (1663 (1603)), preface (unpaginated).

[24] *Ibid.*, 39.   [25] Burnett, 'Circumcision Incident', 140.

[26] See Stephen G. Burnett, *From Christian Hebraism to Jewish Studies: Johannes Buxtorf (1564–1629) and Hebrew Learning in the Seventeenth Century* (1996) 54–102.

Figure 1 Johannes Buxtorf, *Synagoga Judaica*, Basel, 1680, frontispiece, depicting a circumcision and a scholastic scene.

half of the century over the appropriate use and status of Hebrew scholarship. At Leiden, Hebrew was taught in accordance with academic conven-
tion as a propaedeutic subject within the faculty of letters, and theologians
there insisted that linguistic study should remain clearly subordinate to the
higher, dogmatic study of the Bible.[27] Constantijn L'Empereur, Professor
of Hebrew at Leiden from 1627 to 1646, and alongside Johannes Buxtorf
the Younger the most important Christian Hebraist of the second quarter
of the seventeenth century, devoted considerable energy to the justification
of his scholarship to his colleagues. In his inaugural lecture, L'Empereur
vigorously expounded the unique value (*dignitas*) and usefulness (*utilitas*)
of Hebraic study, and also devoted a lengthy excursus to 'the blinding of
the Jews', in which he explained that their imperviousness to the truths so
clearly demonstrated in the Hebrew scriptures was due to their persistent attachment to the 'fables' of the Talmud and other rabbinic literature.[28] This
attack on the Talmud established the theological acceptability of Hebraist
scholarship, and also enabled L'Empereur to demonstrate his erudite familiarity and competence with rabbinic texts, which were his central scholarly
interest.[29] In 1633, L'Empereur was additionally appointed as Professor
Controversiarum Judaicarum, and this specific responsibility to write *adversus Judaeos* further legitimated his interest in rabbinic writings. However,
for L'Empereur, as for other leading Christian Hebraists, the conversion of
Jews did not appear to be a practical concern.[30] Paradoxically, an essentially
purely scholarly fascination in rabbinic literature could only be publicly
justified through the denigration of the intellectual value of these texts.

VOWELS AND DOUBTS

The emergence of new scholarly controversies further problematised
Christian Hebraist study. In 1616, Pietro della Valle brought back to Europe
a copy of the Samaritan Pentateuch that he had bought in Damascus, which
contained as many as 6,000 differences from the Masoretic Hebrew text.[31]
This caused considerable confusion, and posed a troubling challenge to
the traditional identification of the physical text of the Bible with its true
meaning. From the 1620s, the Huguenot Academy at Saumur emerged as
the centre of a new, critical approach to the biblical text. Louis Cappel,
Professor of Hebrew at Saumur, first argued in his anonymous *Arcanum
Punctationis Revelatum* (1624) that the vocalisation signs in the Masoretic

---

[27] Van Rooden, *Theology*, 51.   [28] *Ibid.*, 85–9.   [29] *Ibid.*, 88.   [30] *Ibid.*, 232.
[31] David S. Katz, 'Isaac Vossius and the English Biblical Critics, 1670–1689', in Richard H. Popkin and
A. Vanderjagt, eds., *Scepticism and Irreligion in the Seventeenth and Eighteenth Centuries* (1993) 171.

Bible were a textual accretion. This thesis was essentially an appropriation of a familiar non-traditional rabbinical argument, originally advanced in Elias Levita's *Masoret ha-Masoret* (1538) and already rebutted at length by the elder Buxtorf, that the vowel points were invented by scholars at some stage after the composition of the Talmud.[32] Cappel's *Critica Sacra*, completed in 1634 but because of the controversy it provoked not published until 1650, extended this argument, identifying corruptions in the main body of the Hebrew text, and arguing that the use of critical judgement was necessary to ascertain, case by case, the most probably accurate biblical reading.[33] In rebutting Cappel, the younger Buxtorf made extensive use of rabbinical literature in insisting on the divinely inspired Mosaic origin and uncorrupted perfection of every detail, including vowel points, of the standard Masoretic text. At stake in this dispute between the 'rabbinic' and 'critical' schools of Christian Hebraism was the fundamental issue of the sacred status of the Hebrew language, which according to Buxtorf and his allies was undermined by the new critical approach.[34] Cappel's arguments unintentionally cast the very conceptual basis of Hebraist scholarship into controversy, and placed the issue of the reliability of the early postbiblical Jews as a central point of dispute.

These scholarly tensions echoed the wider epistemological upheaval of the period, centred around the rise of the mechanistic worldview. Although Cartesianism and biblical criticism were not explicitly brought into alliance until the publication of the work of Spinoza and his allies in the 1660s and 1670s, Cappel's critical rationalism, despite his theological orthodoxy, opened the pathway towards such arguments. Already in the 1630s a self-undermining dynamic had emerged in Hebraist scholarship: the application of critical logic to the Hebrew Bible destabilised the assumptions on which the study of this text was based. Seen from this perspective, the publication of Spinoza's *Tractatus Theologico-Politicus* (1670) simply posed in far more devastatingly relentless terms a critique of transparent biblical exegesis the essence of which had already been dimly visible on the intellectual horizon for several decades.

The increasing paradigmatic instability of Christian Hebraism was compounded by a creeping uncertainty regarding its cultural worth. In the late seventeenth century the notion of reason emerged as a key theological concept for Protestants of all denominations. The value of abstract reasoning

---

[32] Burnett, *Christian Hebraism*, 205–39.   [33] Van Rooden, *Theology*, 222–7.

[34] See Daniel Droixhe, 'La Crise de l'hébreu langue-mère au XVIIe siècle', in Chantal Grell and François Laplanche, eds., *La République des lettres et l'histoire du judaïsme antique* (1992) 91–6; Georg Schnedermann, *Die Controverse des Ludovicus Cappelus mit den Buxtorfen über das Alter der Hebräischen Punctation* (1879).

was widely invoked against the opposing dangers of deistic atheism and enthusiastic excess, of which excessive immersion in Hebrew texts was often taken as prime example.[35] In the decades around 1700 rabbinic scholarship was widely caricatured as the quintessence of useless learning. However, the categorical dismissal of Jewish learning was resisted in scholarly circles. A rational approach demanded that all potential sources of knowledge should be considered objectively and with scrupulous care, and particularly those relating to the fundamentally important subject of the accurate interpretation of the Bible. Attitudes towards Christian Hebraism were thus pulled in two contrary directions: suspicion of obsessive obscurantism and doubt as to the ultimate worth of Hebrew texts were offset by the desire to adhere to high standards of fair-mindedness and intellectual thoroughness. This tension was heightened by the more general anxiety concerning standards of erudition that afflicted the rapidly growing and intensely self-conscious Early Enlightenment 'Republic of Letters'. The new monthly literary periodicals which circulated across Europe from the 1680s onwards made it much easier for would-be savants to acquire a veneer of up-to-date erudition. However, this led to a widespread anxiety that book reviews were being used as a substitute to reading the actual books, and that the mastery of the ancient languages, and Hebrew in particular, was being neglected.[36]

The treatment of Hebraic subjects in these periodicals offers a valuable insight into the dynamics of this ambivalence. The francophone literary reviews published in the Dutch Republic from 1684 onwards, and circulated across Europe, were among the most important cultural institutions of the Early Enlightenment. The first three journals, Pierre Bayle's pioneering *Nouvelles de la République des Lettres* (1684–7), its successor the *Histoire des Ouvrages des Savans* (1687–1709), edited by Henri Basnage de Beauval, and its main early rival, Jean Le Clerc's *Bibliothèque Universelle et Historique* (1686–94), were rivalled in influence only by the authoritative but staid *Acta Eruditorum* of Leipzig (1682–1731), and were central to the establishment of the Dutch Republic as the undisputed European hub of bookselling and intellectual exchange in this period.[37] All three journals gave extensive

[35] Michael Heyd, *'Be Sober and Reasonable': The Critique of Enthusiasm in the Seventeenth and Early Eighteenth Centuries* (1995) 176, 180–1.
[36] Goldgar, *Impolite Learning*, 54–114.
[37] See Graham Gibbs, 'The Role of the Dutch Republic as the Intellectual Entrepôt of Europe in the Seventeenth and Eighteenth Centuries', *BMBGN* 86 (1971) 323–49; Hans Bots, 'La Rôle des périodiques néerlandais pour la diffusion du livre, 1684–1747', in *Le Magasin de l'Univers: The Dutch Republic as the Centre of the European Book Trade* (1992) 49–70; Eugène Hatin, *Bibliographie historique et critique de la presse périodique française* (1866) 28–39.

coverage to books dealing with Hebraic and Jewish subjects.[38] Pierre Bayle's journal exhibited a particularly strong interest, with on average at least one article in each monthly issue dealing substantially with a Jewish-related theme. The journals gave detailed coverage both to new editions of classic Christian Hebraist texts and to new scholarly works, many of which were extremely narrow in their focus of interest. In April 1685, for example, Bayle's *Nouvelles* carefully reviewed an anonymous volume titled *Polygamia Triumphatrix*, a study of Jewish laws and customs with regard to polygamy, which used rabbinical sources to argue that this practice is acceptable to God and in accordance with the Mosaic Law. The appearance in 1688 of a Latin *Life* of Johann Reuchlin was warmly welcomed in the *Histoire des Ouvrages des Savans* and in the *Bibliothèque Universelle et Historique*, both of which commented on the great usefulness of Hebrew texts for the interpretation of the Bible.[39] In March 1689, the *Histoire des Ouvrages des Savans* reviewed a new edition of Louis Cappel's Old Testament commentaries, rehearsing at length the now long-standing controversy over the authenticity or otherwise of the biblical vowel signs.[40] In 1695, the same journal reviewed J. Ludolf's *Dissertatio de Locustis*, in which the author used philological argument to establish his case that the Israelites had fed on locusts, and not quails, when wandering in the desert.[41]

The thorough reviewing of Hebraist studies in these journals reveals the extent to which this mode of erudition continued to be accorded respect. However, submerged beneath their scholarly conservatism the journals evinced distinct unease regarding the status of Jewish texts. Writing in the *Histoire des Ouvrages des Savans* on a Hebrew edition of the Talmud published in Amsterdam in 1688, the editor Henri Basnage (whose brother Jacques was later to write his multi-volume *History of the Jews*) lamented his inability actually to read the text under review:

We might have adorned the heading of this article with a title in Hebrew, which might perhaps have earned us much honour. However, it is better for me to admit this language is beyond my sphere of knowledge, and that I find myself shamefully reduced to writing in French the title of a book that is entirely written in Hebrew.[42]

While proclaiming at the outset of the review his support for the study of the Talmud by Christians, Basnage nonetheless noted that the subject was a controversial one: some scholars, he writes, 'view the Talmud with disdain,

---

[38] A thematic index to the *Histoire des Ouvrages des Savans* shows that about 3 per cent of texts reviewed in the journal were by Jewish authors. See Hans Bots and Lenie van Liesholt, *Henri Basnage de Beauval et sa correspondance à propos de l'Histoire des Ouvrages des Savans* (1984) 185–323.
[39] *HOS* (February 1688) 274–85; *BUH* (1688) 485–506.   [40] *HOS* (March 1689) 3–23.
[41] *HOS* (September 1695) 37–42.   [42] *HOS* (May 1688) 35.

as a heap of impertinences and fantasies', whereas other 'fairer and more moderate' authorities value the text for what it can reveal about Jewish antiquity.[43] He himself judged only the Mishnah to be of value, stating that the Gemara contained 'only dull and ridiculous stories, and tedious disputes between exegetes'.[44]

The final publication by Willem Surenhuis in Amsterdam, between 1698 and 1703, of the first translation of the entire Mishnah into Latin was warmly welcomed in the *Histoire des Ouvrages des Savans* with an article forcefully recapitulating the arguments in favour of the usefulness of this text.[45] This publication, the culmination of a project commenced by the Middelburg Hebraist Adam Boreel six decades previously, in 1639, was a major scholarly achievement.[46] However, by the time of its final appearance at the beginning of the eighteenth century the study of Jewish texts had declined dramatically in prestige, becoming a more marginal form of erudition. The stance of Henri Basnage was typical of Protestant intellectuals in this period, who, while committed in theory to the study of Hebrew texts, had very limited inclination towards it in practice, and remained highly disdainful of what they regarded as rabbinic absurdities and excesses.

PROTESTANT JEWS AND CATHOLIC JEWS

Despite the aspiration of the Republic of Letters to transcend rigid denominational divides, theological rivalry between Protestants and Catholics remained a central element of much learned debate. Both camps strove to assert their superior scholarly credentials, and the issue of the correct handling of Hebrew texts was a key domain of such competition. In particular, the publication of Richard Simon's *Histoire Critique du Vieux Testament* in 1678 thrust the issue of the authority and status of the Jewish interpretative tradition into the epicentre of an intense inter-confessional dispute. This text was a bold response to Spinoza's trenchant attack on the authority of the Old Testament, in which Simon accepted that all available versions of the Bible were corrupted with numerous later additions and adaptations. By acknowledging the reality of some of the contradictions and paradoxes that Spinoza had identified in the Pentateuch, but insisting that they did not

---

[43] *Ibid*.   [44] *Ibid*., 36.   [45] *HOS* (April 1703) 147–57.

[46] See Ernestine van der Wall, 'The Dutch Hebraist Adam Boreel and the Mishnah Project', *LIAS* 16 (1989) 239–63; Richard H. Popkin, 'Two Treasures of Marsh's Library', in Alison P. Coudert, Sarah Hutton, Richard H. Popkin and Gordon M. Weiner, eds., *Judaeo-Christian Intellectual Culture in the Seventeenth Century* (1999) 5–8; Peter van Rooden, 'The Amsterdam Translation of the Mishnah', in William Horbury, ed., *Hebrew Study from Ezra to Ben-Yehuda* (1999) 257–67.

undermine the spiritual truth of the underlying pure text, Simon hoped to provide an intellectual bulwark against 'all the false and pernicious consequences' that Spinoza had claimed to draw from these textual cruxes.[47] However, Simon's case was also avowedly anti-Protestant: precisely because the Scriptures were so riddled with inaccuracy and uncertainty, he argued, it was essential to interpret them according to the authoritative tradition of the Church, without which 'we can hardly be sure of anything in matters of religion'.[48]

Unsurprisingly, Protestant theologians took immediate exception to this argument. Attempting to refute Simon's case and to defend the validity of the Protestant commitment to the unmediated interpretation of Scripture, Jean Le Clerc insisted that, while not always transparent in detail, the Bible was invariably clear on essential points.[49] Le Clerc accused Simon of excessive reverence towards rabbis, a charge that Simon vociferously denied in a pseudonymous counter-attack:

The method that he [Simon] has given us for the interpretation of the Holy Books clearly shows that does not give way entirely to the authority of rabbis. But he also does not believe that we should reject them all, because several of them are very learned scholars of Scripture. He believes we should take from them what is useful, and ignore their fantasies: but in order to do this considerable erudition is required, which none of the Protestants possess. This is why M. le Clerc sweepingly condemns the rabbis.[50]

In his rejoinder, Le Clerc sustained his attack on Simon's claim of a continuity of authority from the ancient Jewish law to the hierarchy of the Catholic Church. He also defended himself against some of the specific accusations of exegetical error raised by Simon, but with distinct impatience, stating that he had no desire 'to follow M Simon into the quibbles that he raises concerning matters of little importance'.[51]

In accusing Simon of uncritically echoing Jewish exegetes, Le Clerc implicitly portrayed his adversary as 'rabbinic' in his love of devious, sophistic argument and irrelevant minutiae. However, Simon's riposte placed Le Clerc in an awkward position. He could not, of course, concede that he was indeed less learned in rabbinics than was his adversary, because this

---

[47] Richard Simon, *Histoire Critique du Vieux Testament* (1685 (1678)) ii.   [48] *Ibid.*, viii.

[49] See Jean Le Clerc, *Sentiments de Quelques Théologiens de Hollande sur l'Histoire Critique du Vieux Testament* (1685).

[50] Richard Simon, *Réponse au livre intitulé 'Sentiments de Quelques Théologiens de Hollands sur l'Histoire Critique du Vieux Testament', par le Prieur de Bolleville* (1686) 15–16.

[51] Jean Le Clerc, *Défense des Sentiments de Quelque Théologiens de Hollande sur l'Histoire Critique du Vieux Testament, Contre la Réponse du Prieur de Bolleville* (1686) 306.

would amount to an admission that he had been arguing from a position of ignorance. However, if he retaliated, and attempted to demonstrate
his equal knowledge of rabbinic literature, he risked allowing himself to be
drawn on to his opponent's scholarly terrain, and in so doing muddying the
distinction between the clear, logical simplicity that he regarded as the core
principle of Protestant theology, and the obfuscating pedantry of which
he accused Simon and other Catholics. Le Clerc's position on this subject
was thus extremely precarious. He acknowledged that Hebraic study was
of a certain potential value, but maintained that rabbinic argument was in
essence fundamentally alien to Protestantism, and in excess a dangerously
pernicious influence.

The casting of Catholics as pedantically 'rabbinic' stretched back at least
to the early seventeenth century, when the idea seems first to have been
juxtaposed with a fanciful Protestant self-identification with the newly
discovered non-rabbinic Karaite sect.[52] While this image powerfully encapsulated the sense, among Huguenot refugee Calvinists particularly, of
their own difference to and superiority over the Catholics, it was difficult
to reconcile with the critical values of the Republic of Letters, according to
which Protestants and Catholics alike were committed to the refinement of
objective, rational methods of interpretation.[53] Because Jewish texts were so
strongly associated with the opposing polar notions of either utter purity or
extreme obscurantism, they posed the deepest challenge to the aspirations
of critical scholarship towards clarity and consensus. Texts such as Jean Le
Clerc's *Ars Critica* attempted to establish an undogmatic methodological
basis for textual exegesis, focusing in particular on the difficulties of biblical
interpretation, but applicable to the critical reading of all texts.[54] However,
the need to interpret Scripture in such a way as to reinforce particular theological positions destabilised this project. Whereas before the Cartesian
revolution the rivalry between Protestantism and Catholicism had stimulated Christian Hebraism, by the closing decades of the seventeenth century the embroilment of Hebraist scholarship in inter-confessional disputes
stood embarrassingly at odds with the self-image of the Republic of Letters
as a cosmopolitan sphere that transcended such rivalries. The explicit denominational polemics that shaped the reception of Simon's work also

[52] Yosef Kaplan, ' "Karaites" in Early Eighteenth-Century Amsterdam', in David S. Katz and Jonathan
I. Israel, *Sceptics, Millenarians and Jews* (1990) 226–7; Simon Szyszman, *Le Karaïsme* (1980) 94–5;
Nathan Schur, *History of the Karaites* (1992) 151ff.

[53] See Jean-Michel Vienne, 'De la Bible à la science: l'interprétation du singulier chez Locke', in Guido
Canziani and Yves Charles Zarka, eds., *L'interpretazione nei secoli XVI e XVII* (1993) 771–88.

[54] Jean Le Clerc, *Ars Critica* (1698) esp. 135–41; see also Maria Cristina Pitassi, *Entre croire et savoir: le
problème de la méthode critique chez Jean Le Clerc* (1987) 49–65.

highlighted the difference between the confessional division of Christian Hebraism and the unimpeded internationalism of other fields of inquiry, above all in the sciences, that in contrast with Hebraism were in this period decisively in the ascendant.

TWILIGHT HEBRAISTS

The production of weighty tomes of Christian Hebraist scholarship nonetheless continued throughout the latter half of the seventeenth century. In England in particular (as we shall see in greater detail in the section below on politics), the wave of identificatory fascination with the Jews during the Interregnum period was very pronounced, and its impact on scholarly life was not extinguished with the Restoration.[55] Up to his death in 1675 John Lightfoot maintained a prolific production of distinctive Hebraist studies, applying rabbinic literature to the elucidation of the New Testament. In his *Hebrew and Talmudical Excitations upon the Gospel of Saint Matthew* (1658), Lightfoot powerfully expressed the deep ambivalence typical of the Christian Hebraist attitude towards rabbinic writings: 'The almost unconquerable difficulty of the Stile, the frightful roughness of the Language, and the amazing emptiness and sophistry of the matters handled, do torture, vex and tyre him that reads them . . . There are no Authors do more affright and vex the Reader, and yet there are none, who do more intice and delight him.'[56] However, from 1650 onwards Christian Hebraism increasingly lost its intellectual vitality and self-confidence. In his preface to Lightfoot's collected *Works*, published posthumously in 1684, George Bright noted and lamented his contemporaries' tendency to neglect Hebraic study in preference for easier subjects.[57] The decline of Hebrew was particularly pronounced in its traditional continental centres such as Basel and Leiden, while the discipline strengthened in more intellectually marginal parts of Europe. The most notable Hebraist project of the late seventeenth century was the work of an Italian, Giulio Bartolocci, who from 1651 held the post of Professor of Hebrew at the Collegium Neophytorum in Rome, a college for Jewish converts to Christianity.[58] Bartolocci's vast four-volume *Bibliotheca Magna Rabbinica* was published from 1675 to 1693, the final volume (and a fifth supplementary volume and index) completed after

---

[55] See David S. Katz, *Philo-Semitism and the Readmission of the Jews to England, 1603–1655* (1982) esp. 76–88.
[56] John Lightfoot, *Works* (1684) II, 95–6; see also Manuel, *Broken Staff*, 130–2.
[57] George Bright, 'Preface to the Reader', in Lightfoot, *Works*, I.
[58] *Encyclopaedia Judaica* IV, 263–4.

Bartolocci's death by his student, Carlo Imbonati.[59] In these daunting folio volumes, Bartolocci listed, summarised and in many cases excerpted every rabbinic text that he could find, either directly or through references in earlier compendiums such as the elder Buxtorf's *Bibliotheca Rabbinica* (see figure 2).

Bartolocci's scholarship did not simply amount to tireless cataloguing; interspersed through the *Bibliotheca* are a number of thematic digressions dealing with important or controversial scholarly issues such as the status of angels and devils in Judaism, the differences between Jewish sects and the interpretation of Hebrew cantillation marks. However, these were essentially summaries of basic knowledge, rather than the product of original research or argument. In sheer voluminous comprehensivity, Bartolocci's scholarship marks the highpoint of Christian Hebraism. However, such a retreat into encyclopaedism should, paradoxically perhaps, be interpreted as a further sign of a crisis in attitudes to Jewish learning. Bartolocci offered no global interpretation of the intellectual status and value of the vast body of material he had assembled. He expressed acceptance of the orthodox view that Jewish writings were not of interest in themselves, but only as a tool for conversionism and for the elucidation of the Bible. Nonetheless, his alphabetical catalogue preserved a strict tone of descriptive neutrality, while Imbonati's thematic indexing highlighted the fact that the *Bibliotheca* was potentially an extremely rich resource not only on theological issues, but also on such subjects as medicine, geometry and philosophy. The apparent confidence of the vast edifice of Bartolocci's work in fact veils considerable confusion about the status of Judaic learning. Advances in Hebraism itself – both in awareness of the ambiguities of the biblical text and in the broadened range of rabbinical texts made accessible – had highlighted new complexities, and severely weakened the confidence that had prevailed at the beginning of the seventeenth century. The availability of translations and brief book reviews, and the expansion of the intellectual world to incorporate a wider and more impatient public, broke the exclusive link between the study of the Hebrew language and access to Jewish arguments. By 1700 rabbinic learning was no longer the preserve of a small but proficient intellectual elite. It now loomed more broadly as a bewilderingly vast, intimidatingly difficult and epistemologically confusing intellectual edifice, which could not easily be either accepted or dismissed.

[59] See Manuel, *Broken Staff*, 98–101.

קרית ספר

והוא חבור גדול שבו נכתבו כל ספרי היהודים חברו ויסדו חכם
הכולל בדורו דן יוליום בֿרטולוקי אבא מחברת
הקדושה ציסטירציאינצי :

BIBLIOTHECA MAGNA
RABBINICA

De Scriptoribus, & scriptis Hebraicis, ordine Alphabetico
Hebràicè, & Latinè digestis.

PARS PRIMA,
Tres primas Alphabeti literas complectens א'ב'ג'

*In qua complures identidem interseruntur dissertationes, & digressiones, quarum
Elenchus habetur post Prafationem ad Lectorem.*

Cum Indice rerum, nominum, & locorum Sacra Scripturæ locupletissimo.

AVCTORE
D. IVLIO BARTOLOCCIO DE CELLENO
Congregat. S. Bernardi Ref. Ord. Cistercien. & S. Sebastiani ad Catacumbas Abbate.

ואם לא עכשיו אימתי ; פרקי אבות פ.

Et si non modo, ecquando? Cap. Patrum Cap. 1.

Πάντα δοκιμάζοντε; , τὸ καλὸν κατέχετε. Πρὸς Θεσσαλ. Κεφάλ. ε.

Omnia probate: quod bonum est tenete. 1. Thessal. 5.

ROMÆ, Ex Typographia Sacræ Congregationis de Propaganda Fide.
Anno Iubilei MDCLXXV.

SVPERIORVM PERMISSV.

Figure 2   Giulio Bartolocci, *Bibliotheca Magna Rabbinica*, volume 1, Rome, 1675, title page.

In the early eighteenth century, original Hebraist scholarship ceased almost totally, and new publications tended towards increasingly derivative synthesis. Johann Christoph Wolf's *Bibliotheca Hebraea* (1715), a much more compact four-volume work which listed and very briefly described the writings of over 2,000 Hebrew authorities, was to a considerable extent a distillation from Bartolocci. Even more explicitly than the Roman work, Wolf's tome was purely a reference guide, with no pretensions towards interpretation. The works of these two scholars remained throughout the eighteenth century the key reference texts in the increasingly moribund field of Christian Hebraism. Only in 1802 did a new work of reference appear, by Giovanni Bernardo de Rossi, Professor of Oriental Languages at Parma. This vastly slimmer work, entirely based on seventeenth-century scholarship, is testimony to the dramatic decline of non-Jewish interest in Jewish learning over the course of the Enlightenment.[60]

The eighteenth-century turn away from Hebraica was by no means universal. A notable exception to the decline in Hebraic publication was the work of Biagio Ugolini, whose immense thirty-four-volume compendium of almost every text he could find relating to Judaism was published in Venice between 1744 and 1769.[61] The overwhelming immensity of this work, however, both diminished its usability and marked it sharply apart from the practical, reformist culture of the Italian Enlightenment. Ugolini's preservationist zeal was animated by an instinctive notion of Jewish learning as a precious and vulnerable relic, of vital importance in illuminating the study of the Bible.[62] While his work reflects an intense, religiously motivated commitment to Hebraism, his relentless accumulation of texts cannot truly be considered as scholarship, and his interpretative innocence places him firmly outside the intellectual mainstream of his day.

The significance of Hebraism within Protestant culture also continued to evolve. The foundation of Johann Heinrich Callenberg's Institutum Judaicum in Halle in 1728 marked the emergence of a new phase in this relationship. Despite the Pietists' emphasis on linguistic and textual study, their approach to rabbinic texts was very different from that of the leading scholars of preceding generations. Whereas conversionism tended to be little more than a legitimating pretext for these earlier Hebraists, for the Halle Pietists erudite study was ancillary to the practical missionising tasks of the dissemination of conversionist texts, the education and

---

[60] Giovanni Bernardo di Rossi, *Dizionario storico degli autori ebrei, e dalle loro opere* (1802).

[61] Biagio Ugolini, *Thesaurus antiquitatum sacrarum* (1744–69).

[62] Angelo Vivian, 'Biagio Ugolini et son *Thesaurus antiquitatum sacrarum*: bilan des études juives au milieu du XVIIIe siècle', in Grell and Laplanche, eds., *La République des lettres* 115–45.

assistance of converts and the promotion of the moral reform of all Jews.[63] Various eighteenth-century mystical and millenarian organisations, including most notably the Swedenborgians, drew extensively on Hebraic sources and imagery.[64] However, both missionary and messianic groups, while in varying ways drawing on the ascendant scientific and socially inclusive language of the period, were essentially part of very different and more marginal cultural trajectories than that of the High Enlightenment. As institutional religion steadily lost its intellectual centrality over the course of the eighteenth century, the status of Hebraist scholarship ineluctably subsided with it.

Retrospectively, the eclipse of the dry erudition of Christian Hebraism by the wit and polemic of the Enlightenment perhaps appears as a natural and inevitable process. However, at least until the 1720s no such easy inevitability was apparent to contemporaries. On the contrary, the relationship of the Hebrew language and Hebraist scholarship to the new values of reason and criticism remained a vexed and confused question. This issue provoked such passion and uncertainty because it was intimately associated with a set of wider issues at the heart of the confrontation of religion and philosophy. Much wider issues than mere philology and scholarly competence were at stake in disagreements over the interpretation of the Old Testament. In parallel and in association with these at times arcane debates between Hebraists, the historical, social and political significance of the Jewish Bible and its rabbinic exegesis was also comprehensively reconsidered over the course of the seventeenth century and the Early Enlightenment.

[63] See Christopher Clark, *The Politics of Conversion: Missionary Protestantism and the Jews in Prussia 1728–1941* (1995); Christoph Bochinger, 'J. H. Callenbergs Institutum Judaicum et Muhammedicum und seine Ausstrahlung nach Osteuropa', in Johannes Wallman and Udo Sträter, eds., *Halle und Osteuropa* (1988) 331–48.

[64] David S. Katz and Richard H. Popkin, *Messianic Revolution: Radical Religious Politics to the End of the Second Millennium* (1999) 119–34.

CHAPTER 2

Hebraic politics: Respublica Mosaica

Christian Hebraist scholarship in the seventeenth century was not a sealed, inward-looking enterprise. While leading specialists such as the Buxtorfs, L'Empereur and Cappel focused their attention on textual and ceremonial issues raised directly by their study of the Jewish interpretative tradition, a wider interest in Judaic themes simultaneously percolated into other spheres of European thought and culture in the decades around 1600. Hebraism naturally overflowed its disciplinary boundaries, providing stimulus to debates on a wide range of theoretical, historical, social and political topics. The nature of language itself was reconsidered in the light of the increased scrutiny of Hebrew texts. The notion that Hebrew was the first, divinely created language had been widely accepted since the first centuries of Christianity, and features in the writings of Augustine.[1] In the sixteenth and early seventeenth centuries, however, the originary status of Hebrew was widely contested, most forcefully by the late sixteenth-century Flemish linguist Johannes Goropius Becanus, who, to the amusement of most speakers of other languages, attempted to show that the mother of all languages was Dutch.[2] The increasing sophistication of Christian Hebraist scholarship placed increasing strain on the elevation of Hebrew to eternal status, but nonetheless Hebraists such as the younger Buxtorf insisted that the language had been preserved exactly as Adam had spoken it in Paradise. Fascination with Hebrew was a key element in the widespread seventeenth-century dream of a perfect language, which reached a notable crescendo in England during the tumultuous mid-century decades.[3]

Hebraic interests had also by the middle of the sixteenth century begun to cross-fertilise with Christian political thought. Prior to the Reformation

---

[1] François Laplanche, *La Bible en France: entre mythe et critique* (1994) 16.
[2] See Katz, *Philo-Semitism*, 55–7; Anthony Grafton, *Joseph Scaliger: A Study in the History of Classical Scholarship*, vol. ii (1993) 86–9.
[3] See Katz, *Philo-Semitism*, 43–88; Daniel Droixhe, *La Linguistique et l'appel de l'histoire (1600–1800)* (1978), esp. 41–2; Umberto Eco, *The Search for the Perfect Language* (1995).

Humanist biblical scholarship had eschewed explicitly political themes, while Machiavelli and other late Humanist political theorists defended republicanism in terms of the secular values of liberty and civic virtue.[4] Lutheran theology, with its insistence that all political authority is ordained by God, inaugurated a more political approach to the Bible. However, Luther's political doctrines, which from the spread of the German Peasants' Revolt in 1525 onwards starkly emphasised non-resistance, were grounded above all on Paul's injunction to submit to the secular authorities.[5] Calvinist political theology, in contrast, placed more political emphasis on the Old Testament. The social and governmental structures of the ancient Hebrews fascinated Calvin and his collaborators, who interpreted them as a divine model for the regulation of a godly community. Bonaventure Corneille Bertram's *De Politica Judaica*, published in Geneva in 1574, celebrated the biblical regime of the ancient Hebrews. Bertram emphasised that the Mosaic Law existed in order to control sin, and implicitly drew an extended parallel between its structures and sanctions and the theocratic moral regulation of Calvinist Geneva.[6]

SECOND ISRAELS

The study of the political institutions of what became known as 'The Republic of the Hebrews' emerged at this time as a new genre in Humanist scholarship. At least twelve major works were published on this theme between 1546 and 1710.[7] A major source for these scholars was Josephus' *Jewish Antiquities*, which was widely read in this period.[8] The subject was not exclusively a Protestant interest: one of the most important early texts, Carlo Sigonio's *Republica Hebraeorum*, was written and published in Bologna in 1582.[9] However, among Reformed Protestants the theme resonated most powerfully, as both practically relevant to their own politics and intensified by a strong sense of identification with the imagined biblicism, piety and intermittent suffering of the ancient Hebrews. Moyse Amyraut (1596–1664), one of the leading professors at the Huguenot Academy of Saumur, wrote

---

[4] See Quentin Skinner, *The Foundations of Modern Political Thought* (1978) vol. I, 152–86.

[5] *Ibid.*, vol. II, 15–19.

[6] François Laplanche, 'L'Erudition chrétienne aux XVIe et XVIIe siècles et l'état des hébreux', in *L'Ecriture sainte au temps de Spinoza et dans le système Spinoziste* (1992) 139–42.

[7] *Ibid.*, 133–47.

[8] See Mireille Hadas-Lebel, 'La Lecture du Flavius Josèphe aux XVIIe et XVIIIe siècles', in Chantal Grell and François Laplanche, eds., *Histoire du judaïsme* (1992) 101–13.

[9] On Sigonio see Laplanche, 'L'Erudition', 134–9; C. R. Ligota, 'Histoire à fondement théologique: la république des hébreux', in *L'Ecriture sainte au temps de Spinoza*, 154–6.

extensively on the Mosaic Republic,[10] while the most majestic and endur-
ing of all the seventeenth-century texts on the subject was written by Petrus
Cunaeus, Professor of Theology at the University of Leiden. Cunaeus' *De
Republica Hebraeorum* (1617) exalted the political organisation of the Mosaic
Republic, admiring in particular the equity of its agrarian laws and its institution of the Jubilee. Following the model established by Bertram, he
presented the Old Testament laws as an idealised vision of pure theocracy.
His text examines in detail the legal and political structures of the Hebrew
Republic, discussing the precise roles of judges, priests and the Sanhedrin,
and the details of sacrificial temple worship. In his preface, addressed to
the regents of Holland and West Friesland, he proudly drew attention to
the contemporary relevance of this political model: 'Honoured and powerful sirs, allow me the liberty to present to you...the Republic of the
Hebrews: the holiest and the best there has ever been. We can find there
material of great usefulness to kings, princes, and those who hold the reins
of republics.'[11] The regents of Holland had particular reason in 1617 to look
to Hebraic models for political inspiration. Cunaeus' text was published at
a moment of high drama in the United Provinces, which had only been
constituted, in the pioneering form of a federal republic, by the Union
of Utrecht less than forty years previously in 1579. Since the start of the
twelve-year truce with the Spanish in 1609, the patrician republicanism
advocated most powerfully by the scholar-regent Hugo Grotius and his
'Remonstrant' party had been under increasingly strident attack from the
more zealously Calvinist 'Counter-Remonstrants'. By 1617 this conflict had
reached crisis pitch, culminating in the following year with the overthrow of
the Remonstrant regime in Holland.[12] The theological and political aspects
of this dispute were so tightly intertwined as to be almost inextricable. The
self-image of the Dutch in this period – as a vulnerable, righteous nation,
establishing a new and virtuous polity in sharp contrast to the corruption of
their Spanish oppressors – bound religion and politics together extremely
closely, and placed an extremely high stake on their nexus. It is in no sense
surprising that Cunaeus' study, the hitherto most explicitly political reading of the Old Testament, appeared in the Dutch Republic at this early
moment of conflict over the nature of its republicanism.

---

[10] See François Laplanche, *L'Écriture, le sacré et l'histoire: érudits et politiques protestants devant la Bible
en France au XVII siècle* (1986) 496–516.

[11] Petrus Cunaeus, *La République des hebreux* (1705 (1617)) 1, 5.

[12] For a summary of these events, see Jonathan I. Israel, *The Dutch Republic: Its Rise, Greatness and
Fall, 1477–1806* (1995) 433–49.

The intensely theologico-political culture of the Dutch Republic shared much in common with that of its neighbour across the North Sea. Both England and the Dutch Republic in the early seventeenth century were imbued with a strong sense of national particularism and pride, associated with their respective unique post-Reformation pathways. In both nations there emerged a similar rhetorical self-identification with the ancient Jews, imagined, like themselves, as a small, plucky, internally divided but nonetheless unquestionable special people. The identification of England as a 'second Israel' was perhaps first expressed in John Foxe's immensely popular martyrology, the *Acts and Monuments* (1563).[13] The defeat of the Spanish Armada in 1588 brought to the fore key elements of this neo-Judaic national mythology: resilience, the rejection of slavery by mightier opponents and a sense of divine election. At a time when notions of nationhood were themselves in the process of emergence, it is redundant to argue whether the English saw themselves as the exclusive chosen nation, or as part of a wider whole. The parameters of the English sense of 'chosenness' were highly elastic, intermittently also embracing the Scottish, and at times all Protestants.[14] The political and theological elements of divine election could not easily be demarcated, because it was precisely the relationship between these spheres that was most profoundly at issue in the early seventeenth-century struggles, in both England and the Dutch Republic, between those who saw the nation essentially as a moral entity and those who preferred a more inclusive model.

As we have already noted, the close relationship between politics and religion gave Christian Hebraist scholarship in these two countries a particular impetus. The politicisation of the Bible, however, penetrated beyond the cloisters of academe. Nowhere was this more explicitly the case than in England immediately before and during the revolutionary upheavals of mid-century. In this period, as never before and never since, England was a culture saturated in the Bible. Available widely in the vernacular since the appearance of William Tyndale's translation in the 1530s, a century later the Bible was firmly established as a primary source in political argument both for radicals and traditionalists.[15] For early seventeenth-century Puritans, striving to make the English into a 'godly people', the governmental and legal structures of the ancient Hebrews were understood as intensely relevant

---

[13] This argument was first advanced in William Haller, *Foxe's Book of Martyrs and the Elect Nation* (1963). See also J. G. A. Pocock, *The Ancient Constitution and the Feudal* Law, 2nd edn (1987) 315–7.

[14] Christopher Hill, *The English Bible and the Seventeenth-Century Revolution* (1993) 264–70.

[15] *Ibid.*, esp. 3–44.

to their contemporary struggle.[16] Hebraic identification in this period was extremely widespread, and in the prelude to the civil war grew increasingly polyvalent. Of the approximately 150 surviving 'fast sermons' delivered to the Long Parliament between 1640 and 1645, almost five times as many are devoted to the Old Testament as to the New, and many of these focused on apocalyptic themes.[17] During the 1640s and 1650s the radicalism of groups such as the Levellers, Diggers and Quakers was profoundly inspired by the Old Testament, and propagated through biblical rhetoric that made intensive use of the moral polarities of Abel and Cain, Jacob and Esau, and Israel and Amalek.[18]

The most influential strand of English Hebraic politics, however, was set in motion before the revolutionary period. The conflict between Crown and Parliament emerged against a background of increasingly widespread Erastianism among parliamentary Puritans. Convinced, particularly after the promotion of the traditionalist William Laud to Canterbury in 1633, that an autonomous Church would never be an effective vehicle for the moralisation of the English nation, these parliamentarians grew increasingly concerned to assert their own authority in religious matters. The articulation of this Erastian agenda was closely associated both with Judaic identification and Hebraic scholarship. The ideal of national godliness harked back to the 'second Israel' theme, while scholars closely studied the Old Testament, and the political structures of the Republic of the Hebrews in particular, as sources for the correct regulation of religious and moral affairs. Even at the mid-century peak of the Hebraic suffusion of English discourse this project still provoked some anxiety and embarrassment. Thomas Coleman, a Lancashire rector and one of the leading advocates of Erastianism in the 1640s, was also a noted Hebraist; so much so that he was satirically nicknamed 'Rabbi Coleman'.[19]

JOHN SELDEN: HEBRAISM AND THE AUTHORITY OF LAW

By far the most erudite and influential political Hebraist of the early seventeenth century, however, was John Selden. The primary focus of Selden's career was the law: he practised at the bar in London, and wrote extensively on legal history. His juridical interests, though, flowed naturally into his fascination with Hebraica. This was already evident in his first major work, The *History of Tithes* (1618), in which he presented a meticulous historical

---

[16] See William M. Lamont, *Godly Rule: Politics and Religion, 1603–60* (1969).
[17] Hill, *English Bible*, 83.   [18] *Ibid.*, 196–250.   [19] Lamont, *Godly Rule*, 115.

study of tithe-paying, in order to demonstrate that the practice was based on civil rather than canon law. This thesis pointedly challenged the traditional authority of the Church, and thus also the divine right theory of kingship. Such was the ensuing controversy that Selden was compelled by the Privy Council to retract his claims.[20] In establishing his case, Selden made extensive use of English primary sources such as Bede and the Domesday Book, in which he found little evidence of tithing.[21] The foundational second chapter of the text, however, is devoted to Jewish tithing practices prior to their suspension at the time of the destruction of the second temple. Selden here highlights the complexity of ancient Jewish tithing, and the importance of successive legal judgements in defining and refining the regulations that governed it.[22] This excursus into Jewish law is in no sense a mere adornment to Selden's overall argument. He presents the Jewish case, based on biblical sources, as paradigmatic in his overall theologico-political argument for the paramountcy of law in human affairs. By demonstrating the importance of the mediation of the law in the divinely ordained theocracy of ancient Judaism, Selden established the firmest possible biblical basis for his wider challenge to clerical and royal autonomy.

In his later work Selden grew more explicitly Hebraist in orientation. His *De Jure Naturali* (1640) consisted of a detailed comparison of Jewish and Gentile laws on murder, incest, idolatry and many other matters, while in his *Uxor Ebraica* (1646) he presented a detailed analysis of Jewish marriage laws.[23] Unlike his contemporaries on the continent such as L'Empereur and the Buxtorfs, Selden was a pure autodidact, working without any contact with living Jews. This inevitably limited his perspective, and to a large extent explains certain eccentricities and errors in his use of some rabbinic sources, and his heavy reliance on Maimonides' *Mishneh Torah*.[24] However, also unlike his continental peers, Selden was directly engaged in politics as well as scholarship: both these Hebraist works appeared while their author was serving as member for Oxford in the Long Parliament. Selden's Hebraist studies were intimately connected to his Erastian politics. By establishing the intricacy and historicity of the ancient Jewish law, and the supreme authority of its legislative institutions, Selden repudiated at the most fundamental level the notion that the moral authority of the

[20] See Paul Christianson, *Discourse on History, Law and Governance in the Public Career of John Selden (1610–1635)* (1996) 63–83.

[21] John Selden, *The History of Tithes* (1618) 276–80.   [22] *Ibid.*, 10–24.

[23] John Selden, *De Jure Naturali & Gentium juxta Disciplinam Ebraeorum* (1640); *Uxor Hebraica* (1646) ed. and trans. Jonathan R. Ziskind (1991).

[24] Jonathan R. Ziskind, 'Introduction' to John Selden, *Uxor Hebraica* (1991) 27–8.

Church transcended the institutional power of the law.[25] This argument was most systematically advanced in Selden's final work, his immense three-volume *De Synedriis & Praefecturis Juridicis Veterum Ebraeorum* (1650–3). Selden here meticulously traces the relationship between ancient Jewish legal structures, procedures and sanctions and those of the Classical and Arabic worlds and of primitive and post-Apostolic Christianity. Crucial to his argument was the identification core of 'natural law' on which both Jewish and all subsequent legal systems were based. This core was divinely revealed to the Jews in the seven 'Noachite precepts' – the universal ethical commandments included within the Decalogue – and have formed the basis of all legal authority ever since.[26]

The Jews were central to Selden's theory of law. It was through their historical relationship with God that the natural law basis of justice was originally revealed; and it was uniquely in their earliest polity that all laws – both the 'natural' core and its 'civil' elaboration – were divinely ordained. The essence of Jewish law was universal, but its theocratic totality was unique. This complex duality is succinctly summarised in Selden's *Table-Talk*: 'God at first gave laws to all mankind, but afterwards he gave peculiar laws to the Jews which only they were to observe. Just as we have the common law for all England, and yet you have some corporations that, besides that, have peculiar laws and privileges to themselves.'[27] There is a revealing slippage in Selden's positioning of the Jews over these two sentences. Although his phrasing in this passage does not make it absolutely clear, it was axiomatic to Selden, and fundamental to the theological orthodoxy that framed his argument, that both the universal, natural law and the 'peculiar' Jewish laws were historically revealed by God to Moses and the Jewish people. At this moment in history, the universal and the particular were unified within the Jewish law. The civil law was subsequently amplified and embellished by the legal authorities of the ancient Hebrews, who thereby set in motion the process of legal development that is the central focus of Selden's interest.[28] In the case of England, however, the relationship between sacred and 'peculiar' law is less clear. All law, Selden is at pains to argue, incorporates both divine and human elements. The English common law, like the Jewish law, consists of a civil tradition based around

[25] See Richard Tuck, *Natural Rights Theories* (1979) 94–9; D. R. Woolf, 'Erudition and the Idea of History in Renaissance England', *Renaissance Quarterly* 40 (1987) 32–47.
[26] John Selden, *De Synedriis & Praefecturis Juridicis Veterum Ebraeorum*, 3 vols. (1679 (1650–3)) esp. vol. I, 4–10; see also Tuck, *Natural Rights Theories*, 82–100.
[27] John Selden, *Table-Talk* (1819 (1777)) 70–1.
[28] Selden summarises his historical analysis of the law in *Uxor Hebraica*, 33–6.

a core of universal natural law. However, Selden here more explicitly draws an analogy not between Jewish law and English common law (though it is precisely this analogy that animates his interest in the subject) but between Jewish law and the 'peculiar laws and privileges' of certain corporations.

This ambiguity is fundamental to Selden's legal philosophy. In attempting to historicise natural law theory, Selden sought to position divine universalism within the specific narrative of human legal development. Despite the intricacy of his analysis, he could not overcome the inescapable tension between these two dimensions of his theory. Selden read Jewish law as the most explicit and elaborate intertwinement of natural and civil elements, and was profoundly drawn to it for this reason. His fascination was very much in step with the widespread identificatory affection and admiration for Jews in England in the decades immediately prior to their readmission there in 1655.[29] Selden's personal high estimation of the self-sufficiency, solidarity, prosperity and usefulness of contemporary Jews is recorded in his *Table-Talk*.[30] However, these positive attitudes were not an entirely stable element in his thought. His presentation of Jewish law as paradigmatic of all law left him with no bulwark against the accusation of Judaisation, and the associated fear of a subordination of English particularity to an alien Jewishness. It was both intellectually and politically essential for Selden to reconcile his fascination with Hebraica with an orthodox theology that clearly asserted the supremacy of Christianity and the error of postbiblical Judaism. Against this context Jewish rabbinic law most readily appeared as not in any sense exemplary, but rather as an obscure and obsolete cultural artefact. Selden was unavoidably caught between these two perspectives of Hebraic centrality and particularity. He lavished his abundant scholarly energy almost exclusively on Jewish legal matters, while simultaneously acknowledging the limited, local significance of this subject alongside the many other traditions of civil law in human history.

HOBBES, HARRINGTON AND THE HEBRAIC COMMONWEALTH

Selden's approach to legal history was an important influence on other English thinkers, most notably including Thomas Hobbes.[31] Although no Hebraist, Hobbes shared with Selden a serious interest in the legal and political history of the Jews. The third of the four books of *Leviathan* (1651),

---

[29] See Katz, *Philo-Semitism*, esp. 175–6.   [30] Selden, *Table-Talk*, 71.
[31] Richard Tuck has emphasised the originality and influence of Selden: see his *Natural Rights Theories*, esp. 119. For a contrasting view, see J. P. Somerville, 'John Selden, The Law of Nature, and the Origins of Government', *Historical Journal* 27 (1984) 437–47.

although titled 'Of a Christian Commonwealth', dwells in almost as much detail on the political affairs of the ancient Hebrews. In a fashion structurally similar to Selden's historicisation of legal authority, Hobbes' historical exposition of his theory of contractual politics is grounded on the Mosaic covenant of the Jews with God. Taking issue with the tendency of sermonisers to interpret biblical references to the 'Kingdom of God' metaphorically, he insists that the phrase almost always refers to a literal kingdom: 'a *Kingdome properly so named*, constituted by the votes of Israel in peculiar manner; wherein they chose God for their King by Covenant made with him'.[32] The Israelite commonwealth thus stands as the original and perfect paradigmatic example of the Hobbesian commonwealth. As God's 'Lieutenant', Moses, under God, exercised sovereignty over the Hebrews, overseeing all matters just as Hobbes had argued in the first half of *Leviathan* that a sovereign should. Hobbes also stressed that the basis of Moses' authority was in accordance with his general theory of contractualism: as with 'all other princes', Moses' rule was 'grounded on the Consent of the People, and their Promise to obey him'.[33] The subsequent history of the Jews, as he narrates it, further exemplifies his political analysis. The troubles of the Jews began after the death of Joshua, in the era of Judges, when there was 'no king in Israel'. The Jews' recurrent rebellions and lapses into idolatry weakened the political element of their divine covenant, and began their uneven descent into conditions of life that, if not short, were in Hobbes' eyes often unquestionably nasty and brutish.[34]

In the third book of *Leviathan* the divine voice is a powerful presence. Hobbes examines at length the meaning of biblical references to the 'Word of God', and the various means by which God exceptionally communicated with Moses and the prophets.[35] In the first book of his text, however, he presents the Mosaic commonwealth in a seemingly somewhat different and more mundane fashion. All religions, he here argues, whether 'divine' or 'gentile', are similarly designed to promote among their followers the social values of 'Obedience, Lawes, Peace, Charity and civill Society'.[36] The disjuncture between these two perspectives is immediately striking from a modern perspective, and has lead many of Hobbes' readers, from his own time to the present day, to conclude that his professed privileging of Judaeo-Christianity was insincere guise. However, this argument does not convince. Most scholarly attention has been concentrated on the first two books of *Leviathan*, in which Hobbes expounds his contractual

---

[32] Thomas Hobbes, *Leviathan* (1651) III, §35.   [33] *Ibid.*, III, §40.   [34] *Ibid.*
[35] *Ibid.*, III, §36.   [36] *Ibid.*, I, §12.

notion of government in relentlessly logical and secular fashion. However, the contrastingly theological final two books, of equal length and polemical intensity, also demand interpretation.[37] *Leviathan* is in many ways a frontier text, encompassing both scientific rationalism and bibliocentric theology. As we shall see, in the latter half of the seventeenth century these two perspectives strained increasingly powerfully against each other, until their fusion became untenable. For Hobbes, however, we have no reason to believe that any such incompatability was apparent: he expounds both aspects of his argument with equal conviction. The tension between them, however, is inescapable. Nowhere is this fracture in Hobbes' thought more starkly highlighted than by his exceptional treatment of the Jewish covenant, which he treats as politically paradigmatic and foundational, but in its sacred uniqueness also external to the normal flow of human history.

A fascination with Hebraic politics is even more pronounced in the work of Hobbes' contemporary, James Harrington. Like Hobbes, Harrington read the Old Testament as a fundamentally political text, and both men intended this hermeneutic act as an explicit challenge to the clerical orthodoxy. By demonstrating that the Mosaic covenant had established a theocratic polity in which there was no distinction in kind between civil and religious authority, both *Leviathan* and Harrington's *Oceana* (1651) struck a blow at traditional ecclesiological arguments that based the autonomous authority of the Christian Church on its succession from the Hebrew priesthood. However, *Oceana* was as much a rebuttal of *Leviathan* as it was a reinforcement. Whereas Hobbes saw the Hebraic commonwealth as an absolute monarchy, Harrington presented it as the perfect example of his own preferred form of government: a republic.[38] *Oceana* is an intensely practical text, less a utopia than a visionary statement of the form of republican regime that Harrington hoped would be established in England in the near future.[39] He presents a wide range of exemplary models for this polity, including most prominently the ancient constitutions of Athens, Sparta

---

[37] This point was first made in J. G. A. Pocock, 'Time, History and Eschatology in the Thought of Thomas Hobbes', *Politics, Language and Time: Essays on Political Thought and History* (1971) 158–62. See also Richard Tuck, 'The civil Religion of Thomas Hobbes', in Nicholas Phillipson and Quentin Skinner, eds., *Political Discourse in Early Modern Britain* (1993) 120–38.

[38] On the relationship between Hobbes' and Harrington's thought, see J. G. A. Pocock, 'Historical Intoduction' to Pocock, ed., *The Political Works of James Harrington* (1977) 77–99; Jonathan Scott, 'The Rapture of Motion: James Harrington's Republicanism', in Nicholas Phillipson and Quentin Skinner, eds., *Political Discourse in Early Modern Britain* (1993) 154–163; Blair Worden, 'James Harrington and *The Commonwealth of Oceana*, 1656', in David Wootton, ed., *Republicanism, Liberty and Commercial Society* (1994) 90–1.

[39] J. G. A. Pocock, 'Introduction' to James Harrington, *The Commonwealth of Oceana* (1992) xvii.

and republican Rome, as well as modern Venice. The commonwealth of Israel, however, is singled out for unique attention.

Oceana opens, like *Leviathan*, with an abstract analysis of what Harrington describes as 'the Principles of Government'. Midway through his first chapter, however, Harrington moves to a new terrain of argument. Having 'transcribed these principles of a commonwealth out of nature', he states that he will now 'appeal unto God and to the world.'[40] This statement signals his turn from abstraction to exemplification, which he subdivides into two categories: the divine example of the commonwealth of Israel, and the secular example of the various historical republics. Harrington clearly marks this distinction between the Israelite republic, through which he makes his appeal to divine authority, and all others, which together form a tradition of 'ancient prudence'.[41] However, he repeatedly describes the features of the Israelite republic in parallel with those of subsequent republican regimes, highlighting their fundamental similarity. He supports his argument that religious matters should naturally fall under the jurisdiction of the commonwealth, for example, by showing how this had been the case in a sequence of republics from Israel to Rome.[42] The Jewish past is thus ambiguously positioned in *Oceana*, standing in some senses within the usual weft of human history, while at the same time, in the period of the Israelite republic, at least, uniquely embodying a divinely ordained polity. Here again Harrington echoes Hobbes in his intellectually awkward but rhetorically compelling integration of biblical and rational politics.

The peculiarity of Harrington's presentation of the relationship of Judaism to history is brought to the fore in his single reference in *Oceana* to the Jews of his own time. This discussion features prominently in the introduction to the work, which consists of a mellifluous panegyric to Oceana, which, it is made clear, is to be understood as England in the immediate post-civil-war future. Harrington pays particular attention to the problems of the fertile but degenerate 'neighbour island' of 'Panopea' or Ireland: 'the soft mother of a slothful and pusillanimous people'.[43] His suggestion is that the island would best be settled with Jews, who, he confidently asserts, would flock there in large numbers if allowed 'their own rites and laws'. In Panopea the Jews would retain their mercantile skills, and also rediscover their ancient talent for agriculture, presenting the possibility of a uniquely profitable arrangement both for the tenant Jews and for the landlord commonwealth of Oceana.[44]

---

[40] James Harrington, *The Commonwealth of Oceana* (1992 (1656)) 25.   [41] *Ibid.*
[42] *Ibid.*, 39–40.   [43] *Ibid.*, 6.   [44] *Ibid.*

This suggestion is clearly a response to contemporary events both in England, where debate had recently raged at the Whitehall Conference over the possible readmission of the Jews, and in Ireland, where Cromwell was attempting to implement a brutal policy of native transplantation.[45] Harrington's position here is implicitly critical both of Cromwell's strategy in Ireland (the settlement of Jews would have been the best policy there, he writes, 'if it had been thought upon in time'[46]), and of the *de facto* acceptance of Jewish settlement in England, which had effectively been established only a few months prior to the publication of *Oceana* in the autumn of 1656.[47] In contrast to the newly acknowledged Jewish colony living and working in the heart of London, Harrington's proposed plantation of Ireland with Jews was designed to quarantine them from others: 'To receive the Jews after any other manner into a commonwealth were to maim it; for they of all nations never incorporate but, taking up the room of a limb, are of no use or office unto the body, while they suck the nourishment which would sustain a natural and useful member.'[48] Harrington may have been hostile to the settlement of Jews in Oceana proper because he believed that they would bring with them an economic culture of vigorous financial speculation, which would destabilise the virtuous, property-based society he envisioned.[49] Whatever his reason, however, it reflects a notion of Jews that curiously blurs ancient virtue with contemporary stereotype. Harrington idealises the agrarian and mercantile skills of the Jews, but simultaneously regards them as irreducibly alien and potentially dangerous. The indeterminacy of the relationship of sacred and secular history in *Oceana* is here projected directly on to an actually existing community. Seventeenth-century Jewry, in Harrington's mind, paradoxically straddles these two spheres, standing both as an unchanging marker of divine utopianism and as a living minority requiring the attention of public policy.

In later writings Harrington returned at greater length to Hebraic themes. His final major work, *The Art of Lawgiving* (1659), focuses on Jewish law and is heavily indebted to the scholarship of John Selden.[50] Harrington's account here of the legal development of the Israelite commonwealth places a very distinctive emphasis on the role of Jethro, Moses' Midianite father-in-law, who advised Moses how to organise his judicial system.[51] Jethro is

---

[45] See S. B. Liljegren, 'Harrington and the Jews', *Humanistiska Vetenskapssamfundets* (1932) 65–78.
[46] Harrington, *Oceana*, 6.   [47] See Katz, *Philo-Semitism*, 232–8.   [48] Harrington, *Oceana*, 6.
[49] J. G. A. Pocock, *Machiavellian Moment* 391.
[50] On Harrington's use of Selden, and of Talmudic and rabbinic sources, see Liljegren, 'Harrington and the Jews', 81–90.
[51] Exodus 18: 13–27.

important in Harrington's argument because he was a non-Jew, whose advice, based on the model of his own political community, was incorporated
into the structures of the Israelite commonwealth. Harrington uses this example of the fusion of 'heathenish' and Mosaic legal elements to repudiate
the accusation that his comparison of ancient Israel to other republics was
'irreverent or atheistical'.[52] The Israelite commonwealth, although divine,
was also human, and therefore legitimately stood at the head of Harrington's lineage of historical republics. This emphasis on the influence of Jethro
reflects Harrington's desire to attenuate the exceptionalism of the ancient
Hebrews, and to stress their integration into history. However, it does not
dissolve the central uniqueness of their divine election, or the ambiguity of
the relationship of this to their historical role.

The political history of the Hebrews is, however, a central concern of *The
Art of Lawgiving*. Harrington divides his discussion of the commonwealth
of the Hebrews into two successive epochs: 'Elohim, or the Commonwealth
of Israel, and Cabala, or the Commonwealth of the Jews'. The divine commonwealth of Elohim began to degenerate after the death of Joshua, but
aspects of it endured, according to Harrington, until the dispersion of the
Jews by Emperor Hadrian: longer than any other government since then.[53]
However, after the return from Babylonian exile the Jewish government was
increasingly dependent on the oral law – 'Cabala' – and its interpretation
by the priestly elite.[54] In his earlier *Prerogative of Popular Government* (1658)
Harrington had already examined in great detail the degeneration of the
transmission of authority from *chirotonia* – popular acclaim – to *chiroth-
esia*: the laying on of hands, a closed process creating a self-perpetuating
oligarchy.[55] Through this analysis Harrington recast the decline and loss of
divine favour of the Jews as an essentially political narrative of the corruption of their republican institutions. This narrative forms the blueprint for
the interpretation of history, and particularly of the decline of the primitive
Christian Church into a priest-ridden hierarchy. The Jewish experience is
thus firmly placed at the centre not only of Harrington's republican idealism but also of his understanding of the historical processes of change
and decay. He attempts much more insistently than Hobbes to bridge the
gulf between divine and human history, and to show how the sacred polity
of ancient Israel can legitimately and realistically be used as a model in
revolutionary seventeenth-century England. However, within his biblical

[52] James Harrington, *The Art of Lawgiving* (1659), in Pocock, ed., *Political Works of Harrington*, 629.
[53] *Ibid.*, 635–6.   [54] *Ibid.*, 645–9.
[55] James Harrington, *The Prerogative of Popular Government* (1658), in Pocock, ed., *Political Works of
Harrington*, 516–38.

politics the Jews remain in limbo, neither entirely within secular history nor entirely outside it.

IDENTIFICATION AND INNOCENCE

In the sweeping interpretation of western political thought devised by J. G. A. Pocock, James Harrington serves as a vital linchpin. Pocock sees Harrington as the key reinterpreter of the Machiavellian language of civic Humanism and virtue into an English republican idiom. Via Harrington, he argues, the Renaissance tradition of civic republicanism exerted a fundamental influence on the ideology of English Whig 'neo-Harringtonians' from 1675 onwards, and on the economic and constitutional thought of eighteenth-century America.[56] While this analysis is clearly of considerable persuasive power, Harrington's political use of the Bible highlights the intellectual distance between him and these subsequent generations of thinkers. As Pocock himself has emphasised, in the later seventeenth century new and more sophisticated modes of historical self-understanding began to emerge.[57] This is of crucial importance with respect to the legacy of the biblical politics of the English revolutionary era. The ambiguities of the approach of both Harrington and Hobbes to the Jewish historical record by no means disappeared in subsequent generations; but the innocence of their elision between sacred and secular very soon became untenable.

In part this was due to the political exhaustion of the Bible in England by the end of the Interregnum. The diversity and boldness of the radical readings of the Old Testament during this period had made it evident that the text was abundantly open to multiple interpretation. In response, English scholars in the period immediately after 1660 retreated from the most contentious issues of textual hermeneutics.[58] Elsewhere in Europe, however, the intellectual climate moved according to different patterns. Above all, it was the impact of Spinoza's historicist reading of the Pentateuch that transformed the political usage of the Bible from the 1670s onwards. The radical religious politics of later seventeenth-century England, although owing much to Harrington, were characterised by a much more strident rhetoric of anticlericalism,[59] and by a much more complicated understanding of the

---

[56] Pocock, *Machiavellian Moment*, esp. 383–422; Pocock, 'Machiavelli, Harrington and English Political Ideologies' *Politics, Language and Time* (1971) 104–47. For a penetrating critique of Pocock's argument, see David Wootton, 'Introduction: The Republican Tradition: From Commonwealth to Common Sense', in Wooton, ed., *Republicanism*, 10–19.

[57] Pocock, *Machiavellian Moment*, 401–2.   [58] See Hill, *English Bible*, 413–35.

[59] See Mark Goldie, 'Priestcraft and the Birth of Whiggism', in Phillipson and Skinner, *Political Discourse*, 209–31.

historical status of the Bible and of the Jews. We will therefore turn to these writers later in this book, after we have examined the intervening currents of intellectual change that marked their arguments apart from those of the revolutionary era.

Uncomplicated identification with the ancient Israelites by no means died in England with the Restoration. British high culture in the Augustan era, from Dryden's *Absalom and Achitophel* (1684) to Handel's patriotic *Israel in Egypt* oratorio (1738), abounds with the allegorical conflation of ancient Hebrews and modern Britons as God's chosen people, associated with pluck, resilience and liberty.[60] However, after 1660, and more emphatically after 1688, the 'second Israel' fancy was divorced from its puritan roots and its radical political connotations, becoming in the eighteenth century a stock image in the crafting of a consensual British patriotism.

The blunting of the polemical edge of Hebraic politics in the later seventeenth century was an international phenomenon. Shadowing the rise of Christian Hebraic scholarship in Catholic Europe just as in the Protestant world the discipline had begun to lose momentum, so the culture and politics of the ancient Hebrews emerged in this period, belatedly but decisively, as a popular subject within Catholic orthodoxy. The most confident Hebraic text of the late seventeenth century was written in France by the Abbé Claude Fleury, a prominent ecclesiastical historian and close associate of Fénelon. His *Les Moeurs des Israélites* (1681) was an immense success, rapidly establishing itself as the standard French account of the ancient Hebrew polity, and going through at least sixty reprints in the course of the eighteenth century.[61] Echoing earlier writers on the subject, Fleury stated that the ancient Hebrew regime was a pure theocracy, directly governed by God by means of his revealed law.[62] His emphasis, however, was less on politics than on the utopian evocation of Hebrew society, which he portrayed as an idyll of rustic simplicity. Like Cunaeus, he claimed that the ancient Hebrews offered a practical example for his own contemporary world: 'The people that God chose to preserve the true religion up to the preaching of the Gospel offer an excellent model of human life most fully in accord with nature. We find in their customs the most rational approach to subsistence, labour and social life: we can learn from them not only morals, but also about economics and politics.'[63] Fleury's text presents an innocently straightforward vision of an Old Testament

---

[60] For an survey of this strand of Hebraic imagery in British literature, see Howard D. Weinbrot, *Britannia's Issue: The Rise of British Literature from Dryden to Ossian* (1993) 408–45.

[61] Israel, *European Jewry*, 218; Hertzberg, *French Enlightenment*, 41.

[62] Claude Fleury, *Moeurs des Israélites* (1683 (1681)) 147.   [63] *Ibid.*, 1.

Utopia, insouciantly disregarding all complexities of textual interpretation and historical verisimilitude. The huge popularity of this work throughout the eighteenth century is testimony to a widespread and enduring desire to flee these dilemmas, and to return to the interpretative certainties of the pre-Enlightenment world. However, already at the time of the publication of *Les Moeurs des Israélites* such certainties could no longer confidently be sustained. The rise of textual criticism, as we have seen, had cast the assumptions of literalist Hebraic scholarship into doubt. More fundamentally, the rise of history as subject of intellectual inquiry had raised difficult questions concerning the relationship of the Jewish past to that of other civilisations, and in so doing had profoundly destabilised the seamless integration of sacred and secular history exemplified by figures such as Harrington, Hobbes and, less systematically, Fleury. It is to this gradual erosion of the traditional understanding of the place of the Jews in the wider historical schema that we shall now turn.

CHAPTER 3

Meaning and method: Jewish history, world history

The theological meaning accorded to the Jews in pre-Enlightenment Christianity was profoundly embedded in history. As recipients of the original Mosaic revelation, as the faithful preservers of God's word in their sacred texts, as a reminder in their dispersion and misery of the wrath of God towards those who rejected His son, and as providentially destined to convert to the true faith at the dawn of the end of history, the Jews were the linchpin of the Christian conception of time, past, present and future. The medieval church had in large measure interpreted the biblical narrative in allegorical terms. The Reformation, however, brought with it a more analytical and literalist approach to the Bible, which led to an increasing focus on the interpretation of Scripture above all as history.[1] This project raised many difficulties. The meticulous examination of the Hebrew Bible by Christian Hebraist scholars, and the rising awareness of its ambiguities, called into question the notion of the ancient Jews as transparent and fully reliable historical record-keepers. More broadly, such critical textual scrutiny increasingly destabilised the entire edifice of the Christian theory of history, and thus raised two related and pressing questions. How, if at all, could an ordered structure of historical meaning be established on a more robust and certain basis? And if Jewish history was to be displaced from its sacrosanct status and subjected to critical analysis, on what terms should the Jews and their texts be accounted for and interpreted?

Historical criticism was not born with the Enlightenment. Later historians owed a large debt to fifteenth- and sixteenth-century Humanist scholarship, from Petrarch and Valla to Patrizzi, Bodin and Pasquier, who produced a great wealth of historical writing, inspired by a striving towards both universality of scope and accuracy of method.[2] However, the intellectual upheavals of the seventeenth century had a powerful impact on

---

[1] See Peter Harrison, *The Bible, Protestantism and the Rise of Natural Science* (1998) 121–9.
[2] See Peter Burke, *The Renaissance Sense of the Past* (1969); Donald R. Kelley, *Foundations of Modern Historical Scholarship* (1970); George Huppert, *The Idea of Perfect History* (1970).

historiographical reflection and practice. The advent of Cartesianism and the geometric method challenged the status of historical enquiry: for Descartes, because reason alone, rather than mere human authority or opinion, could be considered a truly valid source of knowledge, history was inevitably demoted below science to the ranks of those fields of enquiry that could only aspire to likelihood or probability of accuracy, and not to truth itself.[3] In the later seventeenth century historians responded to Descartes in various ways. Some scholars, such as La Mothe Le Vayer in his *Discours du peu de certitude qu'il y a dans l'Histoire* (1668), reasserted the poetic tradition of the *ars historica*, and recommended that history should primarily aspire to moral usefulness rather than factual truth. As we shall soon see in more detail, others, and above all Pierre Bayle, appeared positively to relish the puzzles and inscrutabilities of historical erudition, while still others, and above all Bishop Bossuet, firmly reasserted the enduring validity of traditional bibliocentric history. The old broad consensus, however, was unambiguously ruptured.

In this period of philosophical upheaval, the identity and purpose of historical writing was uncertain and much disputed. The discipline was deeply embroiled in key intellectual controversies concerning the relationship of past to present, of nature to culture, of the sacred to the profane, of erudition to true knowledge, and of non-western histories and religions to the Classical and Christian traditions. Jewish themes figured prominently in the discussion of all of these issues. Close to the core of all of them, in different guises, was a challenge to the historical status of the Old Testament, and the privileged narrative of Jewish history contained within it.

These scholarly debates had powerful cultural and political resonances. The assertion of national cultural pride and historical identity – a leading historiographical concern from the late seventeenth century onwards – brought to the fore new mythic narratives that often stood in implicit tension with the overarching structure of biblical history. The nature of national cultures was central to the famed quarrel between 'Ancients and Moderns' that raged in both England and France in the 1690s. Against the insistence of the Ancients on the unity, uniqueness and unquestionable superiority of Classical literature, the Moderns sought to valorise the distinctiveness of different cultures, and the achievements of their own.[4] In England, leading moderns such as William Wotton strongly asserted the

---

[3] Carlo Borghero, *La certezza e la storia* (1983) 3–46; Ian Hacking, *The Emergence of Probability* (1975) 43–8.

[4] See Joan DeJean, *Ancients Against Moderns: Culture Wars and the Making of a Fin de Siècle* (1997) 124–50.

value of Hebraic learning as well as the study of Classical texts.[5] Here as in so many other contexts, Judaism emerged as a key point of intellectual reference. The biblical narrative, because of its status both as the standard account of historical origins and as the archetypal national history, recurrently stood as the central point of comparison to which other histories and cultures were either harmonised or contrasted. To a very considerable extent, much Early Enlightenment historiography was a proxy attempt to renegotiate the complex relationship of European culture to its own mythic Judaic origins.

BIBLICAL CHRONOLOGY: TIME OUT OF JOINT

To the humanist mind, fundamental to the understanding of history was a firm grasp on the basic contours of time itself. The numerical discipline of historical chronology towered over narrative forms of historiography; and at the beginning of the seventeenth century the monumental works of the Leiden professor Joseph Scaliger towered over those of all other chronologists. Most sixteenth-century chronologies had been heavily influenced by the medieval chronologies of Annius of Viterbo, which elaborated fancifully on Persian, Babylonian and Egyptian records, and intertwined them with ancient myths and biblical history.[6] Scaliger, in his *De emendatione temporum* (1583), rejected Annius' forgeries, but recognised the authenticity of some of his key Greek and Egyptian sources. The Bible remained the cornerstone of Scaliger's chronology, but his scholarship was distinguished by a prodigious versatility, drawing on astronomical data as well as a close analysis of Christian, Jewish, Greek, Roman, Persian and Egyptian calendrical systems.[7]

The fusion of these various sources, however, posed serious difficulties. Based on his harmonisation of the Jewish and the Julian calendars, Scaliger dated the creation of the world to the autumn of 3760 BCE.[8] However, this did not accord with the Egyptian dynastic lists recorded by Manetho, an Egyptian priest whose work survived through fragmented quotations and references in Josephus, Eusebius and other ancient writers, and whom Scaliger essentially regarded as an authoritative source. (In making this judgement he disagreed with his contemporary, Isaac Casaubon, and foreshadowed the assessment of modern Egyptologists.) In order to

[5] See Joseph M. Levine, *The Battle of the Books* (1991) 402–7.
[6] Anthony Grafton, *Defenders of the Text* (1991) 76–103.
[7] See Anthony Grafton, 'Joseph Scaliger and Historical Chronology: The Rise and Fall of a Discipline', *History and Theory* 14 (1975); *Defenders of the text*, 104–44; *Joseph Scaliger*.
[8] Grafton, *Joseph Scaliger*, 188–9.

accommodate these dynasties into his calendrical system, Scaliger devised the mind-bending notion of 'proleptic time': this encompassed dates prior to historical time, which started with the Creation. He based this idea on an intricate calendrical mathematics, centred on his concept of the 'Julian Period', a cycle of 7,980 calendrically unique years that he calculated as having begun in 4713 BCE. Manetho's dynasties, however, extended still further back into proleptic time, so Scaliger dated their beginning within the previous 7,980-year calendrical cycle.[9]

Scaliger responded with impatience and derision to the baffled response of most of his contemporaries to his chronological scholarship. He had set his peers an intelligence test, he commented, which almost all of them had failed.[10] However, despite the magisterial erudition of Scaliger's work, it is not surprising that few people could make sense of his invention of a dating system extending prior to the Creation. In his *De theologia gentili* (1641), Gerhard Vossius took a much more straightforward approach to the problem posed by Manetho. By arguing that several of the Egyptian dynasties in his list ran concurrently rather than successively, Vossius managed to contain them within a biblical chronology. He was aided in this task by choosing to base his biblical calculations on the Septuagint, which offered scope for a lengthier chronology than did the Masoretic Bible. In order to justify his turn to the Septuagint, and to explain the divergences between the Greek and Hebrew biblical texts, Vossius reiterated the old accusation that after the translation of the Septuagint the Jews had deliberately falsified their own Hebrew version, in order to confound the Christians.[11]

Vossius' challenge to the authority of the Hebrew Bible destabilised the traditional historical understanding of the Jews as a 'witness people'. If, as Vossius, argued, the Jews were fundamentally unreliable as the record-keepers of divine testimony, then not only was the value of Christian Hebraic scholarship implicitly called into question, but an important element of the theological significance of contemporary Jewry for Christians was tacitly undermined. Scaliger also, in theorising epochs beyond biblical time, unwittingly weakened the assumed historical centrality of the Bible and of the Jewish people. Both Vossius and Scaliger saw themselves as orthodox Calvinist scholars, and sought not to challenge but to reinforce the authority of the traditional Bible-based interpretation of history. However, their speculations opened up vast new terrains of uncertainty and ambiguity, which inexorably led to the opposite result.

This terrain was soon much more boldly explored. The relationship of Jewish history to the past of other peoples was dramatically and

---

[9] *Ibid.*, 681–720.   [10] *Ibid.*, 394.   [11] See Katz, 'Isaac Vossius'.

scandalously reinterpreted by the peripatetic French scholar Isaac La
Peyrère, in his two audacious texts, *Du Rappel des Juifs* (1643) and *Prae-
Adamitae* (1655). Raised as a Calvinist in Bordeaux, and most probably of
Marrano descent, La Peyrère developed a highly original personal theology, the crux of which was his insistence that Adam was the progenitor
not of all humanity but solely of the Jews, and that other Gentile peoples
had pre-existed him on Earth. The Pentateuch, La Peyrère argued, had not
been written down by Moses: it was so 'confus'd and out of order, obscure,
deficient' that it was evidently 'a heap of Copie confusedly taken'.[12] This
argument enabled La Peyrère to explain the at times eccentric differences
between the conventional interpretation of the Pentateuch and his own.
The Divine Law had not been given to Moses, he argued, but to Adam;
and in transgressing it, Adam had become the first man only in the sense
that he was 'the first sinner'.[13] La Peyrère here drew a sharp distinction
between Jewish and Gentile history. He regarded non-Jews as descendants
of the pre-Adamites, and therefore saw their history as utterly separate
from the biblical narrative. He thus dissolved the problem of the potential
incommensurability of Jewish and Egyptian or other chronologies.

On the basis of this separation, however, La Peyrère asserted the theological primacy of Jewish history with renewed vigour. He was a convinced
millenarian, and in his preface to *Prae-Adamitae* specifically addressed his
text to 'all the Synagogues of the Jews, dispersed over all the face of the
Earth', announcing with great excitement the imminence of their great
Restoration, to be marked by their return to Jerusalem and the reconstruc-
tion of the Temple.[14] The Jews, he believed, were the unique carriers of
historical meaning, with which the histories of the Gentiles were associated
only by 'similarity'. There was therefore no need for non-Jewish histories to be reconciled with the Bible. La Peyrère argued that this removed an
important obstacle to the spread of Christianity among non-European peoples, who, if brought to see the Bible not as displacing their own histories,
but simply as more spiritually meaningful than them, 'will willingly receive
the History of *Genesis*, and more willingly become Christians'.[15] Unsurprisingly, almost nobody else shared this enthusiasm. La Peyrère's opinions were
widely condemned, and in 1657, having abruptly converted to Catholicism,
he was forced to recant his theories before Pope Alexander VII himself.[16]

---

[12] Isaac La Peyrère, *Men Before Adam* (1655–6 (1655)) 11, 208.
[13] *Ibid.*, 1, 3–6, 56ff.   [14] *Ibid.*, preface.   [15] *Ibid.*, 60–1.
[16] On La Peyrère, see R. H. Popkin, *Isaac La Peyrère (1596–1676): His Life, Work and Influence* (1987);
History of Scepticism, 214–28; 'Millenarianism and Nationalism – A Case Study: Isaac La Peyrère', in
John Christian Laursen and Richard H. Popkin, eds., *Continental Millenarians: Protestants, Catholics,
Heretics* (2001) 77–84.

The controversy over La Peyrère's pre-Adamite theory highlighted the extreme delicacy of the relationship between sacred and profane history. In attempting to secure beyond all chronological quibbling the spiritual centrality of Jewish history, La Peyrère had largely sacrificed the privileged temporal status of the Jewish past. To virtually all his contemporaries this was unacceptable: the moral and the historical authority of the Bible were imagined as inextricably bound together. However, all attempts to situate the biblical narrative within a wider historical context were inevitably to some extent corrosive of the traditional status of Scripture – and of its subject, the Jews. Over the course of the seventeenth century, as overarching historical schemas proliferated, the meaning of Jewish history for European intellectuals became increasingly controversial and confused.

The separation opened up by La Peyrère between the chronological authority of the Bible and the wider cultural significance of Jewish history was soon taken in a very different direction. In his *Canon Chronicus* (1672), John Marsham effectively inverted La Peyrère's argument, restoring biblical chronology to its traditional status as the framing structure for all human time, while at the same time dramatically de-emphasising the historical centrality of the ancient Jews. Adopting Vossius' device of assuming that various Egyptian dynasties ran concurrently, Marsham managed to fit Manetho's lists within a post-diluvian chronology. He included detailed historical tables in his text, displaying Egyptian, Jewish and Classical history in parallel.[17] However, he argued that Egyptian society was considerably more venerable than that of the Hebrews, having been well established even before the birth of Abraham. He used the information contained within his comparative chronological tables as evidence that the Hebrews had adopted many of their customs, such as the practice of circumcision, from the Egyptians.[18]

Marsham also introduced into chronological scholarship ideas from a very different lineage. Reviving the esoteric Renaissance conflation of Moses with the mystic wisdom of Hermes Trismegistus, he argued that before the Exodus Moses had been well versed in Egyptian magical arts.[19] Despite the outward orthodoxy of Marsham's staid, steady chronological study, his discreet drawing on distinctly unorthodox notions of *prisca theologia* implicitly undermined rather than reinforced the authority of the Bible. Although intended to clarify rather than confuse, with respect to the status

---

[17] John Marsham, *Canon Chronicus Aegyptius, Ebraicus, Graecus et Disquisitiones* (1676 (1672)) e.g. 17–21, 76–9.

[18] *Ibid.*, 73–5.

[19] See Frances Yates, *The Rosicrucian Enlightenment* (1972) 216–9; Jan Assmann, *Moses the Egyptian: The Memory of Egypt in Western Monotheism* (1997) 18–20.

of Jewish history Marsham's text betrays an underlying uncertainty of purpose: although Jewish culture and traditions are subordinated to those of
the Egyptians, Egyptian history is nonetheless forced to conform to the
Hebrew timespan.

A similar uncertainty is evident in Paul Pezron's *L'Antiquité des Tems
Rétablie et Défendue* (1687). Pezron, a Cistercian monk and Doctor of
Theology at the University of Paris, revived and elaborated Vossius' argument that the Septuagint should be preferred to the Hebrew Bible. He
provided a detailed reconciliation of the Egyptian and Babylonian dynasties with the 5,500 years of pre-Christian history allowed for, according to
his calculations, by the Septuagint. This lengthier chronology, he argued,
not only accommodated extra-biblical histories but was also proven by the
biblical prophecy that Messiah would come in the sixth millennium.[20] The
Jews of the first centuries after Christ, Pezron claimed, had deliberately
falsified their own texts in order retrospectively to confound these fulfilled
prophecies. He amplified this accusation in his second book, *Défense de
l'Antiquité des Tems* (1691), in which he identified Rabbi Akiba and his
circle as the likely culprits, motivated by their hatred of the early Christians
in their midst.[21] Pezron's arguments both strengthened and undermined the
Jews' historical status. He reaffirmed that Jewish history was the template
for all history, but he also dismissed Jewish sources and heavily emphasised
the Jews' unreliability and deceit. At once privileged and derided, the Jews
stand at the heart of Pezron's conception of history, but the precise nature
of their role and significance is veiled in ambiguity.

Anthony Grafton has described Pezron's *L'Antiquité des Tems* as a 'very
silly book', marking the degeneration of the once-glorious discipline of
historical chronology from the masterly erudition of Scaliger into a mere
sophistic search for a convenient system for the reconciliation of biblical
and temporal history.[22] However, the gradual dilution of the chronologist's
craft was not simply due to a decline in scholarly standards, but rather to
the transformed intellectual context in which chronological argument was
conducted towards the end of the seventeenth century. Historical scholars
of Pezron's generation could no longer retreat into recondite obscurantism.
A growing educated public was now anxious to explore and understand
the relationship between biblical and non-biblical history. By the 1680s,
it was widely apparent that learned chronologists, despite their erudition,
were very unlikely to provide a satisfactory resolution of this problem.

[20] Paul Pezron, *L'Antiquité du Tems Rétablie et Défendue* (1687) 37–45.
[21] Paul Pezron, *Défense de l'Antiquité des Tems* (1691) 172, 401.   [22] Grafton, 'Joseph Scaliger', 178ff.

Chronological tomes were still given serious attention in the literary periodicals, but a tone of increasing weariness with the discipline is unmistakable. As Pierre Bayle commented at the beginning of his review of *L'Antiquité des Tems*: 'There is no subject more full of confusion and obscurity than Chronology.'[23]

In response to the increasing uncertainty surrounding the historical status of the Old Testament, a number of late seventeenth-century theologians attempted to defend and clarify the Christian view of the past. In his *Origines Sacrae* (1662), the leading English latitudinarian Edward Stillingfleet forcefully asserted the historical authority of Scripture, contrasting the obscurity and unreliability of all other ancient history and chronology with 'the certainty of the writings of Moses'.[24] Explicitly condemning La Peyrère's pre-Adamitic thesis,[25] Stillingfleet painstakingly attempted to demonstrate the absolute and unique reliability of the Jewish historical record. By establishing that 'the Israelites were the most certain conservatours of the ancient History of the world', Stillingfleet believed that he had provided an incontrovertible and purely rational proof of the truth of Christianity.[26]

By far the most resonantly self-confident historical work of the late seventeenth century was Bishop Bossuet's *Discours sur l'Histoire Universelle* (1681). This text was ostensibly written for the edification of the Dauphin, but more importantly was intended resoundingly to quash the dangerous trend towards the critical examination of sacred history, which the writings of Spinoza and Richard Simon in the preceding decade had alarmingly fortified. Covering the entire sweep of human history from the Creation to Charlemagne, Bossuet imperiously brushed aside the uncertainties that troubled so many of his contemporaries, boldly setting out a total history within which, he believed, all events were accorded their proper place and significance.

The *Discours* asserts above all the intimacy of the connection between sacred and profane history. In the first section of the book the past is divided into twelve epochs, within each of which Classical and biblical history are interwoven. The fall of Troy, for example, is placed between the epoch of Moses and that of Solomon; the epoch of Romulus and the foundation of Rome immediately follows that of Solomon, and is followed by Cyrus of Persia. Bossuet's declared scope of the work is double-pronged, aiming to cover 'the history of God's people and that of the great empires',[27]

---

[23] *NRL* (June 1687) 939.   [24] Edward Stillingfleet, *Origines Sacrae* (1662) esp. 107.
[25] *Ibid.*, 533–8.   [26] *Ibid.*, 134.
[27] Jacques-Bénigne Bossuet, *Discourse on Universal History* (1976 (1681)) 110.

which are each treated separately in the remaining two sections of his text. However, Bossuet's coverage of secular history is perfunctory in comparison to his treatment of the history of the ancient Jews up to the establishment of Christianity. The demonstration of a direct line of succession through Moses and the Jewish High Priests to the continuing Papal succession is, for Bossuet, the most perfect establishment of religious certainty: 'what greater authority can there be than that of the Catholic Church, which centres in itself all the authority of past ages, and the ancient traditions of mankind back to its origins?'[28]

The excellence of Jewish history is central to Bossuet's argument. He is unstinting in his praise for Moses and for the Mosaic Law – 'a Law holy, just, wise, provident and simple'[29] – and stresses God's merciful and tender treatment of the Jews, whom he treats 'like disobedient children, whom he returns to their duty by correction, and then, moved by their tears... forgets their faults'.[30] Above all, though, it is on the fall of the Jews, 'whose every circumstance bears testimony to the Gospel',[31] that Bossuet dwells at greatest length:

The Jews, who have been the prey of those ancient nations so celebrated in history, have survived them all, and God, by preserving them, keeps us in expectation of what he will still do for the unhappy remnant of a people once so highly favoured. However, their obstinacy contributes to the salvation of the Gentiles and affords them the advantage of finding in trusted hands the Scriptures, which have foretold Jesus Christ and his mysteries. We see among other things in these Scriptures both the blindness and the misfortunes of the Jews, who so carefully preserve them. Thus we profit by their downfall; their infidelity is one of the foundations of our faith; they teach us to fear God and are a standing example of the judgements he executes upon his ungrateful children, so that we may learn never to glory in the favours shown to our fathers.[32]

The Jews, for Bossuet, unequivocally prove the truth of the Catholic conception of history: 'Condemned by their own books, they establish the truth of religion; they bear, so to speak, its whole history written upon their forehead.'[33]

The extreme judaeocentrism of this historical account is essentially a reiteration of the traditional medieval explanation and moralisation of the plight of the Jews. Bossuet's unwavering reassertion of these arguments was intended to convey a magisterial conviction of the validity of the orthodox historical worldview. However, he offered little of substance to shore up

---

[28] *Ibid.*, 289.   [29] *Ibid.*, 141.   [30] *Ibid.*, 162–3.
[31] *Ibid.*, 213.   [32] *Ibid.*, 206.   [33] *Ibid.*, 292.

a historical edifice that by the 1680s appeared at the very least somewhat wobbly. The thundering rhetoric of the *Discours* enabled Bossuet simply to charge through potential objections to numerous points of detail in his argument. Both millenarian expectancy and the study of chronology, which underpinned the structure of his text, were by the 1680s extremely controversial subjects. On both matters, however, Bossuet restricted himself to generalities, expressing impatience with 'those who would try to obfuscate a clear thing by quibbles over ... useless subtleties'.[34] On the problems posed by attempts to integrate Asian and American history into the European worldview he remained resoundingly silent.

Throughout the Enlightenment, Bossuet's *Discours* was widely read and much respected: more than thirty editions were produced in the century following its first publication.[35] However, Chantal Grell is surely right to detect in the numerous eulogies to it amongst the proceedings of the *Académie des Inscriptions et Belles Lettres* of the early eighteenth century a strong element of nostalgia for an authoritative, integrated view of history that had by then largely been shattered.[36] Already at the time of the publication of the *Discours* challenges to received theological wisdom, although often presented in a spirit of orthodoxy, were ramifying dramatically. Thomas Burnet's *Telluris Theoria Sacra* (1680), for example, which argued that the surface of Earth must have been smooth until the time of the flood for there could not otherwise have been enough water to cover it, offered a new, proto-geological account of the post-diluvian formation of mountains, valleys and volcanoes. Burnet carefully insisted on the harmony of his theory with the account given in the Old Testament.[37] However, he appeared almost impatient with the 'prophetic' and uneven style of Scripture,[38] and was clearly more stimulated by arguments from reason and observation. Bossuet's avoidance of engagement with the intellectual debates of his period is symptomatic of the complexity and awkwardness of these controversies, to which he could not respond with renewed argument, but only with more powerful rhetoric.

---

[34] *Ibid.*, 71.

[35] Günter Pflug, 'The Development of Historical Method in the Eighteenth Century', in *Enlightenment Historiography: Three German Studies* (1971) 17.

[36] Chantal Grell, *L'Histoire entre érudition et philosophie* (1994) 97–8.

[37] Thomas Burnet, *The Sacred Theory of the Earth* (1965 (1680)) 71–81. See also Paulo Rossi, *The Dark Abyss of Time* (1984) 33–41; Scott Mandelbrote, 'Isaac Newton and Thomas Burnet: Biblical Criticism and the Crisis of Late Seventeenth-Century England', in James E. Force and Richard H. Popkin, eds., *The Books of Nature and Scripture* (1994) 149–78.

[38] Burnet, *Sacred Theory*, 79–80.

WHOSE FABLES?

The desire of theologians such as Stillingfleet and Bossuet to reconcile divine and secular history while marking a clear difference in status between the two was, however, undermined by the intellectual curiosity of many of their contemporaries. In England, Stillingfleet's work was intended in part as an explicit challenge to the attempts by the Cambridge Platonists to integrate Christianity with pagan philosophy.[39] Ralph Cudworth and Henry More, the leading figures in this group, were fascinated with the notion of a mystical *prisca theologia*. In his *True Intellectual System of the Universe* (1678) Cudworth argued that all the pagan gods were 'derived from one self-existent Deity'.[40] He particularly emphasised the proto-Christian insight of Plato and his followers, and their albeit disguised and imperfect recognition of 'that Divine Cabala of the Trinity'.[41] Cudworth's argument upheld the centrality of the Mosaic revelation as the originary source of the *prisca theologia*. Thereafter, however, he almost entirely ignored Jewish history, tracing an alternative lineage of the transmission of philosophical wisdom to the Greeks via the Egyptians, in particular via the writings of Hermes Trismegistus. Cudworth revived the Renaissance Hermetic tradition, which had almost been extinguished six decades earlier by Isaac Casaubon's claim that the Hermetic texts were not authentically Egyptian, but probably Christian forgeries from the late antique period. For Cudworth, the bulk of the Hermetic corpus was genuine, and it revealed the esoteric, monotheistic truths that constituted the 'arcane theology' of the ancient Egyptian royal and priestly elite.[42]

In the context of the historical controversies of the late seventeenth century Cudworth's Hermetic revival carried overtones of controversy that had not been present in the late Renaissance. Cudworth's argument posed an explicit challenge to the notion that the Jews had been the first and only ancient people to adopt monotheism, which was one of the most crucial premises underpinning the historical interpretation of the Bible. However, he regarded himself as a loyal and responsible Christian, and saw his work as extending rather than undermining the authority of Christianity. A fundamental ambiguity characterised Cudworth's position regarding the

---

[39] See Sarah Hutton, 'Edward Stillingfleet, Henry More, and the Decline of *Moses Atticus*: a Note on Seventeenth-century Anglican Apologetics', in Richard Kroll, Richard Ashcraft and Perez Zagorin, eds., *Philosophy, Science and Religion in England, 1640–1700* (1992) 68–84.

[40] Ralph Cudworth, *True Intellectual System of the Universe* (1845 (1678)) 1, 414ff.

[41] *Ibid.*, 11, 363ff.

[42] Assmann, *Moses*, 80–90. See also Frances A. Yates, *Giordano Bruno and the Hermetic Tradition* (1964).

historical source of the *prisca theologia*, which he simultaneously represents as a universal and eternal 'true system' and as the essence of the historically specific Judaeo-Christian tradition.[43] This blurring of the relationship between history and religion left Judaism exposed in a uniquely undetermined position. While latitudinarians such as Stillingfleet based their gentle critique of Platonism on the reassertion of the historical centrality of the Jews, Platonists themselves exhibited considerable uncertainty on the subject. While Cudworth and his allies minimised the importance of the Old Testament narrative and evinced almost no interest in rabbinics, they by no means abandoned all interest in Judaism. As we shall see later, Cudworth's close Cambridge associate Henry More was fascinated by the Kabbalah, which he saw as a key source of the *prisca theologia*.[44]

Cudworth's abstracted euhemerism was in some sense echoed by another, almost simultaneous attempt to integrate the beliefs of different cultures. Whereas Cudworth focused his attention on philosophy, Pierre-Daniel Huet, the prolific Bishop of Avranches, attempted to systematise the relationship between Christianity and the myths and fables of all other traditions. In his immense *Demonstratio Evangelica* (1679), Huet responded to the challenge of critical rationalism and Spinozism by using their deductive procedures to reach very different conclusions. The *Demonstratio* is expounded in a tightly logical structure reminiscent of and to some extent indebted to Spinoza's geometric method: as in Spinoza's *Ethics*, published only two years previously, the text opens with a sequence of definitions and axioms.[45] Huet argued that all pagan histories and mythology were based on an Old Testament matrix, from which they were all ultimately derived. He meticulously elaborated this case, firstly by arguing that Osiris, Bacchus, Zoroaster and the leading Indian, Chinese and Japanese deities were all veiled representations of Moses, and that all principal goddesses were representations of Moses' wife Zipporah.[46] The myths and fables of all cultures, Huet claimed, were corrupted renderings of Mosaic history, an awareness of which had in the distant past been transmitted across the globe.

Huet's work immediately won the endorsement of many other leading clerics, including Bossuet. He firmly established the comparative approach

[43] See Peter Harrison, *'Religion' and the Religions in the English Enlightenment* (1990) 32–4; Marialuisa Baldi, 'Il "Vero Sistema" dell'universo e il conflitto delle tradizioni in Cudworth', in Guido Canziani and Yves Charles Zarka, eds., *L'interpretazione nei secoli XVI e XVII* (1993) 185–208; J. A. Passmore, *Ralph Cudworth: An Interpretation* (1951) 79–89.
[44] See Allison Coudert, 'Henry More, the Kabbalah and the Quakers', in Kroll, Ashcraft and Zagorin, eds., *Philosophy*, 47–56.
[45] Pierre-Daniel Huet, *Demonstratio Evangelica* (1679) 7–12.   [46] *Ibid.*, e.g. 73–88, 95–9.

to the study of religions, which influenced many studies over subsequent decades.[47] The comparison of cultures, however, did not necessarily lead to the reinforcement of the centrality of the Jewish tradition. A strikingly contrasting argument was soon put forward by John Spencer, a noted Hebraist and contemporary of Cudworth at Cambridge. In his *De Legibus Hebraeorum* (1685), a work of highly erudite Hebraist scholarship strongly influenced by Maimonides, Spencer attempted to offer a rational and historical analysis of the Mosaic ritual laws. He argued that the Israelites had been strongly influenced by their sojourn in Egypt, and that this was reflected in many similarities between Jewish and Egyptian religious customs. Accepting Marsham's case for the earlier sophistication of Egyptian society, he judged that the Mosaic religion was derived from Egyptian models, rather than vice versa, and attempted to demonstrate in detail the Egyptian sources for almost all aspects of Jewish temple worship.[48] Spencer thus reversed Huet's chronology: rather than presenting Judaism as the blueprint for all myths and religions, he argued that it was itself derivative.

Most fundamental to Spencer's argument was his explanation of the Mosaic Law in terms of its relationship to ancient Egyptian religion. These laws were designed, he argued, in order to inhibit the Israelites' tendency towards idolatry and superstition.[49] In itself, this assertion was a commonplace. Spencer, however, did not stop here: he attempted to show that the Mosaic Law was devised as a specific inversion of Egyptian customs. Whatever pagan practices the Jews had been exposed to in Egypt, the Mosaic Law expressly prohibited, while it mandated certain rituals, such as the sacrifice of the paschal lamb, that directly violated Egyptian religious taboos.[50]

Spencer's detailed historicisation of the Jewish law applied the analytical approaches of Early Enlightenment rationalism to the Old Testament in a challenging and highly innovatory fashion. However, his argument left important ambiguities unresolved. To an important extent Spencer was influenced by the positive valorisation of Egyptian culture put forward in the work of Marsham and Cudworth. Not only did he emphasise the sophistication of ancient Egyptian society, but he also echoed Cudworth in his identification of the 'inner meaning' of the Mosaic Law with the mystical secrets that Moses had learnt in Egypt.[51] In general,

---

[47] See Laplanche, *La Bible en France*, 39–40; Harrison, *'Religion'*, 139–46.
[48] John Spencer, *De Legibus Hebraeorum* (1685) 519–635.   [49] *Ibid.*, esp. 21ff.
[50] For a detailed analysis of this, see Assmann, *Moses*, 57–74. See also Justin Champion, *The Pillars of Priestcraft Shaken: The Church of England and its Enemies, 1660–1730* (1992) 155–6; Amos Funkenstein, *Theology and the Scientific Imagination*, 241–3.
[51] Assmann, *Moses*, 77–9.

though, Spencer was contemptuous of Egyptian idolatry and paganism. His historical interpretation of the Mosaic Law was not intended to undermine its meaningfulness, but, on the contrary, to strengthen it: even the seemingly most redundant regulation, Spencer believed, had been carefully designed to reinforce the Hebrews' monotheism by weaning them from their Egyptian bad habits. Ultimately, though, this argument presented the Jewish law as of parochial and transient significance. The practical legalism of the Old Testament served a specific purpose at a specific time, but in Spencer's eyes it was utterly superseded by the pure spirituality of Christianity. Despite the sophistication of his scholarship, it is difficult – perhaps impossible – to disentangle the interweaving strands of admiration and denigration of both Jewish and Egyptian culture in Spencer's work.

The uncertain implications of Spencer's argument reflected the increasing confusion of the late seventeenth-century debate on historical origins, which each attempt at clarification seemed only to complicate still further. The generally favourable review of Spencer's study in Pierre Bayle's *Nouvelles de la République des Lettres* highlighted the delicate balance of his thesis from the standpoint of the conventional Protestant understanding of Judaism. In his review Bayle drew on Spencer to mock the apparent absurdity of the Jewish law: why, he asked, should God in certain circumstances insist on the immolation of a lamb, rather than a ram? However, he also stressed the importance of a thorough comprehension of the legal system on which Christianity was historically based.[52] Although few if any readers were as sharply aware of it as Pierre Bayle, the analysis of *De Legibus Hebraeorum* was beset with a profound underlying contradiction: in exploring the historicity of the Mosaic Law in order to elucidate its religious significance, Spencer undermined the assumptions on which Christian belief in that significance was based.

Dismissive and reverential views of the Jewish past jostled for position in the writings of the next generation of historical theorists. Although Huet had majestically integrated all histories into the Judaeo-Christian tradition, his argument appeared increasingly strained when set against the detailed dissenting scholarship of Spencer and others. Most prominent amongst those who attempted to mediate between these contrasting perspectives was Antoine Banier, a member of the *Académie des Inscriptions et Belles-Lettres*, whose three-volume *L'Explication Historique des Fables* (1710–15) was recapitulated and extended in a further three-volume work, *La Mythologie et les Fables Expliquées par l'Histoire* (1738–40). Although he held Huet's work

---

[52] *NRL* (April 1686) 431, 442.

in very high esteem, Banier argued that he had over-stretched his case in seeing Moses, Zipporah and Miriam as the models for all pagan divinities.[53] While he acknowledged the appeal of this argument as a fortification of the true religion, he believed it was historically implausible that the myths of all peoples were based on the history of the Jews – if only because the Jews' own secrecy, and the contempt in which they were held by their neighbours, made such wide diffusion of their cultural memory highly unlikely.[54]

Self-consciously adopting a more flexible critical approach, Banier argued that fables emerged from a variety of sources: travellers' tales, the embellishment or falsification of records, and invention in the face of ignorance.[55] Nonetheless, he discerned an underlying resemblance to Judaeo-Christianity in the fables and myths of other cultures. The theogony of the Chaldeans was, he noted, very similar to the theory of the Androgynes in Plato's *Symposium*, and both were clearly connected to the Genesis account of the creation of Eve from Adam's rib.[56] The Chinese religion, based on the worship of a single Supreme Being, was evidently derived from the 'natural law' that God had engraved in the hearts of the descendants of Noah.[57] Banier as much as possible maintained an integrated view of history, while minimising the universalisation of specifically Jewish traditions. This attempt to retain the sweep of Huet's Christian understanding of the global past while attenuating its most blatantly implausible aspects resulted in an awkward compromise between history and theology. The most prominent symptom of the instability of this compromise was Banier's sustained ambivalence towards the position of the Jews in his historical account.

A much more trenchantly unorthodox interpretation of history was offered by Bernard de Fontenelle. In his essay *De l'Origine des Fables* (1724), Fontenelle pointedly avoided reference to biblical history, and emphasised the isolation and barbarism of the earliest human civilisations. Rather than tracing the transmission of archetypal fables, Fontenelle regarded them as the natural product of the ignorance and intellectual crudeness that reigned in the earliest centuries.[58] A very similar ignorance and primitivism, he argued, had pervaded the beliefs of all cultures, from the native Americans to the ancient Phoenicians and Greeks.[59] By evoking the universal barbarism and foolishness of the distant past, and conspicuously failing to make an exception for the ancient Hebrews, Fontenelle introduced a subtly

---

[53] Antoine Banier, *La Mythologie et les Fables Expliqués par l'Histoire* (1738–40) I, 10.
[54] *Ibid.*, 49–50.   [55] *Ibid.*, 33ff.   [56] *Ibid.*, 76ff.   [57] *Ibid.*, 121ff.
[58] Bernard de Fontenelle, *De l'Origine des Fables* (1968 (1724)) 223–6.   [59] *Ibid.*, 233–4.

subversive element into his argument. This radicalism is most clearly hinted at in the closing paragraph of his text:

> Let us therefore not search for anything in fables other than the history of the follies of the human spirit... It is no science to fill the mind with all the eccentricities of the Phoenicians and the Greeks; but it is a science to know what led them to these eccentricities. All men are so similar that there is no people whose foolishness should not make us tremble.[60]

The unequivocality of the word 'all' at the beginning of this final sentence is surely intended as a pointed inclusion of the one ancient people who have been conspicuously absent from Fontenelle's argument: the Jews. Using a similar strategy to that of his *Histoire des Oracles* (1686), in which his discrediting of the pagan oracles implicitly also discredited Christian legitimation claims based on the miraculous demise of the oracles at the time of Christ,[61] so Fontenelle here subtly undermined the historical basis of Christianity without even explicitly addressing the subject. The Jews, Fontenelle implied, were no different from other peoples, and their fables no less foolish. Beneath the embryonic comparative historical anthropology of this essay there lay an unspoken but pointed challenge to the privileged historical status of the Old Testament and of the Jews.

THE AMERICAS AND THE JEWS

The comparison and correlation of cultures in this period was not only a historical activity, but was increasingly also applied to the varied civilisations of the contemporary world. The early proto-anthropology stimulated by the exploration of the Americas was from the outset powerfully driven by a desire to situate native Americans within the framework of biblical history. The notion that the Americans were descended from the ten lost tribes of Israel had been suggested by several Spanish writers in the sixteenth century, and was most influentially reiterated in Thomas Thorowgood's *Jewes in America* (1650). This text included a translation of a recent account by the Dutch rabbi Menasseh ben Israel of the discovery by a Portuguese crypto-Jew, Montezinos, of a tribe of Jews in the Andes. Montezinos reported that these Jews claimed descent from Reuben, recited the *Shema* prayer and warmly welcomed him as their brethren.[62] The volume is suffused with

---

[60] *Ibid.*, 238.
[61] See Bernard de Fontenelle, *Histoire des Oracles* (1686), itself based on a work by the Dutch Anabaptist, Anton van Dale, *De Oraculis* (1683).
[62] Thomas Thorowgood, *Jewes in America* (1650) 129–39.

millenarian excitement, reflecting a conviction that the Jewish Indians were eager to learn about Christianity, and that their conversion was imminent.[63] However, Thorowgood's case was immediately rebutted, with his leading critic, Hamon l'Estrange, swiftly pointing out the tenuousness of the alleged cultural similarity between Americans and Jews. This debate persisted into the Early Enlightenment, during which it stood as a key point of tension between Christian and critical history.[64]

Attempts were also made to associate Jewish religion and customs with the civilisations of India. In his *Conformité des Coutumes des Indiens Orientaux avec celles des Juifs et des autres Peuples de l'Antiquité* (1704), M. de la Crequinière traced similarities between modern Indians and ancient Jews in worship, dress, attitude to outsiders and even in economic behaviour: the Indians, he noted, like the Jews, were great usurers, but only in their dealings with non-Indians.[65] The underlying unity between the two groups, he argued, was their common simplicity: they had both in large measure conserved 'the simplicity of the first peoples', avoiding change and innovation because 'they knew that evil can slip in much more easily than virtue'.[66] Crequinière primarily regarded Indian religion and culture not as a subject of interest in itself, but as a precious relic of ancient times, further confirming and illuminating the biblical text.[67] However, a palpable artificiality runs through this attempt to integrate ethnographical research and theological orthodoxy. Such evidently partisan interpretation of factual evidence was by the early eighteenth century extremely vulnerable to critical scrutiny. In attempting to fortify the historicity of the Old Testament by enlisting contemporary Indians as surrogates for ancient Jews, Crequinière further stretched and strained the weight of historical meaning freighted on Judaism.

On his return to France after five years missionising among the Iroquois, the Jesuit Jean-François Lafitau put forward a further attempt to integrate biblical history with observational anthropology. In his *Moeurs des sauvages amériquains, comparées aux moeurs des premiers temps* (1724), Lafitau argued insistently that the so-called barbarians of America in no measure deserved such a description: 'Not only have the people whom we call

---

[63] *Ibid.*, 59–128.

[64] Hamon l'Estrange, *Americans no Jews* (1651). See also Claire Jowett, 'Racial Identities? Native Americans, Jews and the English Commonwealth', in Siân Jones, Tony Kushner and Sarah Pearce, eds., *Cultures of Ambivalence and Contempt* (1998) 154–6; Richard H. Popkin, 'The Rise and Fall of the Jewish Indian Theory', in Yosef Kaplan, Henry Méchoulan and Richard H. Popkin, eds., *Menasseh ben Israel and his World* (1989) 63–82.

[65] M. de la Crequinière, *Conformité des Coutumes des Indiens Orientaux* (1704) 178–9.

[66] *Ibid.*, 221–2.　　[67] *Ibid.*, esp. iii.

barbarous a religion, but this religion has...great conformity with that of the first times.'[68] Although twentieth-century anthropologists have admired Lafitau's meticulous field research into the language, kinship structures and hunting practices of the Iroquois, his central concern was to show that their religious beliefs were based in essence on a universal originary human credo.[69] He established his case by amassing evidence of the similarities between native American religious and cultural traditions and those of early European civilisations, and in particular of ancient Greece. Although he expressed his profound admiration for Huet, Lafitau rejected his attempt to base the universality of human religion on the Mosaic revelation.[70] In his alternative genealogy of religion, which he believed to be less vulnerable to attack by atheists, all fundamental truths had been included in the original religion bestowed by God on Adam and Eve. The question of which branch of Adam's descendants the Americans belonged to – and whether they were descended from the lost tribes of Israel – was for Lafitau an issue of little importance, on which he could only offer 'vague conjectures'.[71] Although he considered in detail the various possible origins of the Americans, ultimately concluding that the continent was probably first settled from Greece, he stressed that his central concern was simply to demonstrate the conformity of American customs with those of the 'first peoples'.[72]

By positing the pre-Judaic religion of Adam as the source of universal faith, Lafitau limited the historical importance of Judaism to the Judaeo-Christian tradition alone. Although this move was intended to defend orthodox belief against the deistic argument that only an intuitive natural religion was necessary in order to live virtuously, Lafitau's positing of an originary pre-Mosaic religion encompassing all fundamental religious truths amounted to a partial assimilation of Deist theology. Despite the implacable mutual contempt between Jesuits and Deists, there was a striking similarity to their attempts to understand extra-European history. At the core of Deism was a primitivist impulse to contrast an originary age of simple, natural faith with the subsequent corruption of artificial priestly religion. Although the Jesuits of course utterly repudiated any negative evaluation of hierarchical Catholicism, in their eagerness to identify the essence of Christianity in Chinese, American and other cultures they implicitly

[68] Jean-François Lafitau, *Moeurs des sauvages amériquains*, 2 vols. (1974 and 1977 (1724)) 1, 30.
[69] See Margaret T. Hodgen, *Early Anthropology in the Sixteenth and Seventeenth Centuries* (1964) 346–9; Harry Liebersohn, *Aristocratic Encounters: European Travelers and North American Indians* (1998) 21–2; Mary Baine Campbell, *Wonder and Science: Imagining Worlds in Early Modern Europe* (1999) 289–310.
[70] Lafitau, *Moeurs*, 1, 31–2.   [71] *Ibid.*, 37.   [72] *Ibid.*, 79–81.

recognised a similarly minimalist credo as the basis, although emphatically not the sum, of true religion.

By the 1720s historical theorists had generated many such ironic surprises: it was clear that attempts to fortify traditional religion could often appear to have the opposite effect. Increasingly, orthodox theologians avoided the quicksands of historical speculation, restricting their arguments to surer terrain. In his massive apologetic, *La Vérité du Christianisme Prouvée par les Faits* (1722), the Abbé Houtteville criticised earlier defenders of Christianity, including Huet, Bayle and Leibniz, for their excessive complexity and conjecture. Avowedly eschewing such boldness, he declared his intention to restrict himself to the 'proof of facts', which he regarded as the 'simplest and most convincing' form of argument.[73] Leading Protestant theologians such as Jean Pierre de Crousaz also attempted to put forward more straightforwardly authoritative defences of Christianity.[74] However, despite the desire of these controversialists to side-step the complexities and ambiguities of universal history, by the early eighteenth century no such easy escape was possible. The simple biblical 'facts' that Houtteville sought to reassert were, starting from his cornerstone of Moses' divinely inspired authorship of the Pentateuch, irreversibly mired in historical and critical controversy.

The history of the Jews, uncomfortably straddling the faultline between sacred and profane history, inescapably stood at the centre of this debate. Although the ethnographic studies of figures such as Lafitau and Crequinière, in broadening the comparative tableau of global history, seemed to dilute interest in the Jews, they offered no resolution of the fundamentally dualistic paradox of the place of Judaism in the historical imagination of enlightened Christianity. While conventional theologians increasingly over the first half of the eighteenth century retreated from Enlightenment debate, and reverted to the relatively unthinking reiteration of old and now intellectually marginal biblical orthodoxies, bolder thinkers were driven towards two contrasting, and no less problematic, approaches to the Jewish past. Either Jewish history, as a sacred record, could be treated as uniquely external to normal criteria of historical criticism, or this sacred significance could be repudiated, and the Old Testament interpreted purely as an unprivileged historical source document. The former position is most clearly enunciated in Vico's *Scienza Nuova*, while the latter, initiated by Spinoza, was a central argument of the radical strand of the Enlightenment.

---

[73] Claude François Houtteville, *La Vérité du Christianisme Prouvée par les Faits* (1873 (1722)) 134–5, 155–6.

[74] See Jean Pierre de Crousaz, *Cinq Sermons sur la Vérité de la Religion Chrétienne* (1722) esp. on the Jews, 24–5.

VICO: JUDAISM CONTRA HISTORY

Giambattista Vico has widely been regarded as an intellectually isolated figure, prefiguring nineteenth- and twentieth-century thought rather than reflecting the concerns of his own age.[75] However, in his *Scienza Nuova* (1725) Vico put forward a theory that carefully and consciously responded to the contemporary controversy concerning the relationship between biblical and secular history. Almost at the outset of this text Vico declared his rejection of Marsham and Spencer's arguments for the originality of Egyptian rather than Hebrew culture, as well as of Chinese claims for the great antiquity of their own civilisation.[76] The age of the world, he asserted, was as stated in the Bible, which, because the Hebrews alone had maintained accurate records since the beginning of time, provided a uniquely authoritative account of history.[77] Vico is explicit that the sacred history of the Jews stands outside the tripartite cycle of the ages of gods, heroes and men that is the crux of his interpretation of all Gentile history. Although he echoes Huet in discerning an underlying correspondence between the Bible and the early fables of other cultures, which all contain within them a trace representation of the universal historical experience of the flood, he insists that the Hebrews alone worshipped the true God.[78] Emphasising the diversity in nature, customs and historical experience of different peoples, he explicitly repudiated the natural law theories of Grotius, Selden and Pufendorf, on the grounds that their universalism violated both the varying specificities of non-Jewish histories and the unique status of Jewish law: 'they took no account of the particular assistance which a single people received from the true God'.[79]

Vico thus abandoned the traditional theological ambition of integrating sacred and profane history.[80] Having discarded this project, he was able to analyse the development of the Greeks and other civilisations in purely secular terms; it is this dimension of the *Scienza Nuova* that resonates so strongly with post-Enlightenment historiography. However, this modernity is undercut by the fundamental ambiguity of Vico's exceptionalist stance towards Jewish history. Twentieth-century readers have tended to follow Benedetto Croce in dismissing Vico's view of sacred history as a peripheral 'religious scruple' of no real consequence in his philosophy, but

---

[75] See, most influentially, Isaiah Berlin, *Vico and Herder* (1976) 90–107. For a contrasting view see Paulo Rossi, *Le sterminate antichità: studi vichiani* (1969) 68–77.

[76] Giambattista Vico, *New Science* (1968 (1725, 3rd edn 1744)) §44.

[77] *Ibid.*, §53, 126.   [78] *Ibid.*, §169, 192–4, 473–81.

[79] *Ibid.*, §329. See also §311–13, 445.   [80] See Rossi, *Dark Abyss* 168–81.

the structural centrality of the religious theme in the *Scienza* at least as powerfully invites the contrary interpretation: that Vico's secularisation of Gentile history is primarily intended to defend the unique divinity of Jewish history.[81] Both aspects of Vico's philosophy of history, however, predicate and enable the other. His strikingly modern interpretation of the cultural history of the Ancients is inextricably dependent on his exclusion of the Jews from the otherwise universal pattern of historical development.

In contrast with Vico's sharp segregation of secular and sacred history, the radical current of the Early Enlightenment tended with increasing outspokenness to reject this distinction. Spinoza's insistence in his *Tractatus Theologico-Politicus* that the Jews were in no sense 'above other nations' marked the first unequivocal application of a rationalist historical herme-neutic to the biblical text.[82] As we shall see, this approach was extended and rendered more polemical by numerous later writers across Europe, while John Spencer's Egyptological arguments were re-cast in more radical form by the English Deist John Toland. The problems raised by these attempts to construct a convincing counter-history to the biblical narrative will be a central theme of later chapters. The desire to reconcile the authority of the Bible with a rational interpretation of history remained, however, extremely resilient. The status of the Bible as a traditional rock of Christian historical certainty was at stake in this aspiration, as were wider epistemological issues. The reinterpretation of Jewish history probed the possibilities and limits of scholarship; and it starkly highlighted the tension between religious faith and critical reason. These tensions were most sustainedly confronted in the work of two leading Huguenot refugee intellectuals in the Dutch Republic around the turn of the seventeenth century. Jacques Basnage's monumental *Histoire des Juifs* (1716) was the most comprehensive attempt to reassess Jewish history during the Enlightenment, while the significance of Judaism stood at the heart of Pierre Bayle's enigmatic and intense interrogation of the relationship between reason and belief.

---

[81] See Mario Reale, 'Vico e il problema della storia ebraica in una recente interpretazione', *La cultura* 8 (1970) 81–107.
[82] *TTP*, 99.

CHAPTER 4

The limits of erudition: Jacques Basnage and Pierre Bayle

Louis XIV's revocation of the Edict of Nantes in 1685 had many unintended consequences. The mass emigration of French Protestants that followed Louis' abolition of the rights that had been accorded to them in 1598 did great damage to the French economy, and brought significant gains to England, the Dutch Republic, Brandenburg-Prussia and elsewhere where large numbers of Huguenots settled, bringing their commercial, financial and industrial skills with them. More surprising, however, was the striking Huguenot impact on European intellectual life in the decades following 1685. Huguenot intellectuals settled in large numbers in the urban centres of Holland, where they brought a new scholarly and journalistic energy to Rotterdam and Amsterdam. It was largely due to their presence that these cities rapidly emerged as the undisputed hubs of European news-gathering and dissemination. The newly diasporic nature of the Huguenot world gave a unique impetus to the establishment of strong international communication networks, as did their concern for the plight of remaining communities in France.[1] The most significant dimension of the Huguenot role in the Early Enlightenment was, though, not practical but conceptual: to a considerable extent the European intellectual agenda of the decades around 1700 was set by Huguenot concerns. While over the first two-thirds of the seventeenth century the political and theological battles in England and the Dutch Republic had provided the stimulus for much bold and controversial scholarly work, by the 1680s – in England, very decisively after 1688 – political debate in both nations had become both less intense and less philosophical in nature. The conflict between the mighty French Crown and its Protestant exiles, however, raised acute political dilemmas that demanded serious intellectual and theological attention.

---

[1] See Graham Gibbs, 'Some Intellectual and Political Influences of the Huguenot Emigrés in the United Provinces, 1680–1730', *BMBGN* 90 (1975) 255–87; Miriam Yardeni, *Le refuge protestant* (1985) 201–7.

In the 1690s the Huguenot community, and its leadership in Holland in particular, was deeply split. The 'zealot' party, led by Pierre Jurieu, trenchantly rejected any accommodation with Catholic power, while the 'moderate' party, strongly influenced by Pierre Bayle, was open to a more conciliatory approach.[2] While this bitter rift was primarily political, it overlaid profound and long-standing theological tensions within French Protestantism. The Huguenot Academy of Saumur had since the arrival of Louis Cappel in 1614 been a centre of heterodox critical theology, and had been locked in a sustained polemical rivalry with the rigorously Calvinist orthodoxy maintained at the other leading Protestant academy in France, at Sedan.[3] Pierre Jurieu had taught at Sedan up to the academy's suppression in 1681, and the political arguments he later developed in exile were based on a strictly traditional theological interpretation of the Old Testament. In his *L'Accomplissement des prophéties* (1686–88) Jurieu focused on the literal truth and inexorable fulfilment of the Old Testament prophecies. By analogical extension from divine promise of the redemption of the Jews, Jurieu argued that the deliverance of the Church from the evil grip of popery was a similar inevitability.[4] Whereas Jurieu responded to the trauma of exile by confidently asserting the scriptural promise of ultimate victory, for Bayle and other moderates the same historical experience confirmed and intensified their commitment to the questioning, open spirit of the Saumur tradition. In responding to the intolerance of Louis XIV the Huguenot community was thus forced also to confront deep disagreements and uncertainties regarding the nature of religious truth itself. These issues, which were central to the underlying controversies of the Early Enlightenment, were posed with unique political and psychological intensity by the Huguenot predicament.

Self-identification with the Ancient Jews was by the late seventeenth century a stock image in the Protestant imagination. Unsurprisingly, it was a prevalent rhetorical theme for the first generation of Huguenot refugees, who repeatedly compared their exile to the traumatic but short-lived captivity of the Jews in Babylon.[5] For this intensely religious and traumatised

[2] See Guy Dodge, *The Political Theory of the Huguenots of the Dispersion* (1947) 94–138; Hubert Bost, *Un 'intellectuel' avant la lettre* (1994) 65ff.

[3] See François Laplanche, *L'Ecriture, le sacré et l'histoire*, esp. 509–16; Gerald Cerny, *Theology, Politics and Letters at the Crossroads of European Civilization: Jacques Basnage and the Baylean Huguenot Refugees in the Dutch Republic* (1987) 27–8, 62.

[4] Pierre Jurieu, *L'Accomplissement des prophéties* (1686) esp. 11, 239–69. See also Harry M. Bracken, 'Pierre Jurieu: The Politics of Prophecy', in Laursen and Popkin, eds., *Continental Millenarians*, 85–94.

[5] See Cerny, *Theology*, 61; Elizabeth Labrousse, *Pierre Bayle–1* (1963) 201–3.

minority, Jewish peoplehood offered a powerfully sustaining model of cultural survival, and the Jewish narrative of exile and redemption provided the vital inspiration of historical purpose and hope. However, many Huguenot intellectuals were keenly aware of recent scholarly debates, and of the hermeneutical uncertainties and difficulties they had raised concerning the moral and historical status of the Old Testament. It is not surprising, therefore, that the most intensive scrutiny of Judaism and the Jewish past in the decades around 1700 was undertaken by two of the leading scholars of the Dutch Huguenot refuge: Jacques Basnage and Pierre Bayle.

BASNAGE'S *HISTOIRE DES JUIFS:* ERUDITION AND AMBIGUITY

Jacques Basnage's *Histoire des Juifs* was one of the boldest publishing endeavours of the Enlightenment. Its first edition, published by the Rotterdam entrepreneur Rainier Leers in 1706–7, immediately attracted great interest. A full English translation appeared in 1708, and a pirated and bowdlerised French version, adapted for a Catholic readership, appeared anonymously, and to Basnage's outrage, in Paris two years later. In 1716 Basnage published the revised and definitive nine-volume edition of his *Histoire*, which he subtitled as a continuation up to the present of Josephus' early history. In his preface he proudly asserted that the comprehensive scope of his work was unprecedented in both Christian and Jewish scholarship.[6] While his text is without doubt notable in its monumentality, much of its bulk consists of extensive borrowings from earlier works. Of much greater interest, however, is the methodology of the study. Basnage sustainedly attempted to apply the methods of modern critical scholarship to his subject. In so doing, he brought the competing theological and secular approaches to history into direct and intimate confrontation with each other.

Basnage was born in Rouen in 1653, and educated at Saumur, at the Academy of Geneva – where he established a life-long friendship with his fellow-student Pierre Bayle – and at Sedan, where he was taught by Jurieu. In October 1685, after the Protestant Church of Rouen, where he was employed as minister, had been razed to the ground, he emigrated to the Dutch Republic, serving as pastor first of the Walloon Church of Rotterdam, and then from 1710 until his death in 1723 in The Hague.[7] According to his biographer, Gerald Cerny, Basnage was 'a conservative and orthodox Calvinist':[8] although closely allied with Pierre Bayle, he did

---

[6] Jacques Basnage, *Histoire des Juifs* (1716) 1, xix.
[7] See Cerny, *Theology*, 11–178.   [8] *Ibid.*, 312–13.

not share his friend's philosophical profundity and originality. However, Basnage had in his early life been exposed to a wide range of intellectual influences. He had been a student in Geneva at the height of the controversy over Jean-Robert Chouet's introduction of Cartesianism into the scientific curriculum.[9] He had directly experienced the traumatic persecution of his community in Rouen in the years and months leading up to the Revocation of the Edict of Nantes, and soon after arriving in Holland found himself awkwardly drawn into the bitter confrontation between Jurieu and Bayle.[10] The impact of this early buffeting can be detected in the unsettled jostling of competing priorities and perspectives within the text of the *Histoire des Juifs*.

The predominant intellectual concern of Basnage's career was to reconcile these disputes, by integrating sound theology with critical reason. This problematic drew him naturally to biblical themes, his approach to which was delicately caught between opposing pressures and aspirations. His objectivity as a historian strained against his partisanship as a Protestant Christian; a scholarly desire to treat all texts and traditions equally offset a commitment to a sharp distinction between good and bad hermeneutics; and his fascination with otherly exoticism distracted from his desire to maintain an integrated and distinctively Christian interpretative perspective. These tensions are already apparent in Basnage's 1705 edition and translation into French of Petrus Cunaeus' *De Republica Hebraeorum*. Basnage was powerfully attracted by Cunaeus' presentation of the Mosaic Rupublic as political model for his own nation.[11] However, he was troubled by a number of points of detail in Cunaeus' argument, which he published in a separate two-volume commentary to the text under the title *Antiquités Judaïques* (1713). Basnage's rationalist, thorough scholarship did not allow him to accept Cunaeus' unhesitant representation of every detail of the Mosaic revelation as a foreshadowing of the Christian message. This careful balancing of historical evidence and theological dogma remained a powerful strain running throughout the *Histoire des Juifs*.

Basnage was not the first to aspire to write a continuation of Josephus' *Jewish Antiquities*. In the 1650s Menasseh ben Israel frequently mentioned the imminent publication of his own history, titled *La historia Iudiaca, o continuación de Flavio Josepho hasta nuestros tiempos*, but the work never reached the presses, and no manuscript has ever been located.[12] The scope of

---

[9] *Ibid.*, 26–7. See also Michael Heyd, *Between Orthodoxy and Enlightenment: Jean-Robert Chouet and the Introduction of Cartesian Science in the Academy of Geneva* (1982) esp. 69–86.

[10] Cerny, *Theology*, 102, 107–11.

[11] Jacques Basnage, 'Préface' to Petrus Cunaeus, *La République des Hebreux* (1705) i.

[12] Menasseh ben Israel, *The Hope of Israel* (1987 (1652)) 102, 158.

Basnage's work, however, embraced Jewish religious traditions and beliefs as well as history. As his introductory comments make clear, he saw his study as the starting-point for an even vaster endeavour that was almost encyclopaedic in scope:

having formed the plan of writing the history of all the religions that have diverged from Christianity, I realized that I should start with Judaism, because it is necessary to understand a religion from which the first heretics drew some of their dogmas and barbarous expressions. It is also useful to know more about a nation whose place we have taken, and who one day will take back our place, or who, at least, will be reunited with Christians in one body. It is no mere tedium to follow the dispersion of this poor people in the east and the west, and to see where today are to be found the debris of this nation that God loved for so long. Finally, the singularity of the subject, which nobody has fully examined in a vernacular language, obliged me to go further...[13]

A tension is immediately apparent here between the scholarly and the theological dimensions of this project. In part, Basnage is drawn to his subject by a general curiosity, and by a desire to proceed from a logical starting-point in his cataloguing of all deviations from Christianity. However, he also mentions other, unique reasons for his interest in Judaism. Although he does not here emphasise specific millenarian expectations, it is clearly within this optic that Basnage infuses Jewish history with religious meaning. Once God's favoured people, and destined to be so again, the sufferings of the Jews since the time of Jesus Christ are not simply to be regarded as the product of historical forces, but also as the sign and consequence of the withdrawal of divine favour from them, in punishment for their rejection of Jesus.

The scholarly detail and critical rigour of Basnage's text is almost throughout of an extremely high standard. Some sections are heavily dependent on single sources: most notably, the lengthy account of Jewish 'rites and ceremonies' largely repeats the standard seventeenth-century source on this topic, Rabbi Leone of Modena's *Historia di gli riti hebraici*.[14] However, in general his range of scholarly references is extremely wide. Basnage extensively cites the Talmud and later rabbinic literature, as well as leading Christian Hebraists such as the Buxtorfs, John Lightfoot and Johann Wagenseil, and in the 1716 edition a recently inspected collection of rare seventeenth-century Sephardic anti-Christian polemics.[15] He assesses his various sources dispassionately and calmly, evincing a strong empathetic

[13] Basnage, *Histoire*, I, 10.

[14] *Ibid.*, I, 18 and VII; cf. Leone Modena, *Historia di gli riti hebraici* (1637).

[15] On this collection see R. H. Popkin, 'Jacques Basnage's *Histoire des Juifs* and the Biblioteca Sarraziana', *Studia Rosenthaliana* 21 (1987) 154–162.

interest in the minutiae of the Jewish historical experience. He carefully considers the claim that the King of Khazar, in Tartary, converted to Judaism in the eighth century, but rejects it as a fantasy, on the grounds that nobody has been able to locate the state.[16] He also offers a detailed account of Benjamin of Tudela's twelfth-century journey through the Jewish communities of Europe and the Near East,[17] and devotes a chapter to the Jewish 'great men' of the twelfth century, very respectfully discussing the work of Maimonides, Ibn Ezra and others, and even signalling reports of a prodigiously learned Jewess somewhere in the East.[18]

Basnage also discusses the history of Christian persecutions of the Jews. He devotes particularly close attention to the blood libel, endorsing the exposure by Jews of the malicious falsity of these charges.[19] Concluding a detailed and extensively documented study of the various magical accounts associated with blood libel accusations, he dismisses them all as Christian fabrications.[20] His opposition to the persecution and ill-treatment of the Jews is clearly sincere and deeply felt, as is his pride in the contrasting tolerance of Holland, where, he writes, Jews live more peacefully and prosperously than anywhere else in Europe. However, despite his personal commitment to tolerance, Basnage glanced away from enunciating an explicit argument against the traditional Christian hostility towards Jews: 'Christians may believe that they have deserved their exile and other suffering, because of their cruelty in crucifying Jesus Christ, and their obstinacy towards him. However, others who are more fair-minded would wish that they had been treated with more humanity.'[21] This generalised advocacy of moderation does not truly engage with the conventional argument it opposes. Indeed, Basnage accepted the standard view of Jewish misery as a manifestation of divine punishment. His commitment to toleration is animated by a powerful aversion towards the superstitious, anti-rationalist enthusiasm that he regarded as fuelling most anti-Jewish persecution. However, he was unwilling to depart too markedly from traditional Christian arguments that cast the suffering of the Jews, if not their deliberate ill-treatment, as natural and divinely ordained.

The ambiguity is particularly apparent in his approach to the history of Christian treatment of Jews. Basnage frequently equated Jewish and Huguenot suffering: in his lengthy and particularly outraged description of the forced baptism of the Jews by the French medieval king Chilperic, an analogy is clearly implied between this tyrant and his successor, Louis XIV,

---

[16] Basnage, *Histoire*, IX, 18–22.   [17] *Ibid.*, 189–253.   [18] *Ibid.*, 254–98.
[19] *Ibid.*, 372.   [20] *Ibid.*, 372–93.   [21] *Ibid.*, 350.

and between persecuted Jews and persecuted Huguenots.[22] However, this identification is not sustained throughout the text. Basnage did not exonerate all actions by Protestants: while approving of Luther's vigorous attacks on Jewish beliefs, he noted that at times his impetuosity had led him 'beyond moderation'.[23] It was still more awkward for him to account for the long-standing Jewish presence in Rome. Basnage presented this as an example of Catholic hypocrisy, noting that no regime had been 'more gentle to the circumcised' than that of the Popes, who favoured Jews while at the same time persecuting Christians who rejected their authority.[24] Whereas elsewhere in his text Jews stand synecdochically for the true faith, here they are represented as a particularly undeserving counterpoint to it. This oscillation highlights the underlying instability of Basnage's attitude towards his historical subject.

The representation of Judaism in Basnage's *Histoire* was in several passages clearly shaped by the exigencies of contemporary theological disputes between Protestants and Catholics. However, the text was not primarily intended as a confessional polemic: while Basnage fitfully drew an analogy between Catholicism and rabbinic Judaism, this was not developed into a sustained allegorical argument.[25] The association of Popish authoritarianism with rabbinical excess was a long-standing Protestant rhetorical trope, but, as the interchange between Jean Le Clerc and Richard Simon in the 1670s had highlighted, it was difficult to sustain within the scholarly culture of the Early Enlightenment. Moreover, as a rigorous historian Basnage aspired to transcend confessional boundaries: he expressed the hope that his work would gain the approval of Catholics, and even of Jews themselves.[26] Cordiality between members of different churches was assiduously maintained within the Republic of Letters, of which Jacques Basnage, with his deep commitment to the values of moderation and politeness, was an exemplary member.[27] Religious ideology did influence Basnage's portrayal of Jewish history, but it infiltrated his arguments in an intermittent, unresolved and often somewhat uncontrolled way, rather than as a deliberate and sustained intellectual position.

However, a pointedly partisan and anti-Catholic intent is unambiguous in Basnage's idealised description of the Karaite sect. In keeping with

---

[22] *Ibid.*, VIII, 420ff.; Miriam Yardeni, 'New Concepts of Post-Commonwealth Jewish History in the Early Enlightenment: Bayle and Basnage', *European Studies Review* 7 (1977) 247.

[23] Basnage, *Histoire*, IX, 935.   [24] *Ibid.*, 543.

[25] I here disagree with the reading suggested by Jonathan Elukin, 'Jacques Basnage and the *History of the Jews*: Anti-Catholic Polemic and Historical Allegory in the Republic of Letters', *JHI* 53 (1992) 603–30.

[26] Basnage, *Histoire*, I, i–ii.   [27] See Goldgar, *Impolite Learning*, 174–218.

long-standing Protestant tradition, Basnage presented the Karaites in an extremely positive light, emphasising their piety and devotion to Scripture and implying a strong similarity between their theology and that of Reformed Protestants: 'They recognize only two guiding lights in matters of religion: one is *The Lamp of Scripture*, and the other, *that of Understanding*... Truth is recognised, according to them, through the use of *Reason*, which draws it from the bosom of the Prophecies.'[28] For Richard Simon, this brief section was the most provocative of Basnage's entire text, and was the focus of detailed and trenchant criticism in his attack on the *Histoire* published pseudonymously in the *Nouvelle Bibliothèque Choisie* of 1714. Simon based the interpretative authority of Catholicism very firmly on its inheritance from Judaism: he had earlier written that the two faiths were 'one and the same religion in substance'.[29] In his response to the *Histoire* Simon reiterated similar arguments to those he had aired in his quarrel with Jean Le Clerc more than thirty years previously. He accused Basnage of falsely stating that the Karaites rejected all tradition, in order to mount a tendentious attack on the inherited authority of Catholicism. Responding to Simon in the preface of the 1716 edition of the *Histoire*, Basnage indignantly rejected his accusation of distortion. Had he been attempting to attack the Catholic Church, he commented, 'the sin would not have been enormous'; but his portrayal of the Karaites was strictly non-partisan and accurate.[30] In his text he did indeed note the very small size of the Karaite community, and their descent into 'misery' and 'ignorance'.[31] Basnage's historical scholarship here once again strained against his theological interpretation, raising an awkward question that he neither attempted to disguise nor to resolve: if the Karaites adhered to such an enlightened school of Judaism, then why had they been so drastically unsuccessful as a community?

Basnage's attitude to rabbinical Judaism was similarly ambiguous. Although he was in general scornful of the authority of rabbis and wary of their argumentative methods, he was nonetheless anxious to display his interpretative competence and scholarly respect for Hebrew literature. He was forthrightly dismissive of the distinction between the written and oral law on which the authority of the Talmud is based, mockingly observing that it enabled the rabbis to 'make God say whatever they wanted',

---

[28] Basnage, *Histoire*, 11, 381. See also Lester Segal, 'Jacques Basnage de Beauval's *L'Histoire des Juifs*: Christian Historiographical Perception of Jewry and Judaism on the Eve of the Enlightenment', *Hebrew Union College Annual* 54 (1983) 316.

[29] Le Sieur de Simonville [Richard Simon], *Comparaison des Cérémonies des Juifs, et de la Discipline de l'Eglise* (1681) 25.

[30] Basnage, *Histoire*, I, xxiv–xxvi.   [31] *Ibid.*, 11, 440.

and to multiply and change the commandments at whim.[32] Although he claimed that much of the Talmud was foolish and useless, he nonetheless argued against its censorship or repression. Such is its absurdity and blasphemy, he alleges, that its study can only fortify Christians in their contempt for Judaism, just as exposure to the gross superstitions of popery can only harden visitors to Rome against Catholicism.[33] In later passages, though, Basnage shifts towards a more emollient attitude to Jewish learning. He insists that it is essential to learn Hebrew in order to understand Jewish rites, from which many Christian traditions are derived, and he acknowledges the great usefulness of rabbinic writings in the elucidation of Scripture.[34] He here adds a caveat: 'Let us simply note that it is not necessary to fall into excess.'[35] This plea for moderation, couched in the ubiquitous Early Enlightenment language of hostility to 'enthusiasm', scarcely veils the unresolved tension between Basnage's respect for erudition and his scorn for rabbinism.

At the end of the *Histoire* Basnage reverts to an explicitly Christian mode of historiography. His lengthy final chapter is devoted to the subject of the conversion of the Jews, the inevitability of which he does not question. He quotes extensively and approvingly from Jurieu's *L'Accomplissement des Prophéties*, highlighting his reminder that 'we must remember that the Messiah belongs to the Jews, and that he has been promised to the Jews'.[36] Addressing the question of how to herald this event, Basnage rejected forcible conversions, and also attempts to missionise among Jews 'using their own weapons' by locating Christian truths within rabbinic texts, which he regarded as a dishonest strategy because it often distorted the rabbis' intended meaning.[37] Echoing conventional opinion, he blamed the failure of Christian conversionism on the obstinacy and insularity of the Jews, and on their dogged attachment to the absurdities of the Talmud. Despite these obstacles, he insisted that Christians must persevere in their attempts to demonstrate to the Jews 'the absurdity of their texts'.[38] Basnage's concluding comments at the end of this vast work reaffirm his conversionist and loosely millenarian attitude towards the Jewish people:

A Christian will speak with more confidence if he has a large number of proofs to hand; and the Jew, attacked in so many sensitive places where the error of his teachers is revealed, will have less courage and fortitude to resist. But in the final analysis these are only external means, and God alone knows when he will recall *this elect Nation*.[39]

---

[32] *Ibid.*, 111, 112.   [33] *Ibid.*, 189–90.   [34] *Ibid.*, 192–208.   [35] *Ibid.*, 210.
[36] *Ibid.*, IX, 1107.   [37] *Ibid.*, 1118   [38] *Ibid.*, 1137.   [39] *Ibid.*, 1140.

Given the underlying traditionalism of Basnage's attitude towards the Jews, it is perhaps surprising that his *Histoire* has tended to be regarded, both at the time of publication and since, as radically open-minded and liberal. Soon after the publication of the first edition, an English critic, Robert Jenkin, attacked Basnage for his excessive sympathy with the Jews and his over-meticulous attention to their writings.[40] The *Histoire* was a key source for Voltaire, Diderot and other leading *philosophes*: the article 'Juif' in Diderot's *Encyclopédie* was entirely composed of extracts from Basnage's work.[41] The text also influenced the development of history-writing among Jews. In the early 1790s, a group of Berlin Jews associated with Moses Mendelssohn commissioned Solomon Maimon to translate Basnage's work from French to Hebrew, for the instruction of the Jews of Poland; a project that Maimon commenced but never completed.[42]

Twentieth-century historians have also tended to celebrate Basnage's work as unambiguously progressive. According to Gerald Cerny, Basnage was a pioneer of the rational demystification of Jewish history, while Miriam Yardeni has identified the *Histoire* as 'the origin and inspiration of the pro-Jewish tradition in the Enlightenment'.[43] It is undoubtedly true that the boldness and sweep of Basnage's project was strikingly original, and that his respect for historical accuracy and his criticisms of the harsh treatment of Jews were liberal even by the relatively modern standards of early eighteenth-century Holland. However, Basnage's rationalist objectivity and tolerance is repeatedly undercut by his Calvinist theology. He attempted to study Jewish history simultaneously as an objective historian and as a doctrinally committed pastor, and it is the tension between these two perspectives that most crucially characterises his text.

As a historian, Basnage was committed to the application of objective critical methods to his material, and of just ethical standards to the Jews as a people. However, for Basnage the theologian the Jews necessarily remained beyond the normal standards of historical explanation. From this perspective he defined Jewish survival itself as miraculous: 'the greatest of all imaginable miracles is the conservation of the Jewish people, in the midst of all the miseries they have suffered for the past 1700 years'.[44] At

---

[40] Robert Jenkin, *Remarks on Some Books Lately Published* (1709) 1–49.

[41] See Miriam Silvera, 'L'ebreo in Jacques Basnage: apologia del cristianesimo e difesa della tolleranza', *Nouvelles de la république des lettres* 1 (1987) 115.

[42] Solomon Maimon, *Lebensgeschichte* (1792), trans. J. Clark Murray, *Autobiography* (1947) 96–7. See also Michael A. Meyer, 'The Emergence of Jewish Historiography', *Essays in Jewish Historiography* (1988) 164–9.

[43] Cerny, *Theology*, 189–90, 200–2; Yardeni, 'New Concepts', 246.　　　[44] Basnage, *Histoire*, VII, 1.

the core of the subject that Basnage sets out to investigate historically there stands an enigma that he ultimately regards as beyond the reach of historical explanation. The implications of this suppressed paradox suffuse his text, which, despite its determinedly lucid and professional scholarship, is for this reason above all a work of profound ambiguity.

BAYLE'S *DICTIONNAIRE:* JUDAISM AS DIVINE PARADOX

The philosophical temperament of Pierre Bayle was very different to that of his friend. Whereas Basnage consistently avoided directly confronting the tension between reason and faith, the exploration of this delicate relationship was the central theme of Bayle's work. In his eulogy for Bayle, published soon after Bayle's death in his brother Henri Basnage's *Histoire des Ouvrages des Savans*, Jacques Basnage gently chided Bayle for pushing his sagacity so far 'as to find difficulties'.[45] However, it was the relentless probing of difficulties that was the very essence of Bayle's philosophical approach, most spectacularly exemplified in his controversial but extremely influential *Dictionnaire Historique et Critique* (1697).

This immense work is unlike any other historical dictionary. Its substantive articles, devoted to a bizarre assortment of historical figures, are for the most part brief and uncontroversial. Of far greater interest are the copious and eclectic notes appended to them, which contain a trove of anecdotes, suggestions and arguments that are often only tenuously related to the ostensible subject of the article, but which penetrate to the core of Bayle's philosophical preoccupations. In these 'remarks' Bayle repeatedly highlighted intellectual paradoxes of all kinds, focusing mercilessly on the irrationality of religious beliefs, and on the equal insufficiency of human reason. Of particular fascination to Bayle was the relationship between reason and the Bible, which, in contrast to the more optimistic view of almost all his contemporaries, he regarded as fundamentally incompatible with each other. This clash is brought to the fore above all in the large number of articles in the *Dictionnaire* that are devoted to Old Testament themes. (The New Testament, in contrast, is represented only by one brief article on John the Evangelist.[46]) As we shall see, the prominence of Judaism in Bayle's thought is far from coincidental. More explicitly than any other

---

[45] *HOS* (December 1706) 555.
[46] This contrast is noted as 'curious' in R. H. Popkin, 'The Image of the Jew in Clandestine Literature circa 1700', in Guido Canziani, ed., *Filosofia e religione nella letteratura clandestina* (1994) 33.

text of the period, his *Dictionnaire* demonstrates the profound ensnare-
ment of Judaism within the Early Enlightenment confrontation of reason
and faith.

Bayle's personal beliefs have been subject to extremely varied interpretation since his own lifetime, and remain so today. While his biographer,
Elizabeth Labrousse, has emphasised his basic commitment to an idealised
vision of the Christian Church,[47] other scholars have read Bayle as a covert
atheist,[48] a libertine,[49] an agonized doubting believer,[50] and as someone
whose private beliefs remain an enigma.[51] It is, however, ultimately inappropriate to scour the *Dictionnaire* for an underlying authorial voice. Bayle's
deliberately open and mobile intellectual approach frustrates this search at
every turn. Almost all of his writings were published either anonymously or
pseudonymously, and many of them present a plurality of opinions without
any final authorial adjudication between them. His political pamphlet *Ce
que c'est que la France toute Catholique sous le règne de Louis le Grand* (1686),
for example, is made up of three different letters, each purportedly written
by a different Huguenot author, and each expressing a differently tempered
response to Louis' persecution. Bayle offers no indication of his own opinion: rather than aspiring to convince his readers of a single viewpoint, his
aim is to present the full philosophical complexity of the issues and choices
faced by the Huguenot community.[52] Writing was for him very often more
an act of intellectual exploration than of persuasion. Nowhere is this more
emphatically the case than in his *Dictionnaire*, thoughout which he rigorously sustains an indeterminate position on key issues of epistemology and
belief.

The radical unfixity of Bayle's texts marks them as a conceptual and
stylistic mirror image, at the dawn of modernity, of some of the playful ambiguities of postmodernism associated with that epoch's uncertain
end. Bayle saw the quest for knowledge as by definition inconclusive: he
viewed the essence of scholarship as the correction of others' errors, in the
process inevitably producing new errors that will in their turn also stand
correction.[53] Moreover, he regarded the craft of writing, and also its twin

---

[47] Labrousse, *Pierre Bayle—II* (1964) 597–600.
[48] Gianfranco Cantelli, *Teologia e ateismo: saggio sul pensiero filosofico e religioso di Pierre Bayle* (1969).
[49] David Wootton, 'Pierre Bayle, libertine?', in M. A. Stewart, ed., *Studies in Seventeenth-Century European Philosophy* (1997) 197–226.
[50] Michael Heyd, 'A Disguised Atheist or a Sincere Christian? The Enigma of Pierre Bayle', in *Bibliothèque d'humanisme et Renaissance: travaux et documents* 39 (1977) 157–65.
[51] Jean-Pierre Jossua, *Pierre Bayle, ou l'obsession du mal* (1977) 157, 177.
[52] Pierre Bayle, *Ce que c'est que la France toute Catholique* (1973 [1686]).
[53] For an insightful analysis of this see Luc Weibel, *Le Savoir et le corps: essai sur P. Bayle* (1975) 24–33.

activity of reading, as constitutively open-ended. His texts do not seek to reach closure, and do not invite their readers to seek it.[54]

The fundamental paradox explored in some sense in almost all of the articles of the *Dictionnaire* is that of the radical incommensurability of reason and faith. Both modes of thought, for Bayle, are indispensable, and yet neither can either falsify or be reconciled with the other. He is fascinated by the great power of reason, and by its fatal limits. Critical scepticism is, he insists, the essential motor of scientific and logical thought – but it is utterly redundant and dangerously corrosive when applied to matters of faith.[55] The basis of his vehement disagreement with Spinoza, the subject of the longest article in the *Dictionnaire*, is that he regards Spinoza as having violated this segregation of scepticism and religion. Bayle describes Spinoza as a 'systematic atheist',[56] and the *Tractatus Theologico-Politicus* as 'a pernicious and detestable book' containing 'the seeds of atheism' (see figure 3).[57] He mercilessly ridicules Spinoza's pantheistic notion of God as an infinitely modified universal substance, arguing that this amounts to a God absurdly divided against himself.[58] His overarching polemical target in this article is not the specifics of Spinoza's system, but the general notion of the absolute supremacy of human reason.[59] For Bayle, the mysteries of faith remain impervious to rational elucidation, and any attempt to analyse them philosophically is doomed to collapse into the hubris of atheism.

Bayle's own tightly argued rational critiques of the Bible are not intended to undermine religious faith, but rather to emphasise its autonomous mystery. Reason and faith are presented as two utterly separate realms, which cannot be reconciled within the human mind. While faith alone has no critical strength, rational scepticism alone is equally fallible. Once applied reflexively, scepticism implodes on itself: 'It confounds itself... the reasons for doubting being themselves doubtful. We must then doubt if it is necessary to doubt.'[60] In response to this paralysis, Bayle argues that there can be no alternative other than to renounce reason in favour of a more reliable guide: faith. The power of reason is, he suggests, deeply paradoxical. When placed under rigorous philosophical scrutiny it emerges as utterly

---

[54] For a similar argument see Thomas M. Lennon, *Reading Bayle* (1999) esp. 183–6.

[55] This is perhaps most starkly expressed in remark 'B' of the article on 'Pyrrho', in Pierre Bayle, *Dictionnaire Historique et Critique* (1697, 2nd edn 1702); ed. and trans. Richard H. Popkin, *Historical and Critical Dictionary: Selections* (1991) 194.

[56] *Ibid.*, 288 (art. 'Spinoza').   [57] *Ibid.*, 293–5.

[58] *Ibid.*, 312 (art. 'Spinoza', rem. 'N').

[59] See Geneviève Brykman, 'La "Réfutation" de Spinoza dans le *Dictionnaire* de Bayle', in Olivier Bloch, ed., *Spinoza au XVIIIe siècle* (1990) 17–25.

[60] Bayle, *Dictionary*, 205–6 (art. 'Pyrrho', rem. 'C').

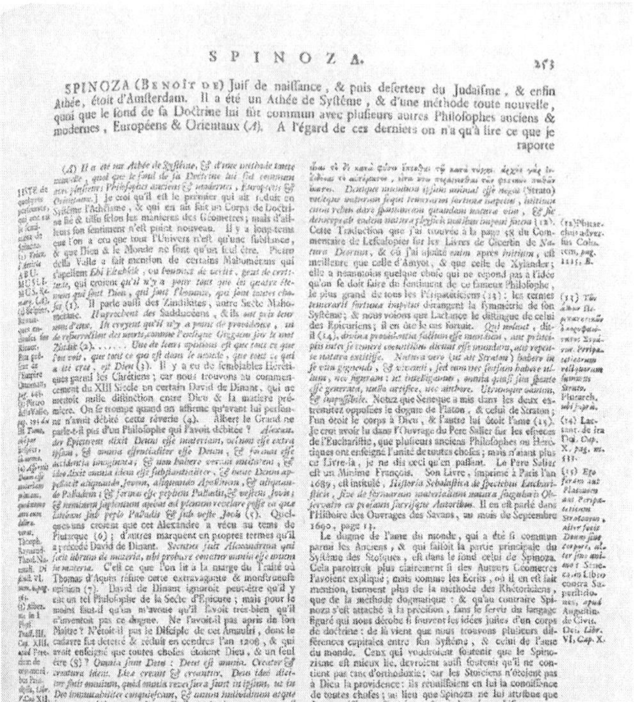

S P I N O Z A. 253

SPINOZA (BENOÎT DE) Juif de naissance, & puis deserteur du Judaïsme, & enfin Athée, étoit d'Amsterdam. Il a été un Athée de Systême, & d'une méthode toute nouvelle, quoi que le fond de sa Doctrine lui fût commun avec plusieurs autres Philosophes anciens & modernes, Européens & Orientaux (*A*). A l'égard de ces derniers on n'a qu'à lire ce que je raporte

Figure 3 Pierre Bayle, *Dictionnaire Historique et Critique*, Rotterdam, 1720, article on 'Spinoza'. As is typical, the footnoted 'remark' on this page, surrounded by its own footnotes, overwhelms the main text itself.

unreliable, but as a tool for everyday thought and argument it is indispensable. Bayle cannot resist the intellectual pleasures of rational analysis, but he maintains an acute sense of the ultimate inadequacy of this approach. Scepticism is thus a process without a goal. In Oscar Kenshur's apt words, 'the essence of Bayle's sceptical journey . . . is precisely that one never arrives'.[61]

In contrast to Spinoza's rationalist reading of the Bible as Jewish secular history, Bayle was fascinated by what he saw as the unbridgeable gulf between reason and Scripture. The Old Testament offered him the most fertile and compelling terrain for the exploration of the antinomy of reason and faith. A recurrent theme in the footnotes to his biblical articles is the discrepancy between rational standards of morality and the behaviour of leading Old Testament protagonists. In posing the unanswerable question of why the leaders of God's chosen people so often behaved in such an ungodly fashion, Bayle mapped the mystery of faith on to the historical record of the Jewish people.

This dynamic is most clearly in evidence in the lengthy article on King David. Bayle here revels in his witty exposure of David's immorality, drawing out the dissonance between his lofty status – 'one of the greatest men in the world, and a man after God's own heart'[62] – and his deceit, licentiousness, brutality and injustice. The tone of Bayle's criticisms vary from the teasingly understated to the uncompromisingly severe. Commenting on David's inaction in response to the rape of his daughter Tamar by his son Amnon, he observes ironically that '[David] was the best father that was ever seen. His indulgence towards his children went beyond reasonable limits.'[63] On his plan to slaughter all the family and the herds of Nabal in order to punish him for his inhospitality, he is contrastingly blunt: 'Is it not indisputable that David was going to commit an extremely criminal action?'[64] Bayle was uncompromising in his assessment of David's brutality in warfare, which he deemed even worse than the moral outrages of his own day:

Can it be said that this way of waging war is not to be condemned? Have not the Turks and the Tartars a little more humanity? And if a vast number of pamphlets complain every day about the military executions of our time, which are really cruel and much to be blamed, although mild in comparison to David's, what would the authors of these pamphlets not say if they had the saws, the harrows,

---

[61] Oscar Kenshur, 'Pierre Bayle and the Structures of Doubt', *Eighteenth-Century Studies* 21 (1988) 300. See also Harry Bracken, 'Bayle's Attack on Natural Theology: The Case of Christian Pyrrhonism', in Popkin and Vanderjagt, eds., *Scepticism*, 254–66.

[62] Bayle, *Dictionary*, 45 (art. 'David').   [63] *Ibid.*, 54 (art. 'David', rem. 'F').

[64] *Ibid.*, 52 (art. 'David', rem. 'D').

and brick kilns of David, and the general slaughter of all the males, young and old, to condemn?[65]

Bayle nonetheless argued that his criticisms of David's behaviour did not contradict the greater judgement of Scripture: 'I recognise . . . that the failings of this prophet are no argument against his having been a man full of piety and extraordinary zeal for the glory of the Lord.'[66] However, he insisted that the principles of morality were timeless and universal, and could not allow for any exceptions, even in the case of David:

Great harm would be done to the eternal laws and consequently to true religion if libertines were given a chance to object to us that, as soon as a man has a share in the inspirations of God, we . . . do not dare to condemn those actions that are diametrically opposed to the conceptions of equity when it is he who has committed them. There is no middle ground. Either these are unworthy actions, or actions like these are not wicked.[67]

Without challenging the religious and historical authority of the Old Testament, Bayle thus presented it as a text extremely deficient in moral judgement. This might readily seem to constitute a scarcely veiled attack on the Bible, and was indeed interpreted as such by many of Bayle's early French readers, who were used to winnowing out the hidden meanings of texts written to fool the censor.[68] However, within the wider context of Bayle's philosophical work it seems clear that his intention was not to launch such blatantly irreligious critique, but rather to underline the baffling, inescapable distance between the simplicity of rational ethics and the authority of God. The striking amorality of the life of David stood for Bayle as a powerful example of the inscrutability of Scripture, and of the non-rational mystery of faith.

Bayle's emphasis on the amoral behaviour of the biblical Jews placed them at odds with his general view of ethics, which he regarded as self-evident and universal. In the opening chapter of his earlier *Commentaire Philosophique* (to which we will return in detail in a later chapter), Bayle had strenuously asserted the universality of the divinely instilled 'natural light', which he described as a resource of the soul 'for infallibly distinguishing truth from falsehood'.[69] The paramount authority of this inner 'natural light' is central to Bayle's understanding of ethics. His moral theology extends to its

[65] *Ibid.*, 60 (art. 'David', rem. 'H').   [66] *Ibid.*, 62 (art. 'David', rem. 'I').   [67] *Ibid.* 62–3.
[68] See Elizabeth Labrousse, 'Reading Pierre Bayle in Paris', in Alan Charles Kors and Paul J. Korshin, eds., *Anticipations of the Enlightenment in England, France and Germany* (1987) 7–16.
[69] Bayle, *Commentaire Philosophique* (1686), trans. Amie Godman Tannenbaum, *Philosophical Commentary* (1987) 29.

limits the Protestant emphasis on the inner voice of conscience: no external authority, he argues, Scripture included, can trump this individual and private source of ethical certainty. It is at this level of personal moral certainty that Bayle ultimately rejects unmitigated scepticism.[70] Judaism, however, is positioned in a unique and troubling relationship to his morality of conscience. Bayle regards the divine principles of the natural light as eternal, and thus external to the Sinaitic revelation. Judaism, as a religion formed in its every detail in that moment of revelation, is therefore by implication a tradition in which the internalised voice of godly morality is uniquely and crucially absent.

This ethical lack is for Bayle the defining characteristic of Judaism. The Jews of the Old Testament were subject to the divinely ordained temporal authority of the Mosaic Law, which regulated all aspects of life, and obliterated all space for the operation of individual conscience. In conformity with traditional Christian beliefs, Bayle regarded the Mosaic Law as having been superseded by the moral teachings of Jesus Christ. It is therefore not surprising that he applied his critical biblical hermeneutic exclusively to the Old Testament. In the New Testament all tension between Scripture and ethics was regarded as having been dissolved: Jesus' purely ethical teachings erased all dissonances between divine morality and divine law. Judaism, both in pre-Christian times and since, thus stood as the cultural repository of this mysterious originary gap between the rationality of ethics and the transcendental authority of faith.

Bayle's view of Judaism as a religion fundamentally lacking in true ethics does not imply that he regarded all Jews as intrinsically amoral. On the contrary: his love of paradox drew him with particular relish to examples of Jewish virtuousness. In an article on the little-known German Jew Benjamin d'Arodon, Bayle praises the morality of his subject's conduct book for Jewish women, *Precetti da esser imparati dalle donne Ebree*, published in Venice in 1652. Discussing d'Arodon's precept that 'a husband and wife are ordered not to say a word during the performance of their conjugal duty, and to have only pious thoughts without any regard to pleasure', and that 'if they should act in any other manner, their children will be born deformed', Bayle comments that '[t]his ethic is excellent'.[71] Indeed, its excellence puts many Christians to shame:

In a word, it is certain that if this man had received with an entire faith the doctrine of Jesus Christ, and if he had been infused with the spirit of grace, he would not

[70] See Sean O'Cathasaigh, 'Skepticism and Belief in Pierre Bayle's *Nouvelles Lettres Critiques*', *JHI* 45 (1984) 421–433.

[71] Bayle, *Dictionary*, 23.

have given advice more worthy of evangelical purity. This ought to shame those teachers of looseness of morals who are so common among Christians.[72]

In this highly characteristic example of Bayle's argumentative indeterminacy, a multiplicity of ironies are superimposed on each other. Firstly, Bayle's praise for such impossibly restrained standards of modesty, and for the manifestly superstitious beliefs associated with them, is clearly not intended seriously. He to some extent appears to ridicule d'Arodon's teachings; but he is utterly logical in presenting them as the pinnacle of Christian ideals of chastity. On one level, the article can also be read as a satire of the moral zeal of puritanical Christians. Further ironies lie beyond this. In using pagan superstition in the service of moral discipline, d'Arodon exemplifies the paradoxical compatibility of virtue and nonsense. Ultimately, though, Bayle suggests the indefinability of ethics themselves. The twists of this article cumulatively imply that rational argument cannot elucidate true morality: such truths can only be known inwardly, through the individual conscience.

In deploying Jewish examples in his arguments, Bayle's concern is not to reach an assessment of Judaism itself. He chooses to discuss d'Arodon's text not for its intrinsic interest, but because it offers a particularly useful springboard from which to explore the contorted complexities of moral judgement. It is, therefore, inappropriate to search for and impossible to ascertain Bayle's inner opinion of Judaism. Scholars who have attempted to do so have reached widely divergent conclusions. Richard H. Popkin has speculated that Bayle's uncommon depth of knowledge of Jewish sources and his explicit commitment to the political toleration of Judaism suggests that at heart he might have been 'a Judaizing Christian, or a genuine Judaeo-Christian, or even a secret Jew'.[73] In contrast, Miriam Yardeni has concluded that although Bayle harboured no racial animosity towards the Jews, he was nonetheless ultimately 'anti-Jewish', because he regarded the religion as morally deficient.[74] It is undoubtedly the case that Bayle was deeply and respectfully fascinated by both ancient and modern Judaism, but also that he regarded it as an ethically alien and inadequate tradition. However, it is precisely because of this tension that Judaism plays such an important role in his thought. The anomaly of Judaism stands as the quintessence of the

---

[72] *Ibid.*, 24.

[73] R. H. Popkin, 'Introduction' to *Pierre Bayle – Historical and Critical Dictionary: Selections* (1991) xxvi.

[74] Miriam Yardeni, 'La Vision des juifs et du judaïsme dans l'oeuvre de Pierre Bayle', in M. Yardeni, ed., *Les Juifs dans l'histoire de France* (1980) 86–95.

fundamental philosophical paradox of the incommensurability of reason and faith.

The philosophical significance of Judaism for Bayle is unique and distinct. He characterises this religion by its one defining absence: its silencing of the voice of individual conscience. Judaism is thus constructed as intrinsically alien to the notion on which Bayle's own ethical principles are absolutely dependent. In the system of binary opposites that underpin Bayle's thought, the Jews occupy the negative excluded space. They stand outside the conceptual sphere within which Bayle's philosophy applies, and it is only in opposition to this exclusion that his positive philosophy can be defined. In contrast to Jewish theocratic legalism, Bayle's Christianity is defined as purely spiritual and politically neutral. Whereas in Judaism individual moral judgement is effaced by the laws of the Covenant, for Bayle independent attention to the divine inner light is the crux of all faith. Most fundamentally, Judaism is regarded as an authoritarian, absolutist system within which all tension between reason and faith is extinguished. For Bayle, it is the eternal tussle between these two intellectual forces, which strain so powerfully in opposing directions, that is the very essence of philosophical thought. Judaism, understood as a legally ordained religion impervious both to personal faith and to reason, is thus not only placed outside the realm of ethics, but also positioned as starkly alien to the practice of philosophy itself.

Bayle thus defines his philosophy through an unstated but structurally essential opposition to Judaism. However, his own philosophical system is not a closed one, and the ambiguities that cling to the Jewish case particularly highlight this incompleteness. As we have seen, in the clash between reason and faith Bayle ultimately judges faith to be paramount. Nonetheless, he offers no final resolution of their relationship: paradoxically, were he to do so, this would undermine the perpetual vitality of the tussle between these intellectual forces, from which the very concept of faith draws its meaningfulness. Faith remains for Bayle a profoundly problematic entity, subject to infinite mysteries and uncertainties, and diversely experienced in the mind of each individual.

The core of faith, he believes, resides in the individual conscience: a notion that is central to his theology, and which, while he loosely associates conscience with the similarly private faculty of rational thought, he acknowledges as ultimately personal and therefore varied. His view of religion thus offers no guarantee of agreement between different independent consciences. As we shall see in detail when we turn to Bayle's crucial place in the history of Enlightenment theories of toleration, this absence of any final trumping authority over the moral commitments of others is of crucial importance in his thought. His adherence to it, even in the face of the considerable difficulties it posed in his attempt to formulate the outer limits of the tolerable, demonstrates once again the resolute unfixity of Bayle's philosophy, in this context also defined against the imagined legalistic rigidity of Judaism.

This opposition was not simply based on the classic juxtaposition of Christian ethics and Jewish law. In his article on Spinoza and elsewhere, Bayle explicitly rejected the paring down of Christianity to a minimal form of natural religion. He understood the Christian God to be manifest not only in abstract ethics, but also in Scripture. Whereas in the New Testament he saw these two dimensions of the divine as closely integrated, the Old Testament posed for him the fundamental mystery of their stark incommensurability. Despite their election, the Old Testament Jews (and also the Old Testament God, although Bayle is significantly reticent on this subject) do not, in Bayle's reading, conform to the absolute principles of morality and ethics. In their imperviousness to moral truth, they stand as representative of that residue of faith most radically unassimilable to reason. This deafness to reason places them outside philosophy, and positions them in a renewed sense as a 'witness people', now bearing witness not to the historical truth of Christianity, but to the eternal imperviousness of religion to the critiques of rational scepticism.

Both Bayle and Basnage were committed to the Early Enlightenment renewal of historical scholarship, based on the critical values of scrupulous accuracy, impartiality and erudition. Although Bayle's philosophical intricacy and scandalous iconoclasm bore an aspect of intellectual playfulness, his work was always also deeply serious, underpinned by a determination to further human knowledge and understanding through level-headed argument and rigour. This was not simply a matter of personal intellectual taste.[75] The Huguenot diaspora in the immediate aftermath of the 1685 expulsion, despite its general well-being in material terms, was intellectually deeply divided, torn between widely differing views of the nature of both civil and ecclesiastical authority. The stakes in this dispute were high, and Bayle's relentless expansion of the envelope of serious analytical debate stood in stark and deliberate counterpoint to the passionate polemics and autocratic tendencies of Pierre Jurieu and others.[76]

---

[75] On Bayle's historical method see Ruth Whelan, 'The Anatomy of Superstition: a Study of the Historical Theory and Practice of Pierre Bayle', *SVEC* 259 (1989) esp. 233–40; Antonio Corsano, *Bayle, Leibniz e la storia* (1971) 15–37.
[76] See Dodge, *Political Theory*, 198–228.

Even the most meticulous erudition, however, could not bridge the inescapable lacuna that separated sacred from secular history. In contemplating the historical and theological status of Jews, Bayle and Basnage confronted this problem directly, but their attempts to resolve it were not and could not be conclusively successful. While breaking down old taboos, myths and prejudices, they simultaneously placed the Jews at the centre of a new and equally dense conceptual knot.

Bayle's unwavering exploration of the inescapable incommensurability of reason and faith pushed erudite learning to its philosophical limits. He could imagine a harmonisation of these two clashing realms only in the mind of God, at which utopian level he maintained a highly abstracted and deferred notion of intellectual holism. This positive vision enabled him to sustain a life as both a rigorously critical scholar and a committed Calvinist. To less agile minds, though, such a rarified and remote reconciliation of reason and religion was not a possibility. Most readers understood Bayle's deconstructive critiques of the Bible as constituting a severe assault on the authority of the Church, and the self-consciously radical tradition of the Early Enlightenment soon drew great strength from his arguments. Beyond the respectable world of public scholarship, within which both Bayle and Basnage were prominent participants, very similar debates and intellectual tensions were simultaneously being addressed in ways that far more outspokenly challenged the shibboleths of mainstream Christianity.

PART II

Judaism and the formation of Enlightenment radicalism

CHAPTER 5

Religious dissent and debate in Sephardi Amsterdam

Spinoza's early non-Jewish admirers portrayed his expulsion from the Amsterdam Sephardi community as a confirmation of the contrast between his isolated genius and the petty-minded dogmatism of the Jewish world into which he had the misfortune to be born. A lingering assumption of the ghetto insularity of the Amsterdam community survives in some modern historiography.[1] More generally, it is widely assumed that until the beginnings of the *Haskalah* in the late eighteenth century – a belated 'Jewish Enlightenment' – European Jewry was largely oblivious to the wider intellectual climate that surrounded it. However, the Sephardim of western Europe were far from isolated from the impact of the Enlightenment, and in the early eighteenth century increasingly absorbed the fashions and values of the prevailing secular culture. The declining respect for rabbinic authority and traditional scholarship in this period was symptomatic of a more general communal crisis in the face of the Enlightenment.[2] However, Sephardi intellectual life in the immediate pre-Enlightenment period, especially in Amsterdam, was characterised by a vibrancy and dynamism strikingly in contrast with this later crisis. Theologico-political dissent within the community, and lively cross-fertilisation with ideas from outside, produced a rich literature of theological argument, which both prefigured and directly influenced later non-Jewish Early Enlightenment debate.

JUDAISM BETWEEN CATHOLICISM AND PROTESTANTISM

The Jews of the seventeenth-century northern European Sephardi diaspora were subject to a uniquely intricate variety of diverse cultural and religious influences, memories and allegiances. The degree to which the *converso* Jews of the Iberian peninsula retained private, 'crypto-Jewish' practices

---

[1] Richard H. Popkin, 'Spinoza and La Peyrère', *The Southwestern Journal of Philosophy* 8 (1977) 179–80.
[2] Israel, *European Jewry*, 237–62.

from 1391 onwards, when they were subject to considerable assimilatory pressures culminating in the forced conversions of the 1490s, remains a topic of historical controversy and uncertainty.[3] However, after several generations of at least outward observance of Catholicism, and for the vast majority at least some degree of internalisation of a Catholic identity even when supplemented by an enduring sense of Jewishness, those Marranos who settled in Hamburg, Amsterdam and a few other North Sea settlements from the 1590s onwards were able for the first time to live openly as Jews. Most of these migrants quickly conformed, at least nominally, to orthodox Judaism, and unhesitatingly accepted the authority of the newly formed Jewish communal structures.[4] However, not all arrivals immediately accepted the differences between the rabbinically enforced Judaism they discovered in northern Europe and the syncretic Judaeo-Catholicism with which they were familiar.

Internal dissent was compounded by external influences: Dutch and German Protestants responded to the Sephardim in a very different way from the inquisitorial Catholics in Spain. In Amsterdam in particular, the high degree of interest in Judaism among Hebraists, theologians and other intellectuals led to a relatively high level of intellectual contact between Jews and Protestants. In the middle third of the century both communities experienced a parallel phenomenon of heightened religious instability and millenarian excitement. This culminated among Jews in 1665, with the wave of enthusiastic fervour unleashed by the news that an Izmir Jew, Shabbatai Zevi, had proclaimed himself the Messiah, and humiliatingly dashed in the following year by Zevi's conversion to Islam.[5] The economic instability of Dutch Sephardi Jewry in the mid seventeenth century, heightened by the community's heavy exposure in the colonial tussle between the Dutch and the Portuguese over Brazil, contributed to a wider sense of spiritual and religious upheaval.[6]

The Sephardim of seventeenth-century northern Europe possessed a powerful sense of their cultural distinctiveness. Refugees from the Inquisitorial oppression of the 'lands of idolatry', as they habitually described the

---

[3] See Cecil Roth, *A History of the Marranos* (1941) 168–94; Benzion Netanyahu, *The Origins of the Inquisition in Fifteenth Century Spain* (1995); Henry Kamen, *The Spanish Inquisition: A Historical Revision* (1998) 28–65.

[4] Daniel M. Swetschinski, *Reluctant Cosmopolitans: The Portuguese Jews of Seventeenth-Century Amsterdam* (2000) 221–4.

[5] On this movement see Gershom Scholem, *Sabbatai Sevi: The Mystical Messiah* (1973).

[6] See Jonathan Israel, 'Dutch Sephardi Jewry, Millenarian Politics and the Struggle for Brazil (1640–1654)', in David S. Katz and Jonathan Israel, eds., *Sceptics, Millenarians and Jews* (1990) 76–97.

Iberian peninsula, they nonetheless retained strong intellectual and material ties with their former homeland. Alongside a conscious preservation of memories of suffering and oppression as forced *conversos*, the Sephardim of Amsterdam and other smaller communities simultaneously cultivated a strong attachment to and identification with Spanish literary culture. The collective psychology of these communities was characterised by a complex interpenetration of Jewish and Iberian patterns of thought. The members of the 'Portuguese nation', as the Amsterdam community described itself, possessed a powerful sense of communal loyalty and pride, based at least as much on traditional Iberian notions of purity of blood and ethnic exclusivity as on a specifically religious sense of affiliation.[7]

On arrival in the city, many Marranos possessed only a limited knowledge of Judaism, and religious education was therefore a major communal concern.[8] Even amongst those who were unequivocally eager to adopt normative Judaism, dissonant concepts derived from long-standing Catholic observance often remained deeply rooted within personal systems of belief. Several migrants, however, were resistant to the imposition of an orthodox conformity on them by the Amsterdam community establishment.[9] The challenge posed to rabbinical authority by these overlapping currents of dissidence and syncretism was compounded by the presence in the city of a significant minority of ex-*conversos* who lived alongside the Jewish community but took no part in its institutional and religious life. Several of these individuals retained close connections with the Iberian peninsula, and on occasion travelled there for business purposes, which was severely forbidden to community members.[10] The ambiguous status of this community – and also of those ethnic Jews, including many relatives of those in Amsterdam, who still lived in 'the lands of idolatry' and maintained

---

[7] See Miriam Bodian, *Hebrews of the Portuguese Nation: Conversos and Community in Early Modern Amsterdam* (1997) esp. 76–95; ' "Men of the Nation": The Shaping of *Converso* Identity in Early Modern Europe', *Past and Present* 143 (1994) 48–76; Richard H. Popkin, 'The Jews of the Netherlands in the Early Modern Period', in R. Po-Chia Hsia and Harmut Lehmann, eds., *In and Out of the Ghetto* (1995) 311–6; Gérard Nahon, 'Amsterdam, metropole occidentale des séfarades au XVIIe siècle', *Cahiers Spinoza* 3 (1980) 15–50; Gordon M. Weiner, 'Sephardic Philo- and Anti-Semitism in the Early Modern Era', in G. M. Weiner and R. H. Popkin, eds., *Jewish Christians and Christian Jews* (1994) 189–209; Swetschinski, *Reluctant Cosmopolitans*, 278–314; Yosef Kaplan, 'The Self-Definition of the Sephardic Jews of Western Europe and Their Relation to the Alien and the Stranger', in Benjamin R. Gampel, ed., *Crisis and Creativity in the Sephardic World, 1391–1648* (1997) 121–45.

[8] See Yosef Hayim Yerushalmi, 'The Re-Education of Marranos in the Seventeenth Century' (1980).

[9] See Yosef Kaplan, 'From Apostasy to Return to Judaism: The Portuguese Jews in Amsterdam', in Joseph Dan, ed., *Binah* 1 (1989) 99–117, esp. 110–12; 'De joden in de Republiek tot omstreeks 1750', in J. C .H. Blom *et al.*, eds., *Geschiedenis van de Joden in Nederland* (1995) 164–6.

[10] See Yosef Kaplan, 'The Travels of Portuguese Jews from Amsterdam to the "Lands of Idolatry" ', in Kaplan, ed., *Jews and Conversos: Studies in Society and the Inquisition* (1985) 197–224.

an outward observance of Catholicism – problematised the relationship of Jewish religious practice to Jewish identity.[11] This blurring of the outer boundaries of Jewishness to some extent undermined the attempts of leaders to enforce communal unity, and contributed to the striking ideological instability and intellectual permeability of the Amsterdam community.

The degree of religious heterodoxy and debate in Sephardi Amsterdam is difficult to gauge, but the survival in large numbers of controversialist anti-Christian manuscripts, often written in response to the questions of doubting Marranos, suggests that theological disagreement and uncertainty was widespread. The catalogue of the Amsterdam seminary, *Ets Haim*, lists more than thirty manuscript copies of these texts.[12] The composition, translation and copying of these manuscripts continued into the early eighteenth century, suggesting that theological doubt and dispute was a sustained phenomenon in Sephardi Amsterdam. The argumentation and texture of these polemics offer a valuable insight into the nature of Jewish responses to non-Jewish theology and philosophy in the decades prior to the expulsion of Spinoza.

The first major text in this genre, Isaac of Troki's *Hizzuk Emunah* (Fortification of the Faith), was written in a very different environment, by an Ashkanazi Karaite in 1590s Lithuania.[13] However, translations of this extremely trenchant anti-Christian text were soon diffused across Europe.[14] In his preface, Troki declared that his work was intended both to glorify God and to assist Jews in defending their 'true faith' against Christianity.[15] A more complicated mixture of motivations animated the slightly later Sephardi authors of anti-Christian polemics. These texts were not primarily intended for use in debate with Christians: even in Amsterdam such audacity would have been a foolhardy endeavour. Designed for use within the Jewish community, they aimed to reinforce the Jewish faith of potential doubters, and to counter the impact of Christian missionising. Most

---

[11] The possibility of salvation for Jews unable to observe the Mosaic Law was a serious anxiety, and the subject of intensive theological debate. See Alexander Altmann, 'Eternality of Punishment: A Theological Controversy within the Amsterdam Rabbinate in the Thirties of the Seventeenth Century', *Proceedings of the American Academy for Jewish Research* 40 (1972) 1–88.

[12] Henry Méchoulan, *Etre juif à Amsterdam au temps de Spinoza* (1991) 101.

[13] However, a parallel can be drawn between these two contexts. As a Karaite, Troki also wrote against a background of internal Jewish dispute. He was also influenced by the intense theological disagreements among his Christian neighbours, directly citing contemporary Polish and Lithuanian Unitarian writers. See Robert Dán, 'Isaac Troky and his "Antitrinitarian" Sources', in Robert Dán, ed., *Occident and Orient: A Tribute to the Memory of Alexander Scheiber* (1988) 69–82.

[14] Copies in Dutch, Spanish, French, Portuguese and Hebrew are listed in L. Fuks and R. G. Fuks-Mansfeld, *Hebrew and Jewish Manuscripts in Amsterdam Public Collections* (1975).

[15] Isaac Troki, *Hisuk Emuna, dat is Versterkinge des Geloofs* (Dutch translation from Hebrew), HS Ros. 494, preface.

importantly, though, the texts were an assertion of Jewish religious dignity and pride. Surviving volumes of Jewish controversialist writings owned by members of the Amsterdam community are expensively bound and meticulously calligraphed. They were clearly cherished by their owners as prized and valuable possessions, symbolic of a new prosperity and self-confidence (see figure 4).

The first important Sephardi anti-Christian polemicist was Eliahu Montalto, whose refutation of the Christian interpretation of the 53rd chapter of Isaiah was probably written in Venice in the first years of the seventeenth century.[16] This extremely polemical text never directly names its target: Christians are always periphrastically but scathingly referred to as 'os Depravadores da Divina Ley' (slanderers of the Divine Law).[17] Montalto argues uncompromisingly against numerous tenets of Christian belief such as original sin, and identifies and ridicules various contradictions and inconsistencies in the gospels, drawing on a detailed knowledge of the New Testament gained during his Marrano past.[18] Montalto died in Paris in 1616 whilst serving as doctor to Marie de Médicis. His student Saul Levi Morteira brought his body to Amsterdam for burial, and later himself became a leading rabbi in the Amsterdam community. Morteira also wrote several anti-Christian polemics, in which he vigorously confronted various key points of friction between Judaism and Christianity, such as the nature of sin and salvation, the Trinity and the issue of the Messiah.[19]

Both the most interesting and most widely circulated of Morteira's works is his final *Tratado de la Verdad de la Ley de Moseh* (1659), in which he engages not with Catholic but with Protestant arguments. During the 1650s, Morteira, like his probable *cheder* pupil, Spinoza, was in close contact with Socinians and other radical Christian groups in Amsterdam.[20] In this treatise, Morteira puts forward a highly original response to Calvinism and Socianianism, tinged with suspicion but also with empathy and excitement. While alarmed by their disrespect for the Mosaic Law, he nonetheless

[16] Israel, *European Jewry*, 84–5; Ralph Melnick, *From Polemics to Apologetics* (1981) 24–8; Bernard Cooperman, 'Eliahu Montalto's "Suitable and Incontrovertible Propositions"', in Isadore Twersky and Bernard Septimus, eds., *Jewish Thought in the Seventeenth Century* (1979) 469–97.

[17] E. Montalto, *Tratado do Doctor Montalto Sobre o principio do Capitulo 53 de Jesaias*, HS Ros. 76.

[18] *Ibid.*, 5, 73–6.

[19] See, e.g., S. L. Morteira, *Preguntas que se hizieron de un clerigo de Ruan a Amsterdam*, HS Ros. 127. See also Melnick, *Polemics*, 29–32; Marc Saperstein, *'Your Voice Like a Ram's Horn': Themes and Texts in Traditional Jewish Preaching* (1996) 118–25.

[20] Henry Méchoulan, 'Morteira et Spinoza au carrefour du socinianisme', *Revue des études juives* 135 (1976) 51–65. See also Myriam Silvera, 'Il *Tratado de Verdade da Ley de Moisés* di Saul Levi Mortera e i "miracoli nascosti" nella natura e nella storia', in Paolo Cristofolini (ed.), *The Spinozistic Heresy* (1995) 13–24.

PROVIDENCIA DE DIOS,
CON YSRAEL
Yverdad de la Ley de Moseh y nulidad de
mas leyes

Figure 4 Saul Levi Morteira, *Providencia de Dios con Ysrael*, Amsterdam, 1664, page 1.
This folio manuscript was uniquely and lavishly calligraphed by the Dutch-Portuguese
master calligrapher Luis Nunes Dovale.

envisages a possible theological alliance between Judaism and non-Trinitarian Christianity, based on the observance of the core biblical precepts and a common rejection of idolatry. This optimism suggests that Morteira hoped to reach not only Jews but also radical Christians, referred to in the text as 'nuevos reformados', whom he hoped to encourage to extend the Reformation to what he regarded as its logical conclusion: the adoption of a minimalist and universal Noachite faith based purely on the Old Testament.[21] He praises the 'newly reformed' for rejecting what he sees as the idolatrous veneration of the Cross and literalist Eucharistic beliefs,[22] and engages in detail with John Calvin's *Institutes of the Christian Religion*, mostly arguing oppositionally, but also at times expressing approval. He assents to Calvin's arguments against the worship of images, but argues that they must apply also to 'invisible images', and should therefore logically lead to the rejection of the Trinity.[23] He argues particularly insistently against Calvin's claim that the Mosaic Law is now obsolete, concluding the text with a triumphant celebration of its 'grace and mercy'.[24]

Unlike most Sephardi controversialist writings, it is clear that the primary purpose of this text was not to dispel the anxieties of Marranos, whose theological notions were much more intermeshed with Catholicism than with Calvinism. The breadth of Morteira's educational ambitions is reflected in his sermons, which range far beyond basic doctrinal inculcation and encompass the interpretation of both Jewish and non-Jewish history.[25] In this text he projects his historical analysis into the future, offering a preliminary sketch of a new, far more harmonious relationship between Judaism and Christianity. Although he maintains an insistence that for Jews the Mosaic Law remains binding in its entirety, his vision of a minimalist Christianity based on the rabbinic doctrine of the seven ethical commandments revealed to Noah after the flood is very close to a form of 'rational religion'. Writing at a time of intense millenarian expectancy amongst radical Protestants, and only a few years before Jewish Amsterdam was profoundly shaken by Shabbatean messianism, Morteira's final treatise reflects this general spirit of transformative anticipation. He subtly inverts the widespread hopes amongst Christians of an imminent conversion of the Jews, envisaging instead dramatic change within Christianity itself. His

---

[21] See H. P. Salomon, 'Saul Levi Mortera en zijn Traktaat Betreffende de Waarheid van der Wet van Mozes' (1988) esp. 1261–4.

[22] Saul Levi Morteira, *Providencia de Dios con Ysrael y Verdad de la Ley de Moseh*, HS Ros. 542, §1.

[23] *Ibid.*, §40.   [24] *Ibid.*, §65–68, 71.

[25] Morteira's positive assessment of the Reformation is discussed in his sermons at least twice: see Marc Saperstein, 'History as Homiletics: The Use of Historical Memory in the Sermons of Saul Levi Morteira', in Elisheva Carlebach, John M. Efron and David N. Meyers, eds., *Jewish History and Jewish Memory* (1998) 123, 126.

text thus bears witness both to the sophisticated level of theological communication between Jews and Christians in the mid seventeenth century, and to the radicalising consequences of this dialogue, even for a community stalwart such as Morteira.

The most prominent Jewish protagonist in cross-communal dialogue in this period was Menasseh ben Israel, whose intensive interaction with radical Protestants has been described by Richard Popkin as constituting an attempt 'to formulate a Judaeo-Christianity'.[26] Against a background of considerable chiliastic expectancy amongst both Jews and Protestants in the mid seventeenth century, many Christians believed that Christianity and Judaism were destined to grow ever closer, and ultimately to fuse together.[27] In the minds of Christian millenarians, Jewish messianic hopes were readily elided with their own expectations: Jews and Christians, it was widely believed, were united in their eager anticipation of the same imminent event. This was clearly the opinion of the prominent Amsterdam theologian Petrus Serrarius, who maintained a close relationship with Menasseh ben Israel.[28] The great respect in which Menasseh was held by a number of prominent figures in England was also of crucial importance in securing the *de facto* re-admission of the Jews there in the mid 1650s.[29]

In his most important work, *Mekveh Israel* ('The Hope of Israel') (1650), Menasseh carefully considered the issue of messianism, and discussed in detail the recent claim of the Marrano explorer Antonio de Montezinos to have encountered a Hebrew-speaking Jewish tribe in the Andes Mountains. Menasseh accepted Montezinos' claim to have discovered a trace of the Ten Lost Tribes of Israel, but emphasised that the Bible described the scattering of the Ten Tribes at various times to various places, so the Indians could represent only a small fraction of the tribes' descendants, the remainder of whom remained dispersed across the globe.[30] His response to this report was thus more cautious than that of Christians such as Thomas Thorowgood, who welcomed it with considerable excitement.

Menasseh's use of messianic arguments may to some degree have been strategically designed to encourage philosemitic sentiment in England.[31]

---

[26] R. H. Popkin, 'Some Aspects of Jewish-Christian Theological Interchanges in Holland and England, 1640–1700', in J. van den Berg and Ernestine G. E. van der Wall, eds., *Jewish–Christian Relations in the Seventeenth Century* (1988) 24.

[27] Hans-Joachim Schoeps, *Barocke Juden, Christen, Judenchristen* (1965) 10.

[28] Ernestine G. E. van der Wall, 'Petrus Serrarius and Menasseh ben Israel', in Yosef Kaplan, Henry Méchoulan and Richard H. Popkin, eds., *Menasseh ben Israel and his World* (1989) 176–9.

[29] David Katz, 'Menasseh ben Israel's Christian Connection', in *ibid.*, 117–38; *Philo-Semitism and the Readmission of the Jews to England, 1603–1655*.

[30] Menasseh ben Israel, *Mekveh Israel: esto es, Esperança de Israel*, esp. 140.

[31] Harold Fisch, 'The Messianic Politics of Menasseh ben Israel', in Kaplan, Méchoulan and Popkin, eds., *Menasseh*, 237–9.

Certainly, in balancing the excitement and great potential benefits of Judaeo-Christian *rapprochement* against the danger of Christian appropriation of Jewish messianic aspirations, he was caught in a theologically delicate position. While in England Menasseh was repeatedly urged to convert to Christianity,[32] and the cautious tone of *Mekveh Israel* suggests an distinct ambivalence towards millenarian syncretism. For Menasseh, as for Morteira, the possibility of the emergence of a universalistic religion based on the Jewish Bible was a very enticing prospect, but he was also committed to sustaining the distinctiveness of Judaism: a difference that Christian millenarians expressly wished to dissolve. Menasseh thus confronted in a particularly direct way the difficult relationship of abstract universalism to cultural particularism. This problem was to develop into one of the central philosophical dilemmas of the Enlightenment.

The considerable extent to which the Shabbatean messianic movement took grip in Amsterdam highlighted the theological confusion and instability of the community in the 1660s. One of the most prominent Amsterdam Shabbateans, the wealthy patrician Abraham Pereyra, at the dawn of the episode published an impassioned and profoundly penitential apologia, *La Certeza del Camino* (1666), before leaving the city with the intention of reaching the Holy Land.[33] The imagery of this text is extremely redolent of Iberian Catholicism. Pereyra evokes at length the infernal punishments that await those who do not reconcile their souls with God, and is particularly anxious about the souls of those 'idolatrous' Jews still living as Catholics. He repeatedly evokes images of cleanliness and purity, describing religious observance as cleansing the soul 'of all sin and dirt'.[34] The language with which he emphasises the indispensability of atonement at Yom Kippur – 'penitence is the only remedy that can restore the sinner to divine grace'[35] – is heavily laden with Catholic notions of confession and salvation.

A preoccupation with sin and absolution was characteristic of the Sephardi diaspora, and was the subject of numerous rabbinical texts, such as Menasseh ben Israel's *De la fragilidad humana y inclinacíon del hombre al pecado* (1642). Menasseh here expounds Jewish doctrines using terminology clearly influenced by Catholicism. Human sin, he argues, is inevitable, and it is therefore essential to acquire divine grace through the observance of *mitzvot*, the role of which he presents as broadly analogous to the Catholic sacraments.[36] Isaac Cardoso's *Las Excelencias de los Hebreos* (1679), published

---

[32] Richard H. Popkin, 'The Rise and Fall of the Jewish Indian Theory', in *ibid*., 69.

[33] Israel, *European Jewry*, 212.

[34] Abraham Pereyra, *La Certeza del Camino* (1987 (1666)) 203–5, 287–9.   [35] *Ibid*., 301.

[36] See Henry Méchoulan, 'Menasseh ben Israel and the World of the Non-Jew', in Kaplan, Méchoulan and Popkin, eds., *Menasseh*, 94–6.

in Amsterdam although the author was resident in Verona, also exhibits a strong Iberian influence not only in its tone of fierce ethnic pride but also in its use at various points of distinctively Catholic theological language.[37]

The enduring Catholic overtones in the writing of a settler in Italy such as Cardoso are perhaps to be expected; but these influences were equally resilient in Amsterdam. This residual underlay not only influenced the flavour of Dutch Sephardi Judaism, but was also the primary filter through which the migrants responded to Protestantism. The triangular theological exposure of this community produced a particular intellectual fecundity and instability. Over the course of the seventeenth century, the Amsterdam Sephardim did not straightforwardly revert to normative Judaism. They remained culturally exceptional, straddling Iberian and Judaic sensibilities while increasingly imbibing new influences from their Dutch milieu. These cross-fertilisations touched the entire community and influenced the outlook of its leadership. The most striking product of this triple cultural overlap, however, emerged in the minds of those isolated radicals who most insistently explored the intersection between these worlds.

URIEL DA COSTA: MATERIALISM, ALLEGORY AND HERESY

Despite the vigorous efforts of community leaders to impose theological conformity through both persuasive and coercive methods, including frequent recourse to the *herem* (community ban),[38] a significant current of dissent survived. A sequence of bold individuals, stimulated by the range of theological and philosophical ideas to which they could gain access in Amsterdam, challenged the communal orthodoxy. The earliest notable heretic was Uriel da Costa, born in Oporto in about 1584, and in his youth a devout Catholic. Through private study Da Costa became increasingly interested in Judaism, and emigrated to Amsterdam in order to escape the attentions of the Inquisition. However, the personal understanding of Judaism that he had developed in Portugal was markedly different from the rabbinically disciplined Jewish life he discovered there. The publication of his *Exame das Tradições Phariseas* ('Examination of Pharisaic Traditions') (1623), a trenchant attack on rabbinical authority, led to his expulsion from

---

[37] Isaac Cardoso, *Las Excelencias de los Hebreos* (1679) esp. 1–22, 35–51. See also Yosef Hayim Yerushalmi, *From Spanish Court to Italian Ghetto – Isaac Cardoso* (1981) 350–412, esp. 379–80.

[38] Yosef Kaplan, 'The Social Functions of the *Herem* in the Portuguese Jewish Community of Amsterdam in the Seventeenth Century', in J. Michman, ed., *Dutch Jewish History*, I (1984) 111–56; 'Deviance and Community in the Eighteenth Century', in J. Michman, ed., *Dutch Jewish History*, V (1993) 103–5.

the synagogue under a *herem*. Da Costa took temporary refuge in Hamburg and his text was burned, and was believed to be lost until in 1990 a single surviving copy was located in the Royal Library in Copenhagen.[39]

Da Costa's attack in his *Exame* is closely aimed at rabbinic authority. He repudiates the rabbinically mediated oral law, arguing that the notion that Scripture needs to be supplemented by an oral tradition scandalously implies that the written law alone is imperfect.[40] He attacks at length the practice of the wearing of *tefillin* (phylacteries) while praying, on the grounds that they are not mentioned in Scripture. The biblical verses traditionally given as the basis for this law should, he argues, be interpreted figuratively rather than literally. 'To be in harmony with the spirit of the lawgiver,' he writes, 'it is necessary to understand allegorically.'[41] He goes on to attack other shibboleths of the oral law, such as the dietary separation of meat and milk.[42] Throughout the text, he characterises the rabbis as legalistic, unspiritual Pharisees: a stock image of Christian anti-Jewish rhetoric, undoubtedly absorbed by Da Costa during his earlier life as a practising Catholic. His stress on the self-sufficient perfection of the biblical text, on the other hand, suggests the influence of Protestantism. Although there is no direct evidence of Da Costa's contacts with Protestants, it seems unlikely that once in Amsterdam a man of his religious inquisitiveness would not rapidly and easily have informed himself about Protestant theology. Already at this early stage in the history of Sephardi radicalism, the interpenetration of Jewish, Catholic and Protestant modes of thought was of crucial importance.[43]

Da Costa was most vociferously condemned not for his attack on rabbinic and Talmudic authority, but for his denial of the immortality of the soul. This doctrine, he argued, implied divine cruelty: only a sadistic God would inflict the souls of sinners to torment in purgatory. He accused the rabbis of using this doctrine as a metaphysical disciplining device, designed to deflect attention from this world to the world to come. The soul was in truth physically present in the blood, and died together with the body.[44] This theory was immediately and vehemently rebutted by Samuel da Silva, a doctor and member of the Hamburg community. In his *Tratado*

[39] See H. P. Salomon, 'A Copy of Uriel da Costa's *Exame das Tradições Phariseas* Located in the Royal Library of Copenhagen', *Studia Rosenthaliana* 24 (1990) 153–68.
[40] Uriel da Costa, *Examination of Pharisaic Traditions*, trans. and ed. H. P. Salomon and I. S. D. Sassoon (1993 (1623)) 271–2.
[41] *Ibid.*, 290–3.   [42] *Ibid.*, 298–9.
[43] On Da Costa's crypto-Jewish background, see I. S. Révah, 'La religion d'Uriel da Costa, marrane de Porto', *Revue de l'histoire des religions* 161 (1962), 45–76.
[44] Da Costa, *Examination*, 416–9.

da Immortalidade da Alma (1623), Da Silva throughout refers to Da Costa indirectly as 'our ignorant adversary', and argues sustainedly against his 'mad opinion that the human soul dies together with the body'.[45] He engages in detail with Da Costa's arguments, arguing that hope in an afterlife is not a mere distraction, but brings with it positive benefits in this life.[46] Da Silva quotes Da Costa extensively, thus unintentionally ensuring that even after the mass destruction of Da Costa's own text knowledge of his ideas and arguments survived in some detail.

The sources for Da Costa's theory of the soul are uncertain: Servetus, Averroës and Pomponazzi have all been put forward as possible influences.[47] Da Costa's knowledge of Judaism was somewhat confused, and his use of notions such as purgatory reveal an idiosyncratic fusion of Jewish and Catholic theology.[48] Although it is impossible to identify his formative influences with any confidence, it is clear that his heresy was a product of the clashing and mixing of the wide range of ideas to which interested ex-Marranos in Amsterdam were newly able to gain access. Alongside anxieties concerning the nature of religious authority, salvation and textual interpretation, the question of the nature of the soul became a recurrent and troublesome focus of debate within the Amsterdam community. No fewer than five treatises asserting the immortality of the soul were written by members of the Amsterdam rabbinate between 1624 and 1640,[49] as well as important later texts dealing with the theme, such as Menasseh ben Israel's *Nishmat Hayyim* (1652) and Raphael Moses Aguilar's brief *Tratado da Immortalidade da Alma*.[50] The numerousness of these polemics suggest that rabbis believed that this heresy continued to circulate within the community, and required sustained refutation.

Despite the suppression of his text, there was a significant level of awareness of Uriel da Costa's ideas in mid seventeenth-century Amsterdam. It can safely be assumed that the young Spinoza, who was eight years old at the time of Da Costa's suicide in 1640, would have acquired detailed knowledge of his opinions. However, Spinoza was not the only dissident in Sephardi Amsterdam in the mid 1650s. His older associate, Juan de Prado,

---

[45] Samuel da Silva, 'Treatise on the Immortality of the Soul', trans. H. P. Salomon and I. S. D. Sassoon (1993 (1624)) 427–551.

[46] *Ibid.*, §27.

[47] See Leo Strauss, *Spinoza's Critique of Religion* (1965 (1930)) 57–8; H. P. Salomon and I. S. D. Sassoon, 'Introduction' to Costa, *Examination*, 38ff.

[48] José Faur, *In the Shadow of History: Jews and Conversos at the Dawn of Modernity* (1992) 110–41.

[49] Salomon and Sassoon, 'Introduction', 48–50. See also Marc Saperstein, 'Saul Levi Morteira's Treatise on the Immortality of the Soul', *Studia Rosenthaliana* 25 (1991) 131–48.

[50] Faur, *Shadow*, 135; Joseph Dan, 'Menasseh ben Israel's *Nishmat Hayyim* and the Concept of Evil in Seventeenth-Century Jewish Thought', in Twersky and Septimus, eds., *Jewish Thought*, 63–75.

who arrived in Amsterdam from Spain (after a brief sojourn in Hamburg) in 1655, had a communal *herem* pronounced upon him in February 1657, seven months after Spinoza had been similarly punished.[51] None of Prado's own writings remain extant, but it is possible to reconstruct his arguments from the three counterblasts written against them by the prominent community member Isaac Orobio de Castro (*c*.1617–87). The first and most extensive of Orobio's tracts, of which many copies survive in manuscript,[52] reveals in its title the essence of Prado's natural law theology: *Epistola Invectiva contra Prado un Philosopho Médico que dudava o no creia la verdad de la divina Escritura, y pretendió encubrir su malicia con la afectada confessión de Dios y la Ley de Naturaleza*.[53] This text was written in 1663, when rumours reached Amsterdam from the Antwerp crypto-Jewish community, where Prado was then living in exile, that the heretic was prepared to recant his views.

Orobio presents a detailed defence of rabbinic and Talmudic authority and of the validity of the *Halakhah*, which we can therefore presume were for Prado central issues of contention. Most interestingly, though, Orobio also discusses abstract philosophical issues. The third chapter of his text makes the titular claim to 'prove that the Law of Moses and the sacred Scriptures conform to natural reason, and are therefore worthy of full respect'.[54] By explicitly basing his argument at this point on philosophical reason, rather than on scriptural authority, Orobio is presumably seeking to rebut an attempt by Prado to differentiate between reason and religion – which was precisely the claim made by Spinoza in the preface to his *Tractatus Theologico-Politicus*.[55] It seems likely that Spinoza and Prado were in close contact between 1655 and 1659, when it appears that Prado finally left Amsterdam.[56] From the fact that regular donations from Spinoza are listed in the community records up to December 1655, we can surmise that Spinoza was an unalienated participant in community life up to this date, which closely coincides with the arrival of Prado in Amsterdam.[57] Evidence of their association appears in a 1659 deposition to the Spanish Inquisition in Madrid by an Augustinian friar, Fray Tomás Solano y Robles, who mentions that he encountered them both while recently in Amsterdam, and describes them as close associates.[58]

[51] See Yosef Kaplan, *From Christianity to Judaism: The Story of Isaac Orobio de Castro* (1989) 122–78; I. S. Révah, *Spinoza et le Dr Juan de Prado* (1959) 13–20.

[52] See Kaplan, *Orobio*, 147, 431–3.

[53] BL MS Harley 3430, 165ff. See also a printed version in Révah, *Spinoza*, 86–129.

[54] Orobio, *Epistola*, in Révah, *Spinoza*, 95–8.

[55] *TTP*, 9.   [56] Kaplan, *Orobio*, 146.   [57] *Ibid*., 131–5; Révah, *Spinoza*, 27.

[58] Kaplan, *Orobio*, 133–4, Révah, *Spinoza*, 31–3, 61–5.

Spinoza's ideas can therefore be seen as the culmination of a long-standing tradition of radical thought within the Amsterdam Sephardi community. With the almost immediate notoriety gained by Spinoza after the publication of the *Tractatus Theologico-Politicus* in 1670, the distinctively Jewish dimension to his thought was studiedly neglected by most parties. Spinoza himself had no wish to emphasise the formative influence on him of his Jewish and Marrano heritage. Within the Jewish community, where even any mention of Spinoza was technically banned, there was an even stronger desire to disassociate Judaism from his scandalous philosophy. Among non-Jews, as we shall soon see, responses to Spinoza's Jewishness were intricate and highly significant. However, he was universally regarded as a very special case: Jewish intellectual culture in general over the course of the late seventeenth century was increasingly seen as intrinsically inimical to philosophical thinking. Texts by Montalto, Morteira and Orobio de Castro were read with great interest by early eighteenth-century radicals, and Jewish themes continued to be intensively debated, but after the debate between Philip van Limborch and Orobio in 1684 respectful, serious discussion between living Jews and Christians effectively ceased. While remaining fascinated by Judaism, the Enlightenment for the most part suppressed any consciousness of its possible indebtedness to currents of thought from within the Jewish world. This erasure has scarcely been challenged even in the twentieth century. The internal dynamics of Jewish life in Amsterdam also changed in the late seventeenth century. The ignominious denouement of the Shabbatean upheaval in Shabbatai's conversion to Islam in 1666 provoked ridicule and scorn from outside and great trauma within the community. This episode vastly shook Jewish confidence, and opened a new sore of internal division: the Shabbatean movement maintained a small but significant following in much of the Jewish world, including amongst its adherents at least one leading Sephardi rabbi in early eighteenth-century Amsterdam.[59] The rising infamy of Spinoza across Europe must also have contributed to a sense of anxiety within the community. Articulate challenges to rabbinic authority did not cease after the 1650s: in 1712 three self-proclaimed 'Karaites' were expelled from the Sephardi community.[60] Moreover, the strengthening Enlightenment gravely sapped Jewish intellectual and cultural self-confidence. After the 1680s, the Jewish contribution to the Early Enlightenment was essentially limited to disembodied texts. However, through

---

[59] Lajb Fuks, 'Sebastianisme in Amsterdam in het begin van de 18e eeuw', *Studia Rosenthaliana* 14 (1980) 20–8.

[60] See Yosef Kaplan, '"Karaites" in Early Eighteenth-Century Amsterdam', in David S. Katz and Jonathan I. Israel, eds., *Sceptics, Millenarians and Jews* (1990) 196–236.

these texts, and above all through the key prism of Spinoza, the distinctively intense tensions of early Sephardi Amsterdam had a powerful and destabilising impact on the intellectual life of Europe as a whole. This early crucible of theological dissent not only in some senses anticipated but also contributed to the ideas and arguments of the wider European Enlightenment, as it gathered force in the closing decades of the seventeenth century.

CHAPTER 6

Judaism in Spinoza and his circle

After his expulsion from the Portuguese Jewish community in July 1656, when he was still only twenty-four years old, Spinoza, unlike Da Costa, Prado and almost all others subjected to a communal *herem*, made no effort to have this order revoked. For the next two decades, until his death in 1677, he lived a uniquely and unprecedentedly secular existence, without affiliation to any religious community. Spinoza's social distance from organised religion has encouraged numerous critics to interpret his philosophy as similarly remote from all theological concerns. According to Leo Strauss, Spinoza was fundamentally uninterested in Scripture, and only accorded it serious attention in his *Tractatus Theologico-Politicus* (1670) because he needed to overthrow its authority in order to make true philosophy possible.[1] For Strauss, the exoteric meaning of the *Tractatus* deliberately conceals its radically anti-religious esoteric meaning, designed only to be understood by receptive, trustworthy readers: 'In the *Treatise* Spinoza addresses potential philosophers while the vulgar are listening.'[2] While it is to some extent valid to regard the *Tractatus* as a preparatory exercise, clearing the necessary philosophical space for the later and utterly non-scriptural *Ethics* (1677), Strauss' theory of double meaning is in this instance cast into severe doubt not only by the already restricted readership of this Latin text, but also by the length and thoroughness of Spinoza's analysis of the Hebrew Bible.[3] The interpretation of Scripture was a central theme of Spinoza's work, and the basis of his interest in it therefore demands explanation.

SPINOZA'S INTERPRETATION OF JEWISH HISTORY

From the 1650s onwards Spinoza communicated extensively with a wide range of progressive Christians, as his surviving correspondence

[1] Strauss, *Spinoza's Critique*, 258–9.
[2] Leo Strauss, *Persecution and the Art of Writing* (1988 (1952)) 184.
[3] Sylvain Zac, *Spinoza et l'interprétation de l'écriture* (1965) 225–9; Alan Donagan, 'Spinoza's Theology', in Don Garrett, ed., *The Cambridge Companion to Spinoza* (1996) 369–71.

testifies.[4] Undoubtedly, his early contact with radical Mennonites and Collegiants, and the influence of his radical Latin teacher, Franciscus van den Enden, was of great importance in shaping his thought, and drawing his attention to the new philosophy of Descartes.[5] It has been suggested that Spinoza's attitude to Scripture was also crucially influenced by his contacts with radical Christians, and particularly with the nucleus of English conversionist Quakers active within Dutch Jewish communities in the 1650s, spearheaded by the Hebraist Samuel Fisher.[6] The language in which Spinoza expresses his notion of the inner experience of philosophical truth – 'the Word of God that speaks in our hearts'[7] – bears an unmistakable affinity with the Quaker emphasis on the divine 'inner light'. However, in contrast with the Quakers, Spinoza's interest in the Bible is primarily historical. It is possible that Isaac La Peyrère may have been an important influence in setting Spinoza on this path: La Peyrère was in Amsterdam in 1655 looking for a publisher for his *PraeAdamitae*, and Spinoza may well have come into contact with him.[8]

It is, though, unnecessary as well as inconclusive to pursue the search for Spinoza's defining antecedents. As we have seen, his concern to historicise the Bible was shared by many contemporary Christian thinkers, orthodox as well as radical. However, in contrast to works such as Bossuet's *Discours sur l'Histoire Universelle*, which sought comprehensively to integrate biblical and secular history while maintaining the absolute supremacy of the former over the latter, Spinoza treats the Bible as an unexceptional local history of the ancient Jews, to be interpreted on exactly the same basis as any other early chronicle. His cautionary observations regarding the unreliability and bias of human historical accounts are stated as general truths, which he happens to demonstrate using the example of the Bible, although he 'could cite many instances in proof of this from the writings both of natural philosophers and historians'.[9]

Spinoza's insistence on the equivalent status of Jewish and non-Jewish records invites his readers to conclude that his focus in the *Tractatus* on the Old Testament is essentially arbitrary, chosen simply as a convenient and familiar example for the illustration of his general thesis.[10] However, an

---

[4] *The Correspondence of Spinoza*, ed. A. Wolf (1928).

[5] See W. N. A. Klever, 'Spinoza's Life and Works', in Garrett, ed., *Cambridge Companion*, 16–23.

[6] Richard H. Popkin, 'Spinoza and the Conversion of the Jews', in C. De Deugd, ed., *Spinoza's Political and Theological Thought* (1984) 171–83.

[7] *TTP*, 197.   [8] Popkin, 'Spinoza and La Peyrère', 189.

[9] *TTP*, 93. For an assessment of the success of Spinoza's equal treatment of biblical and secular history, see Martin D. Yaffe, '"The Histories and Successes of the Hebrews": The Demise of the Biblical Polity in Spinoza's *Theologico-Political Treatise*', *Jewish Political Studies Review* 7 (1995) 57–75.

[10] This argument is developed in Zac, *Spinoza*, esp. 12.

intricate mixture of distance and identification permeates Spinoza's approach to the Jewish past. Although in formal, philosophical terms the Hebrew Bible stands as representative of the exaggerations and inaccuracies of the reports of all ignorant peoples, the complexity of Spinoza's relationship, as a Jew, to the collective memory of the culture of his birth infuses this text with a particular importance and interest. In developing his desacralised reading of Scripture, he is also articulating his understanding of the community he has left, and his response to the rabbis who expelled him.[11]

Certain characteristically Marrano motifs of Jewish communal identity and survival, such as circumcision and the eternity of Israel, retain a positive significance in Spinoza's secular vision of a universal, practical religion for the non-philosophical masses.[12] It is clear that Spinoza retained a sharp awareness of his Marrano background, and some measure of enduring identification with it. In his letter of 1675 to Albert Burgh, a former radical Protestant ally who had recently converted to Catholicism, he discusses the great constancy and suffering of many Jewish martyrs, and mentions his personal knowledge of 'a certain Judah' who died while singing a hymn to his God from amidst the flames of an *auto-da-fé*.[13] However, the broader point that Spinoza seeks to make in this letter is to counter Burgh's arguments in support of Catholicism, by demonstrating that the same claims – venerability of lineage, continuity of authority and abundance of miracles, as well as the courage of martyrs – can all be made even more powerfully on behalf of Judaism. Burgh's defence of the Roman Church, he writes, 'is the same old song of the Pharisees'.[14] Whatever the emotional power of these arguments, they cannot constitute a valid rational defence of any religion.

Of deeper significance than Spinoza's temperamental attitude towards his origins is the manner in which a distinctively Jewish perspective is woven into his philosophical arguments. Spinoza's secularised reading of the Bible segregates the text's ethical content from its historicity. He regards Scripture as useful because it conveys important ethical teachings in a form appropriate for the education of the masses. However, he distinguishes sharply between 'the Divine law, which ... is universal to all men ... and ... ingrained in the human mind' and the non-spiritual 'ceremonial observances' ordained in the Old Testament.[15] The Mosaic ceremonial laws,

[11] For an analysis of Spinoza's attitudes towards Judaism, see Geneviève Brykman, *La Judéité de Spinoza* (1972) esp. 131–5; Edward Feld, 'Spinoza the Jew', *Modern Judaism* 9 (1989) 101–19.
[12] See Yirmiyahu Yovel, *Spinoza and Other Heretics – volume 2: The Marrano of Reason* (1989), esp. 177, 192–7; *TTP*, 56.
[13] Spinoza to Albert Burgh, December 1675, in Spinoza, *Correspondence*, 353–4.
[14] *Ibid.*, 353.   [15] *TTP*, 69.

which 'in no way contribute to blessedness', were 'particularly adapted to the understanding and character of only the Hebrew nation'.[16] This aspect of the biblical record is thus divested of any universal significance, but preserves its parochial interest as an artefact of early Jewish history. Similarly, Spinoza sees little or no ethical value in most of the historical narrative of the Jewish Bible: 'I cannot believe . . . that we cannot understand Scriptural doctrine till we have given heed to the quarrels of Isaac, the advice of Achitophel to Absalom . . . and other similar chronicles.'[17] As imperfect but nonetheless authentic historical accounts, however, these chronicles retain legitimacy. Spinoza devotes three full chapters of his text to a detailed analysis of the Old Testament, in which he attempts to distinguish between accurate and inaccurate passages, and 'to prevent the clear and uncorrupted passages being accommodated to and corrupted by the faulty ones'.[18] At the end of this lengthy section, he briefly explains that he will not progress to a similar analysis of the New Testament, on the grounds that he has insufficient knowledge of the original Greek.[19] While this scruple might straightforwardly reflect Spinoza's respect for philology, his reticence is nonetheless striking in a work directed exclusively towards a Christian readership. The contrasting closeness of his examination of the Old Testament suggests that, despite his alienation from Judaism, this text retained a strong secular interest for him as a unique record of the early history of his own ethnic people.

In general, Spinoza is respectful towards the Jewish tradition of biblical exegesis. He is particularly admiring of the 'enlightened intelligence' of Abraham Ibn Ezra, to whom he attributes his argument that Moses could not be the author of the Pentateuch.[20] However, he sustains a pointed animosity towards Maimonides, in counterpoint to whom he enunciates his own interpretative theory. Spinoza's key exegetical principle is that 'all knowledge of the Bible is to be sought from the Bible alone',[21] which he contrasts to Maimonides' argument that Scripture should be interpreted in accordance with reason.[22] He argues that this approach leads to the metaphorical interpretation of perfectly clear scriptural passages, and therefore rejects it as 'harmful, useless and absurd'.[23]

[16] *Ibid.*, 70.   [17] *Ibid.*, 79.   [18] *Ibid.*, 154.   [19] *Ibid.*, 156.

[20] *Ibid.*, 121–2. See also Shlomo Pines, 'Spinoza's *Tractatus Theologico-Politicus* and the Jewish Philosophical Tradition', in Twersky and Septimus, eds., *Jewish Thought*, 499–521.

[21] *TTP*, 100.

[22] See Moses Maimonides, *The Guide of the Perplexed* (1963) esp. 510–35. See also Sylvain Zac, 'Spinoza et ses rapports avec Maïmonide et Mosé Mendelssohn', in Renée Bouveresse, ed., *Spinoza, science et religion* (1988) 3–9.

[23] *TTP*, 118.

Spinoza's hostility towards Maimonides is at first sight perplexing. *The Guide of the Perplexed* was the boldest work of rational theology of the golden age of Hispanic Jewry, and one might therefore expect Spinoza to be more admiring of it than perhaps any other rabbinical text. In many respects, such as in their conceptualisation of good and evil, the thought of the two men is extremely similar, and there is in general a strong trace of Maimonidean influence in Spinoza's work.[24] However, Spinoza's objection to Maimonides is primarily not philosophical but political. He regards him as a rabbinical elitist, propounding a doctrine that obfuscates the straight-forward reading of Scripture, so that the masses become dependent on the interpretative authority of the rabbis. Against this, Spinoza insists on a democratic vision of learning and study. Repudiating rabbinical 'twisting... about and reversing or completely changing the literal sense' of biblical passages, he advocates a simple reliance on 'the certainty that the masses acquire by candid reading'.[25]

Emmanuel Levinas has argued that Spinoza's attack on such 'pharisaical' sophistry reveals the incompleteness of his Jewish education, and in par-ticular his lack of familiarity with the open-ended discursive approach of the Talmud. He judges that Spinoza was a serious and able Hebrew scholar who at the time of his expulsion had probably not yet reached the level of Talmudic study.[26] According to Spinoza's most recent biographer, Steven Nadler, it is indeed most likely that he abandoned his formal religious education at an early stage, in 1649 or perhaps earlier, having completed possibly as few as the first four years of elementary study.[27] However, there is evidence to suspect that Spinoza was nonetheless involved in some form of organised Jewish study in the early 1650s, perhaps in Rabbi Saul Levi Morteira's *Keter Torah* yeshiva. It is also notable that his private library at his death contained several works of Judaica, including a Talmudic lexicon.[28]

Whatever Spinoza's degree of knowledge of and respect for Jewish study may have been, however, the specifically political cogency of his arguments within a Jewish context stands unaltered. His impatience with rabbinics

---

[24] Zev Warren Harvey, 'Maimonides and Spinoza on the Knowledge of Good and Evil', in Joseph Dan, ed., *Binah: Studies in Jewish Thought* 11 (1989) 131–46; 'A Portrait of Spinoza as a Maimonidean', *Journal of the History of Philosophy* 19 (1981) 151–72; Leon Roth, *Spinoza, Descartes and Maimonides* (1924) esp. 143–5; Steven M. Nadler, 'Spinoza in the Garden of Good and Evil', in Elmar J. Kremer and Michael J. Latzer, eds., *The Problem of Evil in Early Modern Philosophy* (2001) 66–80.

[25] *TTP*, 117–18.

[26] Emmanuel Levinas, 'Spinoza's Background', *Beyond the Verse: Talmudic Readings and Lectures* (1994) 168–76. See also Richard A. Cohen, 'Levinas on Spinoza's Misunderstanding of Judaism', in Melvyn New, ed., *In Proximity: Emmanuel Levinas and the Eighteenth Century* (2001) 23–51.

[27] Steven Nadler, *Spinoza: A Life* (1999) 81.   [28] *Ibid.*, 89–91, 114.

does not imply a dismissal of higher Jewish learning *per se*, but rather a political rejection of what he regards as the authoritarianism of Jewish socio-religious hierarchies. This insistence, undoubtedly intensified by his personal memories of expulsion by the rabbinate of Sephardi Amsterdam, bears a strong resemblance to the earlier arguments of Uriel da Costa. Although the *Tractatus Theologico-Politicus* was published almost fifteen years after the severance of Spinoza's links with organised Jewry, this text represents his political engagement, as a dissident Jew, with issues of Jewish religious and communal authority.

On one level, then, the *Tractatus* can be read as Spinoza's staking of a secular claim on Jewish memory and tradition. To a considerable extent further developing the medieval human-centred exegesis of Ibn Ezra, the *Tractatus* secularises the long-standing theological principle that Scripture was accommodated to the nature and capabilities of man.[29] However, a problematic note of hostility emerges with this step in the argument. In explaining the history of the ancient Hebrews, Spinoza primitivises and infantilises them. Although the essence of the divine law is directly inscribed by God in the human mind, 'to the early Jews religion was transmitted in the form of written law because at that time they were just like children'.[30] Rather than embodying the pure truths of philosophy, the Bible is 'adapted to the intellectual level...of the unstable and fickle Jewish multitude'.[31] Although Spinoza recognises considerable virtues in the Mosaic Law as a code appropriate to its own particular historical moment, when judged in abstract terms it stands above all as testimony to the intellectual and spiritual limitations of the ancient Hebrews. Spinoza's historicisation of the Jewish Bible was not, ultimately, value-neutral, as is underscored by his more positive opinion of the spiritual content of Christianity: 'if Moses spoke with God face to face...Christ communed with God mind to mind'.[32]

Spinoza's identificatory interest, and even pride, in the venerability of Jewish history and culture is undercut by his negative assessment of Judaism as ethically authoritarian. This ambiguous philosophical positioning of Judaism is of crucial importance both in Spinoza's own thought and in his legacy to the Enlightenment in general. Spinoza's reading of the Old Testament was perhaps the most influential aspect of his writings, and was extended by Early Enlightenment radicals into a powerful, polemical critique of established religion. However, from a non-Jewish perspective attacks on Jewish primitivism raised the awkward question of what alternative sense to make of this minority. For Spinoza, this issue did not arise:

---

[29] Funkenstein, *Theology*, 213–21.   [30] *TTP*, 165.   [31] *Ibid.*, 182.   [32] *Ibid.*, 19.

whatever its mysteries and flaws, Jewish history was legitimated *per se*, as the collective memory of his own people. For non-Jews influenced by him, however, Jewish history, once toppled from its privileged theological position, became a problematic anomaly, demanding but powerfully resisting explanation in secular terms. Spinoza's strategy of biblical criticism thus rapidly mutated in the writings of others into a markedly different and often much more trenchantly anti-Jewish form.

LODOWIJK MEYER: CARTESIANISM AND THE BIBLE

In the years immediately following his expulsion from the Jewish community the young Spinoza rapidly became extremely well informed about developments in Cartesian philosophy and observational science.[33] However, as a Jew he remained somewhat distanced from the theological debates in the Dutch universities, which since the 1640s had been dominated by the bitter factional dispute between Voetians and Cocceians over the interpretation of Scripture. Voetius and his followers insisted on the strictly orthodox, literalist interpretation of the Bible, whereas the more flexible camp led by Cocceius advocated the intensive philological scrutiny of Scripture, and was open to allegorical interpretation. By no means all Cocceians were Cartesians, but there was a measure of alliance between the two movements, which were often conflated together in hostile Voetian polemics.[34] Although some theologians, notably Desgabets in France, made determined and tortuous efforts to reconcile Cartesianism with Catholic theology,[35] in the Protestant world a more guarded approach was taken on this issue. By the late 1650s it had become an almost universal strategy amongst Dutch philosophers sympathetic to Cartesianism to insist on the radical separation of philosophy and theology. Given the subordinate, propaedeutic status of philosophy within Dutch universities, such a concession was necessary in order to preserve the academic position of the subject. Even Heereboordt, a notably outspoken Cartesian at Leiden, while vigorously defending the principle of 'libertas philosophandi', acknowledged that with respect to theology it was necessary to resist 'the itch for new opinions'.[36] A

---

[33] See Klever, 'Spinoza's Life', 21–7.
[34] See Jonathan Israel, *The Dutch Republic*, 660–9; J. A. van Ruler, *The Crisis of Causality: Voetius and Descartes on God, Nature and Change* (1995) esp. 303–19; Maria Emanuela Scribano, *Da Descartes a Spinoza: percorsi della teologia rationale nel seicento* (1988).
[35] See J. R. Armogathe, *Theologia Cartesiana* (1977) esp. 114–16.
[36] See Theo Verbeek, 'Tradition and Novelty: Descartes and Some Cartesians', in Tom Sorell, ed., *The Rise of Modern Philosophy* (1993) 196; Malcolm de Mowbray, '*Libertas Philosophandi*. Wijsbegeerte in Groningen rond 1650', in H. A. Krop, J. A. van Ruler and A. J. Vanderjagt, eds., *Zeer kundige professoren* (1997) 33–46.

similar principle of demarcation was maintained by Robert Chouet, who from 1669 onwards introduced Cartesianism into the curriculum at the Calvinist Academy of Geneva.[37] Across the Protestant world, but particularly in the Dutch Republic, the teaching and application of Cartesianism was embroiled in delicate academic politics. Most philosophers sympathetic to the new philosophy preferred to protect the dramatic ascendancy of their discipline by prudently side-stepping the issue of its relationship to the more venerable truth-claims of theology.

The precarious truce between Dutch theologians and philosophers was dramatically challenged by the publication of Lodowijk Meyer's *Philosophia Sancta Scripturae Interpres* (1666), which explicitly denied any separation between the two disciplines. Abandoning all traditional gestures of caution, Meyer asserted that only a philosophical approach could ensure that the Bible was interpreted in accordance with truth: 'Philosophy is the true, certain and indubitable knowledge of things, derived from principles known through the natural light... [Philosophy] can deduce with certainty the true meaning of the Scriptural texts...'[38] Meyer insisted on the perfect compatibility of philosophy and theology. All interpretation of Scripture, he argued, must be in accordance with reason; and any reading incompatible with its truths should be dismissed as inaccurate.[39] Drawing attention to ambiguities within the biblical text, he explicitly repudiated the exegetical slogan of the Reformed Church that 'Scripture is its own interpreter'.[40] He thus denied the autonomy of Scripture, and, reversing the conventional ordering of the disciplines, implied that theology should be subordinated to philosophy.

Meyer's treatise was vigorously and immediately condemned.[41] The most notable moderate refutation of Meyer was that of Johannes de Raey, a leading Cartesian at Leiden, who in his *Cogitata de Interpretatione* (1666) carefully attempted to clarify the boundaries and rules of philosophical discourse, reasserting the conventional argument that the methods of philosophy were not applicable to theology or medicine. The *Tractatus Theologico-Politicus* may have been intended by Spinoza in part as a response to de Raey's refutation of Meyer.[42] Spinoza and Meyer were close and enduring friends: Meyer was Spinoza's personal doctor, and according to

---

[37] See Michael Heyd, *Between Orthodoxy and Enlightenment* 69–86, 236–44.

[38] Lodowijk Meyer, *La Philosophie interprète de l'écriture sainte*, trans. and ed. Jacqueline Langrée and Pierre-François Moreau (1988 (1666)) 115.

[39] *Ibid.*, 89–93.   [40] *Ibid.*, 164–77.   [41] See Israel, *Dutch Republic*, 919.

[42] T. Verbeek, *De Vrijheid van de Filosofie: Reflecties over een Cartesiaans Thema* (1994) 20–1. See also Verbeek 'Spinoza and Cartesianism', in Coudert, Hutton, Popkin and Weiner, eds., *Judaeo-Christian Intellectual Culture*, 173–84.

Spinoza's early biographer Johannes Colerus was in attendance on him at his deathbed.[43] They were also close philosophical allies. As fellow-members of the radical coterie which emerged in Amsterdam in the early 1660s around the Latin school of the radical ex-Jesuit Franciscus van den Enden, Meyer and Spinoza were closely involved in each other's philosophical development, and regarded themselves as participants in a common philosophical project.[44]

However, notwithstanding the close intellectual kinship between these two men, there remains a subtle but important difference of perspective between them. Whereas Spinoza insists that Scripture should be interpreted purely according to internal textual evidence, Meyer advocates precisely the Maimonidean rationalist strategy that Spinoza so explicitly rejects. It is possible the Meyer may have been familiar with Maimonides' *Guide of the Perplexed*, and with the wider medieval Jewish tradition of critical rationalism.[45] However, the tone of his text suggests that he had at most a very cursory knowledge of these arguments. In contrast with the underlying scepticism of Maimonides' negative theology,[46] Meyer enthusiastically presents reason as offering a totally new and utterly decisive interpretative framework. His hostility towards rabbinic learning, and insensitivity to the diversity and disagreement within it, reflects the prevalent Christian attitude of the period. At an early stage in his volume he contrasts the false notion that a biblical sentence can have a plurality of meanings, which he presents as the opinion of all Jewish Kabbalists and rabbis as well as many Catholics, with the truth, upheld by all sincere Protestants, that the Bible has only one meaning.[47] Whereas for Meyer the debate over the relationship between reason and Scripture is framed essentially by the disputes over Cartesianism in the Dutch Republic, for Spinoza, who locates his argument largely within the Jewish tradition, this controversy has a different and considerably longer pedigree. The differing cultural backgrounds of these two philosophers thus led them to hold very different associations with the notion of 'reason' as an exegetical principle.

Several scholars have noted a disjuncture between the philosophies of Meyer and Spinoza, but have tended to minimise its significance.[48] It is

---

[43] Johannes Colerus, *The Life of Benedict de Spinoza* (1706) 89–96. See also Nadler, *Spinoza*, 349–50.

[44] See K. O. Meinsma, *Spinoza et son cercle* (1983 (1896)) 193ff.

[45] On the availability of Maimonides' *Guide* in Latin in the seventeenth century, see Aryeh Botwinick, *Skepticism, Belief and the Modern: Maimonides to Nietzsche* (1997) 5–6.

[46] See *ibid.*, p. 28–111.   [47] Meyer, *Philosophie*, 83–4.

[48] See Manlio Iofrida, 'Linguaggio e verità in Lodiwijk Meyer', in Cristofolini, ed., *Spinozistic Heresy*, 25–35; Jacqueline Langrée and Pierre-François Moreau, 'Louis Meyer et Spinoza', introduction to Meyer, *Philosophie*, 1–19; Klever, 'Spinoza's Life', 30–1.

clear that their philosophies are closely related, and were regarded as such by their authors. Both men attack the autonomy of theology, by arguing that the interpretation of Scripture should be based on some form of common sense: for Spinoza, straightforward reading, and for Meyer, abstract reason. However, the difference between these two hermeneutic strategies is not merely semantic, and is particularly important in the context of the Jewish tradition. Spinoza, despite his deep ambivalence towards Judaism, retains a vision in which the straightforward interpretation of the Bible enables the Jewish populace to access a direct understanding of its common history, reclaimed from the obfuscation of the rabbis. Meyer, in contrast, sees no redeeming historical value in the non-rational content of the Old Testament. All outer aspects of Jewish memory and practice thus implicitly stand in his account as redundant, misleading and devoid of interest. Spinoza's historical and populist reading of Scripture is thus subtly at odds with Meyer's philosophical interpretation.

Reason, for Meyer, is transcendentally almighty and authoritative. The hopes he invests in its imminent triumph are closely related to the prevalent messianic mood of the period: reason occupies a position in his thought similar to that of an all-conquering messianic redeemer. This strand of millenarian ecumenical rationalism is powerfully expressed in the final paragraph of the *Philosophia S. S. Interpres*:

> Besides, a great hope smiles upon us. In these days in which its greatest founder and propagator, René Descartes, has illuminated the world of letters and has endowed it with his example, Philosophy will see its territory expand in every direction through the efforts of those who choose to walk in the footsteps of this author, and we will see appear before God...writings which will bring authority to the interpretation of the Sacred Text, and which will prepare and smooth the path to reunite and gather, in the gentleness of friendship, Christ's Church which has until now been divided and torn apart by continual schisms. Restrained by such tender and such tight bonds, the Church will grow, flourish and strengthen in a united and unanimous future, and will draw to its bosom those nations which are still strangers to it, and finally will joyously triumph in the heavens.[49]

This closing paragraph highlights the extent to which Meyer's thought was inspired by the messianic optimism of the mid seventeenth century, and by an irenic belief that philosophical reason offered the key to the restoration of Christian unity. His final reference to the bringing of stranger nations to the bosom of the Church clearly alludes in particular to the Jews, whose conversion to Christianity had been widely and eagerly anticipated

---

[49] Meyer, *Philosophie*, 249.

in the 1650s and was still regarded as central to millenarian hopes.[50] Jewish difference, as an emblem of all forms of division and difference, thus stands as a problem, to be transcended by the imminent triumph of secular reason. In implicitly situating Judaism as antithetical not simply to Christianity but to reason itself, Meyer injected a sharp hint of hostility into the relationship between Judaism and the radical Early Enlightenment.

ADRIAAN KOERBAGH'S BIBLICAL POLEMICS

The complicated implications of this opposition are more starkly apparent in the work of Meyer and Spinoza's philosophical ally, Adriaan Koerbagh. The fate of Koerbagh was among the most tragic of any prominent Early Enlightenment thinker: he died in prison in October 1669, shortly after being sentenced by the Amsterdam magistrates to ten years' imprisonment for blasphemy.[51] To Spinoza and others, Koerbagh was an early martyr to the cause of philosophy, and a determination to carry forward the battle may well have influenced Spinoza's own decision to go into print in the following year.[52]

Koerbagh's thought was clearly profoundly influenced by Spinoza. However, a distinct philosophical difference can be discerned between the two men. Whereas Spinoza saw philosophy as a pathway towards higher knowledge, transcending theology altogether, Koerbagh, like Meyer, aspired to a union of the two disciplines in a purified theology of rational religion.[53] Despite their friendship, the distinction between the two thinkers remains significant, and is brought into sharp relief by Koerbagh's ambivalent and highly charged treatment of the Old Testament and of Judaism.

Koerbagh's *Een Bloemhof van allerley lieflijkheyd* ('A Flower Garden of All Sorts of Loveliness') (1668) is organised in the deceptively simple form of an alphabetical dictionary. In an ostensible attempt to assert the honourable Germanic purity of the Dutch language, Koerbagh lists and critically analyses the foreign 'bastaard-woorden' that have infiltrated the tongue. However, a brief perusal of the text is sufficient to reveal that his intentions extend well beyond this. Koerbagh's key arguments are philosophical rather than

[50] See Christopher Hill, 'Till the Conversion of the Jews', *The Collected Essays of Christopher Hill* (1986) II, 269–300.

[51] See Meinsma, *Spinoza*, 357–77; P. H. van Moerkerken, *Adriaan Koerbagh (1633–1699): Een Strijder voor het Vrije Denken* (1948); Israel, *Radical Enlightment*, 190–6.

[52] Israel, *Dutch Republic*, 789, 920.

[53] H. J. Siebrand, *Spinoza and the Netherlanders* (1988) 13–24. See also Meinsma, *Spinoza*, 333; Hubert Vandenbossche, *Adriaan Koerbagh en Spinoza* (1978); Gerrit H. Jongeneelen, 'La philosophie politique d'Adrien Koerbagh', *Cahiers Spinoza* 6 (1991) 247–67.

Figure 5 Adriaan Koerbagh, *Een Ligt schijnende in duystere plaatsen*, 1669, pp. 176 v. – 177 r.
The abrupt transition from printed to manuscript text indicates the point at which
printing was suspended by the Amsterdam authorities.

etymological: he rejects the word 'Heresie' on the grounds that it is a nonsense for anybody to judge another person's faith, and radically redefines
'Idolatrie', using a preferred Dutch term, 'Afgodery', as an individual's in-
sincerity to their own personal relationship with God and truth.[54] Beneath
Koerbagh's rejection of the alleged Hebrew, Greek, Latin and French contamination of the plain simplicity of the Dutch language there lies a scantily
cloaked attack on the alien imposition of hierarchical, dogmatic religion
over the transparent simplicity of demotic natural religion.

In his later text, *Een Ligt shijnende in duystere plaatsen* ('A Light Shining
in Dark Places'), Koerbagh expresses his radicalism more outspokenly and
systematically. This book was on the presses at the time of Koerbagh's arrest
in 1669, due to the scandal provoked by *Een Bloemhof*. Printing of the new
text was immediately suspended, with the result that its circulation was successfully suppressed. Only two copies have survived, both in a hybrid form,
with the first half printed and the remainder in manuscript (see figure 5). *Een
Ligt* is essentially a work of biblical criticism, in which Koerbagh, maintaining his linguistic interest, reveals a particular fascination with the original

[54] A. Koerbagh, *Een Bloemhof van allerley lieflijkheyd* (1668) 337–8, 345–6.

Hebrew of the Old Testament. The true meaning of words, he insists, lies not in their outer meaning, but in their inner significance.[55] He expounds this principle through a close analysis of the key words and phrases of the Hebrew Bible, starting with the Tetragrammaton: 'In the *Hebrew* ... *Jehova* ... is simple, single, eternal, without beginning, omnipresent, independent, unchanging, omniscient, omnipotent and supreme. The Hebrews named it so because it truly is becoming and essence, existence and that which exists ... this essence is also *all in everything*.'[56] Koerbagh thus defines the Divine in highly abstracted, ethereal terms, very similar to the immanent notion of God propounded in Spinoza's *Ethics*.[57] Unlike Spinoza, though, Koerbagh painstakingly grounds his argument in the linguistic fabric of the Hebrew Bible. His linguistic definitions closely echo those put forward in the *Tractatus*, and can safely be assumed to derive from collaboration with Spinoza. However, Koerbagh accords the Hebrew language a reverential respect that is markedly different from Spinoza's matter-of-fact approach. He discusses in detail the words *Elohim*, which he defines as 'powerful essence',[58] and *Ruach*, which he interprets as awareness of the unified divine spirit.[59] He puts forward a detailed exegesis of the Hebrew of the first verse of Genesis, which he interprets in accordance with this Spinozian perspective of divine immanence, rejecting the belief that the biblical text offers an account of creation *ex nihilo*.[60] He bases his denial of the Trinity, and his pantheistic conception of a unified divine spirit, on the authority of the inner meaning of the Hebrew *Shema* prayer, of which he offers his own strikingly abstract translation: 'Hear, Almighty, (ISRAEL), the Essence of our power, of our mighty Essence there is a single Essence.'[61]

Most radically of all, and in contrast with the approving opinion of Jesus expressed by Spinoza in the *Tractatus*, Koerbagh not only rejects the notion of an embodied messianic redeemer but also signals no appreciation of Jesus even simply as a moral teacher. He bases his repudiation of Jesus' status on the textual authority of the Hebrew Bible, and implicitly expresses agreement with the Jews' reasons for rejecting his messianic claims.[62] In general, though, Koerbagh adopts an aggressively hostile attitude towards Judaism. He argues that all peoples should unite in one indivisible rational religion, the essence of which he derives from a purified, rationalist interpretation of the Hebrew Bible.[63] This interpretation is contrasted against what Koerbagh regards as the absurdly irrational and unspiritual Jewish

[55] A. Koerbagh, *Een Ligt schijnende in duystere plaatsen*, ed. H. Vandenbossche (1974 (1669)) 1–2.
[56] *Ibid.*, 2.   [57] See Spinoza, *Ethics*, ed. and trans. G. H. R. Parkinson (1989 (1677)) 3–37.
[58] Koerbagh, *Een Ligt*, 13. Cf. *TTP*, 177.   [59] Koerbagh, *Een Ligt*, 14. Cf. *TTP*, 19–20.
[60] Koerbagh, *Een Ligt*, 6–8.   [61] *Ibid.*, 127.   [62] *Ibid.*, 124.   [63] *Ibid.*, 142ff.

reading of the same text. This opposition first emerges in his consideration of the Mosaic Law, only the inner core of which, he argues, is divine, the narrative of the 'outer lawgiving' having been invented by Moses himself.[64] Koerbagh ridicules the Jews' belief in the biblical account: how, he rhetorically asks them, could God have dictated the law to Moses and written the commandments on to stone with his finger, when God has no fingers with which to write, and no mouth with which to speak?[65]

Koerbagh further develops this adversarial challenge to the Jews, posing the imagined Jewish objection that if Moses thought of the law himself it cannot be said to be divine. In response, Koerbagh argues that Moses' 'wisdom and reason', with which he devised the law, was itself a gift from God, and therefore the law has its original source in God.[66] As the rhetoric of his text intensifies, he powerfully attacks the Jews for their refusal to accept the non-material immanence of God:

So I may... ask if is not absurd [to think of] a God who speaks, eats and drinks, and moves around, because he is the omnipresent, infinite, single and unchanging Essence? We have already said, have we not, that this is an absolute contradiction, O ignorant and superstitious JEWS!... What do you now have to say, O stiff-necked and servile JEWS! Will you respect or despise the truth?[67]

In accordance with Spinoza's arguments in the *Tractatus*, Koerbagh denies that the Jews have any special relationship with God, and argues that Ezra was the true author of the Pentateuch. More polemically, he ascribes the Jews' reverence towards their scriptures to a narcissistic preoccupation with texts by and about themselves, and sees in their devotion to the Old Testament miracles mere evidence of Jewish vanity, gullibility and arrogance.[68]

Koerbagh's attitude to Judaism is deeply ambivalent. Central to his project is a desire to deprivilege the biblical narrative, and the special status of Jewish history and destiny enshrined within it. However, he cannot simply dismiss the Bible, which remains the most intensely resonant and familiar point of historical and ethical reference in European culture. He thus inevitably reinterprets Scripture rather than simply rejects it. His reinterpretation contains within it opposing elements of idealisation and of repudiation, both of which crystallise in his attitude towards the Jews. Positively identifying with what he regards as the true message of the Bible, he locates the essence of the true philosophical religion in a purified Judaism. However, he argues that almost the entirety of Judaeo-Christian history has been a tale of manipulated deviation from this natural faith. Concomitant

[64] *Ibid.*, 308. [65] *Ibid.*, 309. [66] *Ibid.*, 310. [67] *Ibid.*, 319–20. [68] *Ibid.*, 320–1, 443.

with Koerbagh's reclaiming of the distilled meaning of the Hebrew Bible is, therefore, his particular denigratory anger towards those who first distorted and misunderstood this simple truth: the early Jews themselves.

For none of the members of the radical coterie in Holland in the 1660s was the status of Judaism consciously considered to be a question of central importance. Spinoza, Meyer and Koerbagh all strove to establish the basis for a universal philosophy, against which all cultural particularisms would fade into the background. However, because of the centrality of the Bible in the thought of the period, Judaism inescapably assumed a special significance in the thought of all three philosophers. In addressing this theme, Spinoza's own Jewishness was of crucial importance. Reappraising the Old Testament as a secular history, Spinoza regarded this text as an honest if not always accurate record of the past of his own people. For non-Jews such as Koerbagh and Meyer, such a relatively straightforward rereading of the Old Testament was not available, because from their perspective the Jewish historical record, once divested of any special theological significance, had no obvious claim to attention simply in itself. Attempting to claim the Bible for rational philosophy, the philosophical universalism of these radicals clashed with Jewish particularism in this common textual space. In the writings of Meyer and Koerbagh we can discern the early emergence of the problematics generated by simultaneous but conflicting desires to deprivilege the status of the Jews and yet to retain in some form the positive centrality of the biblical text. This repressed contradiction, which is particularly evident in Koerbagh's *Een Ligt*, was to recur in many different guises and configurations over the course of the later development of the philosophies of the Enlightenment.

CHAPTER 7

Spinoza: Messiah of the Enlightenment?

Spinoza's Jewish origins thus subtly but crucially mark his philosophy apart from the arguments of his closest intellectual collaborators. The precise nature and significance of this difference, through, was something of which his friends, and perhaps even Spinoza himself, were at most only dimly conscious. As partners in a philosophical project that was powerfully conceived as universalist, it would have been incongruous for members of Spinoza's circle to draw attention to the particular ethnicity of one of their number. After Spinoza's death, there was a perceptible tendency to de-judaise his thought and memory: a process in which Meyer, as his literary executor, is likely to have played an important role. Nonetheless, the repressed fact of Spinoza's Jewish origins was not forgotten, and was of considerable importance in shaping his rise to iconic status among philosophical radicals in the decades following his death.

Almost alone among philosphers, the traditional account of Spinoza's life is unblemished, humanising and inspiringly positive. This humble lens-grinder, we are told, devoted himself solely to his honest craft and to the disinterested, systematic search for truth, with no concern for money, fame or public approval. When for his independence of mind he was expelled and hounded into exile by the Jewish community into which he was born, he accepted his fate calmly and without bitterness. Impervious to the religious dogmatism and bigotry that surrounded him, he quietly devoted the rest of his life to developing his humane, rational philosophy of tolerance and of freedom through self-mastery. This basic narrative of Spinoza's life, which remains deeply lodged in the popular historical imagination, differs very little in essence from the anecdotes that began to circulate almost immediately after the philosopher's death in 1677. Over the past three centuries, profound continuities have marked the enduring iconic status of Spinoza's life, largely transcending wide differences in the interpretation of his philosophy. Whether he has been regarded as an atheist or a pantheist, a dangerous heretic or an inspired genius, a wayward Jew or a true

133

universalist, Spinoza's life, both during the Early Enlightenment and since, has almost always been presented as a distilled, exemplary narrative of serenely virtuous philosophical detachment.

These admiring assessments of Spinoza's life and character may well largely reflect the truth.[1] A perusal of Spinoza's surviving *Correspondence* unquestionably conveys the impression of a scrupulously polite, modest, even-tempered and honest man.[2] No human life, though, is utterly uncorrupted by the complexities of interpersonal interaction; and recent research has enabled the construction of a less hagiographical account of Spinoza's careful management of his relationships and of his philosophical reputation and impact.[3] However, whatever the relationship between myth and reality, the idealisation of Spinoza's life is remarkable both in its intensity and its ubiquity, particularly during the Early Enlightenment. Over the half-century immediately following his death, Spinoza's image was deeply embedded in the formation of the identity of anti-establishment radical philosophy. His importance in this process was not simply his intellectual contribution, but also his unique status as arguably the first thoroughly secular individual in European history. In choosing to remain without even a nominal religious affiliation from 1656 onwards, Spinoza stood radically outside conventional social categories. Because of this independence, he readily stood as representative of the universalism of philosophy in its purest form. This universalistic philosophical aspiration – and his imputed embodiment of it – was, though, troubled and uncertain. The ambiguities of Spinoza's cultural status, and particularly the ineradicability of his Jewish origins, have ever since the Early Enlightenment remained a key prism through which the philosophical difficulties of negotiating both identity and universalism are brought into focus.

THE MAKING OF A PHILOSOPHER-HERO

The oldest known biography of Spinoza, and the source of many enduring hagiographical anecdotes, was almost certainly written within a year of his death. Its author, Jean Maximilien Lucas, was a French Huguenot resident in the Netherlands, and an admiring member of Spinoza's circle. Lucas' account of his subject's life is devoted and at times hyperbolic in tone, portraying Spinoza as a tireless seeker after truth: 'He was so ardent in

---

[1] Two recent biographies largely corroborate this impression. See Nadler, *Spinoza*; Margaret Gullan-Whur, *Within Reason: A Life of Spinoza* (1998).

[2] A. Wolf, 'Introduction' to Spinoza, *Correspondence*, 23–4.

[3] See Klever, 'Spinoza's Life', esp. 35–46.

the search for Truth that, although his health was very poor and required rest, he nevertheless took so little rest that once he did not go outside his lodgings during three whole months.'[4] Lucas' Spinoza is a paragon of virtue. He is utterly modest: when dying, we are told that he requested that his name not be put on his *Ethics*, 'saying that such affectations were unworthy of a philosopher'.[5] He has no desire for riches, and no fear of poverty: 'His virtue raised him above all these things.'[6] Lucas is careful, though, to humanise his hero. He tells us that Spinoza 'was no enemy of innocent pleasures', recounting how he happily chatted with the common people for relaxation, delighting everybody he encountered with his unpretentious, clear and genial conversation.[7] He describes his excellent manners, and notes that '[h]e had a quality which I esteem all the more because it is rare in a philosopher. He was extremely tidy.'[8]

Lucas emphasises Spinoza's equanimity and lack of rancour, reporting his calm, patient response to the many bitter and defamatory attacks on him personally and against the *Tractatus Theologico-Politicus*.[9] He presents the advocacy of Spinoza's ideas as inseparable from the attempt to emulate his life: the virtue of Spinoza's philosophy merges with the virtue of the philosopher. The elevation of Spinoza to the status of a philosophical saint is most clearly enunciated in the concluding paragraphs of the biography, in Lucas' lamentation of his hero's death:

But since he could not escape the lot of all of us that have life, let us strive to walk in his footsteps, or at least to revere him with admiration and with praise, if we cannot imitate him. This is what I counsel to steadfast souls: to follow his maxims and his lights in such a way as to have them always before their eyes to serve as a rule for their actions.

That which we love and revere in great men lives still and will live through all the ages... BARUCH DE SPINOZA will live in the remembrance of true scholars and in their writings, which are the temple of Immortality.[10]

The only other extant early biography of Spinoza was written by Johannes Colerus, a German minister of the Lutheran Church at The Hague. Colerus first came to The Hague several years after Spinoza's death, and it seems that he was originally prompted to write his text when he discovered the coincidence that his own home had earlier housed the infamous philosopher himself. His *Life of Benedict de Spinosa* first appeared in Dutch in 1705, with French and English translations following in the subsequent year.[11] Unlike

---

[4] Jean Maximilien Lucas, 'The Life of the Late Mr de Spinosa', repr. in A. Wolf, *The Oldest Biography of Spinoza* (1927) 60.

[5] *Ibid.*, 62.   [6] *Ibid.*, 64.   [7] *Ibid.*, 64, 71.   [8] *Ibid.*, 63–4.   [9] *Ibid.*, 71.

[10] *Ibid.*, 75.   [11] Siebrand, *Spinoza*, 120.

Lucas, Colerus was a convinced opponent of Spinoza's views, which he regarded as dangerously atheistic: 'This is the true opinion of Spinoza, whatever he might say. He takes the liberty to use the word God, and to take it in a sense unknown to all Christianity.'[12] However, he deals only cursorily with what he describes as Spinoza's 'impious and absurd Doctrines'. For further information he refers his readers to the many published refutations of his philosophy, explaining that he has touched briefly on some of his key ideas 'only to inspire the Christian Reader with the aversion and horror he ought to have for such pernicious Opinions'.[13] Colerus' interest is drawn to more elusive questions regarding Spinoza's life and identity. Although he describes Spinoza's character in a markedly less star-struck fashion that does Lucas, he nonetheless corroborates the image of a mild, serious-minded, modest man. 'He was sober, and very frugal', he tells us, elaborating that although he had numerous friends, a good sense of humour and enjoyed conversation 'even about trifles', he was nonetheless profoundly serious, spending most of his time 'quietly in his own chamber; troublesome to no Body'.[14]

Two moments in Spinoza's life particularly fascinate Colerus: firstly his excommunication from the Jewish community, of which he gives a detailed account, and secondly his death, an analysis of which occupies more than ten pages in a text of barely 100 pages. This is a subject, Colerus writes, on which there have been 'so many various and false reports' that he had determined finally to establish the truth.[15] Amongst the stories he recounts is the belief that Spinoza refused to allow people to visit him while he was dying; 'that he spoke once and even several times these words "O God have mercy upon me miserable sinner" '; and that on the point of imminent death he poisoned himself with 'some Juice of Mandrake' which he had kept by him for this purpose.[16] After detailed research, including an interview with Spinoza's former landlord and landlady, Colerus scotches all these rumours. He takes particular care in his refutation of the final suggestion, providing us with full details of Spinoza's final apothecary bill: 'I find in it some Tincture of Saffron, some Balsam, some Powder, etc., but there is no Opium nor Mandrake mentioned therein.'[17] Colerus thus establishes that the mask of Spinoza's fearless atheism did not slip at the point of imminent death. Despite maintaining allegiance to the conventional religious belief that final reconciliation with God is amongst the deepest of human imperatives, Colerus nonetheless meticulously marshals evidence to demonstrate that

---

[12] Colerus, *The Life of Benedict de Spinosa*, 63.   [13] *Ibid.*, 71.   [14] *Ibid.*, 36, 41–2.
[15] *Ibid.*, 89.   [16] *Ibid.*, 93–4.   [17] *Ibid.*, 97–8.

the case of Spinoza demonstrates the possibility of a death that is both dignified and godless.

Notwithstanding the theological and philosophical differences between Colerus and Lucas, they are both similarly mesmerised by a mythic quality in their subject. For both biographers, Spinoza is exceptional in his fearless transcendence of all the worldly attachments and comforts that for normal folk are so essential. He has no need for material possessions, strong emotional or community ties, or the reassurances of conventional religious belief. For Colerus, as for Lucas, Spinoza represents the epitome of detachment, which both biographers regard as the mark of the true philosopher. While from a theological perspective this detachment is inextricable from Spinoza's alleged 'atheism' to which Colerus is so implacably opposed, he is nonetheless clearly deeply impressed by the exemplarity of Spinoza's noble equanimity. This ideal, so powerfully crystallised in Spinoza, to a considerable extent transcended the philosophical and theological divisions of the period. From the outset, Spinoza's philosophy inspired intense polemic: in Germany alone, more than thirty writers engaged substantially with his philosophy between 1670 and 1700, only three of whom offered an even partially positive assessment.[18] Nonetheless, even the most trenchant refutations of Spinoza's philosophy typically acknowledged the virtuousness of his character, which was nowhere directly called into question. Acceptance of Spinoza's exceptional virtue sat in odd coexistence with the demonisation of him as the arch-systematiser of atheism.

The possibility of non-theological codes of behaviour and ethics was a recurrent focus of interest among transgressive philosophers in the late seventeenth century. The belief that only religious faith made true virtue possible had first been sustainedly attacked by the sceptic philosopher François de la Mothe le Vayer, in his *De la Vertu des Païens* (1642).[19] Pierre Bayle further developed this theme in his *Pensées Diverses sur la Comète* (1683), in which he argued that atheism did not necessarily lead to the corruption of morals.[20] Bayle puts forward various ancient philosophers as examples of virtuous atheists, but the only modern figure he discusses in any detail is Lucilio Vanini, burned in Toulouse in 1619 for alleged atheism.[21] In his later *Dictionnaire Historique et Critique* (1697), however, Bayle draws heavily on

---

[18] Manfred Walther, '*Machina Civilis* oder *Von Deutscher Freiheit*: Formen, Inhalte und Trägergeschichten der Reaktion auf den Politiktheoretischen Gehalt von Spinoza's *Tractatus Theologico-Politicus* in Deutschland, bis 1700', pp. 184–221 in Paolo Cristofolini, ed., *Spinozistic Heresy* (1995) 184.

[19] See J. S. Spink, *French Free-Thought from Gassendi to Voltaire* (1960) 17–18.

[20] Bayle, *Pensées Diverses sur la Comète* (1939 (1683)) II, 5–8.

[21] *Ibid.*, 107–14. Bayle does, however, briefly discuss Spinoza's death elsewhere in the volume: see 134–5.

Lucas in giving an extensive account of Spinoza's virtuous life, alongside a vigorous refutation of his philosophy. Because of the great success of the *Dictionnaire*, it was largely via this conduit that an image of Spinoza as the quintessential virtuous atheist became strongly fixed in the eighteenth-century European mind. As in so many other articles in the *Dictionnaire*, Bayle highlights with relish what he sees as a paradoxical dissonance between beliefs and actions:

> Those who were acquainted with him [Spinoza], and the peasants of the villages where he had lived in retirement for some time, all agree in saying that he was sociable, affable, honest, obliging, and of a well-ordered morality. This is strange; but, after all, we should not be more surprised by this than to see people who live very bad lives even though they are completely convinced of the Gospel.[22]

For Bayle, Spinoza's exemplary life starkly demonstrated the disjuncture between virtuous living and religious devotion. However, for more outspoken critics of conventional religion it was important not only to expose the ethical inadequacy of piety, but also to develop an alternative, secular notion of virtue. Spinoza's philosophy was a key inspiration for these radicals in their search for a new, more rationalist ethic. A brief anonymous essay titled *L'Idée d'un Philosophe*, preserved within a volume of early eighteenth-century French clandestine manuscripts, presents virtue as the path to true happiness. Expounding an argument clearly based on Spinoza's *Ethics*, the author states that the philosopher must devote himself to the mastery of his passions, through the use of natural reason. The ideal philosopher, the text asserts, must not be excessively bookish, is careful to control his passions and lives to the best of his abilities in according to his natural reason.[23]

A similar argument, emphasising the fact that reason alone is adequate as a guide for virtue, is advocated in another anonymous clandestine text, *De la conduite qu'un honnête homme doit garder pendant sa vie*. In striving for virtue, the text argues, 'we have no need for anything other than reason, and when she speaks we must listen and be silent'.[24] The text offers a list of several exemplary virtuous atheists, including Thomas Hobbes, as well as a number of ancient philosophers. Pride of place, however, is given to Spinoza, whose virtuous and irreproachable life is celebrated in detail.[25] For early eighteenth-century radicals, Spinoza's life was thus sanctified as the epitome of philosophical perfection. His virtue was represented as undiluted by any distracting commitments or interests. His romantic unattachment, although never directly highlighted, reinforced his

---

[22] Bayle, *Dictionnaire*, 295.   [23] *L'Idée d'un Philosophe*, MS Aix 814, 1–5.
[24] *De la conduite qu'un honnête homme doit garder pendant sa vie*, MS Maz. 1194, 113.   [25] *Ibid.*, 127.

intellectual individualism and communal autonomy. As the supreme philosopher, all mundane foibles or peculiarities were expunged from his character. Spinoza's uniquely isolated and autonomous social status made him an ideal exemplar of detachment and neutrality. Whereas all of his disciples remained at least to some extent bounded in their thinking by their specific national, cultural and religious allegiances, Spinoza alone appeared totally free of such attachments. His life could thus readily be universalised as one of total liberation from all social roots and bonds.

The exemplary universalisation of Spinoza's life intersected problematically, however, with the biographical fact of his Jewish origins. Spinoza's ethnicity is invariably obscured in idealised representations of him, but the mechanisms of this occlusion are highly intricate and revealing. Spinoza's biographers appear unequivocally certain that on renouncing Judaism Spinoza no longer remained in any sense a Jew. Bayle presents the stages of Spinoza's life in linear sequence: Spinoza was 'a Jew by birth, and afterwards a deserter from Judaism, and lastly an atheist'.[26] Colerus similarly seems to be in no doubt about the totality of this erasure: Spinoza, he tells us, was 'originally a Jew' but 'after he had forsaken Judaism he changed his Name, and call'd himself Benedict in his Writings, and in the Letters which he subscribed'.[27] However, Spinoza's status as a Jew who had rejected Judaism placed him in a uniquely indeterminate category. The ambiguity of Spinoza's identity was an omnipresent issue, but was always treated with considerable delicacy. In his biography, Lucas makes only one substantive reference to Spinoza's Jewishness. However, this isolated statement makes it clear that he sees this fact as highly significant:

But what I esteem most in him is that, although he was born and bred in the midst of a gross people who are the source of superstition, he had imbibed no bitterness whatever, and that he had purged his soul of those false maxims with which so many are infatuated . . . He was entirely cured of those silly and ridiculous opinions which the Jews have of God.[28]

Spinoza is here implicitly represented as something almost miraculous: a Jew who has utterly transcended the mark of his origin. A powerful echo resonates of the life of an earlier Jew who, it was believed, had rejected the narrow dogmas of his people. This echo is reinforced by Lucas' explicit assimilation of Spinoza into his own brand of enlightened Christianity: 'The Law of Jesus Christ leads us to the love of God and of our neighbour, which is precisely what reason inspires us to do, according to the opinion of Mr de Spinoza.'[29]

[26] Bayle, *Dictionnaire*, 288.   [27] Colerus, *Life*, 1.   [28] Lucas, *Life*, 69.   [29] *Ibid*.

This portrayal of Spinoza as the Jesus Christ of Reason reflects the powerful associations for Lucas and others of Spinoza's exit from Judaism. Millenarian expectancy, so intense amongst radicals in the mid seventeenth century, remained a potent strand in the thinking of many minority Christian groups throughout the Early Enlightenment and beyond.[30] Henry Oldenburg, the secretary of the London Royal Society and an admiring and enthusiastic correspondent of Spinoza, was an avid millenarian, and saw Spinoza's abandonment of Judaism as extremely significant in this schema.[31] As we have seen, a millenarian element can also be discerned in Lodowijk Meyer's work, and it seems likely that similar hopes may have animated other members of Spinoza's circle, for whom his 'conversion' could not have failed to appear meaningful.[32] Evoking submerged but powerful Christian imagery, Lucas uses Spinoza to cast the heralding of the new insights of natural, rational religion as truths laid bare by a prophetic Jew. Once again, a Jewish outcast upholds the deepest spiritual truths of Judaeo-Christianity, in rebellion against the dogmatic and primitive group that first, and most drastically, corrupted this message. The dawn of Enlightenment is thus given a subliminally millenarian tinge, with Spinoza performing the key Messianic role as its necessarily originally, and then no longer, Jewish harbinger.

THE SPECTRE OF JUDAISM AND THE SPIRIT OF SPINOZA

From the late 1670s onwards, Spinoza's iconic status penetrated rapidly into the various subcultures of the radical Enlightenment. From the outset, his works were banned almost everywhere; even in the liberal climate of the United Provinces, pre-existing, anti-Socinian censorship legislation was used to drive underground the circulation and sale of the *Tractatus Theologico-Politicus*. Nowhere could Spinoza's ideas be publicly discussed or referred to approvingly.[33] The numerous published refutations of his ideas – most prominently Bayle's *Dictionnaire* article and Christopher Wittich's *Anti-Spinoza* (1690) – became the main source through which some idea of the substance of Spinoza's thought was made accessible to an educated readership. The transgressive nature of Spinoza's philosophy heightened his interest to groups of freethinkers and religious radicals, particularly in

---

[30] See, e.g., J. van den Berg 'Priestley, the Jews and the Millennium', in Katz and Israel, eds., *Sceptics*, 256–74.

[31] Sarah Hutton, 'Henry Oldenburg and Spinoza', in Cristofolini, ed., *Spinozistic Heresy*, 106–19.

[32] R. H. Popkin, 'The Convertible Jew', in *ibid.*, 119–22.

[33] Jonathan Israel, 'The Banning of Spinoza's Works in the Dutch Republic', in Wiep van Bunge and Wim Klever, eds., *Disguised and Overt Spinozism Around 1700* (1996) 8.

the late seventeenth-century Dutch Republic. These early 'chrétiens sans église', to use Leszek Kolakowski's phrase, were in various ways engaged in redefining the relationship between private faith, reason and the organised church, and were often powerfully drawn both to Spinoza's ideas and to his own 'sans église' status.[34]

Responses to Spinoza were charged with an extra-textual symbolic power. To theological conservatives, the term 'Spinozist' very rapidly came into use as a hostile broad-brush synonym for 'atheist', and was widely used to brand opponents of almost any non-orthodox hue. Even Wittich, who had attempted to refute Spinoza from a Cartesian perspective, on the grounds that he had misapplied the Cartesian method, found himself accused by Voetian anti-Cartesians of Spinozism.[35] To self-conscious radicals, allegiance to Spinoza became in itself a transgressive gesture; and celebration of the exemplarity of his life could stand as a coded implication of sympathy with his ideas. 'Spinozism' in the Early Enlightenment is an elusive and shifting phenomenon, far more often evoked by conservatives than explicitly identified with by radicals. Ideas branded as 'Spinozist' were varied in nature, and often diverged considerably from Spinoza's own philosophy. Nonetheless, by the 1690s materialist ideas to some extent influenced by Spinoza, and strongly associated with him, were being propagated and popularised in the Dutch Republic with increasing boldness. Two decades later, Spinoza's reputation as the most seductively dangerous modern philosopher was firmly established across continental western Europe.[36]

The text that most powerfully linked Spinoza's name to the materialist philosophical underground of the Early Enlightenment was the most infamous treatise of the early modern age: the anonymous *Traité des Trois Imposteurs*. The origins of this polemic are still extremely uncertain and mysterious. Its central theme has extremely long antecedents: Moses, Jesus and Mohammed, the three great religious leaders, are presented as cynical impostors, inventing the details of their respective creeds in order to gain political mastery over the gullible masses. This thesis was traditionally associated with Machiavelli, but can be traced back much further. The notion that Jesus was an impostor appears in early Jewish satires such as the *Toledot Yeshu*, the existence of which was known to Christians by the ninth century.[37] Claims of the existence of a prototype *Three Impostors* text

---

[34] See Leszek Kolakowski, *Chrétiens sans église* (1969) 206–17.   [35] Siebrand, *Spinoza*, 100–7.

[36] See Wiep van Bunge and Wim Klever, 'Introduction' to *Disguised and Overt Spinozism Around 1700* (1996) esp. vii–viii.

[37] B. E. Schwarzbach and W. Fairbairn, 'History and Structure of our *Traité des Trois Imposteurs*', in Silvia Berti, Françoise Charles-Daubert and Richard H. Popkin, eds., *Heterodoxy, Spinozism and Free*

extend back to the thirteenth century: a common putatative author was the Emperor Frederick II, who was excommunicated by Pope Gregory IX in 1239 allegedly for this heresy.[38] The same blasphemy was also widely attributed to Avveroës, who was an even earlier candidate for the original authorship of the text. Although there were many reported sightings of the manuscript during the early modern period, we have no safe evidence of the existence of any such text until around the end of the seventeenth century, when various slightly differing versions began to circulate clandestinely, often under an intriguing alternative title: *L'Esprit de Spinosa*.

In the form that it then surfaced, the text largely consisted of a composite of various unattributed extracts, sometimes tendentiously translated, from Vanini, La Mothe le Vayer, Naudé, Charron, Hobbes and Spinoza, including a large extract from the *Ethics*. It is still unclear when, where and by whom this manuscript was assembled, but it seems probable that it was compiled around 1700 by Jan Vroesen, a judicial official of Brabant resident in The Hague.[39] It is also unclear how or exactly when the 'Spirit of Spinoza' title first came into use, but as almost all copies of the *Esprit* are preceded by a version of Lucas' life of Spinoza, it seems that the decision to link these two texts together was the stimulus for the renaming of the main treatise. By 1716, much the same text was circulating both as *Le Fameux Livre des Trois Imposteurs* and as the latter part of *La Vie et l'Esprit de M Benoît de Spinoza*.[40] In 1719 the *Vie et l'Esprit* was published for the first time, by Charles Levier, a Huguenot bookseller in The Hague. This was the first time that a major clandestine manuscript had been printed, and was therefore a notable publishing event.[41]

The relationship between Spinoza's own philosophy and the overall argument of the *Esprit de Spinosa* is somewhat tenuous. This text does not expound a faithful account of Spinoza's ideas, but instead selectively

Thought in Early-Eighteenth-Century Europe (1996) 81–90; Samuel Krauss and William Horbury, *The Jewish–Christian Controversy: Volume 1 – History* (1995) 12–13.

[38] See H. S. Nisbet, '*De Tribus Impostoribus* : On the Genesis of Lessing's *Nathan the Wise*', *Euphorion* 73 (1979) 368.

[39] Silvia Berti, 'l'Esprit de Spinosa: ses origines et sa première édition dans leur contexte Spinozien', in Berti *et al.*, *Heterodoxy*, 3–50; '*La Vie et l'Esprit de Spinosa* e la prima traduzione francese dell'*Ethica*', *Rivista storica italiana* 98 (1986) 5–46; 'Jan Vroesen, Autore del *Traité des Trois Imposteurs*?', *Rivista storica italiana* 103 (1991) 528–43. On the convoluted evolution and particular process of authorship of this treatise, see Miguel Benítez, 'Une histoire interminable: origines et développement du Traité des Trois Imposteurs', in Berti *et al.*, *Heterodoxy*, 53.

[40] See Françoise Charles-Daubert, 'Les Traités des Trois Imposteurs et *l'Esprit de Spinosa*', *Nouvelles de la république des lettres* 1 (1988) 21–50; '*L'Esprit de Spinosa* et les *Traités des Trois Imposteurs*: rappel des différentes familles et de leurs principales caractéristiques', in Berti *et al.*, *Heterodoxy*, 131–89.

[41] See John Christian Laursen, 'The Politics of a Publishing Event: The Marchand Millieu and *The Life and Spirit of Spinoza* of 1719', in Berti *et al.*, *Heterodoxy*, 273–96.

assimilates them into an older tradition of 'libertinage érudit'.[42] Not only is the tone of the text generally much more polemical and impassioned than Spinoza's own writings – the Bible is swiftly dismissed as a product of 'rabbinical fantasy'[43] – but its philosophical preoccupations diverge from his own. This is particularly pronounced in the exposition of a totally materialist philosophy with which the *Esprit* culminates. The materiality of the soul, described as 'an extremely nimble substance, in continual movement',[44] is discussed in great detail, whereas no such argument is even touched on by Spinoza.

Why, then, was this only very loosely Spinozist text given its secondary title? And what was the perceived relationship between Spinoza's hagiographical *Life* and his impassioned, impatient *Spirit*? The mild, temperate tone of Lucas' *Life* contrasts markedly with the philosophical and political vigour of the *Spirit*, and this poses a paradoxical disjuncture between the two texts: the fiery *Spirit* does not at all seem to be in the spirit of Spinoza as he is portrayed in the *Life*. It is on a different, less literal level that the *Esprit de Spinosa* is worthy of its name. The two texts share a common theme of outsiderness, and of the rejection at the most fundamental level of religious tradition. Because Spinoza's adult life was lived outside the structures of organised religion, his 'spirit' could be claimed as that of the repudiation of all religious authority, which is the central message of the 'Three Impostors' thesis. The iconic sanctification of Spinoza's life is thus extended through this selective rewriting to apply also to his philosophy. His own metaphysics is displaced by a new representation of his ideas as imbued with a generalised spirit of anti-religious subversion. In these combined texts, the libertarian ideals of the radical Enlightenment find their fullest expression. Together, the *Life* and the *Spirit* present Spinoza as the perfect embodiment of escape from all dogma and constraining traditions, through the attainment of absolute philosophical wisdom and freedom.

The idealisation of Spinoza was complicated, however, by the fact of the philosopher's Jewish roots. Not only did this ethnic particularity jar with the universalisation of his image, but Judaism itself was widely regarded as the epitome of unenlightened superstition and legalism: the very opposite of the values associated with Spinoza himself. Claiming Spinoza fully for radical philosophy thus required the erasure of all traces of Jewishness from

---

[42] Françoise Charles-Daubert, 'L'Image de Spinoza dans la littérature clandestine et l'*Esprit de Spinoza*', in Olivier Bloch, ed., *Spinoza au xviiie siècle* (1990) 64–5. See also Silvia Berti, ed., *Traité des Trois Imposteurs* (1994 (1719)) 92 (editorial note); Richard H. Popkin, 'Spinoza and the Three Impostors', in Edwin Curley and P.-F. Moreau, eds., *Spinoza: Issues and Directions* (1990) 347–58.
[43] *Trois Imposteurs*, 96.   [44] *Ibid.*, 228.

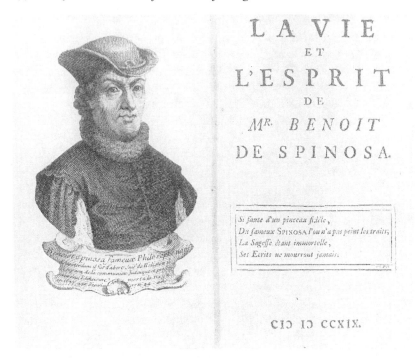

Figure 6 *La Vie et l'Esprit de Mr Benoit de Spinosa*, The Hague, 1719, frontispiece
and title page.

his identity. In Levier's 1719 publication, this editorial operation can be
clearly traced. Levier interpolated into Lucas' *Life* a physical description
of Spinoza based on the information given by Colerus in his biography.
Colerus, however, explicitly describes Spinoza as characteristically Jewish:
'He was of a middle size, he had good features in his face, his skin somewhat black, black curl'd Hair, long Eyebrows, and of the same Colour, so
that one might easily know him by his Looks that he was descended from
Portuguese Jews.'[45] In Levier's version, Colerus' words are subtly amended:
'He was of average size, with well-proportioned facial features, dark skin,
black, curly hair, eyebrows of the same colour, small, dark and lively eyes,
a fairly attractive physiognomy, and a Portuguese air.'[46] This description,
and the vagueness of its concluding 'Portuguese' reference, cleanses Spinoza
of any explicit trace of his Jewish ethnicity.[47]

　　This conscious erasure is more explicit in the choice of image and words
on the frontispiece of Levier's edition (see figure 6). Opposite the title page,

[45] Colerus, *Life*, 39.　[45] *Trois Imposteurs*, 56.
[47] Silvia Berti, 'Introduzione' to *Trattato dei Tre Impostori*, xxxvii–xxxix.

a portrait of Spinoza appears that is immediately striking in its total lack of resemblance to any other surviving portrait of the philosopher. A print of an engraving by Étienne-Jahandier Desrochers, later appointed 'graveur du roi' at the French court, it has been identified as a representation not of Spinoza at all, but of René 'the Good', Duke of Anjou and King of Naples in the fifteenth century.[48] Significantly, the rhyme appearing on the title-page opposite the image amounts to an admission that the portrait is not a genuine one:

> Si faute d'un pinceau fidéle
> Du fameux SPINOSA l'on n'a pas peint les traits;
> La Sagesse étant immortelle,
> Ses Ecrits ne mourront jamais.[49]

> [If, for lack of a reliable brush,
> We have not depicted the famous Spinoza's traits,
> Wisdom being immortal,
> His writings will never die.]

Together, the poem and the portrait seem implicitly to make the claim that the transcendental immortality of his wisdom render irrelevant the precise details of Spinoza's personal appearance. As representative of the quintessence of philosophical goodness, it matters little if his individual looks are blurred with those of another semi-mythical archetype of goodness, René of Anjou, who reputedly retired from kingship to a life devoted to Provençal poetry and agriculture. As Silvia Berti has argued, the editors of the volume were clearly concerned to de-judaise Spinoza, by representing him with an image that offered no hint of his Jewishness.[50] A conscious decision was made not to use any of the portraits of Spinoza painted during his life, which typically depict him with much more characteristically Jewish features.[51]

However, it is not simply the case that Desrochers' image is intended to erase all awareness of Spinoza's Jewish origins. The cartouche directly beneath the bust indeed specifically mentions this fact: 'Benedict Spinosa, famous philosopher and native of Amsterdam. He was first a Jew by religion; he left the Jewish communion and thereafter professed Atheism. Died in The Hague in 1677, aged about 44 years old.'[52] This strikingly un-Jewish portrait thus attracts attention in its own caption to the fact that it is of a Jewish subject. Spinoza's Jewish origins are not simply concealed, but

---

[48] Ernst Altkirch, *Spinoza im Porträt* (1913) 70–1.   [49] *Trois Imposteurs*, frontispiece.
[50] See Berti, 'Introduzione', xl.
[51] See Altkirch, *Spinoza im Porträt*; Simon L. Millner, *The Face of Benedictus Spinoza* (1946).
[52] Berti, 'Introduzione', xxxviii–xxxix.

positively highlighted, in order subsequently to be erased. Spinoza's separation from 'la communion Judaïque' is presented not only as significant, but as absolute to the extent that even all visual traces of his Jewishness are overcome by it. The insistence on Spinoza's universality is here revealed as in a sense dependent on his Jewish origins. His ethnic specificity represents the photographic negative of his philosophical idealisation: it must not be forgotten, so that it can be deliberately inverted and thus erased. Paradoxically, though, the need to maintain the visibility of this act of erasure also guarantees its inconclusiveness. The attempt to obliterate all remnants of Spinoza the Jew in Spinoza the philosopher cannot, ultimately, succeed, particularly when the strained artificiality of this process is rendered so explicit. Spinoza's ineradicable Jewishness thus lingers as a powerful destabilising faultline in the narrative of universal philosophical exemplarity constructed around him.

The image of Spinoza was a central site of contestation in the early formation of modern philosophy, as a distinctive and autonomous cultural practice. Universalism was fundamental to the identity of the Enlightenment: in contrast with the culturally and textually specific truth claims of religion, philosophy in its purest form was defined by its rejection of these horizons of thought. Both for the detractors and the proponents of this emergent intellectual culture, Spinoza stood as the archetypal philosopher, epitomising pure detachment and abstraction. However, he also represented the limits of this vision. Taking their lead from Bayle, those who saw Spinoza as a dangerous atheist typically juxtaposed his mild-mannered life against his pernicious ideas, thus underlining the deceptiveness of secular philosophising. For more uncompromising radicals, identification with Spinoza enabled symbolic identification with an internally contradictory self-image that was simultaneously respectably virtuous and fearlessly subversive, and both abstractly universal and concretely individual. The excavation of the deployment of Spinoza in Early Enlightenment radicalism exposes these paradoxical fissures within this tradition of thought.

More than three hundred years after his death, the figure of Spinoza still retains a particular inspirational power. Exactly what Spinoza represents remains highly contested: in recent decades, he has been claimed as a proto-Marxist, a proto-Zionist, a postmodernist and a bulwark against the excesses of postmodernism.[53] Spinoza's spirit thus still stands in a very

---

[53] Antonio Negri, *The Savage Anomaly: The Power of Spinoza's Metaphysics and Politics* (1991); Yirmiyahu Yovel, *Spinoza and Other Heretics*, 190; Gilles Deleuze, *Expressionism in Philosophy: Spinoza* (1992); Christopher Norris, *Spinoza and the Origins of Modern Critical Theory* (1991), esp. 251–74. For a recent, nuanced attempt to apply Spinoza to contemporary concerns, see Moira Gatens and Genevieve Lloyd, *Collective Imaginings: Spinoza, Past and Present* (1999).

uncertain relationship with his historical, embodied life. Echoing Derrida's evocation of Marx as a spectral presence that perpetually and inescapably haunts the political conscience of the capitalist world,[54] we should perhaps also identify the presence of Spinoza's spirit as another philosophical apparition who refuses to be exorcised. Spinoza's spectrality is that of the ideal of a pure philosophy, embracing both personal wisdom and universal reason. In the radical Early Enlightenment, this aspiration was powerfully alive, and its envisioned realisation was encapsulated in an image of Spinoza simultaneously as an exemplary individual and as the universal voice of philosophical truth. However, this universalisation was destabilised by the particular specificity of which it was an inversion: Spinoza's ineradicable Jewish origins. In the ultimately unwinnable battle to escape the confines of cultural particularism, the biblical *Urkultur* of Judaism was widely positioned by Early Enlightenment radicals as a proxy enemy, standing metonymically for the much more nebulous target of the inescapable constraints of their own cultural horizons. The universalisation of Spinoza represented the enactment of this strategy, but the inevitable inconclusiveness of the eclipsing of his Jewishness discreetly undermined it from within. The complexity and the precariousness of this idealisation highlights the ambiguities inherent in the universalistic aspiration of the Enlightenment, and their problematisation by the enduring presence of Judaism.

[54] Jacques Derrida, *Specters of Marx* (1994) 3–48.

CHAPTER 8

Enlightenment and Kabbalah

The mystical texts and techniques of the Kabbalah, it is claimed, enclose the hidden inner truths of the Torah. The nature and status of this esoteric knowledge, however, and its relationship to the exoteric interpretation of the Jewish Bible and Jewish law, has always been a subject of extreme uncertainty and disagreement. The historical development of Kabbalah is equally disputed: the relationship between ancient Jewish mysticism, its later flowering in thirteenth-century Languedoc and Catalonia, centred on the interpretation of the inscrutable *Zohar*, and the variation developed in sixteenth-century Safed, in Galilee, by Isaac Luria and his followers, remains under intense scholarly debate.[1] The role of external influences on the development of Jewish mysticism is also controversial. However, it is clear that ancient Gnostic and Neoplatonic thought was a significant force in shaping Jewish philosophical and mystical notions of the relationship between the material world and the ineffable realm of divine perfection.[2] The Kabbalah thus in itself forms part of a wider, long-standing western tradition of esoteric speculation. Christian interest in Kabbalah, however, first emerged in the Renaissance and Reformation periods, driven, like Christian Hebraism as a whole, by a desire to establish a firmer basis in Jewish sources for the truths of Christianity. As Christian engagement with Judaism grew increasingly complex, these most mysterious and ambiguous of all Jewish texts posed many difficulties for their non-Jewish readers. For those who sought to find a universal core buried within the historical particularism of Judaism, however, the Kabbalah provided an exceptionally rich and exciting source.

---

[1] The key texts in this debate are still Gershom Scholem, *Major Trends in Jewish Mysticism* (1955); Moshe Idel, *Kabbalah: New Perspectives* (1988).

[2] See Steven T. Katz, 'Utterance and Ineffability in Jewish Neoplatonism', in Lenn E. Goodman, ed., *Neoplatonism and Jewish Thought* (1992) 279–98; Moshe Idel, 'Jewish Kabbalah and Platonism in the Middle Ages and Renaissance', in *ibid.*, 319–51; Gershom Scholem, *Origins of the Kabbalah* (1987) 12–24.

148

When Pico della Mirandola and other Neoplatonists turned their attention to Jewish mysticism in the late fifteenth century, they did not simply perpetuate the tradition of crudely Christological manipulation of the Kabbalah which had been initiated by converted Jews in medieval Spain. However, although they regarded their investigations as a form of serious theosophical speculation, the mystical demonstration of Christian truths remained important to the Neoplatonic Kabbalists: Pico asserted that 'no science can better convince us of the divinity of Jesus Christ than magic and the Kabbalah'.[3] In Johannes Reuchlin's slightly later work the manipulation of the Kabbalah for explicitly Christian ends is more starkly evident. Reuchlin's most insistently laboured argument is his justification for the insertion of an extra letter – a *shin* – into the Tetragrammaton, to give the holy name Yehoshua, or Jesus.[4] However, despite this blatant distortion, the fascination with the Kabbalah of scholars such as Reuchlin was genuine.[5] The apparent hermeneutic power of basic Kabbalistic techniques – particularly numerology, the *ars combinatoria* and the finding of hidden meanings within the sacred texts – stirred great excitement and curiosity. Although the Christian Kabbalah continued to attract suspicion during the sixteenth century, it increasingly gained acceptance as a valid branch of theological inquiry, and leading practitioners such as Guillaume Postel (1510–81) and the Venetian Franciscan Francesco Giorgio (1460–1541) commanded wide respect.[6]

At this time, however, the Kabbalistic tradition itself was in considerable flux, due to the impact of the teachings of Isaac Luria (1534–72). Although the extent to which Luria's ideas represent a radical break with earlier Kabbalistic tradition remains disputed, the Lurianic theory of creation was immensely influential in both Jewish and Christian circles. According to this account, the creation of the world was preceded by *tsimtsum*: the withdrawal of the divine – *En-Sof* – into a single point, in order to vacate space for the creation of the Universe. There then followed the act of creation itself, which ended with the calamity of the 'breaking of the vessels', causing imperfection in the world. The task of humanity is *tikkun olam*: the cosmic repair of the world, by reconstituting the broken vessels and restoring creation to its intended perfection.[7]

---

[3] Cited in Gershom Scholem, *Kabbalah* (1974) 197. See also Bernard McGinn, 'Cabalists and Christians: Reflections on Cabala in Medieval and Renaissance Thought', in Popkin and Wiener, eds., *Jewish Christians*, 11–34.

[4] See Reuchlin, *De Arte Kabbalistica* (1993 (1517)) 17; Scholem, *Kabbalah*, 198.

[5] See Scholem, *Kabbalah*, 199. For a counter-argument see Idel, *Kabbalah*, 256–7.

[6] Scholem, *Kabbalah*; Yates, *Rosicrucian Enlightenment*, 226–9; François Secret, *Le Zôhar chez les kabbalistes chrétiens de la Renaissance* (1958).

[7] Scholem, *Major Trends*, 244–86.

Whether or not Luria's teaching should accurately be understood as suffused with a yearning for mystical redemption,[8] it was certainly in these terms that it was predominantly interpreted by Christians. In the charged atmosphere of millenarian enthusiasm in much of mid seventeenth-century Europe, the discovery of the Lurianic Kabbalah stirred considerable interest. The Lurianic emphasis on *tikkun olam* resonated powerfully with the millenarian and utopian hopes of idealists who envisioned an imminent end to religious conflict and division. These aspirations, which were closely associated with a proto-Enlightenment commitment to the triumph of some form of 'natural religion', were also, however, characterised by a pronounced hostility towards the perceived legalism and exclusivity of rabbinic Judaism. The Kabbalah thus provoked profoundly ambivalent and contradictory responses. By the late seventeenth century a complex philosophical matrix had emerged within which these contrary impulses strained against each other.

PHILOSOPHY AND MYSTICISM: THE *KABBALAH DENUDATA*

The popularisation of the Lurianic Kabbalah in the late seventeeth-century Christian world was largely the work of two men: Christian Knorr von Rosenroth (1636–89), the son of a Lutheran minister in Silesia, and the charismatic Flemish mystic, Francis Mercurius van Helmont (1614–98). Van Helmont was one of the most famous peripatetic visionaries of mid seventeenth-century Europe, and was throughout his life preoccupied by Judaism. His first major work, *Alphabeti veré Naturalis Hebraici* (1667), written in prison in Rome after his arrest by the Inquisition, is a eulogy to the holy language, which he regarded as the perfect union of orthography and phonetics.[9] He provides an elaborate diagrammatic analysis of the vocal production of the sound associated with each Hebrew letter, arguing that these movements of tongue, lips and breath form the basis of the form of the written letter itself. He was also deeply impressed by the emphasis in Judaism on study and education, writing a detailed analysis of the teaching techniques of the *Beit HaMidrash* of the Second Temple period, which, he argued, should be used as a model for Christian religious instruction.[10] Van Helmont turned to Judaism as part of his search for the mystical, unified essence of divine truth, and was therefore particularly drawn to the most mystical aspects of Judaism itself.

---

[8] On this debate, see *ibid.*, 287–324; Idel, *Kabbalah*, 256–67; Peter Schäfer and Joseph Dan, eds., *Gershom Scholem's 'Major Trends in Jewish Mysticism': 50 Years After* (1993).

[9] See Allison P. Coudert, *The Impact of the Kabbalah in the Seventeenth Century: The Life and Thought of Francis Mercury van Helmont (1614–1698)* (1999) 58–99.

[10] F. M. van Helmont, *The Paradoxical Discourses of F. M. van Helmont* (1685) 184–200.

Knorr von Rosenroth was animated by a similar idealism. While travelling extensively across Europe in the 1660s he developed an intense interest in religious mysticism. While in Amsterdam, he studied with rabbis and acquired manuscript copies of Kabbalistic texts.[11] From 1668 onwards he settled in Sulzbach, in northern Bavaria, where he enjoyed the patronage of the local Prince, Christian August. It was in Sulzbach that he prepared and published the two volumes of his masterwork, the *Kabbalah Denudata* (1677, 1684). Van Helmont was a key collaborator on this project, which also involved the Cambridge Platonist Henry More. These men embarked in this bold editorial project because they believed that the Kabbalah offered vital insight into the uncontaminated, original *prisca theologica*: the purified philosophy revealed orally by God to Moses on Mount Sinai. Knorr and van Helmont shared a deeply irenic vision of religious unity and peace, and believed that Kabbalistic study could reveal the core, primeval truths of pure, universal religion, and thus lead to the healing of denominational divisions within Christianity (see figure 7).

The *Kabbalah Denudata* consists of a bulky compendium of Kabbalistic texts, either in Latin only, or, in the case of the *Zohar*, in Hebrew with parallel Latin translation. It also includes an extensive supporting apparatus of indices, synopses, glosses, references to both rabbinic and Christian scholarship, a glossary and lengthy editorial commentaries. For the first time, an extensive range of Kabbalistic material was made available to non-readers of Hebrew. While Knorr's translations are far from flawless, they are clearly the product of extremely serious and scrupulous scholarship.[12] However, although he implicitly presents his opus as comprehensive in scope, the *Kabbalah Denudata* in fact offers a selective and carefully mediated perspective, reflecting his own philosophical and political concerns.

Knorr and van Helmont were drawn above all to the Lurianic Kabbalah, which they interpreted in a particularly optimistic and philosophical vein.[13] Both volumes of the *Kabbalah Denudata* give prominence to the writings of Abraham Cohen Herrera, an otherwise relatively obscure figure who first encountered the Lurianic Kabbalah in Italy towards the end of the sixteenth century, and after later settling in Amsterdam wrote two texts in Spanish which presented Luria's thought in a strikingly Platonic fashion.[14]

---

[11] Scholem, *Kabbalah*, 416.   [12] *Ibid.*   [13] See Coudert, *Impact of Kabbalah*, 118–25.

[14] On Herrera, see Gershom Scholem, 'Abraham Cohen Herrera: Leben, Werk und Wirkung', in Friedrich Haußermann, ed. and trans., *Sha'ar Hashamayim, oder Pforte des Himmels* (1974) 10–22; Nissim Yosha, *Myth and Metaphor: Abraham Cohen Herrera's Philosophic Interpretation of Lurianic Kabbalah* (in Hebrew with English summary) (1994); Alexander Altmann, 'Lurianic Kabbalah in a Platonic Key: Abraham Cohen Herrera's *Puerta del Cielo*', in Twersky and Septimus, eds., *Jewish Thought* 1–38; Kenneth Krabbenhoft, 'Kabbalah and Expulsion: The Case of Abraham Cohen de

Figure 7 Christian Knorr von Rosenroth, *Kabbala Denudata*, volume 1, Sulzbach, 1677, frontispiece. The Kabbalah symbolically inspires a semi-clad young woman, enabling her to approach the open doorway to the palace of secret knowledge, with the keys to the Old and New Testaments around her wrist.

For Herrera, the Lurianic notion of *tikkun* – the healing of the lower, shattered vessels using the divine power contained within the higher, unbroken vessels – was identical to the relationship of lower and higher intellects in the Neoplatonic philosophy of Marsilio Ficino and others.[15] His metaphorical interpretation of the Lurianic Kabbalah was profoundly influenced by non-Jewish thinkers, most notably Plotinus, Ficino, Thomas Aquinas and Pico della Mirandola, whose work had been easily accessible to him as a Jew from a Tuscan Marrano background, whose family had left Spain only shortly before his birth.[16]

Herrera's arguments strongly resonated with Knorr and van Helmont's own metaphorical understanding of *tikkun* as the healing of religious division in the world. The extract of Herrera's *Puerta del Cielo* (The Gate of Heaven) included in the *Kabbalah Denudata* is explicitly presented as a harmonisation of Kabbalistic and Platonic philosophy.[17] Herrera's explicitly non-literal understanding of the Kabbalah marginalised his work within the Jewish world, where it had very little influence. However, this same aspect of his work made him particularly accessible and attractive to Christians.[18] By presenting Herrera's work as much more authoritative than it was recognised as among Jews, Knorr was able implicitly to elide the Kabbalah with his own philosophy of mystical ecumenical irenicism.

The *Kabbalah Denudata* stands in the intersection of the Renaissance and the Enlightenment. Knorr's compendium has been interpreted as a late work of mystical speculation that was profoundly at odds with the prevalent proto-Enlightenment rationalism of the 1670s,[19] but also as a forward-looking work, based on quintessentially Enlightenment values of tolerance, ecumenicalism and an optimistic commitment to social and scientific progress.[20] It is, though, impossible to demarcate between the mystical and the progressive elements of Knorr's thought. In the *Kabbalah Denudata*, the Kabbalah simultaneously represents both a mystical *prisca theologica* and the pinnacle of abstract philosophy; both a domain of divine contemplation and the fruit of meticulous critical scholarship; and both a specifically Jewish esoteric tradition and the basis for a universalist metaphysical optimism. As a work of scholarship, the *Kabbalah Denudata* reflects both a continued reverence for long-standing traditions

---

[15] Abraham Cohen Herrera, *Puerta del Cielo* (1974 (*c.*1630)) 265–6.

[16] Yosha, *Myth*, vi–ix; 'Abraham Cohen de Herrera: An Outstanding Exponent of Prisca Theologica in Early Seventeenth-Century Amsterdam', in Jozeph Michman, ed., *Dutch Jewish History*, v (1993) 117–26; Kenneth Krabbenhoft, 'Syncretism and Millennium in Herrera's Kabbalah', in Matt D. Goldish and Richard H. Popkin, eds., *Jewish Messianism in the Early Modern World* (2001) 65–76.

[17] *Kabbalah Denudata* I (1677), book 3, title page.   [18] Scholem, 'Herrera', 9.

[19] Kurt Salecker, *Christian Knorr von Rosenroth (1632–1689)* (1931) 1–2.

[20] Allison P. Coudert, 'The *Kabbalah Denudata*: Converting Jews or Seducing Christians?', in Popkin and Weiner, eds., *Jewish Christians*, 75.

of learning and a commitment to the more rigorous standards of critical textual analysis and interpretation characteristic of the Early Enlightenment. Philosophically, it is also a Janus-faced text: in its yearning to unify all fields of thought and knowledge, it resonates equally powerfully with Renaissance esotericism and with the practical universalism of the Enlightenment.

While the power of the *Kabbalah Denudata* was reinforced by these dualities, they also inflected it with a measure of ambiguity, most starkly brought to the fore in its simultaneous exoticisation and universalisation of Judaism.[21] Knorr believed that the Kabbalah revealed universal truths that transcended Judaism, and in so doing extinguished it. Although Jewish mystical sources provided the blueprint for his Christian ecumenicism, there was no space for Judaism itself within this vision. Knorr and his collaborators certainly regarded themselves as unambiguously philosemitic: their second volume opens with the words 'Lectori Philebraeo Salutem!'[22] Nonetheless, the Sulzbach project ultimately sought to appropriate the Kabbalah, and through this process to erase Jewish particularism within a general ecumenicalism. Their approach combined a profound scholarly respect for Jewish sources with a fundamental belief in the obsolescence of Judaism itself. The *Kabbalah Denutata* was predicated on a suppressed paradox: it sought to use specifically Jewish traditions of mystical reflection in order to establish the obsolescence of religious specificity in all its forms. This simultaneous privileging and erasure of Judaism produced a significant strand of confusion and internal contradiction submerged beneath the surface of the text.

The members of Knorr's circle were not impervious to these internal strains. The precariousness of their project is highlighted by the intellectual trajectory of Knorr's early associate, Henry More. In his early writings More regarded the Kabbalah as the original source of the deepest truths of Neoplatonism. The motion of the Earth, the 'praeexistency of the Soul', and the 'Atomick Philosophy' were all derived, he argued, from the 'Philosophick Cabbala'.[23] However, having been drawn into Knorr's circle after writing his *Conjectura Cabbalistica* (1653), during the preparation of the *Kabbalah Denudata* he grew impatient with the intricacies of the subject. In a critical essay that he insisted was included in the compendium, he attacked Kabbalism as both unnecessarily complicated and

[21] See esp. *Kabbalah Denudata* II (1684) 18–19, 30–2.
[22] *Ibid.*, I. See also Coudert, *Impact of Kabbalah*, 133–6.
[23] See A. Rupert Hall, *Henry More* (1990) 109–11.

falsely materialistic and pantheistic.[24] Having previously admired the universalism of the Kabbalah, he now condemned it as narrowly Jewish. He associated Judaism with the failure to distinguish adequately between the material and the divine, discerning this shortcoming both in the Kabbalah and in Spinoza's philosophy.[25] Having lost his former conviction that Jewish mysticism could provide a universal underpinning for his own scientific and metaphysical beliefs, More's attitude towards this tradition flipped into an almost diametrically opposed position. No longer a *prisca theologica*, the Kabbalah was instead cast as the epitome of obscurantist, unspiritual parochialism.

GEORG WACHTER: SPINOZISM, JUDAISM AND DIVINE PRESENCE

A very similar cluster of shifts and ambiguities appears in the writings of one of the most intriguing philosophical radicals of the German Early Enlightenment, Johann Georg Wachter. Like More, Wachter also wrote repeatedly on the Kabbalah, and also radically revised his opinion of it. His assessment, however, moved in the opposite direction, from denigration to indealisation.[26] In his first book on the subject, *Der Spinozismus in Judenthumb* (1699), Wachter alleged that Spinoza had been a secret Kabbalist, and that it was this alien belief system that had inspired his dangerous, absurd and intrinsically Jewish philosophy. This argument provoked considerable controversy, in response to which Wachter wrote a second work, *Elucidarius Cabalisticus* (1706), in which he discreetly but crucially amended his argument. He here maintained his insistence on the Kabbalistic roots of Spinoza's thought, but rather than using this as the basis for a critique of his philosophy, he now professed agreement with the fundamental truths of the Kabbalah, which Spinoza had merely elucidated. Wachter effected this important intellectual shift extremely casually. He did not explicitly retract his earlier work, and seemed not to regard his two texts as being in direct contradiction with each other, although to a modern reader they

---

[24] Henry More, *Fundamenta Philosophiae Sive Cabbalae Aeto-Paedo-Melissaeae*, in *Kabbalah Denudata* 1, 293–312. See also Allison P. Coudert, 'A Cambridge Platonist's Kabbalist Nightmare', *JHI* 35 (1975) 647–8; Sarah Hutton, 'Henry More, Anne Conway and the Kabbalah: A Cure for the Kabbalist Nightmare?', in Coudert, Hutton, Popkin and Weiner, eds., *Judaeo-Christian Intellectual Culture*, 27–42.

[25] See Sarah Hutton, 'Reason and Revelation in the Cambridge Platonists, and their Reception of Spinoza', in Karlfried Gründer und Wilhelm Schmidt-Biggemann, eds., *Spinoza in der Frühzeit seiner religiösen Wirkung* (1984) 192–3.

[26] On Wachter, see Winfried Schröder, *Spinoza in der Deutschen Aufklärung* (1987) 59–124; Rüdiger Otto, *Studien zur Spinozarezeption in Deutschland im 18 Jahrhundert* (1994) 95–101.

self-evidently appear to be so. The key to an understanding of this puzzle lies in Wachter's deep ambivalence towards Judaism. For Wachter, as for so many Early Enlightenment thinkers, Judaism in general, and Jewish mysticism in particular, provoked simultaneous reactions of repulsion and attraction, and impulses towards both repudiation and assimilation.

Wachter's original decision to engage critically with Spinoza seems to have been spurred by alarm. While in Amsterdam in 1698–9, Wachter encountered the famous convert to Judaism, Moses Germanus, who, as a Christian and under the name Johann Peter Spaeth, had first encountered the Kabbalah whilst working under Knorr van Rosenroth on the editing of the *Kabbalah Denudata*. Spaeth had been so impressed by what he discovered that, having already converted from Catholicism to Lutheranism and then, like Van Helmont, to Quakerism, he converted to Judaism and settled in Amsterdam under his new name.[27] Wachter was troubled by this example of the Kabbalah exercising precisely the opposite conversionary power from that which had been conventionally claimed for it by Christian Kabbalists. He therefore entered into debate with Spaeth, and published the essence of his adversarial arguments against him as *Der Spinozismus in Judenthumb*.[28] However, his text is not simply a polemic against this eccentric and isolated Jewish convert. Wachter also here uses the Kabbalah as a launching site for an exploration of the central issues of metaphysics, such as the nature of creation and the relationship between God and the material and inhabited world.

Wachter was known in Germany as a religious and philosophical freethinker.[29] Although he unambiguously considered himself a Christian, he was not concerned to defend the orthodoxies of any brand of mainstream Christianity. His intellectual ambition was to elucidate the parameters of 'natural religion', which he understood as truths self-evident to human reason, requiring no recourse to elaborate theology. It is obvious by the 'light of reason', Wachter argued, that God must exist as a distinctive entity clearly separate from the created world.[30] Spinoza's immanent view of God, he claimed, contradicted this self-evident common sense. Spinoza's God, he insists, is nothing other than the hidden, infinite *En-Sof*: the mystical concept of divine omnipresence elaborated in the Zoharic theory of the tree of the *Sephirot*, or divine potentialities. This theosophical outlook of the 'Vergötterung der Welt' – the denial of the distinction between God and

---

[27] See Winfried Schröder, 'Einleitung' to Georg Wachter, *Spinozismus in Judenthumb* (1994) 13–15.
[28] *Ibid.*; Gershom Scholem, 'Die Wachtersche Kontroverse über den Spinozismus und ihre Folgen', in Gründer and Schmidt-Biggemann, eds., *Spinoza*, 15–25.
[29] Schröder, 'Einleitung', 7–8.
[30] Georg Wachter, *Der Spinozismus in Judenthumb* (1994 (1699)) 14–15.

the world – is, he argues, the cornerstone of Spinozism, of the Kabbalah and of Judaism in general.[31] He strenuously repudiated this notion, setting out a fifteen-point table of distinctions between God and the material world, cross-referenced with another list of God's immaterial attributes and perfections.[32]

Wachter's argument effectively conflates Judaism with Kabbalism. He does not acknowledge any diversity within the Kabbalah, drawing on both Zoharic and Lurianic concepts indiscriminately, and assumes that Spinoza, as a Jew, must also have been a Kabbalist. The Jews' 'most basic teaching', he asserts, is that the world's creation occurred in space emptied by the 'drawing together of the infinite': a notion that he condems as 'impossible and contradictory'.[33]

The question of creation plays an important part in Wachter's argument. Largely on the basis of this hasty interpretation of Lurianic *tsimtsum*, he concludes that the Kabbalah starts from the classic philosophical conundrum that nothing can come of nothing: 'ex nihilo nihil fit'.[34] He argues that this falsehood is inextricably connected to a view of God that is indistinguishable from matter, and that such a worldly God cannot be the subject of true religion.[35] He contrasts this Jewish view of God with the higher spirituality of natural religion, which is based on the naturally prescribed denial of the sinful actual world, and the quest for the hidden divine.[36] This distinction between a higher, hidden, loving God and a lower, lawgiving, 'Jewish' God echoes the ancient arguments put forward by the second-century Gnostics, which have been described by Gershom Scholem as 'metaphysical anti-semitism in its profoundest and most effective form'.[37] Wachter concludes the main body of his text very much in this vein, describing the two religions in carefully counterpointed contrast:

Christianity is a religion that has as its aim and destiny the immateriality and hiddenness of God, the eternal, great, wise and holy being; and which by its nature leads . . . to all virtues, and in particular to humility.

Judaism is a *contradictory*, worthless jumble of religion and atheism, which has as its aim and destiny the substance and creatures of the present time, and transient, parochial, foolish and material being; and which by its nature leads . . . to all sins, and in particular to hatred.[38]

The intense hostility towards Judaism that is clearly manifest in *Der Spinozismus in Judenthumb* compounds the puzzle of Wachter's later intellectual career. Only seven years later he advanced in print a seemingly utterly contrasting position of deep respect towards the Kabbalah. It is

---

[31] *Ibid.*, 20–1. [32] *Ibid.*, 199ff. [33] *Ibid.*, 185. [34] *Ibid.*, 223. [35] *Ibid.*, 244ff.
[36] *Ibid.*, 252ff. [37] Scholem, *Major Trends*, 322. [38] Wachter, *Spinozismus*, 256.

possible that he encountered or experienced something during this period that led him to revise his attitude towards Judaism. However, beneath Wachter's apparent volte-face it is possible to discern a convoluted but nonetheless comprehensible continuity of approach.

Spinozismus provoked a considerable and largely hostile response, in part in reaction to which Wachter published his *Elucidarius Cabalisticus* (1706). As a Latin text, this work was written in a very different cultural register, and was aimed at a much more restricted readership. Wachter here once again argues in detail that Spinoza's philosophy is in essence Kabbalistic. However, directly reversing his earlier criticism of Spinoza's allegedly Kabbalistic 'Vergötterung der Welt', he now stresses the positive nature of this theosophical affinity. Spinoza's notion of God, Wachter argues, is that of the Kabbalistic infinite *En-Sof*, encompassing both spiritual and material domains.[39] Rather than claiming that this implies a base materialisation of the divine, he interprets this integration positively, as a mystical spiritualisation of matter. A pantheistic spiritual monism, and an emanationist view of the relationship between God and the world, are presented by Wachter as fundamental both to Spinoza's system and to the Kabbalah, and indeed to all pure philosophy. He has such enthusiasm for the illuminatory power of the Kabbalah that in the final chapter of *Elucidarius* he insistently presses for the incorporation of Kabbalistic study into the philosophy curricula of European academies and universities.[40]

Wachter's opinions clearly underwent significant revision over the few years between the writing of these texts. However, there is an underlying similarity between the two works: in both cases, Wachter attempts to enunciate a radical notion of God, drawing on Neoplatonic and Gnostic traditions of esoteric thought. This project is only discreetly evident in *Der Spinozismus in Judenthumb*: in this more accessible vernacular text, Wachter chooses not to stray too blatantly from conventional Christian lines of argument. However, he nonetheless appeals to natural reason rather than to Christian theology in establishing his case against Spinoza's 'Vergötterung der Welt', and he contrasts the baseness of Judaism against an extremely abstracted, elliptical vision of Christianity. In *Elucidarius Cabalisticus*, Wachter's Neoplatonic theological radicalism is more clearly manifest. Wachter here effectively co-opts both Spinoza and the Kabbalah to his own, profoundly Neoplatonic conception of natural religion.[41]

In neither text is Wachter most fundamentally concerned either with Spinoza or with Kabbalah. These two philosophical perspectives, bracketed

---

[39] Georg Wachter, *Elucidarius Cabalisticus* (1995 (1706)) 44–5.
[40] *Ibid.*, 46ff.   [41] See Winfried Schröder, 'Einleitung' to *Elucidarius* (1995) 20.

together, are used in the first text as a counterpoint and in the second as a support for his own faltering attempts to articulate his notion of a proto-Enlightenment natural religion. Even in *Elucidarius Cabalisticus*, he shows little interest in the question of the structural relationship between the ten divine *Sephirot*, which was a central strand of Jewish Kabbalistic speculation. In contrast to these intricate arguments, with which he expresses a distinct impatience, Wachter offers a straightforwardly Neoplatonic interpretation of the Kabbalah, for which Herrera's writings were clearly a key influence and source.[42] There is, then, contrary to initial appearances, a distinct line of continuity between Wachter's two texts. As with the case of Henry More, the oscillations in Wachter's arguments are indicative of the more general instability that characterised the prevalent Early Enlightenment response to Judaism.

Wachter later returned to Jewish themes. He was fascinated by the possibility of an ancient Judaic source of natural religion, and in his *De primordiis Christianae religionis* (1717) put forward the hypothesis that Christianity had originated as a Jewish sect closely related to the ancient Essenes.[43] This theory, which the discovery of the Dead Sea Scrolls has shown to be far from foolish speculation, was a natural supplement to his attempt in *Elucidarius Cabalisticus* to ground natural religion in the Kabbalah, and so to imbue it with the authority of a primeval source. In *De primordiis* Wachter approached this same goal from a more historical perspective. By associating the originary essence of Christianity with a timeless, mystical form of purified Judaism, he effectively placed natural religion outside of history. His argument in a sense echoed Vico's segregation of sacred and secular history, but with the crucial difference that Wachter's separation was based not on the authority of Scripture, but on the eternality of the Kabbalah, and sought to establish the timelessness not of institutional Christianity, but only of its minimal philosophical core.

Wachter's celebration of the Essenes as early exponents of natural religion did not imply any sustained positive reassessment of Judaism as lived and practised by actual Jews. In his later writings Wachter saw the Kabbalah as the philosophical essence of an eternally transcendent Judaic core of true knowledge. Although he was reliant on the elucidation of this philosophy from within the Jewish rabbinical elite, he was nonetheless deeply ambivalent towards the Jewishness of his sources. In *Der Spinozismus in Judenthumb* he regards the Kabbalah as profoundly Jewish, and denigrates it on this basis; in *Elucidarius Cabalisticus*, concomitant with his revalorisation of

[42] *Ibid.*, 20–1.   [43] Georg Wachter, *De primordiis Christianae religionis* (1995 (1717)) 113.

the Kabbalah, he transplants it from the Jewish to the universal realm. Jewish difference is at no stage viewed positively by Wachter. However, he is intensely drawn to the prospect of overcoming the difference by using Judaism as the basis for a universal philosophical sameness. At the heart of Wachter's ambiguities and oscillations on this subject lies his battle to reconcile conflicting universalistic and particularistic readings of Judaism within his own emergent philosophy of natural religion.

MYSTICAL DEMARCATIONS AND CONFUSIONS

The Kabbalah also presented a slippery intellectual terrain for more orthodox thinkers. The most prominent critic of Wachter's arguments was Johann Franz Buddeus, Professor of Philosophy at the newly founded University of Halle, who was deeply alarmed by the claim that the Kabbalah was intrinsically Spinozistic, and thus, in his opinion, atheistic. Buddeus believed that Wachter had heretically tainted with atheism one of the key pillars of the Judaeo-Christian religious tradition. He professed deep respect for the ancient traditions of the Kabbalah, and argued that the accusation that it was Spinozistic could only anger the Jews, and render yet more difficult their conversion to Christianity.[44] In response to Wachter, Buddeus carefully distinguished between the 'ancient Kabbalah', including the Zoharic tradition, which he regarded as unimpeachable, and the 'recent Kabbalah' of Luria and Herrera, which he described as 'impure' and at best of highly dubious authority.[45]

In highlighting this distinction, Buddeus emphasised precisely the historical discontinuity which the *Kabbalah Denudata* and Wachter had silently erased. However, Buddeus' concern to distinguish between the 'ancient' and 'recent' Kabbalah was more strategic than scholarly. Avoiding discussion of the correct interpretation of Lurianic Kabbalah, he simply denied its validity, and restricted his positive arguments to the more secure ground of the older Kabbalistic tradition. His strategy in response to Wachter's subversive challenge was to construct an intellectual bulwark against it, behind which he could defend the core of Jewish philosophy and rabbinics from the aspersions of freethinkers and radicals. Buddeus' scholarship was strongly influenced by the seventeenth-century tradition of Christian Hebraism, and was predicated on the purity and authority of Jewish learning. He

---

[44] Johann Franz Buddeus, 'Defensio Cabbalae Ebraeorum Contra Auctores Quosdam Modernos', in *Observatorium selectarum ad. rem. litterariim spectantium* I (1700) 207–31, esp. 230–1.

[45] *Ibid.*, 221–3; Buddeus, *Introductio ad Historiam Philosophae Ebraeorum* (1702) 306–21.

therefore regarded it as essential to rebut Wachter's unorthodox reading of the Kabbalah, which, like Wachter, he regarded as the philosophical essence of Judaism.

Buddeus' critique of Wachter left him with the challenge of providing an alternative account of the origins of Spinoza's thought. Spinozism, he insisted, had existed long before Spinoza: although he acknowledged the distinctiveness of Spinoza's philosophy, he argued that it was closely related to the ancient atheism of Democritus, Epicurus and others.[46] In his compendious *Theses theologicae de atheismo* (1717), which attempted to encompass all aspects of the causes, varieties and pernicious consequences of atheism, Buddeus devoted particularly close attention to Spinoza. However, he was unsure of how to account for this phenomenon. His historical positioning of Spinoza was ambiguously poised between assimilating him into the heretical mainstream and treating him as in some sense unique.[47] Neither strategy was comfortable: the former failed to take account of Spinoza's Jewishness, while the latter implicitly associated Judaism, through Spinoza, with atheism. Buddeus was concerned to refute Wachter's suggestion of such a link; but he was unable to offer a convincing alternative account of the aetiology of his thought. Spinoza remained an awkward anomaly, straddling the religious, cultural and philosophical categories of the eighteenth century. The enduring mark of his Jewish otherness frustrated Buddeus' attempt to situate him satisfactorily within an overarching account of the history of philosophy.

The question of the source of Spinoza's ideas, once raised by Wachter, could not easily be evaded. Despite Buddeus' attempted refutation of the idea, the relationship between Spinozism and the Kabbalah remained an open controversy in early eighteenth-century German academic debate. Scholarly repudiators of atheism such as Jacob Staalkopf and Jacob Friedrich Reimmann treated this issue cautiously, but tentatively accepted this thesis.[48] Wachter's *Elucidarius Cabalisticus* even inspired the interest of Leibniz himself, whose notes on the text were discovered in the mid nineteenth century. The title under which these notes were then published – *Réfutation Inédite de Spinoza par Leibniz* – gives a misleading impression of the tone and content of this fragmented, meandering text. Leibniz does not

---

[46] J. F. Buddeus, *Exercitatio Historico-Philosophica de Spinozismo ante Spinozam* (1701) in *Analecta Historiae Philosophicae* XI (1724) 324–6; see also Alan Charles Kors, *Atheism in France, 1650–1729* (1990) 231–2.

[47] J. F. Buddeus, *Theses theologicae de atheismo et superstitione variis* (1737 (1717) 248ff., 369ff.

[48] M. Iacobus Staalkopf, *Ab Impiis Detorsionibus Thomae Hobbesii et Benedicti de Spinoza Oraculum Paulinum* (1707) 17–21; Jacob Friedrich Reimmann, *Historia Atheismi et Atheorum falso & merito suspectorum* (1725) 514–9.

here sustainedly refute either Spinoza or Wachter's interpretation of him, but rather uses Wachter's text as a springboard for a series of reflections on the differences between Spinoza's philosophy and his own.[49]

In his published writings Leibniz conformed to the almost universal contemporary condemnation of Spinoza. In these private notes, however, he shows a more contemplative, measured response to his philosophy. The main criticism that he levels at Spinoza is that he confuses spirit and matter, thus obliterating any distinction between the soul and the body, and failing to perceive the subtleties of Leibniz' own monadological theory of substance.[50] As we have seen, it is precisely this element of Spinoza's thought that Wachter regarded as most fundamentally Kabbalistic. Leibniz does not discuss this issue directly, but appears tacitly to accept Wachter's argument. Elsewhere, in his correspondence, Leibniz explicitly identifies the Kabbalah as a key source of Spinoza's philosophy: 'Indeed, Spinoza formulated his monstrous doctrine from a combination of the Kabbalah and Cartesianism, corrupted to the extreme. He did not understand the nature of true substance or monads...'[51] Leibniz' own attitude to the Kabbalah is difficult to discern. In his response to Wachter's *Elucidarius*, Leibniz reveals a considerable degree of informed interest in the subject, and particularly in the Lurianic account of creation. He was a close friend of van Helmont, and there are powerful resonances between his theodicy and ecumenical optimism and the stress on cosmic reparation in Lurianic Kabbalah.[52] However, despite these signs of a measure of Kabbalistic interest and even influence in Leibniz' thought, this is offset by his more hostile stance elsewhere in his work, and by his willingness to accept Wachter's association of the Kabbalah with Spinoza's unacceptable, rival philosophical system. Leibniz' opinion of the Kabbalah, like that of so many of his contemporaries, appears to have been marked by a considerable flexibility and ambivalence.[53]

Early Enlightenment Christians were drawn to the Kabbalah because they imagined it to offer a timeless pathway to eternal truth. Understood as *prisca theologica*, the true Kabbalah was regarded as, by its very nature, impervious to change. It was from this perspective that Leibniz and others saw the Kabbalah as an ancient, universalistic philosophical essence, providing a valuable underpinning for their own attempts to develop a

---

[49] G. W. Leibniz/A. Foucher de Careil, *Réfutation Inédite de Spinoza par Leibniz* (1995 (1854)) 309ff. See also Georges Friedmann, *Leibniz et Spinoza* (1962) 228.

[50] Leibniz, *Réfutation*, 33.

[51] Cited in Allison P. Coudert, *Leibniz and the Kabbalah* (1995) 77.   [52] See *ibid.*, 78–135.

[53] On Leibniz and mysticism in general see Allison P. Coudert, Richard H. Popkin and Gordon M. Weiner, eds., *Leibniz, Mysticism and Religion* (1998).

compelling philosophical universalism. However, Leibniz also exemplifies the precariousness of this universalisation of the Kabbalah, which was very readily destablised by lingering suspicion of its Jewish source. In later writings, such as his *Theodicy* (1710), Leibniz tended to conflate the Kabbalah with his philosophical animus, Spinozism.[54] When writing in this mode, Leibniz regarded the Kabbalah as an alien, characteristically Jewish source of impious, materialistic opinions.

The pervasive uncertainty with which Early Enlightenment thinkers responded to the Kabbalah is classically reflected in Jacques Basnage's *Histoire des Juifs*. Basnage also accepted that Spinoza was essentially a systematiser of the Kabbalah, from which he had derived his axiom *ex nihilo nihil fit* and his determination to reduce everything to a single substance.[55] However, he nonetheless offers elsewhere in this massive text a lengthy and extremely positive discussion of the Kabbalah, which he describes as 'a noble science, which leads men . . . to knowledge of the most profound truths'.[56] However, towards the end of this exposition a contrasting note of frustration slips into his text:

The profundity of [the Kabbalists'] writings is sometimes so obscure that it becomes impenetrable. Reason offers nothing that accords with the terms that fill their writings. After having hunted in vain for a long time, you grow weary; you close the book; you return an hour later; you think you have seen some small glimmer of insight; but it soon disappears . . .[57]

Basnage's respect for the Kabbalah is, then, doubly undercut: by its association with Spinozist atheism, and by his personal admission of fatigue and incomprehension. The higher faculties of reason, he acknowledges, strain in the opposite direction to Kabbalistic mysticism. These uncertainties concerning the philosophical status of the Kabbalah were compounded by a scholarly ambivalence. The inscrutability of Kabbalistic texts brought to the fore more acutely than any other form of study the internal strain in the minds of intellectuals such as Basnage between their reverence for erudition and their rationalist impatience with obscurantism. Unable to reconcile these contrasting perspectives, Basnage leaves his readers with an impression of the Kabbalah that on close scrutiny proves to be fundamentally split and incoherent.

Spinoza's own assessment of the Kabbalah was uncompromising and unambiguous. In the ninth chapter of the *Tractatus Theologico-Politicus*, he writes: 'I have read and known certain Kabbalistic triflers, whose insanity

[54] See Friedmann, *Leibniz*, 230–2.   [55] Jacques Basnage, *Histoire des Juifs*, IV, 294ff.
[56] *Ibid.*, III, 271.   [57] *Ibid.*, 363.

provokes my unceasing astonishment.'[58] This statement appears to have been utterly ignored in the extensive early eighteenth-century debate over Spinoza's alleged Kabbalism: a sure sign that the issues at stake extended far beyond the ostensible subject of the controversy. The crux of this debate was not the interpretation of Spinoza itself, but the wider question of the relationship of Early Enlightenment thought to the mystical core of Judaism.

For Leibniz, Wachter and their contemporaries, Judaism was powerfully associated both with obstinate particularism and with utopian universalism. It therefore resisted fixity, and troublingly haunted the pioneers of the Enlightenment. The tensions that clustered around the interpretation of the Kabbalah in this period were generated above all by the tussle between conflicting particularist and universalist readings of this tradition. Both perspectives were problematic in their stance towards Judaism. Whereas critics of the Kabbalah attacked it as narrowly and characteristically Jewish, idealists such as Knorr and van Helmont erased this particularity, by absorbing the Kabbalah into their own utopian vision of Christianity. Neither assessment, however, could be reconciled readily with the Enlightenment aspiration to encompass both rationalism and cosmopolitanism. Early Enlightenment intellectuals therefore had great difficulty choosing between the two, and often oscillated between the opposing poles of appropriation and distancing, and of celebration and condemnation. The Kabbalah thus stands out as a particularly revealing focus of the difficulties that beset the thought of this period. However, the confusions and indecidabilities highlighted by the Kabbalah are also apparent in Early Enlightenment responses to other aspects of Judaism. For radical thinkers in particular, Judaism provoked widely divergent interpretations, and was heavily invoked both as a positive source of anti-Christian argument and as a negative archetype of unenlightened primitivism.

---

[58] *TTP*, 140. For a discussion of Spinoza's views, see Richard H. Popkin, 'Spinoza, Neoplatonic Kabbalist?', in Goodman, *Neoplatonism*, 387–409.

CHAPTER 9

Judaism, reason and the critique of religion

Christian interest in the arguments put forward by Jews against Christianity dates back at least to the early Middle Ages. Medieval theologians who investigated this subject were motivated by two distinct concerns: while anxious to monitor and repress what they regarded as Jewish blasphemies against Christ, they were also from the thirteenth century onwards increasingly eager to develop cogent counter-arguments, in order to break down the Jews' resistance to Christian conversionism. The early development of Christian Hebraism was largely spearheaded by the desire of Dominican and Franciscan conversionist friars to use Jewish texts in sermons and disputations against the Jews. Although the agendas of the famous disputations at Paris (1240), Barcelona (1263) and Tortosa (1413–14) were narrowly predetermined by the friars, these occasions nonetheless initiated some form of encounter between Christian and Jewish modes of theological argument.[1] In the mid seventeenth century, dialogue between Christians and Jews, particularly in the Dutch Republic, attained an unprecedented level of openness. Even in this environment, the Christian hope of winning Jewish converts was the underlying legitimation of almost all intellectual contact. After the breaking of the mid-century wave of messianic expectancy among both Jews and Christians, however, this unity of perspective began to dissolve, and Christian responses to Jewish arguments and opinions became much more varied and complex.

The dedication of the new, vast Portuguese synagogue in Amsterdam in 1675 eloquently symbolised the rising prosperity and self-confidence of the northern European Sephardi diaspora. The synagogue immediately became a major tourist attraction, boldly showcasing the Jewish community as a presence worthy of attention and contemplation by visitors to the city.[2]

---

[1] See Cohen, *Friars*; Chazan, *Daggers*, esp. 14ff.; Hyam Maccoby, *Judaism on Trial* (1982).
[2] Israel, *European Jewry*, 220.

The increasing visibility of a respectable, bourgeois form of Judaism was accompanied by a rising awareness among non-Jews of Jewish religious and cultural practices – and of Jewish arguments against Christianity. Although more conservative thinkers remained alarmed by these Jewish satires and polemics, they nonetheless often found them intriguing. For Early Enlightenment radicals, however, this argumentative literature stirred great interest as a potential polemical resource. In the early eighteenth century, Jewish anti-Christian arguments circulated widely in clandestine circles, where they lent a transgressive piquancy to the assault on orthodox religion. A proto-anthropology of Jewish customs and beliefs also emerged, which, although at times extremely hostile to Judaism, was in some cases deployed as part of a subtle subversion of Christianity.

OROBIO'S FRIENDLY DISCUSSIONS

Amsterdam in the mid seventeenth century was the hub of a uniquely intense phase of theological interchange between Christians and Jews.[3] In the 1650s and 1660s, members of a tight Anglo-Dutch philo-Judaic circle, including the Amsterdam millenarian Petrus Serrarius, the Middelburg Hebraist Adam Boreel and, in England, John Durie, Samuel Hartlib and others, were involved in a number of projects, including translations of the Mishnah into Latin and of the New Testament into Hebrew, and the collection of funds for the Jewish community in Jerusalem.[4] The meticulously detailed model of Solomon's Temple built in the 1640s by Rabbi Jacob Jehuda Leon (1602–75) fascinated Jews and Christians alike, and for several decades attracted large numbers of visitors in both Holland and England.[5] As commercial contacts between Jews and Christians closened – particularly, from the 1650s onwards, due to the booming Dutch colonial trade with the West Indies[6] – social and intellectual interchange also grew more amicable and commonplace. By the end of the seventeenth century, it was possible for determined Christian intellectuals, particularly in Holland, to gain access to a range of Jewish anti-Christian texts. The circulation of these manuscripts within the Jewish community was an open secret, and it seems very likely that leading Dutch Sephardic patricians

---

[3] See Popkin, 'Jewish-Christian Interchanges', in van den Berg and van der Wall, eds., *Jewish–Christian Relations*, 3–32.

[4] Ernestine G. E. van der Wall, 'The Amsterdam Millenarian Petrus Serrarius (1600–1669) and the Anglo-Dutch Circle of Philo-Judaists', in *ibid.*, 73–94.

[5] See A. K. Offenberg, 'Jacob Jehuda Leon (1602–1675) and his Model of the Temple', in *ibid.*, 101–10.

[6] Israel, *European Jewry*, 154–6.

on occasion proudly showed their sumptuously calligraphed volumes to selected Christian savant acquaintances.[7]

These polemics, as we have seen, were written to address specific doubts and uncertainties within the Sephardi community, and were intended for an exclusively Jewish readership. However, there is evidence of Christian access to them from as early as the 1630s: Constantijn l'Empereur possessed several Jewish polemics, and mentioned in his correspondence that he was engaged in translating one of them into Latin.[8] In the middle years of the seventeenth century Menasseh ben Israel stands out as the member of the Amsterdam Sephardi community with by far the closest interaction with the Christian world. In addition to his extensive contacts in England, Menasseh was a close friend of Petrus Serrarius, and knew many members of his circle very well.[9] Menasseh's Judaeo-Christian milieu, however, was largely shaped by the millenarian excitement of the middle decades of the century. In the period after the Shabbatai Zevi affair, Christian interest in Judaism became less fervid, and was increasingly moulded by the more sober scholarly concerns of the Republic of Letters. In this intellectual climate Jewish philosophical and theological arguments were explored with a new meticulousness and sense of fascination.

The most important mediator between the Christian and Jewish intellectual worlds during the 1670s and 1680s was a man very different in outlook from Menasseh ben Israel: the physician and philosopher Isaac Orobio de Castro (*c*.1617–87). Orobio had trained as a physician in Spain before settling in Amsterdam in 1662.[10] His scientific background not only led him to take a prominent role in rebutting heresies within the Jewish community, such as the opinions of Juan de Prado; it also contributed to his unique status in Dutch intellectual life. His first foray into this world was his *Certamen Philosophicum* (1684), a contribution to the intense controversy over the opinions of Johannes Bredenburg.[11] A member of the radical Protestant Collegiant sect, Bredenburg had in 1675 published a trenchant refutation of Spinoza; to his own alarm, though, he found that while attempting

[7] On Jewish–non-Jewish sociability in this period, see Jonathan I. Israel, 'Gregorio Leti (1631–1701) and the Dutch Sephardi Elite at the close of the Seventeenth Century', in Ada Rapaport-Albert and Steven J. Zipperstein, eds., *Jewish History: Essays in Honour of Chimen Abramsky* (1988) 267–84.

[8] Peter van Rooden, 'Constantijn l'Empereur's Contacts with the Amsterdam Jews and his Confutation of Judaism', in van den Berg and van der Wall, *Jewish–Christian Relations*, 63–4. See also van Rooden, 'A Dutch Adaptation of Elias Montalto's *Tractado Sobre o Principio do Capitulo 53 de Jesaias*', LIAS 16 (1989) 189–204.

[9] See Ernestine van der Wall, 'Petrus Serrarius and Menasseh ben Israel', in Kaplan, Méchoulan and Popkin, eds., *Menasseh*, 164–90.

[10] Kaplan, *From Christianity to Judaism*, 1–109.

[11] On this controversy see Andrew Fix, *Prophecy and Reason* (1994) 225–31.

to condemn his arguments he had effectively been persuaded by them.[12] It seems that Bredenburg himself approached Orobio in the hope that his Jewish perspective might enable him to escape from the clutches of Spinozism.[13]

A similar respect for Orobio's opinions is a notable feature of his most famous encounter: the 'friendly conversation' that took place between him and the leading Remonstrant theologian Phillip van Limborch, a record of which van Limborch published a few years later under the title *De Veritate religionis Christianae: Amica Collatio cum Erudito Judaeo* (1687). Although polite dialogue between Jews and Christians was no longer in itself a cause for excitement in 1680s Holland, the formalised theological debate presented in this volume is unique in the period. The ambiguous dual purpose of this text is reflected in the awkward relationship between the two halves of its title: it is presented both as an assertion of 'the truth of Christianity' and as an open, non-partisan 'friendly conversation with an erudite Jew'. In his encounter with Orobio, van Limborch sought to integrate the traditionally adversarial, conversionist stance of Christianity towards Judaism with respect for the Early Enlightenment values of tolerance, courtesy and scholarly scrupulousness. Their debate in this sense straddles the threshold between medieval and distinctively modern modes of confrontation between Christianity and Judaism.

In contrast with the major medieval disputations, in which the Jewish participants were forced to argue within a framework almost entirely set by their Christian adversaries, in the *Amica Collatio* Orobio opens the proceedings, challenging van Limborch to demonstrate the scriptural basis for the key claims of Christianity.[14] Although Orobio was able to present his case with striking boldness, his approach closely echoed long-standing Jewish anti-Christian argumentative strategies. At least according to his own account, Nachmanides put forward a very similar case in the Barcelona disputation of 1263, arguing both that messianic belief is not fundamental to Judaism and that the scriptural prophecy that the Messiah would bring peace on Earth had manifestly not been fulfilled by Jesus.[15]

[12] Johannes Bredenburg, *Enervatio Tractatus Theologico-Politici* (1675); *Mathematica Demonstratio* (1684). See also Wiep van Bunge, 'On the Early Dutch Reception of the *Tractatus Theologico-Politicus*', *Studia Spinozana* 5 (1989) 230–3.

[13] Kaplan, *From Christianity to Judaism*, 263–6.

[14] Phillip van Limborch, *De Veritate religionis Christianae* (1687) 1–2.

[15] Nachmanides, *Vikuach*, in Maccoby, *Judaism on Trial*, 119–22.

Van Limborch's approach, however, was far from traditional.[16] In response to Orobio's questions, van Limborch makes no attempt to defend the prophetical basis of Christianity in the Old Testament. Rather than putting forward the traditional repudiations of the Jewish interpretation of disputed scriptural passages, he argues that it is neither necessary nor appropriate to try to draw such detailed proofs from the Bible. Eschewing close biblical exegesis, he attempts instead to stress a spiritualised, internal notion of revelation. Reason alone, van Limborch asserts, is sufficient to establish the inadequacy of the 'external cult' of Judaism, and its necessary supercession by the perfected religion instituted by the Messiah.[17] He rejects Orobio's demand that the scriptural basis of Christianity must be conclusively proven, attempting only to demonstrate the 'reasonableness' of the Christian interpretation of the Bible. The grounds on which Jesus is recognised as the Messiah, he argues, are at least as strong as those on which the Jews recognise the authority of Moses.[18]

Van Limborch shared with his close collaborators Jean Le Clerc and John Locke an aspiration towards a rationalist Christian theology, primarily based not on biblical interpretation, but on the universal insights of natural reason.[19] This attempt to integrate Christianity with Enlightenment rationalism implied a dramatic departure from tradition in many respects, including that of the status of the Jews: the truth of Christianity was from this perspective no longer dependent on their traditional, Augustinian role as 'custodians' of the original divine revelation.[20] The reappraised significance of the Jews in van Limborch's mind is, however, far from clear. He was ardently committed to the cause of Jewish conversionism: in his correspondence with John Locke, the debate with Orobio is discussed at length as a conversionist endeavour.[21] However, the importance of the conversion of the Jews was undermined by his own rationalist argument, which stood uneasily alongside the traditional Christian notion of the historical centrality of the Jews. This tension between a normalisation and a continued

---

[16] This assessment differs from the interpretations in Hans Joachim Schoeps, *The Jewish–Christian Argument: A History of Theologies in Conflict* (1965) 88–90 and Kaplan, *From Christianity to Judaism*, 284–5.

[17] Van Limborch, *De Veritate*, 5.   [18] *Ibid.*, 4.

[19] See Luisa Simonutti, *Arminianesimo e tolleranza nel seicento olandese: Il carteggio Ph. van Limborch/ J. le Clerc* (1984) 157–9; Pitassi, *Entre croire et savoir*, esp. 90–3; Jean Le Clerc, *A Treatise on the Causes of Incredulity* (1697) esp. 234–77.

[20] See Peter van Rooden and J. W. Wesselius, 'The Early Enlightenment and Judaism: the "Civil Dispute" between Philippus van Limborch and Isaac Orobio de Castro (1687)', *Studia Rosenthaliana* 21 (1987) 153.

[21] See Nabil Matar, 'John Locke and the Jews', *Journal of Ecclesiastical History* 44 (1993) 50.

exceptionalism of the status of Judaism is echoed in van Limborch's stance towards Orobio himself. Interwoven into the tone of scholarly respect that dominates the debate, he is intermittently extremely dismissive of all Jews, portraying them as intrinsically carnal and material, and therefore unable to respond to the spiritual message of the gospels.[22]

In his polite and respectful demeanour towards Orobio, van Limborch attempted to embrace the critical values and cultural standards of the Early Enlightenment, without sacrificing confidence in the supercessionist authority of Christianity. However, the instability of his representation of Judaism, and of Orobio himself as both a respected scholar and a representative of a people incapable of recognising spiritual truth, subtly undermined this project from within. Over the subsequent few decades, the awkwardness of van Limborch's integrative approach became increasingly apparent, and the last vestiges of consensus regarding the appropriate Christian response to Jewish arguments crumbled rapidly. The 'polite conversation' of the 1680s marked the effective end of the aspiration, born with the disputations of the thirteenth century, to establish the truth of Christianity and the falsity of Judaism through rational debate between members of the two parties. For the next eighty years Jewish arguments continued to resonate powerfully in non-Jewish thought; but they did so in a disembodied form, with little or no sense of their connection to a living, contemporary Judaism.

JEWISH ARGUMENTS AND THE SUBVERSION OF CHRISTIANITY

The *Amica Collatio* drew enduring interest across much of Europe in the early eighteenth century.[23] Other Sephardic anti-Christian polemics also at this time attracted significant attention from Early Enlightenment intellectuals. Several such manuscripts were sold at high prices at the auction in The Hague in 1715 of the 'Biblioteca Sarraziana', the vast private library of G. L. de la Sarraz, a Protestant minister and bibliophile.[24] Jacques Basnage, who was Sarraz' father-in-law, eagerly took the opportunity to consult the library just before its sale, and incorporated much new material from the polemics of Orobio, Morteira, Montalto and Menasseh ben Israel into the third edition of his *Histoire des Juifs* (1716).[25] Basnage treated these texts as striking intellectual curiosities, and described their contents in detail

---

[22] Van Limborch, *De Veritate*, 22 (and elsewhere).
[23] See Israel, *Radical Enlightenment*, 615, 688–90.
[24] Popkin, 'Jacques Basnage's *Histoire des Juifs* and the Biblioteca Sarraziana', 154–62.
[25] *Ibid.*, 157–8; Jacques Basnage, *Histoire des Juifs* (1716) IX, 1043ff.

without attempting to offer any response to them. In more radical circles, however, the same texts were put to inventive and ingenious use.

The most intricate reception of Orobio's writings was within the world of early eighteenth-century French clandestine philosophy. The initiator of this was the Deist Jean Lévesque de Burigny (1692–1785) who, while in Holland in 1720, made contact with learned Jews and had copies made of the anti-Christian texts by Orobio that they had shown him.[26] He then returned to France, and, in collaboration with his friend Thémiseul de Saint-Hyacinthe, introduced these texts into clandestine circulation there.[27] From the 1720s onwards, French manuscript translations of Orobio's writings circulated in various forms and under a variety of titles. At least four distinct French clandestine texts consist largely of translations or excerpts from his works.[28] To the radical readers of these manuscripts, the writings of Orobio and other Jewish controversialists constituted a rich and intriguing seam of arguments against Christian orthodoxy, readily mined for subversive use. However, the specifically Jewish flavour of the texts complicated their reception, and was handled in a variety of ways. While at times Orobio's Jewishness was subtly erased from the manuscript translations, at other times it was deliberately highlighted, in order to achieve an affect of daring, exoticism, indeterminacy or irony.

The most widely circulated manuscript based on Orobio's writings, measured by the number of extant copies, was titled *Dissertation sur le Messie*.[29] The main body of this text consisted of loose translation of selected chapters of Orobio's *Prevenciones Divinas*: his most trenchant attack on the doctrines of Christianity, which had circulated widely within late seventeenth-century Sephardi Jewry.[30] The subtitle of the French version encapsulates Orobio's argument: 'in which it is proven that he [the Messiah] has not yet come, and that, according to the promises of the prophets to the Jews, they are right still to await him'.[31] The overall argument of the French manuscript, however, is transformed by its introductory and concluding chapters, which are clearly written by a non-Jewish, philosophically radical author. These framing chapters, most probably written by Lévesque de Burigny or one

[26] Burigny describes this encounter in a much later letter; see Ira O. Wade, *The Clandestine Organization and Diffusion of Philosophic Ideas in France from 1700 to 1750* (1938) 229–30.

[27] Miguel Benítez, 'Orobio de Castro et la littérature clandestine', *La Face cachée des lumières* (1996) 150–1; Elisabeth Carayol, *Thémiseul de Saint-Hyacinthe, 1684–1746* (1984) 94, 142–5.

[28] See items 30/C XIV, 67/D XXXIII, 91/E XVIII, 145/P VIII and 234 in the inventory in Benítez, *Face cachée*, 20–61. See also Benítez, 'Orobio'; Anthony McKenna, 'Sur l'hérésie dans la littérature clandestine', *Dix-huitième siècle* 22 (1990) 301–13; Kaplan, *Orobio*, 451–57.

[29] Eight copies of this manuscript have hitherto been located; see Benítez, *Face cachée*, 33 (item 67).

[30] Orobio, *Prevenciones Divinas*, BL MS Harley 3430; Kaplan, *From Christianity to Judaism*, 243–5.

[31] *Dissertation sur le Messie*, BN FF 13351, 1.

of his collaborators, combine to cast a powerfully ironic inflection on the main body of the text.

Both interpolated chapters are written in *faux-naïf* style in an anonymous first person voice. The author begins by lamenting the 'absurd situation' of his ignorance of even a single letter of the language in which God dictated the Bible. In order to overcome this, and to satisfy his zeal to follow the biblical commandments 'as exactly as possible', he explains that he has turned for guidance to 'those who have preserved the purity of the holy language': the Jews.[32] Expert instruction from the most learned rabbis has convinced him of the enduring authenticity of Judaism, and of the falsity of Christianity. He then summarises the anti-Christian arguments that are elaborated in the main body of the text, drawn from Orobio. He dismisses the Trinity as contrary both to reason and Scripture, and ridicules the claim that the coming of Jesus Christ abrogated all the laws and ceremonies that are 'so clearly set out in the Pentateuch'.[33]

This fulsome respect for the Mosaic Law, however, is manifestly ironic. The feigned innocence of the authorial voice is intended not to suggest genuine admiration for rabbinic learning, but on the contrary to undermine Christianity by implying that Christian zeal logically reduces to such absurdity. A truly devoted Christian, the text provocatively implies, should become a Jew. In the light of this introduction, the chapters of the text translated from Orobio take on a highly ambiguous gloss. Purely as textual critique, the reader is invited to acknowledge the persuasiveness of their interpretative logic, which is presented as distinctively 'rabbinic'. The argumentative potency of this, however, is utterly reversed when the text is read in the ironic tone suggested by its introduction. Within the terms of scripturally based religion, Orobio's arguments defeat those of the Christians; but, far from suggesting the underlying validity of these arguments, this is intended to demonstrate the utter ridiculousness of all biblical reverence. Superficially, Judaism is presented as posing a telling challenge to Christian theology, but more fundamentally it is cast as a *reductio ad absurdam* of Christianity itself.

The ironic tone of the *Dissertation sur le Messie* is reaffirmed in its concluding editorial interpolation, once again in the voice of our anonymous narrator, who here enthusiastically celebrates the revealed authority of Judaism, established in perpetuity at Sinai.[34] Within the culture of French clandestine philosophy in this period, the irony of this argument is unmistakable: it was the most fundamental radical tenet that faith precisely

[32] *Ibid.*, 1–5.   [33] *Ibid.*, 20, 25.   [34] *Ibid.*, 168.

should not be based on revelation, but on reason. In ostensibly lauding the Sinaitic 'beatific vision',[35] the text in fact pointedly ridicules the allegedly static, dogmatic and irrational nature of Judaism, and implies that Christianity, if pushed to its logical conclusions, is scarcely any different.

Here and in other manuscript versions of Orobio's texts, his arguments are exploited in an extremely mobile and double-edged manner.[36] They are simultaneously used as a highly effective weapon against Christianity and portrayed as even more absurd than the Christian beliefs against which they are deployed. Orobio's voice at times serves almost as a ventriloquistic mouthpiece for Early Enlightenment rationalism, while also representing an archetype of blinkered rabbinism. The Jewish speaking position in these manuscripts is both fundamentally unstable and deeply ironic. These texts capture a powerful subversive pleasure in using the arguments of a Jew to undermine Christian theology. However, sustained identification with these arguments is never entertained. Repeatedly, Jewish victory is ironically undercut, through its portrayal as the inverted triumph of a religion even more absurd than Christianity, as a result of the topsy-turvy logic of irrational scriptural fundamentalism.

Beyond France, Jewish anti-Christian arguments also attracted the attention of the English Deists, and above all Anthony Collins, whose immense library included manuscript apologetics in Spanish by Troki, Morteira and Orobio.[37] Collins' *Discourse of the Grounds and Reasons of the Christian Religion* (1724), in which he argues that the Old Testament prophecies can only lend support to Christianity if they interpreted allegorically rather than literally, is clearly indebted to Orobio's detailed exegesis, in his *Prevenciones Divinas*, of the prophetical books of Daniel and Isaiah.[38] In his later *Scheme of Literal Prophecy Considered* (1727), which he wrote in response to the scandalised outcry provoked by the *Discourse*, Collins more explicitly aligns himself with a 'Jewish' insistence on the literal meaning of these biblical passages. He here attacks traditionalists such as Stillingfleet and Grotius for 'playing upon words', in ignoring the literal sense of the prophecies that was clearly 'intended by the writer', and instead supporting an allegorical interpretation.[39]

---

[35] *Ibid.*

[36] For a close examination of these texts, see Adam Sutcliffe, 'Judaism and Jewish Arguments in the Clandestine Radical Enlightenment', in Gianni Paganini, Miguel Benítez and James Dybikowski, eds., *Scepticisme, clandestinité et libre pensée* (2002) 97–113.

[37] James O'Higgins, *Anthony Collins: The Man and his Works* (1970) 26.

[38] Anthony Collins, *Discourse of the Grounds and Reasons of the Christian Religion* (1724); see also O'Higgins, *Anthony Collins*, 155–99.

[39] Anthony Collins, *A Scheme of Literal Prophecy Considered* (1727) 251.

In his earlier texts, however, Collins' attitude towards Judaism appears somewhat more ambivalent. Praising Josephus in his *Discourse of Freethinking* (1713), Collins expresses regret that his historiographical talents were wasted on 'such an illiterate, barbarous and ridiculous people'.[40] Despite his fascination with Jewish themes, there is no underlying stability to his view of Judaism. While drawing on Morteira and Orobio's literalist scriptural readings in order to challenge the Christian interpretation of biblical prophecy, Collins simultaneously argues in his *Discourse* of 1724 that the Talmud also diverged from the literal meaning of the Bible, and that therefore the allegorical biblical readings of Jesus and his disciples were in some sense characteristically Jewish. He repeatedly divides the Jews into opposing camps, by such means as drawing a sharp contrast between the ancient Sadducees and Pharisees.[41] Such splitting enables him to identify within Judaism the source of both the pure essence of natural religion and the priestly obfuscations that first obscured this wisdom.

For the English Deists, and to an even greater extent for the French compilers of clandestine manuscripts, writing was a performative practice, at least as concerned with the gestural enactment of intellectual transgression as with the formulation of new philosophical truths.[42] The simultaneous exoticism and familiarity of Judaism, and its status within traditional Christian theology as both foundational and abhorrent, made it a perfect site of symbolic confrontation and intellectual play for both English and French radicals. A characteristic mode of many clandestine manuscripts was layered argumentation, in which superficial readings are undermined by more hidden ones. The subversive use of Judaism typically followed this pattern, functioning as a critique that was itself subject to critique. To the authors and readers of these texts, the logical instability of these arguments was overshadowed by their polemical power, and by the intellectual pleasure of the paradoxes and inversions they produced.

Although Jewish arguments against Christianity were of noteworthy importance in the Early Enlightenment, it is not appropriate to consider them, as some scholars have done, as 'sources' of unbelief.[43] The arguments of Orobio, Morteira and others did not in themselves generate doubts in Christian minds, or even strengthen the opinions of radicals by providing

---

[40] Anthony Collins, *A Discourse of Freethinking* (1713) 157.

[41] Collins, *Scheme*, 20–1; *A Philosophical Inquiry Concerning Human Liberty* (1717) 60–1.

[42] See James A. Herrick, *The Radical Rhetoric of the English Deists* (1997).

[43] See Richard H. Popkin, 'Jewish Anti-Christian Arguments as a Source of Irreligion from the Seventeenth to the Early Nineteenth Century', in Hunter and Wootton, eds., *Atheism*, 159–81; Silvia Berti, 'At the Roots of Unbelief', *JHI* 56 (1995) 555–75.

them with new reasons to doubt the traditional truth claims of Christianity. Writers such as Collins and Lévesque de Burigny enthusiastically deployed their arguments not because they found them straightforwardly convincing, but because they constituted an extremely intriguing and versatile polemical resource. These Jewish sources highlighted, however, internal fractures within the formulation of Enlightenment rationalism. While critiquing mainstream Christianity, there was no space unequivocally external to this tradition on which Deists and radicals could ground their arguments. While Judaism in some sense offered such a non-Christian point of departure, it also represented the most fundamental roots of the Judaeo-Christian world view, in opposition to which these critics largely defined their intellectual project. In grappling with this paradox, they confronted their own inextricable philosophical connection to the tradition they sought to overcome.

COLLECTING JEWISH TEXTS; OBSERVING JEWISH CUSTOMS

The most notable late seventeenth-century German collector of Judaica was Johann Christoph Wagenseil (1633–1705), a Lutheran jurist and Professor at Altdorf. Wagenseil travelled extensively on both sides of the Mediterranean in search of Jewish anti-Christian polemics. He published a selection of his discoveries, including the infamous *Toldedot Yeshu*, Nachmanides' *Vikuach* (his account of the Barcelona disputation of 1263) and Isaac of Troki's *Hizzuk Emunah*, in their original Hebrew with his own translations into Latin, in his *Tela Ignea Satanae* ('The Fiery Darts of Satan') (1681).[44] Unlike the later French and English radicals, Wagenseil, as the title of his anthology suggests, regarded these texts with unambiguous revulsion, and provided his own detailed rebuttal of each of them. His preface dramatically warns the faint-hearted reader of the shocking blasphemies that are to follow, and concludes with an intense supplication for the conversion of the Jews.[45] However, despite his conservative adversarial stance towards Judaism, Wagenseil was also profoundly influenced by the intellectual values of the Early Enlightenment. A scholarly fascination with Judaism drew him to these texts, which his own anthology ironically for the first time made readily available to a Christian readership.

Wagenseil was concerned not only with the theological challenges posed by the Jews, but also with the social and political issues raised by their presence in Christian Europe. In a sequence of publications he sought to

---

[44] See Krauss and Horbury, *Jewish–Christian Controversy*, 142–4. Most of Wagenseil's anthology is translated into English in Morris Braude, *Conscience on Trial* (1952).
[45] Johann Christoph Wagenseil, *Tela Ignea Satanae* (1681) 1–5.

integrate a commitment to the authority and dignity of Christianity with a fair-minded, rational approach to Judaism. In his *Denunciatio Christiana* (1703) he anxiously appealed to all Christian princes to prevent the Jews' mocking the Nativity and other Christian symbols and beliefs; two years later, however, he wrote a detailed rebuttal of the blood libel.[46] He also published *Der Jüden Glaube und Aberglaube* (1705), the main body of which consisted of a new edition of a sixteenth-century account of Jewish beliefs and ceremonies by a converted Jew, Anthonius Margaritha, and which also incorporated material by a contemporary convert, Friedrich Albrecht Christiani. Although Wagenseil's introduction to this text is heavily freighted with anti-Jewish and conversionist rhetoric,[47] his volume made accessible a great deal of detailed and largely accurate information on Jewish worship and community life.

Wagenseil's measured, scholarly approach to Jewish anti-Christian arguments contrasted with the polemical stance of other German Hebraists. His contemporary Andreas Eisenmenger, Professor of Oriental Languages at Heidelberg, in best known as the author of the venomous *Entdecktes Judenthum* (1700). In this vast work, extending to over 2,000 pages, Eisenmenger combed the Talmud and other Jewish sources for what he regarded as defamations of Christianity. Although he was a competent textual scholar, Eisenmenger insisted on a coarsely literalist, non-contextual reading of Jewish texts.[48] He was also profoundly hostile towards Judaism, which he saw as irredeemably separatist and contemptuous towards all non-Jews.[49] In the late eighteenth and nineteenth century Eisenmenger's text served as a leading source book for anti-Jewish polemicists. In the context of the Early Enlightenment, however, the work stood out as a relatively isolated reaction against the prevalent emphasis on reasonableness and moderation in academic scholarship. An acknowledgement of its extremism is reflected in the successful petition of the Court Jew Samson Wertheimer to the Holy Roman Emperor, which resulted in an immediate ban on the circulation of *Entdecktes Judenthum*.[50]

Orthodox theological responses to Jewish anti-Christian arguments in this period more typically adopted a tone of self-conscious fair-mindedness. Richard Kidder's *Demonstratio Messiae* (1684–1700), a three-volume treatise

[46] Krauss and Horbury, *Jewish–Christian Controversy*, 143.

[47] J. C. Wagenseil, *Der Jüden Glaube und Aberglaube* (1705) esp. 29–33.

[48] Johann Andreas Eisenmenger, *Entdecktes Judenthum* (1700) esp. 58–61.

[49] See Katz, *From Prejudice to Destruction*, 13–22; Krauss and Horbury, *Jewish–Christian Controversy*, 180–3.

[50] Graetz, 'Court Jews', 39–40.

devoted to the defence of Christianity against all its enemies 'but particularly against the Jews', focused in particular on a hitherto virtually unknown
Latin anti-Christian mansuscript, the *Porta Veritatis*.[51] This text appears to
have been completed in Venice in 1634 by Jacob ben Amram, a former
Marrano who in 1630 had abandoned his senior position in the legal administration of Florence, reverted to Judaism and fled to the Venetian
ghetto.[52] Menasseh ben Israel sold a copy of the manuscript to Ralph
Cudworth when he came to England in the 1650s; it was this copy that
Kidder, then Bishop of Bath and Wells, read and refuted.[53]

Kidder pronounced the author of the text as the greatest Jew of his generation, and 'the sharpest and most considerable enemy to Christianity'.[54]
The *Porta Veritatis* alleged numerous misinterpretations of the Old
Testament and contradictions or errors in the New, each of which Kidder
painstakingly attempted to rebut. In general Kidder sustained a high degree of respect for the acuteness of Amram's arguments, and even appeared
to appreciate them for inspiring his own more comprehensive defence of
Christianity. However, at key moments of argumentative closure he typically slips into a more hostile rhetoric, accusing his adversary of stubborn-
ness, sophistry, contradiction or absurdity.[55] Like Wagenseil, Kidder desired
to engage Jewish texts in a spirit of Enlightenment reasonableness, but was
unable to reconcile this with his conviction of the falsity and perniciousness
of all Jewish challenges to Christian dogma.

Wagenseil's move from traditional Hebraism to the proto-
anthropological study of Jewish customs and beliefs reflected a wider ethnographic turn in Germany in the early eighteenth century. Several scholars,
such as Johannes Böner (1647–1720), Johann Jacob Schudt (1664–1722) and
Johann Bodenschatz, in this period published illustrated studies of Jewish
rituals and customs.[56] These texts were characterised by a close attention
to detail, and a general tone of informative objectivity. Jewish converts to
Christianity played an important role in interpreting this material and lend-
ing it authority. However, the potently anti-Christian invective that had
long been the expected hallmark of writings by Jewish converts was by the
early eighteenth century no longer so popular. The convert Paul Kirchner's
characteristically hostile *Jüdisches Ceremoniel* (1717) was revised and

[51] MS Clark A527M3.P839 1634.
[52] J. M. Hillesum, 'De *Porta Veritatis* van Jacob van Amram', *Het Boek* 17 (1928) 346.
[53] Richard Kidder, *A Demonstration of the Messias* (1726 (1684–1700)) II, ii–iii.
[54] *Ibid.*, III, 138.   [55] *Ibid.*, e.g. 138, 145, 152, 155.
[56] Johann Jacob Schudt, *Jüdische Merkwürdigkeiten* (1714–18); Johann C. G. Bodenschatz, *Kirchliche
Verfassung der heutigen deutschen Juden* (1748–9). See Richard I. Cohen, *Jewish Icons: Art and Society
in Modern Europe* (1998) 52–66.

republished by an amateur Hebraist, Sebastian Jugendres, in 1724. This edition retained some elements of Kirchner's revelatory sensationalism, but in general muted his polemic, and presented itself as an objective and scholarly study of Jewish religious customs.[57] These texts reflect a striking interest among early eighteenth-century Germans in the Jewish communities in their midst – a domestic fascination rising in parallel with the increasing popularity and descriptive detail of travel literature from overseas.[58] All these studies were written from a normatively Christian perspective. However, their emphasis on the open and respectable religiosity of non-Christians, while frequently exoticising or demeaning these communities, could also suggest a similarity between all religions, which implicitly undermined the assumed uniqueness and superiority of Christianity.

Nowhere is this implication more powerfully conveyed than in the Enlightenment's boldest and most thorough work of comparative religion, Bernard Picart's immensely successful *Cérémonies et coutumes religieuses de tous les peuples du monde* (1723). This lavish seven-volume study was almost immediately translated into English and Dutch, and rapidly established itself as one of the most popular and prized books across Europe.[59] Unlike the theologically orthodox German writers on Jewish customs, Picart was a self-conscious freethinker, and during the 1710s was a leading member, along with John Toland, Prosper Marchand and others, of a proto-Masonic secret society in The Hague, the 'Knights of Jubilation'.[60] The son of a Parisian engraver, as a young man he abandoned his father's Catholicism, but perpetuated his profession. Around 1710 he joined the Huguenot refuge in the Dutch Republic, where, under the influence of his friends in the intellectual and publishing worlds, he absorbed a radically deistic, rational worldview. The impact of the *Cérémonies et coutumes*, a collaboration with the publisher Jean Bernard, was above all due to Picart's subtle artistic conveyance of this perspective in the over 200 meticulous engravings that illustrate the work.

Picart's first volume opens with a lengthy study of the ceremonies of the Jews. While much of the text is drawn from standard seventeenth-century accounts by Leone Modena and Richard Simon, the many accompanying illustrations of Jewish domestic and public rituals present an almost obsessively precise and extremely dignified view of Jewish life. Picart depicts

[57] Elisheva Carlebach, *Divided Souls: Converts from Judaism in Germany, 1500–1750* (2001) 205–11; Paul Christian Kirchner, *Jüdisches Ceremoniel* (1724).
[58] See Mary Louise Pratt, *Imperial Eyes: Travel Writing and Transculturation* (1992) 15–37; Shulamit Volkov, 'Exploring the Other: The Enlightenment's Search for the Boundaries of Humanity', in Robert S. Wistrich, ed., *Demonizing the Other: Antisemitism, Racism and Xenophobia* (1999) 148–67.
[59] Cohen, *Jewish Icons*, 43.   [60] See Jacob, *The Radical Enlightenment*, esp. 164–9.

Figure 8 Bernard Picart, *The Ceremonies and Religious Customs of the various Nations of the known world*, London, 1733–9. Engraving of a Sephardi Passover Seder. Note the detailed annotations, and the black servant eating with the family.

most annual festivals and life-cycle rituals, including a circumcision, as well as the procedure for the laying of *tefillin* (phylacteries) for prayer. He expressly notes that his engraving of a domestic Passover seder was drawn from life. This illustration, like many others, is carefully annotated. He draws attention to the confident participation of women in the ritual, and to the fact that Jewish servants are included, and eat at the same table (see figure 8). These elegant images of Jewish domesticity, which were later extremely popular among nineteenth-century bourgeois Jews, powerfully demystified Judaism, and asserted its parity of status alongside all the other religions of the world.[61]

In the context of Picart's wider comparative project, however, this respectful representation is undercut by a subtle but unmistakable critique of

---

[61] Cohen, *Jewish Icons*, 43–52.

The ACAFOTH, or the
Seven turns round the Coffin.   Les ACAFOTH ou les sept
tours autour du CERCUEIL.

Figure 9 Bernard Picart, *The Ceremonies and Religious Customs of the various Nations of the known world*, London, 1733–9. Engraving of the circling of the coffin before a Sephardi burial.

all religious rituals. The introductory prelude makes clear the text's deistic insistence on the human origin of all ceremonies, declaring as its subject 'the various Customs which men have introduced into religious worship in Honour of the supreme Being'.[62] As the study progresses from Judaism and Catholicism, via the religions of North America, Africa and Asia, to Greek Orthodoxy, the major Protestant sects and Islam, the calendrical festivals and rites of passage of these cultures, although exotically varied in their external trappings, appear strongly to echo one other in their underlying structures. The stately circulation of the Amsterdam Sephardim around a coffin about to be buried differs little in essence, for example, from Picart's representation of the funeral ceremony of the natives of Guinea (see figures 9 and 10).[63] These parallels are only gently hinted at, and undoubtedly

[62] Bernard Picart, *The Ceremonies and Religious Customs of the various Nations of the known world*, 7 vols. (1733–9 (1723)) I, 16.
[63] *Ibid.*, I, 243; IV, 445.

FUNERAL CEREMONY
of the NATIVES *of* GUINEA

CEREMONIE FUNEBRE
des HABITANS *de* GUINEE.

Figure 10 Bernard Picart, *The Ceremonies and Religious Customs of the various Nations of the known world*, London, 1733–9. Engraving of a funeral ceremony of the natives of Guinea.

scarcely registered in the minds of many readers, for whom the *Cérémonies et coutumes* probably served largely as an elegant coffee-table book. A sense of the text's subversive implication, however, must often have occurred even to those who only casually flipped through Picart's engravings. The religions of the world, these illustrations gently suggest, are ultimately very similar to each other, with the most significant difference being that in distant continents people seem to experience their rituals more vividly and passionately, and perform them wearing considerably fewer clothes.

FROM BIBLICAL RATIONALISATION TO BIBLICAL SATIRE

Judaism was, however, inescapably of special significance in the formation of Enlightenment rationalism. Despite the attempt of individuals such as Picart to treat it on the same terms as all human religions, the foundational status of Judaism in Christian thought and culture repeatedly brought Early Enlightenment radicals into confrontation with the authority of the Old

Testament. Alternative theologies and counter-histories inevitably focused on the Hebrew scriptures, attempting either to reappraise them in accordance with reason, or, more boldly, to dismiss them as amoral, unreliable or irrelevant. Both these strategies were problematic. The Jewish Bible, because of its unique scope and cultural authority, was extremely resistant both to easy rationalisation and to marginalisation.

The acute difficulties inherent in Early Enlightenment attempts to establish a rational biblical hermeneutics were first brought to the fore in the bitter controversy provoked by the publication of Balthasar Bekker's *De Betoverde Weereld* ('The World Bewitched') (1691). In this text Bekker tried to show from a Cartesian, reasoned perspective that angels and demons could not intervene in human affairs. He insisted on the divinely revealed perfection of the Bible, and argued, echoing Adriaan Koerbagh, that the Hebrew of the Bible was utterly free of superstition: the word *malachim*, for example, should be translated straightforwardly as 'messengers', rather than 'angels'.[64] However, when interpreting key scriptural episodes, such as the Fall, in which the intervention of divine or satanic agents is crucial to the narrative, Bekker fell back on a somewhat different argument. Invoking the long-standing exegetical principle of accommodation – the notion that the language of Scripture was tailored to accord with the intellectual capacities of its original audience – he claimed that the many biblical references to angels, spirits and demons were allegorical embellishments, designed to accommodate the superstitious mentality of the ancient Hebrews.[65]

Bekker's ambition was to provide a convincing integration of the paramountcy of reason and the authority of Scripture. However, the scandal provoked by his text showed that his middle path satisfied few readers: he was widely condemned both by traditional theologians and by other Cartesian philosophers, many of whom dismissed him as a 'Spinozist'.[66] His own argument, moreover, was fundamentally fractured, and this is most clearly apparent in the confusion surrounding his stance towards Judaism. Bekker both privileges the Jews, as the people to whom the truths of pure monotheism were first revealed, and implicitly blames them for the opacity of this message in the Bible: it was due to their superstitious tastes that it

---

[64] Balthasar Bekker, *Le Monde Enchanté* (1694 (1691)) II, 119–26, 283. See also Andrew Fix, 'Bekker and Spinoza', in Van Bunge and Klever, eds., *Spinozism*, 26–7.

[65] See Wiep van Bunge, 'Balthasar Bekker's Cartesian Hermeneutics and the Challenge of Spinozism', *British Journal for the History of Philosophy* 1 (1993) 63–6. On the doctrine of accommodation see Funkenstein, *Theology*, 213–9.

[66] See, for example, the combined refutation of Bekker and Spinoza in F. E. Kettner, *De Duobus Impostoribus* (1694). See also Fix, 'Bekker and Spinoza', 23–5; Jonathan Israel, 'The Bekker Controversies as a Turning Point in the History of Dutch Culture and Thought', *Dutch Crossing* 20 (1996) 1–17.

had been necessary to introduce such misleading imagery into Scripture. He offers a lengthy account of the degeneration of Judaism into its contemporary state of paganised superstition, which he regards as uniquely scandalous because it clashes so absolutely with the originary principles of the religion.[67] The Jews are thus simultaneously represented as uniquely intimate with divine truth and irredeemably distant from it. Bekker's undoubtedly sincere commitment to the authority of the Bible ultimately could not be resolved with his desire to subordinate all texts to the authority of reason. As the recipients and guardians of Scripture, the Jews stand in his text as the embodied historical subjects over whom these opposing intellectual forces strain against each other.

The bitter controversy provoked by *De Betoverde Weereld* underlined the philosophical difficulties inherent in integrating rationalist arguments into a sustainable positive theology. From the 1690s onwards, however, at some level no doubt in response to this realisation, radical writers began to turn away from earnest argument and towards a more playful, satirical approach. A new genre of literary philosophy emerged in the Dutch Republic, pioneered by Johannes Duijkerius' anonymously published *Philopater* novels (1691 and 1697), which mercilessly lampooned established religion. Duijkerius' immensely popular first novel ridicules the sterile theological pedantry of the Dutch Reformed Church. The eponymous Philopater, in training (as was his creator) for the priesthood, wryly observes the absurdities of seminary life, and particularly laments the long hours of Hebrew study to which he is subjected. His fellow-students study the Mosaic religion in such arcane detail, he notes, that it was as if they were themselves intending to become Jewish.[68] As Philopater's opinions progress from orthodox Calvinism to ardent Spinozism, the narrative becomes more outspokenly philosophical. Our hero's discovery of the universal truth of reason is contrasted with the particularism of all three major monotheistic religions.[69] However, Judaism, rather than Christianity or Islam, is repeatedly cast as archetypal of theocratic irrelevance and narrowness.

The use of literary satire enabled writers such as Duijkerius to sidestep the philosophical dilemmas that had beset Bekker, while challenging orthodox opinions with devastating effect. This strategy was soon imitated in French by Simon Tyssot de Patot, a Huguenot refugee in the Overijssel

---

[67] Bekker, *Monde Enchanté*, IV, 185.
[68] Johannes Duijkerius, *Het Leven van Philopater* (1991 (1691)) 83–4. On Duijkerius, see Israel, *Dutch Republic*, 923; Geraldine Maréchal, 'Inleiding' to *Het leven van Philopater, en Vervolg van 't leven van Philopater* (1991) 11–38.
[69] Johannes Duijkerius, *Vervolg van 't leven van Philopater* (1991 (1697)) 164–5.

town of Deventer. Tyssot's *Voyages et Avantures de Jacques Massé* (c.1715) takes the form of meandering travelogue, imbued with much powerful advocacy of reason and parody of conventional religion. Among the characters the narrator meets on his travels is a certain Michob, 'a wandering Jew, who had once been a servant of Pontius Pilate'.[70] Michob entertains a crowd near Bordeaux harbour late into the night with tales from his seventeen centuries of peripatetic existence, including an absurdly literalistic description of the resurrection of the saints in Jerusalem after Jesus Christ's crucifixion. Tyssot here inverts the traditional didactic significance of the Wandering Jew, deploying Michob to ridicule rather than reinforce Christian dogma. Elsewhere, however, Judaism itself is subjected to ridicule. Adopting a polemically charged version of the concept of accommodation, he suggests that only the foolishness of the Jews enabled them to be duped by the preposterous absurdities of the Old Testament: 'There is no doubt . . . that the notion of a God who works and who rests can only be swallowed by an extremely ignorant and primitive people.'[71]

In Germany, radical philosophy followed a similar trend, from the constructive seriousness of such works as E. W. Tschirnhaus' *Medicina Mentis* (1687) and Friedrich Wilhelm Stosch's *Concordia Rationis et Fidei* (1692) to the semi-novelesque style of Johann Christian Edelmann's *Moses mit Aufgedeckten Angesicht* (1740). This text takes the form of a dialogue between the enlightened 'Lichtlieb' and his pious brother 'Blindling', who spends all his time assiduously studying the Bible. Almost the first argument used by Lichtlieb to convince his brother of the futility of this activity is to compare him to the Jews, who study Scripture continually, in its original language, but clearly derive no benefit from it.[72] Edelmann's text expresses explicitly an opposition implicit in much earlier German deistic thought, in which a minimalist rational Christianity is sharply contrasted against the textual dogmatism of Judaism.

JUDAEOPHOBIA AND FRENCH CLANDESTINE PHILOSOPHY

For writers of subversive philosophy Judaism lent itself extremely well to satire. Jews were familiar enough to eighteenth-century readers to be a

---

[70] Simon Tyssot de Patot, *Voyages et Avantures de Jacques Massé* (1714–17) 12.

[71] *Ibid.*, 169–70. On Tyssot de Patot see David Rice McKee, *Simon Tyssot de Patot and the Seventeenth Century Background of Critical Deism* (1941); Audrey Rosenberg, *Tyssot de Patot and his Work, 1655–1738* (1972).

[72] Johann Christian Edelmann, *Moses mit Aufgedeckten Angesicht* (1740) 5–7. See also Rüdiger Otto, 'Johann Christian Edelmann's Criticism of the Bible and its Relation to Spinoza', in van Bunge and Klever, eds., *Spinozism*, 171–88; Walter Grossman, *Johann Christian Edelmann: From Orthodoxy to Enlightenment* (1976) 111–40.

resonant butt of ridicule, but also exotic and abstract enough for an almost limitless range of characterisations and opinions to be projected on
to them. Positioned as the vague inverse of the positive, rational values
of philosophical radicalism, Judaism was an extremely polymorphous target, readily refashioned to suit the needs of the polemical moment. These
arguments were deployed with particular vigorousness in the clandestine
philosophical manuscripts that circulated in France in the first half of the
eighteenth century. Whereas in England and in Germany heterodoxy and
orthodoxy remained in dialogue with each other in this period, the tight
French censorship regime ironically fostered the emergence of a uniquely
outspoken world of clandestine philosophical speculation. The recurrent
themes of this underground literature – scientific speculation, irreligious
polemic and theories of materialism and natural religion – are explored
extensively in a wide range of anonymous clandestine manuscripts.[73] With
striking regularity, Judaism in some form is positioned in these texts as the
defining antithesis of their authors' own implied values and opinions.

The underground circulation of radical philosophy in France was particularly associated with the manuscript form, which offered several advantages over the printed book. Manuscripts could be circulated more discreetly
and produced far more cheaply than books; they could also freely incorporate pirated extracts from printed texts, and could easily be modified from
copy to copy.[74] According to Roger Chartier, the 'author function' was in
the process of emergence in the early eighteenth century: authors were now
increasingly identified as the unique proprietors of their texts, in contrast
to the Renaissance period, when the printer, bookseller, author and reader
were all regarded as equally complicit in the diffusion of subversive ideas
in print.[75] The culture of the French radical Enlightenment was in rebellion against this process: plagiarism, tendentious translation and authorial
ventriloquism or anonymity were all standard practice. Clandestine texts
were regarded as ownerless, and were freely embellished and modified.[76]
The anti-Christian arguments of Orobio de Castro, as we have seen, were
utilised in this clandestine tradition in an extremely mobile and ambiguous fashion. The deployment of Judaism in other texts is similarly slippery,

[73] For an inventory of these manuscripts, listing 213 distinct texts known to have circulated, see Benítez, *Face cachée*, 20–61.
[74] See Ann Thomson, 'Qu'est-ce qu'un manuscrit clandestin?', in Olivier Bloch, ed., *Le Matérialisme du XVIII siècle et la littérature clandestine* (1982) 13–16; François Moureau, 'La plume et le plomb', in Moureau, ed., *De bonne main* (1993) 5–16.
[75] Chartier, *The Order of Books*, 41–2, 50.
[76] See Claudine Cohen, 'La Communication manuscrite et la genèse du Telliamed', in Moureau, ed., *De bonne main*, 59–69; Jeroom Vercruysse, 'Les Trois Langages du Rabbin de Woolston', in Guido Canziani, ed., *Filosofia e religione nella letteratura clandestina* (1994) 352–3.

reflecting a much greater concern for polemic effect than for intellectual coherence. However, Judaism was of key philosophical importance for the authors and compilers of these texts, because it starkly highlighted many of the underlying difficulties inherent in their ambition to construct purely rational accounts of history, politics and religion. The handling of Jewish themes in these texts thus offers a unique insight into the relationship of the Early Enlightenment to these occluded philosophical paradoxes.

The assertion of an alternative account of the past that toppled the historical authority of the Bible was a recurrent theme of several clandestine manuscripts. The discrediting of Scripture, however, was not a straightforward project, and was approached through various exegetical strategies.[77] In each case, the historical status of the Jewish past stood out as a jarringly awkward problem, resistant both to an enduring biblical exceptionalism and to assimilation into the historical mainstream. In the *Traité des Trois Imposteurs*, one of the most widely circulated manuscripts of the early eighteenth century, Moses is cast as a masterful impostor, who took advantage of the ignorance of the Jewish people to assert his authority over them.[78] At times the *Traité* seems to suggest that this is simply a prominent example of the natural pattern of the manipulation of the weak by the strong: 'Ambitious people', it is noted, 'have always been masters of the art of deception.'[79] However, the text also suggests that Moses carries a special culpability, having initiated the tradition of imposture that was later imitated by Jesus and Mohammed. The Jews are also portrayed as uniquely gullible: 'There had never existed a more ignorant, or, therefore, more credulous people.'[80] The *Traité*, like several other manuscripts of the period, hovers awkwardly between attempting to normalise the ancient Jewish past and subjecting it to uniquely intense condemnation.[81]

Some clandestine texts express an extremely strident hostility towards Judaism. In the *Nouvelle Moysade*, the travel narrative of a seeker after wisdom who turns in the hope of inspiration to Judaism, we read a horrified account of our narrator's encounter with Jewish barbarism, absurdity and fanaticism. The text concludes with an intense statement of his revulsion towards Judaism: 'And you, furious people, vile and coarse men, deserving slaves to the yoke that you bear, go, take your books, and get away from

---

[77] For an analysis of these strategies see Winfried Schröder, *Ursprünge des Atheismus: Untersuchungen zur Metaphysik- und Religionskritik des 17. und 18. Jahrhunderts* (1998) 94–122.
[78] *Traité des Trois Imposteurs* (1994 (1719)) 115. See Wade, *Clandestine Organization*, 124–40.
[79] *Trois Imposteurs*, 110.   [80] *Ibid.*, 115.
[81] For examples of this ambiguity in other clandestine manuscripts, see *Dissertation sur Moyse*, MS Maz. 1194, 59–111; *Extrait des ouvrages du Comte de Zinzendorf*, MS Aix 10; *Le rabbinisme renversé*, MS Maz. 1197; *La Nouvelle Moysade*, MS Aix 10.

me.'[82] Such extreme ferocity extends beyond the stylistic norms of satire, and suggests a underlying frustrated anger. No amount of rationalist satire could dislodge the Jewish Bible from its foundational position in the Judaeo-Christian view of history. The anomalous survival of the Jews and their texts was a persistent reminder of the failure of the inconclusivity of attempts to establish a fully convincing counter-history. In an era prior to the development of archaeology and rigorous linguistic analysis, clandestine polemicists had no authoritative extra-textual evidence with which to challenge the Bible. They could only reiterate familiar anti-biblical arguments with increasing insistency and aggression.

One of the most widely circulated clandestine manuscripts, the *Opinions des Anciens sur les Juifs*, assembled at some stage before 1722 by Jean Baptiste de Mirabaud (1675–1760), secretary of the Académie Française, attempted to establish an alternative account of the history of the Jews.[83] Drawing on a wide range of classical sources, including Diodorus Siculus, Strabo, Plutarch, Juvenal, Horace and Martial, the manuscript asserted that the ancients' hatred of the Jews had been universal, and that this had been based on solid grounds: the Jews' customs were absurd, and they were known to be of bad character, absurdly credulous and arrogantly contemptuous towards all non-Jews.[84] By discrediting the reputation of the ancient Jews, Mirabaud obliquely but unambiguously undermined the authority of Christianity. The identification of Jesus as the Messiah, the text noted, was based on the reports of 'a few members of the vilest rabble'.[85] However, this argument was dependent on a polemical assault on Judaism that was itself based on unstable evidence. The shrill tone of Mirabaud's compilation almost made transparent the highly selective and decontextualised nature of its use of classical sources, which were themselves also of possibly dubious reliability.

In a twin compilation titled *Opinions des Anciens sur le monde*, Mirabaud used a similar strategy to undermine the Old Testament account of Creation. Almost all ancient philosophers, as well as most extra-European cultures, he concludes from his survey, believed the world to be eternal: only the Jews, in order to flatter their own antiquity, had invented an account of Creation with which they could associate their own origins.[86] In a similar fashion, Henri de Boulainvilliers, in his *Abregé de l'Histoire Universelle Jusqu'à l'Exode*, puts forward a rationalist reading of Genesis and Exodus that is in fact an anti-biblical counter-history, in which he

---

[82] *La Nouvelle Moysade*, MS Aix 10, 3.   [83] See Wade, *Clandestine Organization*, 205–21.
[84] *Opinions des Anciens sur les Juifs*, BN NAF 4369, 172–82, 206–7.   [85] *Ibid.*, 372.
[86] *Opinions des Anciens sur le monde*, BN FF 14696, 35–6.

systematically belittles Jewish history and emphasises the contrasting sophistication of the Egyptians.[87] These texts challenged the authority of
the Old Testament simply by holding other narratives, such as those of the
Chinese and Indians, against it. Despite the rationalist rhetoric that framed
these challenges, no attempts were made to explore the inner meanings or
epistemological authority of these alternative accounts.[88] In combating as-
sertions with counter-assertions, these clandestine manuscripts established
no logically sturdy basis for their claims. Their argumentative impact was
therefore dependent not on authoritative evidence or on rational proof, but
on the power of their rhetorical invective, the brunt of which was almost
exclusively borne by Judaism.

The natural mode of the clandestine philosophical genre was attack. In
attempting to enunciate new, positive conceptions of metaphysics, history
and religion, radicals had no decisive intellectual tools at their disposal that
could enable them to put forward arguments that were conclusively more
certain than those of the old orthodoxy. Their attempts to establish an
alternative paradigm were therefore largely based on the critique of established opinions, and, more often than not, their basis in the Old Testament.
Judaism was thus uniquely exposed in this tradition as a key polemical target. However, because of the enduring and inescapable dominance of the
Bible in eighteenth-century European thought, Jewish texts and arguments
were also, as we have seen, a vital positive resource for philosophical radicals. Despite the argumentative fluidity of the clandestine tradition, and its
preference for satire and ridicule over sustained prepositional advocacy, at
a certain point these two approaches became inseparable from each other.
It was almost impossible to put forward a sustained critique of Christianity without also to some extent advancing an alternative vision of history,
metaphysics or ethics. These propositions, however, were almost invariably
themselves enmeshed in the same Judaeo-Christian tradition as the orthodoxies against which they were pitted. The inextricable relationship of
Enlightenment radicalism to the narratives and beliefs it sought to overthrow is thus starkly highlighted in the profoundly ambivalent and contradictory stances taken in these clandestine manuscripts towards Judaism.

The early development of Enlightenment thought was characterised by
a number of key ambiguities. Prominent among these was a recurrent
tension between elitism and popularism. The radical slogans of this period are deeply democratising, expressing the demand that knowledge and

---

[87] *Abregé de l'Histoire Universelle Jusqu'à l'Exode*, BN FF 6363.
[88] See Miguel Benitez, 'L'ailleurs dans le littérature clandestine: la Chine comme argument',
Face cachée, 409–10.

truth should be accessible to all. However, in many radical texts there is an implication that the ignorant are not really capable of true philosophical knowledge.[89] This more general ambiguity is echoed in the contrasting philosophical responses to Judaism in this period. The subcultures and traditions within Judaism with which Early Enlightenment radicals at times identified – the Kabbalah, Moses' Egyptian *prisca theologica*, Essenian philosophy – are all understood as elitist traditions of knowledge, accessible only to an initiated few. As a popular mass, however, the Jews are almost invariably represented extremely negatively, as the quintessence of stupidity, legalism and primitivism.

This internally split positioning of Judaism has extremely deep roots. Its theological essence was perhaps most clearly expressed in Blaise Pascal's *Pensées* (1670):

Carnal Jews are half-way between Christians and pagans. Pagans do not know God and only love earthly things; Jews know the true God and only love earthly things; Christians know the true God and do not love earthly things. Jews and pagans love the same possessions, Jews and Christians know the same God.

Jews were of two kinds: one kind had pagan sensitivities, the other Christian ones.[90]

The religiosity of Pascal's statement marks it as deeply Catholic in spirit; however, its structured binary logic in some sense associates it with the spirit of the Enlightenment. While to a considerable extent Enlightenment radicalism was defined in anti-Pascalian terms, it is also possible to discern his positive influence on rationalist thought.[91] In the eighteenth century, Jews were also persistently situated on the middle ground between truth and falsity, predominantly conceived not as the opposition of Christianity to paganism, but as that of reason against superstition. The ideologically necessary but philosophically impossible border between reason and unreason was repeatedly drawn through the middle of the intermediate intellectual terrain where Judaism was exiled.

Thinkers such as Pascal and Bayle were intensely conscious of the delicate incommensurability of reason and faith, and of the indispensability of either realm. Later proponents of Enlightenment, however, tended to have more confidence in the self-sufficiency of reason. Whereas Pascal was acutely aware of his divided stance towards Judaism, in the printed texts

[89] See Miguel Benitez, 'Lumières et élitisme dans les manuscrits clandestins', *Face cachée*, 199–211.
[90] Blaise Pascal, *Pensées* (1995 (1670)) 85.
[91] Anthony McKenna, *De Pascal à Voltaire* (1990) esp. 634–76; 'Les *Pensées* de Pascal dans les manuscrits clandestins du XVIIIe siècle', in Bloch, ed., *Matérialisme*, 131–42.

and clandestine manuscripts of the Early Enlightenment this split was al-most always heavily occluded. These radical texts were almost all written in a tone of brash confidence and finality. However, their repressed contra-dictions, in particular in relation to Judaism, often highlight the premature nature of their argumentative closure.

Polemical anger and violence was a frequent symptom of this philosoph-ical haste. However, the consequences of this impatience were by no means unambiguously negative. A sense of certainty and commitment was nec-essary in order to turn the Enlightenment into a practical project. Radical thinkers in the early eighteenth century were not simply concerned with abstract issues; they were often much more anxious to achieve concrete so-cial and institutional change. Bekker's proof that spirits could not intervene in human affairs may not quite have been philosophically convincing, but it had a practical impact: in 1696, one Prussian woman whose condemna-tion for witchcraft had been overturned by the use of Bekker's arguments travelled all the way to Amsterdam to thank him personally.[92] Similarly, the wider Enlightenment campaign against the dominance of established clerical orthodoxies had a very important social and political dimension, putting forward a new vision of citizenship, and promoting pluralistic tol-eration. These issues were of extremely wide importance, and in some cases particularly so for the Jews. It is in this social and political realm that the ironies of the Enlightenment are apparent in their fullest complexity and significance.

[92] Antonello Scibilia, 'Balthasar Bekker: articulazioni e limiti di una lotta', in Sergio Bertelli, ed., *Il libertinismo in Europa* (1980) 288–9.

PART III

Judaism, nationhood and the politics of Enlightenment

CHAPTER 10

Utopianism, republicanism, cosmopolitanism

The resonance of Judaic imagery in European political thought was utterly transformed over the course of the Enlightenment. In his study of the use of the Exodus narrative in the western tradition of political radicalism, Michael Walzer has noted that while the language of the English Puritan preachers of the mid seventeenth century was suffused with references to the biblical Exodus, the story was conspicuously absent from the rhetoric of the French Revolution. While the Old Testament was the cultural touchstone of transformative politics in England in the 1650s, the French revolutionaries of the 1790s were hostile to the traditional Judaeo-Christian view of history, and seemed deliberately to avoid turning to the Bible for political inspiration.[1] This dramatic shift of perspective occurred gradually, and was far from straightforward. From the 1660s onwards, as religious millenarianism gave way to secular rationalism as the dominant anti-establishment paradigm, expectancy of imminent change waned, and the fervent biblical politics of the mid seventeenth century gave way to a more ambivalent approach to the politics of the Old Testament. The utopian celebration of the Republic of the Hebrews by James Harrington and others unmistakably influenced Early Enlightenment radicals such as John Toland in England and Pietro Giannone in Italy. However, by the early eighteenth century Judaic politics, while still an inspiring source of visionary idealism, was inextricably ensnared in the philosophical controversies of the Enlightenment itself, and could no longer be invoked so innocently.

THE MOSAIC REPUBLIC AND THE DUTCH REPUBLIC

Spinoza places a considerable emphasis in his *Tractatus Theologico-Politicus* on the political organisation of the Mosaic Republic. In accordance with standard Christian opinion on the subject, he stresses the pure theocracy

---

[1] Michael Walzer, *Exodus and Revolution* (1985) 5.

of God's authority over the ancient Hebrews: 'in the Hebrew state the civil and religious authority, each consisting solely of obedience to God, were one and the same'.[2] He examines the laws of the state in some detail, and discusses the advantages of several of them, such as universal legal instruction (among men), the inclusion of all male adults in the army and the return of alienated land in Jubilee years.[3] He particularly emphasises the republicanism of the ancient Hebrews. Their constitution, he comments, functioned excellently for as long as a republic was maintained: only when they instituted a monarchy did civil strife and other problems emerge. This example serves as the crucial basis for his argument that 'every dominion should retain its original form'; and therefore, in pointed opposition to the resurgent pseudo-monarchic Orangism in the Dutch Republic in the late 1660s, that Spinoza's own home dominion should always resist monarchy or over-mighty overlordship.[4]

The *Tractatus Theologico-Politicus* is an intensely political text. It was written by Spinoza in large measure as an urgent defence of the democratic structures of the Dutch Republic, in opposition to the twin threats posed to them by Orangism and religious intolerance.[5] His defence of Dutch republicanism is the closing climax of the treatise, for which all preceding political arguments serve as preparation. However, precisely for this reason it would be a mistake to take the *Tractatus Theologico-Politicus* as Spinoza's final word on scriptural politics. In this text praise for the Mosaic regime is pressed into service as support for the endangered Dutch polity, which had long flattered itself with an imagined similarity to the ancient Hebrew republic. It is striking, though, that in his unfinished *Tractatus Politicus*, in which Spinoza sets out to establish the principles of politics in abstract terms, he makes absolutely no reference to Scripture. In this text Spinoza treats politics as a science, and attempts to ground it on mathematically certain principals, as he had done for morals in his *Ethics*.[6] He therefore avoids textual exegesis, arguing as much as possible directly from principles of abstract reason, supplemented by brief historical examples.

The Hebrew scriptures, for Spinoza, offer a distorted but authentic account of the distant Jewish past. This narrative is of interest in itself because of its uniqueness and venerability, and because it contains much that can be used, as moral or historical evidence, in support of the furtherance of human happiness. It does not, however, contain any unique political wisdom or knowledge. In his first *Tractatus*, Spinoza does not hesitate to use

[2] *TTP*, 219–20.   [3] *Ibid.*, 226–8, 230.   [4] *Ibid.*, 237–44.
[5] This is forcefully argued in Etienne Balibar, *Spinoza and Politics* (1998) 16–24.
[6] Spinoza, *Tractatus Politicus* (1951 (1677)) esp. 288.

scriptural evidence to advance his practical political argument in support of the institutions of the Dutch Republic. In his second *Tractatus*, though, in which he examines politics as an abstract science, he rigorously eschews all discussion of biblical examples. Spinoza's stance towards scriptural politics is utterly consistent with his wider approach towards the historical status of the Old Testament, which, as we have seen, he values as a record of Jewish memory, but does not privilege with any universal significance.

This distinction is not reflected in the work of Spinoza's closest Dutch collaborators. The recent rediscovery of a political treatise by his Latin teacher, Franciscus van den Enden, has underscored the intellectual affinity, in some respects, between the two men.[7] Van den Enden's *Vrije Politijke Stellingen* ('Free Political Treatises') (1665) is the first in the western tradition to assert unequivocally that democracy is the only stable and virtuous form of government. However, although Spinoza and van den Enden (1602–74) are very closely united in their political beliefs, the religious inflection of their arguments differ markedly. Van den Enden powerfully asserts that true Christianity itself consists purely of belief in clear, simple reason, and in the joyous dissolution of the self in communal love.[8] He distils Jesus' message to the simple imperative of love of one's neighbour, from which all divine knowledge flows.[9] This Christian selflessness is explicitly contrasted to Jewish authoritarianism. Jews do not act out of love, he argues, but are cajoled into action by threats, miracles and laws. They are therefore 'childlike', and worthy of contempt.[10]

A streak of infantilising hostility towards Judaism was also present in Spinoza's work, as we shall soon see in more detail.[11] However, whereas Spinoza's critique of Judaism is integrated into his historical interpretation of the Old Testament, for van den Enden a positive vision of politics itself is constitutively dependent on its juxtaposition against Judaic legalism. Echoing the charged anti-Jewish rhetoric in the contemporaneous writings of Adriaan Koerbagh, a member of the same circle, van den Enden's political thought is profoundly inflected by his theological understanding of Judaism as the pure negative of his own positive, minimally Christian values of freedom and love. He ignores the long-standing republican tradition of admiration for the Mosaic polity, and instead casts Judaism as straightforwardly and eternally oppressive.

Van den Enden's rationalist vision of religion as pure joyous love recurs in the most explicitly political text of the next generation of the Dutch Early

[7] See W. N. A. Klever, 'Inleiding' to Franciscus van den Enden, *Vrije Politijke Stellingen* (1992) 99–111.
[8] Franciscus van den Enden, *Vrije Politijke Stellingen* (1992 (1665)) 201.
[9] *Ibid.*, 202.   [10] *Ibid.*   [11] See esp. *TTP*, 165.

Enlightenment: Frederik van Leenhof's *Den Hemel op Aarden* ('Heaven on Earth') (1703). Van Leenhof (1647–1712), a pastor of the Dutch Reformed Church in Zwolle, provoked a major furore in publishing this radically utopian text, which provoked rapid and intense condemnation. Critics were alarmed not simply by the substance of van Leenhof's arguments, but also by the fact that, like Bekker, he had expounded them in the vernacular, thus leading to the diffusion of dangerously subversive notions amongst the uneducated masses.[12] This anxiety is unsurprising given the powerfully antinomian and hedonistic overtones of his arguments. Van Leenhof's key theme is the celebration of joy: the word 'blydschap' – joy, or bliss – recurs throughout the text. In a manner strongly influenced by Spinoza's metaphysics, but also by a large measure of neo-Epicurian hedonism, he equates God with the presence of joy and love in the world, and defines 'blydschap' as embracing all virtues.[13] In the final chapters of the text, he puts forward a practical agenda for spreading 'true joy' throughout the world, imposing a particular responsibility on teachers, public officials and preachers to encourage public blissfulness by always being 'cheerful and jolly'.[14]

Van Leenhof's passionate practical utopianism, although bearing strong philosophical affinities with Spinoza's *Ethics*, is in its political spirit much closer to the demotic idealism of van den Enden and Koerbagh than to Spinoza's serious and elitist emphasis on the importance of wisdom and the exercise of reason. Like Spinoza, however, van Leenhof invokes ancient Jewish examples in support of his case. He identifies Jerusalem, with its temple, as the archetypal city of love and joy.[15] He expresses particular admiration for King Solomon, noting that 'the jolly Solomon' was a ruler thoroughly committed to human happiness.[16] Van Leenhof wrote two earlier texts exclusively on Solomon, in the first of which he recounted his life and praised his character, and in the second turned to a more philosophical analysis of his rule. Solomon's example showed, van Leenhof argued, that it was possible to eradicate all human stupidity and vanity, through the simple, true and wise application of reason.[17]

Van Leenhof's interpretative strategy towards the Old Testament in these texts is neither clear nor consistent. Despite his celebration of Solomon's monarchic rule, his underlying sympathies are unmistakably republican: he

[12] Jonathan Israel, 'Les controverses pamphlétaires dans la vie intellectuelle hollandaise et allemande à l'époque de Bekker et Van Leenhof', *Dix-huitième siècle* 195 (1997) 254–8.

[13] Frederik van Leenhof, *Den Hemel op Aarden* (1704 (1703)) 25, 71.   [14] *Ibid.*, 124–5.

[15] *Ibid.*, 13–14.   [16] *Ibid.*, 88–9.

[17] Frederik van Leenhof, *Het Leven van den Wijzen en Magtigen Konink Salomon* (1700); *De Prediker van den Wijzen en magtigen Konink Salomon* (1700) esp. 438–40.

praises Solomon not for his kingship, but for his wisdom, which led him to realise that power should be subordinate to the law and to the rational interests of society at large.[18] While this might suggest a flexible approach towards the biblical narrative, elsewhere he appears reverential towards the language of Scripture, frequently, like Koerbagh, citing key Hebrew terms in their original script, and providing a gloss of their true, purified meaning.[19] At times he seems to regard the Salomonic episode as a heuristic device with which to further his practical argument: much as Spinoza's use of the Mosaic Republic heightened his defence of the Dutch Republic, this example of good kingship highlights in counterpoint van Leenhof's implied criticism of contemporaneous monarchs such as William III and Louis XIV. However, elsewhere Solomon's reign is elevated to transcendent heights. Jerusalem under his rule is presented as a veritable worldly paradise, where political, religious, individual and social utopianism are perfectly integrated. The Jewish past hovers in these texts in an undefined and indeterminate intellectual territory, straddling both empirical history and idealised fantasy.

These ambiguities might seem to be of little significance. Radicals such as van Leenhof and van den Enden were much more strongly motivated by a desire to promote actual political change than they were by a concern for perfect hermeneutic consistency. However, in fitfully presenting Judaism, or moments from its past, as either the antithesis or the epitome of democratic politics, they tightened the web of confusion that surrounded the political status of Jews as an actually existing minority at the dawn of the modern world. While Spinoza, as an ethnic Jew, was at least mindful of the complicated relationship between real and textual Judaism, the radical Enlightenment tradition most directly influenced by him routinely blurred these categories, and, insouciantly contemptuous of the attempts by traditional theologians such as Huet and Bossuet to integrate Jewish and Gentile history, left the Jewish Bible, and also its contemporary adherents, in a state of epistemological limbo.

JOHN TOLAND: PANTHEISM AND THE POLITICS OF JEWISH ORIGINS

Judaism also figured prominently in English political argument in the early eighteenth century. The radicalism of the English Deists, in contrast with

---

[18] Van Leenhof, *Leven*, 44. See also Jonathan Israel, 'Spinoza, King Solomon, and Frederik van Leenhof's Spinozistic Republicanism', *Studia Spinozana* 6 (1995) 303–17.

[19] Van Leenhof, *Prediker*, 102.

the clandestine or semi-clandestine nature of much radical philosophy elsewhere in Europe, was explicitly engaged with the politics of the public
sphere.[20] Matthew Tindal, Anthony Collins, John Toland and other Deists
were centrally concerned with the political power of writing itself, and were
bound together by their open discussion of themes and ideas that were often
shocking to the political and religious establishment. Their willingness –
and even desire – to provoke outrage was itself a deeply political act, which
was in some ways more important than their actual opinions. Toland's inner
beliefs, in particular, have proved extremely resistant to conclusive interpretation: his professed 'pantheism' – he was the first to coin the phrase – has
been interpreted both as a radical but sincere brand of Christianity and as a
scarcely concealed atheism.[21] Both readings are dependent on an assumed
stability in Toland's thought, which, even if it existed at a private level, is not
accessible through his writings. His primary intellectual concern was not to
develop a consistent theology, but to expand the limits of public discourse.
Rather than trying to pin down Toland, it is more productive to read him –
and the other leading Deists – in the context of their contemporary political
engagement, as mobile and provocative public intellectuals.[22]

To read the Deists' arguments more as process than as product does not,
however, imply that the internal logic of their texts is of no interest. The
exploratory nature of their investigations into materialism, republicanism
and rational religion lend their arguments a particular openness to the implications and pitfalls of various lines of argument.[23] It was such speculative
curiosity that drew John Toland to a sustained fascination with the politics
of the Mosaic Republic, and with the Judaic roots of early Christianity.
Toland's approach to the Old Testament – and, indeed, to many aspects of
his pantheistic and materialist thought – was heavily indebted to Spinoza.[24]
Like Spinoza, Toland sought to deprivilege the Jewish past, by providing
a purely secular, historicist reading of the Old Testament. He was also,

---

[20] See Venturi, *Utopia and Reform*, 53.
[21] For the former interpretation, see Robert E. Sullivan, *John Toland and the Deist Controversy* (1982);
for the latter, David Berman, 'Introduction' to *Atheism in Britain* (1996) vol. 1, xi–xv.
[22] This is persuasively argued for Toland by Justin Champion, in his 'Introduction' to John Toland,
Nazarenus (1999) 13–15, 60–1; see also Champion, 'John Toland: The Politics of Pantheism', *Revue de
synthèse* 116 (1995) 259–80. On the Ramist dimension of Toland's approach to rhetoric see Stephen
H. Daniel, 'Toland's Semantic Pantheism', in Phillip McGuinness, Alan Harrison and Richard
Kearney, eds., *John Toland's 'Christianity not Mysterious': Text, Associated Works and Critical Essays*
(1997) 303–12.
[23] On Deist invovement in debates on materialism, see John W. Yolton, *Thinking Matter: Materialism
in Eighteenth-Century Britain* (1983) 39–45.
[24] See Pierre Lurbe, 'Le Spinozisme de John Toland', in Bloch, ed., *Spinoza au XVIII e siècle*, 33–7;
Rienk Vermij, 'Matter and Motion: Toland and Spinoza', in Van Bunge and Klever, eds., *Spinozism*,
275–88.

though, strongly influenced by the Christian tradition of the idealisation of the Mosaic Republic, which James Harrington had emphatically placed at the core of English republican thought. In 1700 Toland published his own edition of Harrington's works, including such intensely Hebraic texts as *The Art of Lawgiving*.[25] In attempting to integrate this Harringtonian perspective with his simultaneous desire to challenge the centrality of Jewish history, Toland's approach to Judaism was caught, in a particularly heightened fashion, in the same fundamental ambiguity that marked the thought of so many Enlightenment writers on this subject.

Toland projected a major work on the Mosaic Republic, which, although never completed, has survived in essence through three published fragments, which doubtlessly formed part of this wider project.[26] The most important of these is his *Origines Judaicae* (1709), a polemical work written against Pierre-Daniel Huet's *Demonstratio Evangelica*. The text emerged from a sustained epistolary dispute between Toland and Huet in 1707, in which Toland had vigorously challenged the Bishop of Avranches' hypothesis that the mythologies and religions of all cultures were based on a Mosaic blueprint.[27] In the *Origines* Toland stridently accuses Huet of misinterpreting his classical sources. Based on his own reading of the ancients' writings on the Jews, he put forward his own Mosaic counter-history, which radically inverted Huet's exceptionalist treatment of the Jewish past. From Diodorus Siculus Toland took the argument that Moses had been an Egyptian priest; from Tacitus and Strabo the claim that the Jews were a mixed race, from scattered, remote origins; and from Strabo his most provocative argument that Moses had been 'a Pantheist, or, in more recent language, a Spinozist'.[28]

Toland's essay was heavily indebted to the earlier work of John Marsham and John Spencer, who in the 1670s and 1680s had introduced into biblical scholarship the notion that Egyptian society was more venerable and sophisticated than that of the Ancient Hebrews, and that Egyptian influences had profoundly shaped early Jewish customs and laws. However, Toland took this argument into much more radical territory. Rather than using the classical historians in order to elucidate the biblical account of Jewish rituals, as had Spencer, Toland deployed his ancient sources against the Bible.[29] His alternative account systematically negated the providential claims of the Old Testament, and their elaboration in Huet's *Demonstratio*. Far from

---

[25] On Toland's edition, see Pocock, 'Historical Introduction', 141–5.
[26] See Robert Rees Evans, *Pantheisticon: The Career of John Toland* (1991) 187ff.
[27] See Sullivan, *John Toland and the Deist Controversy*, 30.
[28] John Toland, *Origines Judaicae* (1709) esp. 104–9,117.
[29] See Assmann, *Moses the Egyptian*, 91–6.

being a pure and divinely chosen people, Toland's Jews are a mongrel race, dependent on Egyptian sources for the essence of their religion. Their laws are not ordained by God, but are the product of human invention; and their leader, Moses, was inspired not by revelation, but by his training in the Egyptian priestly tradition of esoteric knowledge.

Toland's historical depriviliging of Judaism was, however, not so straightforward. While denigrating the Jewish religion and exceptionalist attitudes to Jewish history, Toland retained a deep admiration for the teachings at the originary core of Judaism: the Mosaic Law. Following Strabo, Toland presents Moses as a secular lawgiver, at the head of a tradition continued with Minos, Lycurgus, Solon and Romulus.[30] Fusing the long-standing esoteric fascination with Hermetic speculation with a newer, rationalist Deism, Toland radically disassociates Moses from anything related to Judaism or to God, and alternatively situates him both within the Hermetic tradition of Egyptian priestly wisdom and within a rational lineage of civic lawgiving. The cult that Moses instituted for the Jews during their Exodus was in every respect simple and restrained, Toland insists. Only at a later stage, after Moses' death, were superfluous rites and superstitions, such as circumcision, sacrifices and purity laws, introduced.[31] Toland thus dramatically reverses Spencer's earlier view of the relationship between the Jewish Law and the customs of Egypt. Spencer had admiringly explained the purpose of the Jewish ritual law in cleansing the Jews of all traces of Egyptian idolatry. In contrast, Toland saw these laws as themselves superstitious, reflecting the Jews' later degeneration from the philosophically eternal but culturally Egyptian pantheistic simplicity that had imbued their original Mosaic cult.

Toland's view of Judaism was thus fundamentally split. He was contemptuous of Jewish rituals and ceremonies, which he saw as marking the beginning of the descent of philosophically pure religion into elaborate systems of priestly domination. However, despite his stress on the Egyptian origins of Moses' philosophy, he nonetheless cast this earliest form of Judaism as the defining crystallisation of rational religion. In his earlier *Christianity not Mysterious* (1696) Toland had attempted to establish the basic principles and historical trajectory of this ideal of religious rationalism. Arguing that all knowledge must be based on reason, he here argues that in its original form Christianity was free of all mysteries, and was 'a Rational and Intelligible Religion'.[32] All magical and superstitious elements in Christianity were derived from 'pagan mystick rites', imported into

[30] Toland, *Origines*, 103–4. See also Champion, *Pillars of Priestcraft*, 130–1.
[31] Toland, *Origines*, 157–8.   [32] John Toland, *Christianity not Mysterious* (1964 (1696)) 46.

the religion by Gentile converts.[33] Toland apportions much blame to the first Christian Emperors, who, he claims, introduced the hierarchical and ceremonial trappings of paganism into the new religion. These rituals were later embellished by the Christian clergy, who discovered that pomp and ceremony could 'stupify the minds of the ignorant people', and so augment the power of the priesthood.[34]

In insisting on the Gentile source of these rituals, Toland preserved the uncontaminated purity of Christianity's Judaic roots. However, elsewhere in *Christianity not Mysterious* Toland ascribes to the Jews a particularly intense penchant for superstition: 'the Jews were infatuated with a fancy that nothing could be true but what was miraculously proved so'.[35] It was purely on account of this that it was necessary for Jesus to supplement his rational teachings with the performance of miracles, in order to convince the 'stiff-necked Jews' of the divine authority of his Gospel.[36] As we have seen, the simultaneous privileging of an abstract, purified Judaism and the dismissal of it as practised by Jews was a recurrent theme both of traditional Christian theology and of Early Enlightenment radicalism. In the context of Toland's detailed historical speculations, however, the tension between these two perspectives takes on a particular complexity.

Toland aspired to establish a secular historical account both of the roots of rational religion and of the superstitious obfuscations that have impeded popular awareness of these simple truths. Both these currents are powerfully associated with Judaism, and in Toland's writings the impossibility of any neat demarcation between them is clearly apparent. Toland's 'good' Judaism and his 'bad' Judaism are both overwhelmingly shaped by the same, biblical source: even his use of classical writers is overwhelmingly defined by their effectiveness as a polemical counterpoint to the Old Testament. At certain points in his *oeuvre* he maximises the historical marginalisation of Judaism: in the second of his *Letters to Serena* (1704) he proclaims the Egyptians as 'the Fountains of Learning to all the East', providing an account of their preeminence in science and philosophical wisdom in which the Jews are scarcely mentioned at all.[37] Elsewhere, however, as to some extent in *Christianity not Mysterious*, he emphasises the Jewish roots of true Christianity. In *Origines Judaicae* he attempts to integrate these perspectives: Moses is both revered as a supremely gifted political legislator and

---

[33] *Ibid.*, 160.
[34] *Ibid.*, 162–72, esp. 171. On this text see also Frederick C. Beiser, *The Sovereignty of Reason: The Defence of Rationality in the Early English Enlightenment* (1996) 245–9.
[35] Toland, *Christianity*, 127.   [36] *Ibid.*, 47.
[37] John Toland, *Letters to Serena* (1964 (1704)) 40. See also Champion, *Pillars of Priestcraft*, 148–9; Sullivan, *John Toland*, 47.

negatively portrayed as the leader of a worthless rabble, himself dependent on what he had learned from the Egyptians. This argument was of great polemical effectiveness: it preserved the politically inspirational power of the Mosaic regime, while profoundly destabilising the legitimating myths of clerical authority. However, while dramatically raising the rhetorical stakes riding on the Old Testament, Toland left the historical status of this text as ambiguous and indeterminate as ever.

Toland's *Hodegus*, which circulated privately from 1708 onwards but was first published as the first part of his *Tetradymus* in 1720, further reflects this underlying ambiguity. The central argument of this essay, which clearly bears the stamp of Spinoza's influence, is that the 'pillar of cloud and fire' by which the Israelites were led through the wilderness was simply a form of 'ambulatory beacon', and was therefore in no sense a miraculous phenomenon.[38] Toland also ridicules other alleged miracles in the Exodus story: it is obvious to all 'men of clear understanding', he writes, that the Hebrews' clothes did not wear out during their forty years in the wilderness simply because they must have included among their multitude plenty of competent tailors.[39] This mode of the rational explanation of biblical miracles closely echoes Spinoza's arguments in the sixth chapter of the *Tractatus Theologico-Politicus*.[40] However, echoing the linguistic preoccupations of Koerbagh, Bekker and others, he also closely scrutinises the original Hebrew of the Jewish Bible, arguing, as Bekker had done, that the Hebrew word for 'angel' has no supernatural connotations, simply signifying any form of messenger.[41] Toland's linguistic rationalisation of the Book of Exodus implicitly idealises the Hebrew language itself – a notion that sits awkwardly with his accusation that the ancient Jews were particularly devoted to fantasy and superstition.

In his *Nazarenus, or Jewish, Gentile and Mahometan Christianity* (1718) Toland most explicitly attempted to establish the universalism of natural religion. In this text he undermines the exclusive claims of orthodox Christianity by simultaneously advancing distinctively Islamic and Judaic interpretations of the Gospels. Toland had been very excited by his discovery in 1709 of the Gospel of St Barnabus: a fifth Gospel of uncertain origins, which followed Moslem belief in recounting the crucifixion of Judas rather than of Jesus, who instead foretells the later revelation to Mohammed. Basing his arguments on this source, Toland lent support to the truth claims of both Islam and Judaism: the original Christians, he argued, were

---

[38] John Toland, *Tetradymus* (1720) 6–7.   [39] *Ibid.*, 30.
[40] *TTP*, 81–97. See also Chiara Giuntini, *Panteismo e ideologia repubblicana: John Toland (1670–1722)* (1979) 420–2.
[41] Toland, *Tetradymus*, 46–8.

members of a Jewish sect, the Nazarenes, who recognised Jesus as their temporal, Jewish Messiah.[42] By putting forward both these arguments in the same text, Toland powerfully connected Jewish, Christian and Islamic theology.[43] True Christianity, he implies, embraces all and none of these specific, mutually incompatible truths: although the religious message might appear in diffferent guises to different peoples, its underlying essence is cross-cultural and universal.

Toland argues that for the Nazarenes, including Jesus himself, the Mosaic Law, signified above all by circumcision, continued to be binding, and would always remain so: there will always be a distinction between Jewish and Gentile Christians within the Church.[44] This claim, which to some extent echoes Wachter's earlier identification of the Essenes as the first and purest Christians, is extremely confused in its attitudinal stance towards Judaism. While in a sense subordinating Christianity to Judaism, insofar as he identifies the core constituency of Christians as eternally Jewish, Toland seems no less to subordinate Judaism to Christianity: he draws a sharp distinction between the Nazarene Jews, who acknowledged Jesus, and those others who did not.

This confusion is heightened in the first appendix to the text, titled *Two Problems Concerning the Jewish Nation and Religion*. This fragment had, like *Hodegus*, circulated in manuscript since around 1709, but was first published with *Nazarenus*. Toland here poses two questions. The first is essentially the mystery of Jewish survival: why, he asks, after 1,700 years of dispersion, have the Jews nevertheless 'preserv'd themselves a distinct people with all their ancient rites' (excepting those connected with temple worship, which could no longer be observed)?[45] Secondly, he asks why, in contrast to their present strict religious observance and segregation from Gentiles, in the period before their dispersal from Palestine the Jews were 'perpetually inclined to the most gross idolatries', and tempted to 'mix and marry' with non-Jews, in contravention of their own laws.[46] This extremely brief text offers no answer to either question. However, the dramatic posing of these two carefully balanced mysteries at the end of one of his most significant texts reflects the intensity of Toland's interest in Judaism, which he regarded with a deep and unresolved fascination.

In the *Two Problems* Toland expresses his most unequivocal enthusiasm for the Mosaic Republic. Moses, he writes, was by far the greatest lawmaker in history, outclassing all rivals in the ancient world, and the originator of

---

[42] John Toland, *Nazarenus* (1999 (1718)) 150–4.   [43] See Champion, *Pillars of Priestcraft*, 123–9.
[44] Toland, *Nazarenus*, 156–60.
[45] John Toland, *Two Problems Concerning the Jewish Nation and Religion* (1999 (1709)) 237.
[46] *Ibid*.

the politically utopian notion of the 'Immortality of a Commonwealth'.[47] Toland concludes on a proto-Zionist note, suggesting to his patron Prince Eugene of Savoy, for whom the essay was originally written, that a possible Jewish return to Palestine should be actively promoted by Christian leaders:

[If the Jews] ever happen to be resettl'd in Palestine upon their original foundation, which is not at all impossible; they will then, by reason of their excellent constitution, be much more populous, rich and powerful than any other nation now in the world. I would have you consider, whether it be not both in the interest and duty of Christians to assist them in regaining their country. But more of this when we meet…[48]

This timeless idealisation of the Jewish polity stands markedly at odds with Toland's distinction, in his *Origines Judaicae*, between Moses' political wisdom and the superstitious primitiveness of the Jewish people as a whole. Although Toland sets out, in that text and elsewhere, to secularise Jewish history, Judaism persistently eludes a fixed rational analysis, and remains in his texts powerfully charged with mythic significance. While he demystifies Judaism in order to undermine the historical authority of Christianity, he simultaneously remystifies it in new terms, as an originary source of natural religion and as a model of utopian politics.[49]

Toland made no attempt to smooth out his various approaches to Jewish themes. His writings on this subject, as on most others, were self-consciously polemical, forming part of a strategic campaign against priestly authority, and in support of an alternative vision of a democratic civil theology.[50] He deliberately deployed the Jewish past flexibly, in order to destabilise Christian arguments to the maximum effect. However, Toland's political engagement was not only critical, but also constructive. He proudly boasted of his friendships with people of all religious persuasions, including Jews,[51] and, as we shall soon see, he made an important practical call for a more inclusively tolerant policy towards Jews in Britain and Ireland. Such political interventions, while important in themselves, cannot be disassociated from the ambiguous overlappings in his texts between the mythic, historical and contemporary guises of Judaism. His suggestion that Christians should take an activist role in reestablishing a Jewish state in Palestine should not be taken as mere empty rhetoric, and constitutes a particularly stark instance of

---

[47] *Ibid.*, 238.   [48] *Ibid.*, 240.

[49] See P. Lurbe, 'John Toland et l'utilisation de l'histoire juive: entre l'histoire et le mythe', in Chantal Grell and François Laplanche, eds., *La République des lettres et l'histoire du judaïsme antique* (1992) 160–1.

[50] See Champion, *Pillars of Priestcraft*, esp. 225–6, 234–6; Stephen H. Daniel, *John Toland: His Method, Manners and Mind* (1984) esp. 139.

[51] Daniel, *John Toland*, 142.

ancient associations shaping attitudes to the Jews of the eighteenth century. More loosely, Toland's Judaic evocations and polemics contributed to a Deistic political culture in which, despite its professed rationalism, Judaism was routinely shrouded in mysteries and contradictions.

Toland's claim that Judaism was profoundly shaped by Egyptian in-fluences was echoed by other Deists. The Third Earl of Shaftesbury, in his *Characteristicks of Men, Manners, Opinions, Times* (1711), discussed the 'servile Dependency of the whole Hebrew race on the Egyptian Nation'.[52] Like Toland, Shaftesbury ascribed Moses' teachings to his priestly training in Egypt; unlike him, however, Shaftesbury cast the Egyptian priesthood in purely negative terms, as utterly ridden with magic and superstition.[53] The identification of Deism with the notion that the Mosaic Law was Egyptian in origin had soon became so established that it was a central point of con-tention in Bishop William Warburton's convoluted refutation of Deism, *The Divine Legation of Moses Demonstrated* (1738–41). Warburton acknowl-edged that Moses had been a master of Egyptian esotericism, but argued that in his divinely inspired legislation for the Hebrew nation he had made these truths available to the masses in a directly accessible form, repudiat-ing the exoteric, pagan superstitions with which the Egyptian priests had concealed them from the general populus.[54]

Warburton's attempt to clarify the relationship between Jewish revelation and Egyptian superstition somewhat backfired, however: most readers saw his arguments as reinforcing rather than repudiating the radical view of the Mosaic Law as an expression of Egyptian esoteric wisdom.[55] By the middle of the eighteenth century the authority of the Bible was no longer a compelling target for most English radicals. However, as traditionalist theologians such as Warburton belatedly attempted to address the Deists' challenges, they found themselves embroiled in puzzles and ambiguities very similar to those that had surfaced in Toland's work at the beginning of the century.

PIETRO GIANNONE'S NOACHITE UTOPIANISM

Toland's writings resonated across Europe: he was a familiar visitor in radical circles in the Dutch Republic, and several of his texts circulated

---

[52] Shaftesbury, *Characteristicks of Men, Manners, Opinions, Times* (1999 (1711)) vol. II, 154.

[53] *Ibid.*, 149–58. See also Lawrence E. Klein, *Shaftesbury and the Culture of Politeness* (1994) 169–74.

[54] William Warburton, *The Divine Legation of Moses Demonstrated* (1846 (1738–41)) vol. II, 298–361. See also Young, *Religion and Enlightenment*, 174–9.

[55] Assmann, *Moses the Egyptian*, 96–100; Young, *Religion and Enlightenment*, 179–90.

clandestinely in France.[56] His writings on Judaism, however, had their most pronounced impact in Central Europe. All of his writings on this topic were sent to his patrons in Vienna, Prince Eugene of Savoy and the Baron Hohendorf, whose libraries jointly constituted perhaps the richest collection of radical texts in Europe.[57] Most notable among the radicals who gained access to Toland's ideas in the Habsburg capital was the Neapolitan jurist Pietro Giannone (1676–1748). Forced to leave his home city by the outcry provoked by his first book, *L'Istoria civile del regno di Napoli* (1723), Giannone took refuge in Vienna, where he discovered the writings of Spinoza, Toland and other radicals, and, considerably under their influence, wrote his own masterwork, *Il Triregno* (c.1730).[58]

The *Triregno* is a polemical history, aimed above all against the relentless self-aggrandisement of the Papacy. As the title suggests, Giannone divides the past into three eras, or 'reigns': the 'terrestrial reign', corresponding to the period of the Old Testament; the 'celestial reign' heralded by Jesus Christ; and the degenerative 'papal reign', from the conversion of Constantine onwards. In a similar fashion to Toland, Giannone contrasts the authoritarianism and hierarchy of established Christianity to the egalitarianism and simplicity of natural religion, which he identifies with the originary essence of the Jewish tradition.

Giannone describes the religion of Noah in rhapsodically minimal terms: 'it was totally pure and simple, without rites, ceremonies, priests, temples or altars'.[59] The Noachite religion, he asserts, consisted purely of a simple belief in an omnipresent, nameless creator-God. Its followers had no conception of the immortality of the soul: they believed that 'death was the end of everything'.[60] Following Toland's *Letters to Serena*, Giannone claims that the Egyptians were the first to imagine that the soul was immortal.[61] The significance of this doctrine was a recurrent focus of controversy in early eighteenth-century radicalism: while Toland acknowledged the social efficacy, although not the truth, of the notion of an afterlife, French clandestine texts such as *L'Ame Matérielle* argued unequivocally that the

---

[56] Margaret Jacob, *Living the Enlightenment* (1991) 91–5; Miguel Benítez, 'Sociétés secrètes philosophiques à l'aube des lumières: pantheistes et naturalistes', *Face cachée*, 191–8.

[57] Dino Carpanetto and Giuseppe Ricuperati, *Italy in the Age of Reason 1685–1789* (1987) 109–10.

[58] On Giannone, see Giuseppe Ricuperati, *L'esperienza civile e religiosa di Pietro Giannone* (1970) esp. 143–264; 'Libertismo e deismo a Vienna: Spinoza, Toland e *Il Triregno*', *Rivista storica italiana* 79 (1967), 628–95; J. G. A. Pocock, *Barbarism and Religion* 11 : *Narratives of Civil Government* (1999) 29–71.

[59] Pietro Giannone, *Il Triregno* (1977 (c.1730)) 8.   [60] *Ibid.*, 15.

[61] *Ibid.*, 16; cf. Toland, *Letters to Serena*, 40.

soul was material, mortal and identical in animals and in humans.[62] In the *Triregno* Giannone implicitly aligns himself with a materialist position: the doctrine of the soul's immortality is presented as one of many corrupting influences that the Jews absorbed from the Egyptians.

Giannone's account of Jewish history is a narrative of degeneration. Having at first embraced a uniquely pure and simple faith, the Jews gradually adopted, from the Egyptians and from other cultures, a panoply of redundant rituals, laws and hierarchies. The 'celestial reign' instituted by Jesus Christ was intended to sweep away these contaminations, and to purify human religion by introducing a new, 'celestial' element of redemptive grace.[63] These reforms, however, were very soon subverted by the Papacy, which, having illegitimately assumed domination over the Church, once again corrupted the truths of natural religion with the pernicious distortions of hierarchy and ritual.

In some respects Giannone was more theologically cautious than Toland, with whom he emphatically differs on the question of Moses' underlying beliefs. He explicitly repudiates Toland's claim in *Origines Judaicae* that Moses was a pantheist: it is clear from the Pentateuch, he argues, that Moses acknowledged 'the distinction between Creation and its Creator'.[64] A sharp division between God and the material world is a fundamental tenet of Giannone's notion of natural religion, and is explicitly included in his description of the originary Noachite credo. He also does not abandon all belief in the positive distinctiveness of Christianity: while he celebrates the this-worldly simplicity of the 'terrestial' Jews, he nonetheless appears to attach importance to the 'celestial' doctrines of reward and punishment introduced by Jesus. His admiration for the Noachite core of Judaism is thus seemingly tempered by a more conventionally Christian commitment to the overcoming of the old covenant by the new.

The theology of the *Triregno* was unmistakably subversive – as the authorities of the Piedmontese regime, which incarcerated Giannone for the last twelve years of his life, unhesitatingly realised. However, although no reader could doubt the intensity of his opposition to the Papacy, Giannone's positive beliefs remain in crucial respects open and ambiguous. As with so many other Enlightenment thinkers, these uncertainties are highlighted by his treatment of Judaism. While he differs from Toland on many significant

---

[62] *L'Ame Matérielle*, ed. Alain Niderst (1969). See also Aram Vartanian, 'Quelques réflexions sur le concept d'âme dans la littérature clandestine', in Bloch, ed., *Matérialisme*, 149–63; John W. Yolton, *Locke and French Materialism* (1991) 55–8; Champion, *Pillars of Priestcraft*, 148–9.
[63] Giannone, *Triregno*, 61–9.   [64] *Ibid*., 51.

points of detail, his simultaneous idealisation and denigration of the religion of the Old Testament, and his failure to draw a clear demarcation between these two stances, reflect a very similar indeterminacy of argument.

Giannone's positioning of Judaism contrasts markedly with that of his Neapolitan contemporary, Vico. Whereas Vico casts Egyptian history, as well as that of the Chinese, Indians and others, as fundamentally mythical, and regards the Jews alone as precociously sophisticated because of their assistance from God, Giannone in a sense inverts this formula, emphasising the inventiveness of the Egyptians and the importance of their influence on the Jews.[65] The underlying philosophical perspectives of the two men were also sharply opposed: while Vico regarded the *Scienza Nuova* fundamentally as an anti-Cartesian tract, Giannone explicitly presents the *Triregno* as a continuation of the rationalist project of 'the incomparable Descartes'.[66] Their divergence with regard to Judaism mirrors this broader disagreement. Whereas Vico strictly segregates sacred and profane history, Giannone, and the radical Enlightenment in general, is committed to the rejection of this barrier. If the Jewish past is to have the power to inspire change in the immediate present, then it must be integrated into human history. However, in imbuing the early Jews with such idealised simplicity, Giannone inescapably also shrouds them in an aura of myth. Once again, Giannone's Jews hover in an indeterminate political space, representing both a utopian fantasy and an exemplary model for his practical reformist vision.

D'ARGENS' *LETTRES JUIVES:* ROOTLESS COSMOPOLITANS?

The political energies of the Enlightenment were pitted not only against theocratic and monarchic authority, but also to some extent against the confining national structures on which government was traditionally based. The nation was a focus of repressed ambivalence for many eighteenth-century philosophers, who, while often heavily invested in the formation of national narratives of political legitimation and cultural identity, nonetheless also aspired to an intellectual cosmopolitanism that transcended all frontiers.[67] The Republic of Letters was self-consciously imagined as an intellectual collectivity so thoroughly transnational that it could be regarded as metaphorically constituting a nation of its own. This ideal of cosmopolitanism stood in stark tension with the relentless institutionalisation of the

---

[65] Rossi, *Dark Abyss*, 181–9.   [66] Giannone, *Triregno*, 36, 56–7.
[67] For a probing analysis of this paradox see Geoffrey Bennington, 'Postal Politics and the Institution of the Nation', in Homi K. Bhabha, ed., *Nation and Narration* (1990) 121–37.

nation state – a clash tacitly acknowledged at the end of the Enlightenment, in the dilution of Kant's vision of global citizenship, in his essay on 'the cosmopolitan point of view' of 1784, to his later, nation-based *Project for a Perpetual Peace* (1795).[68] In the first half of the eighteenth century, however, disillusion had not yet clouded the cosmopolitan ideal. While the enactment of cosmopolitanism by Europeans was compromised by their cross-cutting national identities, it was readily projected on to outsiders, and particularly on to the most visibly transnational minority in Europe: the Jews.

The immense success of Montesquieu's *Lettres Persanes* (1721), of which no fewer than ten editions appeared in the year of its publication, catapulted the fusion of exoticism and satire to the forefront of Enlightenment literature. The central device of the *Lettres Persanes* was not without precedent: most notably, the Italian Giovanni Paolo Marana's purported letters from a 'Turkish spy' at the French court (1694) were widely read in both French and English translations.[69] However, through the wide-ranging social, political and philosophical observations on French society by his Persian travellers, Uzbek and Rica, Montesquieu used the ventriloquistic voice of the outsider with devastating effect. Despite his exotic portrayal of Persian oriental despotism, Montesquieu nonetheless casts his peripatetic critics as idealised cosmopolitans, commenting on European mores from a detached perspective of rationalist objectivity.

Unsurprisingly, this *succès de scandale* soon spawned imitators. The most prolific epistolary satirist of the succeeding literary generation was the philosophically radical marquis d'Argens (1703–71). Argens' most successful work – although its attribution to him remains uncertain – was the infamous *Thérèse philosophe* (1748), which according to Robert Darnton ranked as the fifteenth best-selling illegal book in France over the period 1769–98.[70] This erotic novella, aptly classed by Darnton as 'philosophical pornography', traces the eponymous Thérèse's discovery of both philosophical materialism and sexual pleasure, through a sequence of intellectual discussions and physical liaisons – vividly illustrated – with libertine priests.[71] Argens' earlier work was more respectable, and was explicitly modelled on Montesquieu's epistolary example. His six-volume *Lettres juives* (1736–8)

---

[68] Jonathan Rée, 'Cosmopolitanism and the Experience of Nationality', in Pheng Cheah and Bruce Robbins, eds., *Cosmopolitics: Thinking and Feeling Beyond the Nation* (1998) 77–90.

[69] Giovanni Paolo Marana, *Letters Writ by a Turkish Spy* (1970 (1694)). See also Robert Shackleton, *Montesquieu: A Critical Biography* (1961) 31–2.

[70] Darnton, *Forbidden Best-Sellers*, 63.

[71] Anon., *Thérèse philosophe* (c.1748), repr. in *ibid.*, 249–99. See also Darnton, *Forbidden Best-Sellers*, 85–114; Jacob, 'Materialist World of Pornography', 180–93.

was an immediate success: so much so that they were swiftly followed by two sequel works, the *Lettres cabalistiques* (1737) and *Lettres chinoises* (1739–40).

The literary function of the three peripatetic Jews whose correspondence makes up the *Lettres juives* closely echoes that of Uzbek and Rica in the *Lettres Persanes*, and of the wise Confucian, Sioeu-Tcheou, in Argens' *Lettres chinoises*.[72] Through the voices of Aaron Monseca, who travels in a circuit from France through the Low Countries and England, Jacob Brito, who visits Italy and Spain, and Isaac Otis, a rabbi in the travellers' home city of Constantinople, who eventually travels to Egypt, Argens offers an eclectic, comic and politically trenchant satire of European and Mediterranean society. Like Montesquieu's Uzbek and Rica, Argens' Jewish characters are presented as both exotically oriental and transcendentally universalist. In the *Lettres Persanes* the tension between these two perspectives is stark and persistent: while Uzbek is represented as wise and enlightened, this respectful portrayal is powerfully undercut by Montesquieu's account of the forces of political instability and swirling lust that overrun his home seraglio as a result of his departure. In the *Lettres juives*, Monseca and his correspondents are less closely associated with an exotically alien culture. Jewish difference here jostles against Jewish sameness, while the transnational nature of European Jewry, and particularly of mercantile Sephardi Jewry, reinforces Argens' portrayal of his characters as the most natural and perfect cosmopolitans.

Much of the comedy of the *Lettres juives* is dependent on the *faux-naïf* directness of its Jewish voices. Monseca's seemingly innocent description of Parisian high society thinly cloaks the subversively irreligious implications of his comments, and so imbues them with a heightened satirical piquancy. Fashion, Monseca observes, is an all-consuming preoccupation in Paris: not only are women incessantly updating their wardrobes to keep up with the latest trends, but saints are subject to identical vicissitudes in popularity. At the moment, he notes, St Peter and St Paul are out of favour, but St Geneviève is in.[73]

While these incidental observations are dependent simply on Monseca's social outsiderness, the terms of his response to Christianity are specifically Jewish. Throughout the *Lettres juives* Christians are referred to as 'Nazarenes'. Argens thus inverts the conventional understanding of the relationship between the two faiths, casting Judaism as the more universal

---

[72] On the *Lettres chinoises*, see Wolf Steinsieck, *Die Funktion der Reise- und Briefliteratur in der Aufklärung untersucht am Beispiel der 'Lettres Chinoises' des Marquis d'Argens* (1975).

[73] Jean Baptiste de Boyer, marquis d'Argens, *Lettres juives* (1737) vol. I, II.

creed, and Christianity as its schismatic offshoot. Judaism is here represented as identical to enlightened Deism, as is made clear by Monseca's excited report of his discovery of a coterie of radical freethinkers in Paris:

I have found in Paris a significant number of Jews, who have no knowledge of this fact. This will seem like an invented joke to you; but it is absolutely true. All the people who are here called 'brave spirits' [Esprits-forts], 'light-headed people', and 'women of the world', follow the Nazarene religion only outwardly. In their hearts, they believe very little of it. It is enough for them simply to believe in a God.[74]

Eagerly encouraging his correspondent in Amsterdam, Rabbi Otis, to acknowledge these radicals as part of the Jewish fold, Monseca stresses the identity of their beliefs to those of Judaism:

I do not see how we can deny them the title of Jews. They believe in a God, who created the universe, rewards goodness, and punishes evil. What more do we believe? Is that not the entirety of our religion, apart from a few ceremonies, which our theologians and priests have commanded us to observe? These ceremonies, after all, are not indispensably necessary...[75]

This universalisation of Judaism echoes the long-standing fascination among Enlightenment radicals with the notion that core principles of natural religion were to be found in a minimalist, originary version of Judaism. In keeping with the norms of this tradition, however, Argens clearly marked the difference between this idealised Judaism and its contemporary, rabbinic form. In the final volume of the text Rabbi Otis leaves Constantinople for Cairo, where he encounters the city's large community of anti-rabbinical Karaite Jews. Persuaded of the validity of their arguments, he abandons his vocation and becomes a Karaite himself.[76] The principles of authentic, pure Judaism, Argens thus suggests, undermine the false claims of rabbinic Judaism. Argens also explicitly repudiates the possible misconception that his text suggests any Jewish superiority over Christians: in the preface to the third volume, dedicated to the rabbis of the Amsterdam synagogue, he states that the Jews, like all other peoples, contain only a tiny minority of individuals as enlightened as Brito and Monseca.[77] The apparent cosmopolitanism of Argens' representation of Judaism is ultimately self-undermining, because it is based on the assertion of a philosophical universalism that erases all traces of actual Jewish difference.

Argens was untroubled and explicit about the distance of his own use of Judaism from the beliefs and practices of living Jews in the eighteenth

[74] *Ibid.*, 49.   [75] *Ibid.*, 49–50.   [76] *Ibid.*, vol. v.   [77] *Ibid.*, vol. iii, dedicatory preface.

century. The letters of the 'wise cabbalists' in his *Lettres cabalistiques*, it is almost immediately clear, have nothing to do with Judaism at all: 'Kabbalah' serves simply as a generalised rubric encompassing all aspects of the supernatural, impossible and absurd.[78] However, this tension is nonetheless intellectually troubling, for two key reasons. Firstly, Argens' literary fascination with difference – all his epistolary satires gallop exhaustingly between countries and cultures – is undercut by his underlying philosophical non-acknowledgement of difference. He is at once intoxicated with variety and dismissive of all deviations from a monolithic rationalism. Secondly, the demand that other cultures be respected, which at a surface level is one of the central political challenges of Argens' writings, is also undermined by his own ultimate scorn for all perspectives other than his own. The cultural inclusivity gestured toward in the *Lettres juives* is hollow, because it finally embraces nothing but a unitary sameness of Enlightenment. This gap between abstracted idealisation and actual disdain for Judaism recurs ubiquitously in the political thought of the Early Enlightenment. Nowhere, however, are its implications more pointed than in the most urgent practical debate of the period: the question of the philosophical basis and political limits of toleration.

[78] Marquis d'Argens, *Lettres cabalistiques* (1737).

CHAPTER II

Judaism and the invention of toleration

The proper meaning and application of the concept of tolerance was one of the most intensively debated themes of the late seventeenth century. The nascent literary periodicals of the Dutch Republic published numerous essays on the subject, in which arguments both for and against the principle were aired in detail. Whereas the leading *philosophes* of the mid eighteenth century assumed the case for toleration to be utterly obvious to any rational individual, there was no such easy confidence among the pioneering theorists of toleration in the Early Enlightenment. The three most sophisticated and influential writers on toleration in this period – Baruch Spinoza, John Locke and Pierre Bayle – each developed careful arguments to counter the deeply felt political and theological objections of their opponents. For many Protestant and most Catholic thinkers, toleration was a dangerous and new-fangled absurdity, implying the relativist abandonment of any commitment to the unitary authority of true Christianity. The Catholic scholar Pellison, in his repudiation of Leibniz' advocacy of religious toleration, spoke for many theologians in his airy dismissal of the neologism of 'intolerance', 'of which people accuse the Roman Church as if it were some terrible crime'.[1]

Recognition of the need for some form of stable confessional coexistence was not, of course, an idea without precedent before the Enlightenment. Medieval thinkers such as Peter Abelard and John of Salisbury thought carefully about the possibilities of intellectual interaction between faiths; while in the sixteenth and early seventeenth centuries the devastation caused by religious conflict led to repeated attempts to promote forbearance and concord.[2] However, early modern toleration was a matter

[1] M. Pellison, 'Réponse aux objections envoyées d'Allemagne', in G. W. Leibniz, *De La Tolérance des Religions*, Paris, 1692, 46.
[2] See John Christian Laursen and Cary J. Nederman, eds., *Beyond the Persecuting Society: Religious Toleration Before the Enlightenment* (1998) 13–165; Martin Fitzpatrick, 'Toleration and the Enlightenment Movement', in Ole Peter Grell and Roy Porter, eds., *Toleration in Enlightenment Europe* (2000) 27–9.

of practical necessity rather than moral principle. Leading sceptical thinkers such as Montaigne, Lipsius and Hobbes all considered the issue in fundamentally pragmatic terms; while the codifications of tolerance at the end of the French Wars of Religion and the Thirty Years' War were generally felt to be little more than precarious truces, underwritten not by intellectual commitment but by military exhaustion.[3]

The early seventeenth-century clash between the Arminian and Gomarist factions of the Dutch Reformed Church brought the issue of toleration to the fore. Leading Arminians such as Simon Episcopius, arguing against the authoritarian Calvinism of their adversaries, even went so far in the 1620s as to advocate a comprehensive toleration of all churches.[4] However, it was Louis XIV's revocation of the Edict of Nantes in 1685, and the resulting creation of a large, embittered and articulate Huguenot diaspora, that established the question of toleration as a key public issue, and gave rise to the extensive and tightly argued debate of the closing decades of the seventeenth century. Many leading Huguenot exiles, including Pierre Bayle, regarded a commitment to the principles of toleration and liberty of conscience as the theoretical cornerstone of their opposition to the Revocation, and to the persecution of the Huguenots remaining in France. However, their arguments were vehemently opposed by Pierre Jurieu and his 'zealot' supporters, for whom the idea of toleration implied indifference towards religious truth. Rather than countering absolutism with abstract theories of justice and liberty, Jurieu directed his polemical fury against the evils of popery, in the name of which Louis was oppressing true Christianity. Jurieu envisaged the ultimate triumph of Protestantism, and therefore rejected pluralism, insisting that the right of the prince to crush heretical dissent must in principle be maintained.[5]

The status and rights of the Jews of Europe was, in practical terms, a marginal issue in the toleration debates of this period. The Jews were a small and easily pliable minority, whose conditions of existence carried none of the urgency posed by the fractious disputes between Christian denominations. Nonetheless, the Jewish case was very frequently raised

---

[3] Richard Tuck, 'Scepticism and Toleration in the Seventeenth Century', in Susan Mendus, ed., *Justifying Toleration* (1988) 21–35; Herbert Butterfield, 'Toleration in Early Modern Times', *JHI* 38 (1977) 573–84; Henry Kamen, *The Rise of Toleration* (1967).

[4] Jonathan Israel, 'The Intellectual Debate about Toleration in the Dutch Republic', in C. Berkvens-Stevelinck, J. I. Israel and G. H. M. Posthumus Meyjes, eds., *The Emergence of Tolerance in the Dutch Republic* (1997), 9–21; 'Toleration in Seventeenth-Century Dutch and English Thought', in Simon Groenveld and Michael White, eds., *The Exchange of Ideas: Religion, Scholarship and Art in Anglo-Dutch Relations in the Seventeenth Century* (1994) 17–22.

[5] See Guy Dodge, *The Political Theory of the Huguenots*, 165–97.

in theoretical discussions of toleration. The anomalous social status of Judaism, and its unique, foundational relationship to Christianity, drew the Jews into the heart of the complicated abstract issues raised in this controversy.

Since the beginning of the Diaspora the Jews had lived dispersed among Christians. They therefore in a sense stood as a primary example of a tolerated minority. Some commentators argued that the widely accepted toleration of Judaism clinched the case in favour of the toleration of all religious groups. If even the Jews had been deemed to be tolerable, the argument ran, what possible grounds could there be for denying a similar toleration to any other group? This case is powerfully put in an anonymous essay on civil tolerance in the Dutch Republic, published in the *Histoire des Ouvrages des Savans* in 1692:

> Let us take the example of the Jews. There is no doubt that they are tolerated for no other reason than the advantages they bring for commerce . . . However, taking the Jewish religion into consideration, there is nothing that is more odious to Christianity. The attack, wherever Jews are present, on the victorious Messiah is a blasphemy against Jesus Christ, whom they reject . . . If it is argued that we must tolerate them, because they are destined to be recalled, and miraculously converted, and that there is besides no reason to fear that their impiety might spread, I answer that we must therefore tolerate all idolaters . . . One cannot push tolerance any further than the case of the Jews; and so the implications of their case are unanswerable.[6]

This argument highlights many of the ambiguities that clustered around the concept of toleration in the late seventeenth century. Does toleration entail nothing more than allowing the physical presence of members of a minority, or must this be accompanied by certain rights and guarantees? Can pragmatic considerations, such as the particular theological and economic reasons to encourage a Jewish presence, be incorporated into general, abstract arguments for toleration? Can cogent arguments for universal toleration be derived from an avowedly Christian theological perspective? How compatible can the toleration of a minority such as the Jews be with a deep-seated cultural or religious disdain towards it? These difficulties resonate throughout the Early Enlightenment toleration debate. Despite the aspiration of many Protestant thinkers to develop a philosophical justification for toleration that was free from confessional bias, their frequent reversion to exceptionalist and theological modes of thought when considering the case of the Jews reveals how incomplete and troubled this project was.

[6] *HOS* (January 1692) 240–1.

JUDAISM AND TOLERATION IN SPINOZA'S *TRACTATUS*

Although Spinoza does not directly discuss the concept of toleration in his writings, the right to freedom of thought and expression was fundamental to his philosophy. The *Tractatus Theologico-Politicus* culminates with his claim to have conclusively demonstrated 'that in a free commonwealth every man may think as he pleases, and say what he thinks'.[7] Fundamental to Spinoza's argument is the careful distinction he draws between religious faith and philosophy, which, he states, is 'the main object of this entire treatise'.[8] Whereas faith offers a pathway to salvation for all, through simple obedience to God's revealed commands, philosophy enables the intelligent few to find wisdom and happiness guided by the natural light of reason alone. Spinoza acknowledges that matters of outward religious worship have always rightly been subject to the authority of the sovereign, but argues that philosophical thinking is impossible to control, and must therefore inevitably be free.[9]

Spinoza's argument is thus crucially not put forward in support of *religious* toleration. Perhaps unsurprisingly, given his own religious non-affiliation, he is not concerned to defend diversity in public worship, but only with the right of the individual to freedom of thought and expression. Indeed, the sharp distinction that he draws between authoritarian faith and truth-seeking philosophy is implicitly extremely anti-religious. This hint was seized on by Spinoza's early critics, who interpreted the *Tractatus* as an unambiguously atheistic tract. As J. B. Stouppe argued with horror in his *Religion des Hollandois* (1673), the first published refutation of the *Tractatus*, the text was read as a design 'to destroy all religions, in particular Judaism and Christianity, and to introduce atheism, libertinage, and freedom from all religions'.[10]

Spinoza's criticism of organised religion is in fact somewhat attenuated in the case of Christianity. Although he implies that all structures of religious authority are in essence unphilosophical, he also gives a positive account of Jesus' message, which he summarises as teaching that '[God's] covenant is no longer written in ink or engraved on tablets of stone, but is inscribed by God's spirit in men's hearts'.[11] This minimalist interpretation of Christianity emphasises its private, autonomous nature, and brings it into harmony with Spinoza's own philosophy. His language of internal divinity echoes the Quaker concept of the 'inner light', and perhaps bears the trace of

---

[7] *TTP*, 265.   [8] *Ibid.*, 183.   [9] *Ibid.*, 245–66.

[10] Cited in R. H. Popkin, 'The First Published Reaction to Spinoza's "Tractatus": Col. J. B. Stouppe, the Condé Circle, and the Rev. Jean Lebrun', in Cristofolini, ed., *Spinozistic Heresy*, 7.

[11] *TTP*, 237.

contacts he may have had with English conversionist Quakers who were active within the Amsterdam Jewish community in the 1650s, spearheaded by the Hebrew-speaking Samuel Fisher.[12]

In sharp contrast to this interpretation of Christianity, Spinoza casts Judaism as a religion of total subjection to the authority of God. As we have seen, Spinoza expresses his admiration for many aspects of the theocratic Mosiac Republic. However, this praise is carefully limited to the specific historical context and unique circumstances of the Republic, and also sharply contrasts with his generally extremely negative view of Judaism as fundamentally unphilosophical. He presents the unquestioning obedience to the Mosaic Law required of Jews, both ancient and modern, as diametrically opposed to the spirit of independent philosophical inquiry that he most values. The fact that the Ancient Jews needed such an explicit covenant bears witness to their intellectual underdevelopment: 'Religion was imparted to the early Hebrews in the form of a written law', he writes, 'because they were at that time just like children.'[13] Although these vivid prophecies and rigid laws were appropriate to the predicament and capabilities of the Ancient Jews, they now constitute, as law, an obsolete remnant of an extinct covenant, and as narrative, a text that is purely of historical rather than philosophical interest.

It is hardly surprising to discover in Spinoza a profound hostility towards formal Judaism. 'By the decree of the Angels and the word of the Saints we ban, cut off, curse and anathemize Baruch de Espinoza... with all the curses written in the Torah': thus the communal record book of the Portuguese Jewish community of Amsterdam for 27 July 1656.[14] Spinoza was only twenty-four years old when this punishment for his 'horrible heresies' was pronounced, forbidding all members of the community to have any contact with him whatsoever. It is eminently understandable that, as Yirmiyahu Yovel puts it, '[w]hen it comes to his fellow Jews, Spinoza loses his philosophical cool'.[15] However, Spinoza's personal experiences do not alter or displace the fact that Jewish observance of the Mosaic Law is cast within his writings as the defining polar opposite of his own positive philosophy.

Spinoza's arguments do not explicitly undermine the social or political toleration of Judaism. However, he unambiguously excludes Judaism from his standards of intellectual tolerability. The discipline of Spinoza's

---

[12] Richard H. Popkin, 'Spinoza and Samuel Fisher', *Philosophia* 15 (1985) 219–36; 'Spinoza's Relations with the Quakers in Amsterdam', *Quaker History* 37 (1984) 14–28.
[13] *TTP*, 165 (translation slightly amended). On Spinoza's use of the concept of accommodation see Funkenstein, *Perceptions of Jewish History*, 88–98.
[14] Cited in Yovel, *Marrano of Reason*, 3.   [15] *Ibid.*, 178.

geometrical method sets a standard of rational logic to which all ideas that merited any respect must conform.[16] In the *Tractatus* he represents Judaism as the starkest case of a worldview that does not conform to these standards. Toleration of Judaism thus falls prey to a suppressed paradox: if this religion is intrinsically inimical to any notion of individual intellectual freedom, then how can it be encompassed within the bounds of a toleration that is based on the absolute paramountcy of this ethical value? Spinoza's hostile characterisation of Judaism throws into relief an edge of judgemental inflexibility that problematises the intellectual foundations on which his argument for tolerance is based.

JOHN LOCKE: UNIVERSALISM AND CONVERSIONISM

The most influential English text on toleration in the late seventeenth century was undoubtedly John Locke's *Letter Concerning Toleration*, first published, anonymously and in Latin, in 1689. Unlike Spinoza, Locke was in no sense an uncompromising rationalist: he was fundamentally concerned to establish a demarcation between reason and religion that defended the integrity of both domains, and insulated them from each other.[17] Locke's argument does not advocate an unrestricted freedom of thought. He firmly excludes the rights of atheists, asserting that 'all men know and acknowledge that God ought to be publicly worshipped'.[18] He also implicitly bars Catholicism, by excluding from toleration '[t]hat church...which is constituted on such a bottom, that all those who enter into it, *ipso facto*, deliver themselves up to the protection and service of another prince'.[19]

It is unclear to what extent non-Christians are included within the remit of Locke's argument. At one point in the *Letter*, he proclaims a universal definition of toleration: 'Nay, if we may openly speak the truth, and as becomes one man to another, neither pagan, nor Mahometan, nor Jew, ought to be excluded from the commonwealth because of his religion. The gospel commands no such thing...'[20] Locke specifically endorses the right of the Jews to open public synagogues – a privilege they were still

---

[16] See Efraim Shmueli, 'The Geometrical Method, Personal Caution, and the Idea of Tolerance', in R. W. Shahan and J. I. Biro, eds., *Spinoza: New Perspectives* (1978) 213–14.

[17] See John Marshall, *John Locke* (1994) 357–76; Samuel C. Pearson, Jr., 'The Religion of John Locke and the Character of his Thought', in Richard Ashcraft, ed., *John Locke: Critical Assessments* (1991) 11, 133–50; Jonathan I. Israel, 'Spinoza, Locke and the Enlightenment Battle for Toleration', in Grell and Porter, eds., *Toleration*, 102–13.

[18] John Locke, *A Letter Concerning Toleration* (1991 (1689)) 32.

[19] *Ibid.*, 46.   [20] *Ibid.*, 51.

denied in England, where all Jewish worship still took place in private houses.[21] However, in the first few lines of the *Letter* Locke defines his subject matter as 'my thoughts about the mutual toleration of Christians in the different professions of religion', and frames his argument in explicitly Christian terms: 'I esteem that toleration to be the chief characteristical mark of the true Church.'[22] The importance in Locke's thought of his Christian perspective, and particularly of his Calvinist concept of moral 'calling', has been underestimated in the classic interpretation of him as the supreme prophet of modern secular liberalism.[23] The theological dimension of his politics, however, is starkly apparent in his fractured stance on the toleration of Judaism, which, despite his inclusionary pronouncements, he nonetheless regarded with a fundamental philosophical hostility.

Locke's argument for toleration is fundamentally based on the principle of the rights of conscience. 'The care of each man's salvation belongs only to himself', he writes, insisting that each individual must be free to observe the form of worship that their personal conscience dictates.[24] Judaism, however, stands outside this logic. Echoing the traditional Christian view of the Mosaic Republic, Locke stresses its utterly theocratic nature:

[T]he commonwealth of the Jews, different in that from all others, was an absolute theocracy: nor was there, nor could there be, any difference between that commonwealth and the church. The laws established there concerning the worship of one invisible Deity, were the civil laws of that people, and a part of their political government, in which God himself was the legislator.[25]

The Mosaic Commonwealth, and the Jewish laws that are its legacy, are here defined as a moral universe within which the necessary space for the kind of individual calling that stands at the crux of Locke's politics and ethics is uniquely obliterated. Like Spinoza, Locke characterises Judaism as a religion based on law rather than conscience. He implicitly defines Judaism as intrinsically inimical to the principle of personal conscience on which his notion of toleration is based, and therefore – although he does not address this – presumably radically unassimilable within a regime of toleration grounded on that right.

Locke's *Letter* was swiftly rebutted in print by Jonas Proast, who took particular exception to Locke's extension of toleration to Moslems and Jews, on the grounds that 'such a wide toleration can do no service to the

[21] *Ibid.*; N. I. Matar, 'The Controversy over the Restoration of the Jews in English Protestant Thought', *Durham University Journal* 49 (1987–8) 241.
[22] Locke, *Letter*, 14.   [23] See John Dunn, *The Political Thought of John Locke* (1969) 245–61.
[24] Locke, *Letter*, 32–3, 42.   [25] *Ibid.*, 39.

True Religion'.[26] In response, Locke reiterated his support for the toleration of Jewish worship, but offered a very different defence of his argument:
'[W]e pray every day for their Conversion, and I think it our duty so to
do; But it will, I fear hardly be believed that we pray in earnest, if we
exclude them from the... ordinary and probable means of Conversion;
either by driving them from, or persecuting them when they are amongst
us.'[27] In his correspondence with Phillip van Limborch from 1685 to 1687,
Locke reveals himself to be, like van Limborch, an ardent conversionist,
eager to hasten the mass Jewish conversion that will herald the Day of
Judgement.[28] The casualness with which Locke slides from an apparently
unconditional advocacy of the toleration of Jews to a more traditional and
circumscribed conversionist position demonstrates the superficiality of his
consideration of the Jewish case. More pointedly, though, and taken together with Locke's moral hostility towards Judaism, a tension is apparent
between his willingness to accept Jews as citizens and his pronounced ambivalence over whether they can truly be accepted as Jews. The tangled
jumble of attitudes that Locke displays towards Judaism exposes an un-
thought strand of arrogance and intolerance that lies deeply woven into his
notion of enlightened toleration.

PIERRE BAYLE: TOLERATING INTOLERANCE

For the Huguenot political theorists of the 1680s the ideal of a universal
toleration was problematised much less by Judaism than by Catholicism.
The first extended Huguenot advocacy of the principle of toleration, Henri
Basnage de Beauval's *Tolérance des Religions* (1684), is intensely polemical
in tone. Basnage devotes most of his essay to a vehement attack on the
intolerance of the French Catholic Church since the beginning of the Wars
of Religion, comparing their zeal to the ferocity of 'a tiger intoxicated
by blood',[29] in contrast to the stoic and honourable peacefulness of the
Huguenots, 'who know how to bear misfortune bravely'.[30] Given Basnage's
characterisation of Catholicism as pathologically oppressive, his theory of
toleration falls into the same paradox posed by Spinoza and Locke's hostility
towards Judaism: if Catholicism is itself intrinsically intolerant, it must also
be, at least in this respect, intolerable.

---

[26] Jonas Proast, *Argument of the Letter Concerning Toleration, Briefly Consider'd and Answer'd* (1690)
2–3.
[27] John Locke ['Philanthropus'], *A Second Letter Concerning Toleration* (1690) 2.
[28] Matar, 'John Locke and the Jews', 50.
[29] Henri Basnage, *Tolérance des Religions* (1970 (1684)) 31.   [30] *Ibid.*, 103.

Pierre Bayle's slightly later *Commentaire Philosophique* (1686) addressed the issue with much greater sophistication. This essay was both the most inclusive and the most philosophically rigorous argument for toleration in this period, confronting the dilemmas of the concept more directly than any other Enlightenment writer.[31] Bayle's argument is structured around a refutation of the literal interpretation of Jesus' words in Luke's gospel: 'Go out into the highways and hedges, and compel them to come in, that my house may be filled.'[32] Since the original exegesis of St Augustine this prooftext had been invoked by theologians in justification of coercive methods to drive heretics back to the true faith. Strenuously repudiating this logic, Bayle here argues for the toleration of all sects – with no exceptions, and explicitly including Jews – on the sole condition that they pose no threat to the state.[33]

In a broadly similar but much more outspoken manner than Locke, the linchpin of Bayle's argument in the *Commentaire* is his insistence on the paramountcy of conscience.[34] He opens his text with a lengthy defence of the inescapable need to base all understanding on the inner insights of the individual 'natural light'.[35] For Bayle, the inner voice of conscience is the voice of God, and therefore must in all circumstances be obeyed. His argument against the literal reading of the biblical injunction to 'compel them to come in' is, he states, not theological but philosophical. His conclusions are based on one basic principle of natural light: 'any literal interpretation which carries an obligation to commit iniquity is false'.[36] Such is Bayle's conviction of the self-evidence of this notion that he equates it with sanity itself: 'As long as a man is not mildly mad, he will never consent to anyone being able to command him to hate his God and to scorn his laws clearly and distinctly dictated to conscience and intimately engraven in the heart.'[37] In rebuttal of the argument, advanced by theologians such as Jurieu, that a distinction must be made between the toleration of truth and of falsehood, Bayle insists that 'an erroneous conscience has the same rights as an enlightened conscience'.[38] The individual, he argues,

---

[31] On the historical context of the *Commentaire*, see Amie Godman Tannenbaum, 'Introduction' to *Pierre Bayle's 'Philosophical Commentary': A Modern Translation and Critical Interpretation* (1987); Hubert Bost, *Pierre Bayle et la religion* (1994) 51–62; Elizabeth Labrousse, 'Note sur la théorie de la tolerance chez Pierre Bayle', *Notes sur Bayle* (1987) 173–6; Walter Rex, *Essays on Pierre Bayle and Religious Controversy* (1965) 136ff.

[32] Luke 14:23.   [33] Pierre Bayle, *Philosophical Commentary*, 145.

[34] For a contrasting interpretation of the relationship between Bayle and Locke, see Sally Jenkinson, 'Two Concepts of Tolerance: Or Why Bayle is Not Locke', *Journal of Political Philosophy* 4 (1996) 302–22.

[35] Bayle, *Philosophical Commentary*, 29.   [36] *Ibid.*, 28.   [37] *Ibid.*, 66.   [38] *Ibid.*, 15.

is always morally bound to follow the dictates of conscience, regardless of what those dictates might be, and on what religious conviction they are based.[39]

This commitment leads Bayle to an immediate problem. What of those who believe that their conscience requires them to persecute others? This was effectively the argument of Louis XIV and his supporters in their repression of Protestantism in France, who claimed that as loyal Christians they were obliged to extirpate heresy. Bayle was sharply aware of this problem, which he poses explicitly in his text: 'The ... difficulty proposed is that my doctrine, in its consequences, destroys what I would like to establish. My design is to show that persecution is an abominable thing, and yet everyone who believes himself obliged by conscience to persecute would, by my doctrine be obliged to persecute and would be sinning if he did not.[40] In response to this objection, Bayle redefines the purpose of his argument as being 'to convince persecutors that Jesus Christ has not commanded violence'.[41] Rather than claiming that his case for toleration is incontrovertibly based on abstract reason, he implicitly acknowledges that he must ultimately take recourse to faith, and specifically to Christian faith, in order to convince persecutors of 'those errors of conscience which they may harbour in regard to persecution'.[42] He does not flinch from the ineluctable consequence of his argument: those who remain convinced in conscience of the necessity to persecute others indeed must follow their consciences and do so. He nonetheless unequivocally condemns such beliefs, not in terms of detached philosophical rationalism, but in ethical outrage:

I do not deny that those who are actually persuaded that it is necessary to extirpate sects in order to obey God, are obliged to follow the motions of this false conscience and that, in not doing so, they are guilty of disobedience to God since they do a thing they believe to be in disobedience to God.

But, (1) It does not follow that they do without sin what they do by conscience. (2) This does not hinder our crying out loudly against their false maxims and endeavouring to enlighten their understandings.[43]

This shift brings into sharp relief the outer limit of Bayle's pyrrhonistic argument in favour of tolerance. Sceptical reasoning here arrives at the point of its own inevitable self-undermining, leaving the philosopher with no alternative but to turn to faith. However, this represents not the collapse but the climax of the *Commentaire Philosophique*.[44] The paradoxical

---

[39] On the implications of this argument, see John Kilcullen, *Sincerity and Truth: Essays on Arnauld, Bayle and Toleration* (1988) 59–105.
[40] Bayle, *Philosophical Commentary*, 166.   [41] *Ibid.*, 167.   [42] *Ibid.*   [43] *Ibid.*
[44] I here disagree with the interpretation in Rex, *Essays on Pierre Bayle*, 184–5.

insufficiency of reason is central to Bayle's philosophical investigations, permeating, as we have seen, almost all the articles on the Old Testament in his later *Dictionnaire Historique et Critique*.[45] It is as a moral judgement, impervious to sceptical attack, that he asserts that persecution is sinful – just as moral conviction also underpins his more contentious declaration that no responsible individual could deny the self-evident sinfulness of sodomy and adultery.[46]

This pronouncement highlights the most obvious problem inherent in Bayle's dependence on the individual conscience: it is by no means self-evident that all reasonable people share the same inner notion of sin. The limits of Bayle's argument, however, are most sustainedly highlighted by his extensive discussion of the relationship of Judaism and toleration. As we have already seen in his approach to Jewish history in the *Dictionnaire*, Bayle, like Spinoza and Locke, regarded Judaism as a religion in which personal conscience is erased by the absolute authority of the Mosaic Law. In the *Commentaire Philosophique*, this foundational opposition of Judaism to philosophy emerges not simply as an abstract paradox, but as an exclusion that casts a troubling shadow over the practical implications of his theory of toleration.

In the first chapter of the *Commentaire* Bayle explicitly states that the Old Testament falls within the purview of his argument.[47] The Mosaic Law, he argues, while extending beyond the insights of the universal inner light, is in all respects compatible with it. For the Jews from Moses' time onward it served as a supplement to the natural light, dependent on it and as valid as it, just as deductions in geometry carry the same authority as the axioms from which they are derived.[48] As an elucidation of this, Bayle discusses a case, culled from Guilelmus Arvernus' thirteenth-century *De fide et legibus*, of a group of medieval Jews who renounced Judaism, because they regarded the Mosaic Law as nothing more than 'an infinity of useless or absurd precepts', with no divine authority to endorse them.[49] Bayle is sharply critical of these Jews' apostasy. He judges them guilty of disregarding both 'the incontestable proofs of divinity which God himself had given the mission of Moses' and the 'solid grounds' on which the ceremonial laws were based, given 'the character of the Jewish nation and their penchant to idolatry'.[50]

[45] On the centrality of this strategy to Bayle's treatment of the key problem of theodicy, see Lothar Kreimendahl, 'Das Theodizeeproblem und Bayle's fideistischer Lösungsversuch', in Popkin and Vanderjagt, eds., *Scepticism*, 267–81.
[46] Bayle, *Philosophical Commentary*, 168.   [47] *Ibid.*, 31.   [48] *Ibid.*, 31–2.
[49] *Ibid.*, 32.   [50] *Ibid.*

This curious digression highlights an important paradox in Bayle's argument. Despite his general insistence on the absolute paramountcy of individual conscience, he nonetheless unreservedly condemns these Jews, who followed their consciences in choosing to abandon Judaism. In this case, the rights of conscience are overridden by the authority of the Mosaic revelation, which is 'a general law with regard to the Jews, enunciated absolutely and without restriction to time or place'.[51] Whereas for Christians knowledge of God and of ethics is above all discovered through the individual's personal inner light, for the Jews this is displaced by the binding authority of the Mosaic Law, through which God exceptionally 'limited the immunities of conscience'.[52]

The exceptional suppression of conscience in the case of the Jews is of great significance in Bayle's argument. This transcendental frustration of logic, in the most intimate commandments of God to his chosen people, constitutes, in his eyes, the deepest possible reminder of the mystery of faith. In his typical style of unswerving intellectual honesty, he directly confronts the political consequences of this clash between faith and reason. Since the Mosaic Law allowed absolutely no toleration for idolaters and false prophets, might God not in the New Testament also have commanded a similar intolerance towards heresy?[53] Bayle's response to this imagined objection is blunt and unflinching: 'I avow in good faith that this objection is strong and seems to be a mark that God wishes us to know hardly anything with certainty, by the exceptions He put in His words for almost all the common notions of reason.'[54] In the *Dictionnaire* Bayle's exploration of the incommensurability of faith and reason, also crucially associated with the uniqueness of Judaism, appears for the most part as an intellectually playful celebration of the eternal paradoxes of philosophy. In the *Commentaire*, however, this same argument takes on more sombre overtones, as Bayle starkly recognises its practical implication: no political principle, even one as basic as toleration, can be asserted with absolute certainty and authority.

This conclusion in no sense undermines his argument for toleration: on the contrary, it marks its crucial reconciliation with the rigorous, unbounded scepticism that extends to every corner of Bayle's thought. Just as reason must ultimately cede to faith, Bayle acknowledges that in the political sphere philosophy must ultimately give way to pragmatics. His awareness of the limits of his theory of toleration did not at all restrain his scathing attacks on his opponents – Pierre Jurieu in particular – whose opinions he believed were undermining the possibility of a tolerant society.[55] His final

---

[51] *Ibid.*, 121.   [52] *Ibid.*, 120.   [53] *Ibid.*, 117.   [54] *Ibid.*, 118.
[55] See John Christian Laursen, 'Baylean Liberalism: Tolerance Requires Nontolerance', in Laursen and Nederman, eds., *Beyond the Persecuting Society*, 197–215.

abandonment of the possibility of a philosophically conclusive account of toleration leads him to an acceptance of the messiness of politics, and of the inevitable contingency and variety of the ways in which groups that disagree manage successfully to coexist.[56]

The enduring viability of Bayle's theory of toleration does not, however, displace the troubling implications of its dependence on a profoundly negative view of Judaism. Bayle's explicit advocacy of the political toleration of Jews is destabilised by his representation of Judaism as itself quintessentially intolerant. In casting Judaism as the defining antithesis of the values of individual moral responsibility on which his theory of toleration is based, Bayle explicitly places it outside the realm within which the theory applies. While nominally extending to Jews the right of civil toleration, he also excludes them from the community of the tolerant.

This tension in some sense reflects a philosophical inevitability: the idea of tolerance can only be defined in opposition to a contrasting notion of intolerance.[57] For Bayle, and also for Spinoza and Locke, Judaism filled the rhetorically indispensable role of philosophical negative, in diametric contrast to which the positive contours of toleration could be delineated. In our own era Islam rather than Judaism is much more frequently cast as the inverse of enlightened toleration, in contrast to which 'western' values are defined and reinforced. During the Enlightenment, however, Judaism was the ubiquitous agonistic partner of reason. Bayle's *Commentaire philosophique*, because of the unwavering absolutism and rigour of its sceptical logic, exposes the political implications of this opposition perhaps more starkly than any other text. Like many other essays of this period, but with much greater transparency than almost all of them, Bayle's political argument for the toleration of Jews was undercut by his philosophically fundamental rejection of Judaism.

ABSTRACT ARGUMENTS AND POLITICAL RIGHTS

The Jews of western Europe were not passive bystanders to the toleration debates of the seventeenth century. The first sustained modern advocacy of Jewish toleration, foreshadowing many later Enlightenment arguments on the subject, was Simone Luzzatto's *Discorso circa il stato de gl'Hebrei* (1638). Luzzatto (d. 1663), who succeeded Leone Modena as chief rabbi of Venice, wrote his essay in response to the threatened expulsion of the Jews from

---

[56] For a compelling argument for this view of toleration, see Michael Walzer, *On Toleration* (1997) esp. 1–5.

[57] See Mary Warnock, 'The Limits of Toleration', in Susan Mendus and David Edwards, eds., *On Toleration* (1987) 123–39.

Venice in 1636–7, in the aftermath of a scandal in which several members of the community had been implicated in a major robbery.[58] Luzzatto's apologia is unmistakably rationalist in flavour. Eschewing any theological defence of Judaism, he emphasises instead the practical economic advantages that accrue to Venice thanks to the Jewish presence in the city. He celebrates the Jews' excellence in maritime trade, stresses their civic loyalty and defends the basic ethics of Judaism. The Mosaic Law, he reminds his readers, requires that Jews treat everybody, including non-Jews, with charity and kindness.[59]

Luzzatto was one of the most outward-looking and heterodox Jews of his generation. His other major work, the scientifically oriented *Socrate* (1651), was also written in Italian for a non-Jewish readership.[60] While his political rationalism can be situated within a Jewish intellectual tradition originating with Maimonides, the secular universalism and philosophical scepticism of *Socrate* strongly suggest the influence of Montaigne.[61] Luzzatto should be seen as a significant precursor of the Enlightenment, both with respect to his vigorous defence of science and repudiation of superstition in *Socrate* and to his approach to the politics of toleration in the *Discorso*. Studiously avoiding reference to theology in both texts, he approached both science and politics in starkly secular terms that were extremely radical for his period.

The *Discorso* circulated widely, and Luzzatto's arguments were an important influence not only on Jews such as Menasseh ben Israel and Spinoza, but also on James Harrington's *Oceana* (1656).[62] However, the impact of this text may well have been to some extent double-edged. A lengthy chapter of the *Discorso* is devoted to the refutation of the anti-Jewish arguments of Tacitus, which were little known among Christians in the early seventeenth century, and which Luzzatto perhaps used as a proxy for contemporary slanders and allegations.[63] Rebutting Tacitus' portrayal of the Ancient Jews as superstitious and ignorant, Luzzatto stressed the political order and wisdom of the Mosaic Republic. While this critique was itself influential, it also inevitably drew attention to Tacitus' own arguments, which, as we have seen,

---

[58] Benjamin C. I. Ravid, *Economics and Toleration in Seventeenth Century Venice* (1978) 7–18.
[59] Simone Luzzatto, *Discorso circa il stato de gl'Hebrei* (1638) 8–32, 46–51.
[60] David Ruderman, *Jewish Thought and Scientific Discovery in Early Modern Europe* (1995) 153.
[61] Bernard Septimus, 'Biblical Religion in Simone Luzzatto, Maimonides and Spinoza', in Twersky and Septimus, eds., *Jewish Thought*, 399–433; Ruderman, *Jewish Thought*, 178–84.
[62] Abraham Melamed, 'English Travellers and Venetian Jewish Scholars: The Case of Simone Luzzatto and James Harrington', in Gaetano Cozzi, ed., *Gli ebrei e Venezia* (1987) 507–26.
[63] Luzzatto, *Discorso*, 57–72; Abraham Melamed, 'Simone Luzzatto on Tacitus: Apologetica and Ragione Di Stato', in Isadore Twersky, ed., *Studies in Medieval Jewish History and Literature*, II (1984) 149–50, 158–60.

emerged in the late seventeenth century as a major source of anti-biblical counter-histories and polemics.

In 1714 John Toland published a brief pamphlet titled *Reasons for Natu-ralizing the Jews in Great Britain and Ireland*. In this deliberately provocative essay Toland drew heavily on Luzzatto's *Discorso* to advance his argument for a 'general naturalisation' of all Jews, which would liberate them from all civil impediments.[64] Following Luzzatto, Toland describes the Jews as excellent brokers of trade, and stresses their political loyalty: 'they'll never join with any Party in Civil Affairs, but that which patronizes liberty of conscience and their naturalization, which will ever be the side of Liberty and the Constitution'.[65] He ardently praises the virtues of the Jews, claim-ing that as citizens they are 'as obedient, peaceable, useful and advantageous as any; and even more so than any others', and noting enthusiastically that 'the Jews were anciently excellent soldiers', and therefore potentially could be so again.[66] Toland's unequivocal argument for the political normalisa-tion of the political status of Jews was unprecedented both in its secularism and in its specificity, and has appropriately been celebrated as an important landmark on the historical pathway to Jewish emancipation.[67]

Toland's defence of Judaism was not, however, simply based on a disin-terested concern for the plight of this minority, or even on a primary interest in the Jews' economic usefulness.[68] As we have already seen, Toland's intel-lectual approach to Judaism was complicated, embracing contrary strands of normalisation and idealisation. His hyperbolic praise for the Jews, and particularly his leap from their supposed ancient martial prowess to their contemporary promise, reflects an enduringly exceptionalist view of Jewish history. More profoundly, however, this exceptionalism is also lodged in Toland's thought at a philosophical level. Echoing the argument of his earlier *Origines Judaicae*, Toland finds support in Luzzatto for his sharp distinction between the parochial, accommodated rituals of Judaism, and its universal, philosophical core:

LUZZATTO expressly maintains, that as their religion, consider'd as it is *Jewish*, or distinct from the LAW OF NATURE, was solely calculated for their own Nation and Republic; so they were never commanded to instruct others in their particular

---

[64] I. E. Barzilay, 'John Toland's borrowings from Simone Luzzatto', *Jewish Social Studies* 31 (1969) 75–81.
[65] John Toland, *Reasons for Naturalizing the Jews in Great Britain and Ireland* (1714) 12.
[66] *Ibid.*, 11, 16.
[67] See, for example, Ettinger, 'The Beginning of a Change', 216–19.
[68] For a similar interpretation, see Justin Champion, 'Toleration and Citizenship in Enlightenment England: John Toland and the Naturalization of the Jews, 1714–1753', in Grell and Porter, eds., *Toleration*, 133–56; in contrast, David S. Katz, *The Jews in the History of England, 1485–1850* (1982) 234–7.

rites and ceremonies, tho they are every where enjoin'd to magnify to all the world the divine goodness, wisdom, and power, with those duties of men, and other attributes of God, which constitute NATURAL RELIGION.[69]

Toland's support for Jewish naturalisation was thus closely related to his idealised view of the essence of Judaism, which he sharply differentiated from its modern form. A loosely similar disassociation appears in the writings of other advocates of toleration. Gregorio Leti (1631–1701), a flamboyant Italian émigré of Amsterdam, lavishly praised the economic and cultural benefits of the Dutch toleration of the Jews, but disdainfully described synagogue worship as consisting largely of 'gesti ridicolosissimi'.[70] Toland, however, goes beyond this, effectively conflating a universalised, abstract Judaism with his own positive philosophy, while viewing its existing religious form with political indifference and intellectual disdain. While powerfully combating traditional religious and social prejudices towards Jews, his argument for Jewish naturalisation is based on a highly filtered and fanciful notion of Judaism itself.

The economic functionalism of Toland's pamphlet should also be interpreted in a wider polemical context. Hostility to Judaism was widespread within the conservative 'country party' of early eighteenth-century England. This faction felt their traditional, landed values to be threatened by the rise of commerce and moveable capital, and perceived Jewish and Huguenot immigrant communities as playing a prominent role in this process. Whig thinkers such as Toland expressly sought to counter such rhetoric, and in order to do so turned to a rational analysis of social and economic questions. Bernard Mandeville, another staunch advocate of religious toleration, extended the logic of social rationalism to its fullest extent in his *Fable of the Bees* (1723), in which he famously and shockingly argued that public benefits flowed from the private vice of selfishness.[71] In France, too, economic pragmatism was closely associated with the cause of toleration. In his *Persian Letters* Montesquieu, through the voice of Usbek, welcomed the decline of the Christian 'spirit of intolerance', noting that the persecution of the Jews, like that of the Huguenots, had caused nothing but harm.[72] This practical argument, however, was not in Montesquieu's case linked to any reappraisal of conventional stereotypes of Jews or Judaism. Usbek observes the Jews' 'invincibly stubborn religious conviction, which

[69] Toland, *Reasons for Naturalizing*, 50–1.
[70] Israel, 'Gregorio Leti and the Dutch Sephardi Elite', 269–70.
[71] See E. G. Hundert, *The Enlightenment's Fable: Bernard Mandeville and the Discovery of Society* (1994) esp. 11–15; on religious toleration see Bernard Mandeville, *Free Thoughts on Religion* (1720) xv, 214–51.
[72] Montesquieu, *Persian Letters* (1993 (1721)) 125.

verges on folly', and comments sardonically that 'wherever there is money, there are Jews as well'.[73]

The precariousness of the relationship between the political toleration of Jews and the enduring religious and social hostility towards them was highlighted by the furore that surrounded the passing and subsequent repeal of the English 'Jew Bill'. In April 1753 the government introduced, and both houses of Parliament swiftly passed, a 'Jewish Naturalisation Act', which exempted Jews from the normal requirement of taking the sacrament in order to become naturalised citizens. This act affected only a very small number of foreign-born Jewish magnates, for whom it was intended by the Whig government as a quiet favour. Jews born in England were not subject to the discriminatory 'alien duties' that were the main commercial disadvantage of foreign status; while only the most prosperous Jews could afford the expense of steering a private act through Parliament, which remained the only way to become naturalised. Nonetheless, the passing of the bill provoked a public outcry. Facing a barrage of satire and criticism, the government swiftly initiated the repeal of the bill, which by the end of the following year had been largely forgotten.[74]

The most startling aspect of the 'Jew Bill' controversy is the suddenness with which it both erupted and disappeared, and the casual ease with which the government proponents of the bill reversed their position. Many of the anti-Jewish polemics produced in 1753 approached a near-hysterical level of rhetoric and anxiety. More than sixty pamphlets appeared in the course of the outcry, many of which focused on the intimate peril of circumcision: lurid images were evoked of true-born Englishmen forcibly emasculated by hordes of naturalised Jewish zealots.[75] The straightforwardness with which the bill was initially passed suggests a tacit acceptance within British parliamentary culture of a pragmatic, secular approach to Jewish affairs. However, once the issue erupted, the terms of debate immediately shifted into a very different register. While opponents of the bill portrayed Jews as incorrigibly alien, its defenders also typically cast the Jews in an exceptionalist frame, arguing that a welcoming approach to Jews was the best way to effect their conversion.[76]

---

[73] *Ibid.*

[74] See Thomas W. Perry, *Public Opinion, Propaganda and Politics in Eighteenth-Century England: A Study of the Jew Bill of 1753* (1962); Todd Endelman, *The Jews of Georgian England 1714–1830* (1979) 24–6, 88–91; Katz, *Jews in the History of England*, 240–53; James Shapiro, *Shakespeare and the Jews* (1996) 195–224; Champion, 'Toleration and Citizenship', 136–9; Frank Felsenstein, *Anti-Semitic Stereotypes: A Paradigm of Otherness in English Popular Culture, 1660–1830* (1995) 187–214.

[75] Roy S. Wolper, 'Circumcision and Polemic in the Jew Bill of 1753: The Cutter Cut?', *Eighteenth-Century Life* 8 (1982) 28–36; Wolper, ed., *Pieces on the 'Jew Bill', 1753* (1983).

[76] Endelman, *Jews of Georgian England*, 59–62.

Over sixty years earlier, as we have seen, John Locke moved from a philosophically universalist rationale for the political toleration of the Jews to an
argument based on conversionist strategy. In the midst of the High Enlightenment, attempts to think of Jewish difference in non-exceptional terms
were no less unstable. The theology of Jewish otherness could temporarily
be overridden by the pragmatic logic of the exchange of favours within the
London political and economic elite. However, once Jewishness became
the focus of public debate, abstract notions of toleration were almost immediately displaced in the minds of virtually all parties by deep-seated,
theologically based views of Judaism and Jews as constitutively unique and
alien.[77]

It would perhaps be comforting to be able to draw a sharp separation
between the populist demagoguery of 1753 and the sober, liberal arguments
for toleration developed by Spinoza, Locke, Toland and Bayle. Their arguments paved the way for the possibility of the Jew Bill; and we can imagine
that all four men would have been deeply depressed by the prospect of such
a vehement outpouring of anti-Judaic sentiment more than a generation
after their deaths. However, despite their best endeavours, none of these
thinkers was able to transcend the exceptionalism that structured virtually
all responses to Judaism within the Christian cultural tradition. Even while
explicitly arguing for the sameness of the political rights of Jews alongside
all other peoples, all four thinkers, in distinct but closely related ways, reasserted the underlying unique difference of Judaism. The philosophical
ambiguity towards Judaism in their texts is indirectly echoed – under high
distortion – in the political muddles, contradictions, absurdities and rever-
sals of the English Jew Bill episode. Similar ambiguities in the treatment of
Judaism resonate more widely through the eighteenth century and beyond.
Most starkly, and most infamously, they abound in the writings of the most
celebrated polemicist of the entire Enlightenment: François Marie Arouet,
better known as Voltaire.

---

[77] On the emergence of a newly unified visual stereotype of Jews during this controversy, see Isaiah
Shachar, 'The Emergence of the Modern Pictorial Stereotype of "The Jews" in England', in Dov
Noy and Issachar Ben-Ami, eds., *Studies in the Cultural Life of the Jews in England* (1975) 331–66.

CHAPTER 12

The ambiguities of Enlightenment:
Voltaire and the Jews

Voltaire's reputation is based less on what he wrote – apart from *Candide*, he is relatively little read today – than on what he represents. More potently than any other eighteenth-century figure, Voltaire stands metonymically for the Enlightenment spirit of engaged struggle against intolerance and superstition. This image, carefully constructed over the course of the nineteenth century,[1] has continued to imbue most twentieth-century scholarship on this intellectual hero. For his leading biographer, Theodore Besterman, Voltaire was the very embodiment of the spirit of reason – 'the most absolute kind of rationalist' – and should be given much of the credit for initiating the key social and intellectual battles of the Enlightenment.[2] The tricentennial of Voltaire's birth in 1994 was marked in France with much fanfare, including a major exhibition celebrating his central role in spreading the Enlightenment across Europe.[3] In an era of seemingly increasing political disengagement, Voltaire's tireless intellectual activism continues to hold a considerable inspirational power.

One prominent current in Voltaire's writings, however, strikes a contrary note: his sustainedly disparaging and often vehemently hostile attitude to Judaism. His historical writings and biblical criticism, in particular, are punctuated with polemical attacks on the Jews, whom in one representative passage he dismisses as 'this vile people, superstitious, ignorant, and both scientifically and commercially stunted'.[4] He repetitively reiterates a familiar range of anti-Jewish themes: the absurdity of the Pentateuch, the insignificance and uncreativity of the Jews, and their barbarism, arrogance

---

[1] See Stephen Bird, *Reinventing Voltaire: The Politics of Commemoration in Nineteenth Century France* (2000).

[2] Theodore Besterman, *Voltaire* (1969), 604–5. See also similar comments in Norman Torrey, *The Spirit of Voltaire* (1963) 40; Peter Gay, *Voltaire's Politics* (1959) vii; René Pomeau, *Politique de Voltaire* (1963) 202.

[3] See Françoise Bléchet, ed., *Voltaire et l'Europe* (1994).

[4] *Remarques sur les Pensées de Pascal* (1728) M.xxii.45. All references to works by Voltaire will be made in this format to his *Oeuvres complètes*, ed. Louis Moland, 52 vols, Paris, 1877–85.

and immorality. For Voltaire, Judaism signifies primitivism, legalism, and blind reverence for tradition: the obverse of his own Enlightenment values of progress and rational enquiry. The extent of Voltaire's contempt for the Jews, and the aggressive tone in which it is often expressed, cast a problematic shadow over his commitment to universal toleration. If Judaism represents those values that are most antithetical to the spirit of rationalist justice and toleration, on what terms, from a Voltairean perspective, can the Jewish people themselves be tolerated?

Many attempts have been made to absolve Voltaire of the charge of antisemitism, or to quarantine this flaw from his otherwise triumphant historical reputation. Several scholars have largely discounted his anti-Judaic rhetoric as an incidental product of his stylistic flamboyance and polemical vigour, or as an unthinking reflection of the common assumptions of his time that was in any case powerfully trumped by his abstract commitment to universal toleration.[5] The severity of his diatribes has been speculatively ascribed to the two instances in his life in which he lost money in dealings with Jews: however, his polemics precede by several years the earlier of these incidents, in 1726, when his Jewish banker in London went bankrupt.[6] These exonerating arguments are based on a view of anti-Jewish attitudes as neatly separable from the wider opinions of the person who holds them. However, an examination of Voltaire's writings powerfully suggests the contrary: the problems posed by Judaism stand at the very core of his thought and politics.

Voltaire, it has become almost a cliché to observe, was not a 'system-builder'.[7] His piercing wit and indefatigable political engagement took precedence over philosophical consistency: the many oscillations and contradictions in his texts should therefore, it has been argued, not be accorded too much significance. However, in a sense the precise opposite is the case. Voltaire, unlike more carefully systematic *philosophes* such as Montesquieu or Rousseau, made little sustained attempt to conceal the tensions within his thought. He therefore offers a particularly open view of the antinomies that ran through the eighteenth-century conception of reason. In his immense *oeuvre* Voltaire explored almost every theme that had caught the interest of Enlightenment thinkers up to his time: universal and national

---

[5] Besterman, *Voltaire*, 92; Pierre Aubery, 'Voltaire et les juifs: ironie et démystification', *SVEC* 24 (1963) 69–78; Pomeau, *Politique de Voltaire*, 48; Gay, *Voltaire's Politics*, 352–4; Bertram Eugene Schwarzbach, 'Voltaire et les juifs: bilan et plaidoyer', *Studies on Voltaire and the Eighteenth Century* 358 (1998) 27–91.

[6] Katz, *From Prejudice to Destruction*, 43; Hertzberg, *French Enlightenment*, 283–5. See also Norma Perry, 'City Life in the 1720s: The Example of Four of Voltaire's Acquaintances', in T. D. Hemming, E. Freeman and D. Meakin, eds., *The Secular City: Studies in the Enlightenment* (1994) 42–56.

[7] Ira O. Wade, *The Intellectual Development of Voltaire* (1969) 769.

histories; biblical criticism; alternative theologies and cosmologies; the politics of citizenship and toleration. He contributed little that was strictly original to these debates. However, he masterfully synthesised and rhetorically polished the major ideas and arguments that had emerged since the late seventeenth century.

Voltaire was profoundly intellectually indebted to his recent predecessors, drawing extensively on the work of the English Deists, Pierre Bayle's *Dictionnaire* and the French clandestine manuscript tradition.[8] His eclectic and impatient integration of these sources brings into sharp focus their common philosophical ambiguities and uncertainties. These philosophical problematics, as we have already seen in each of these earlier cases, pointedly intersect in questions concerning the textual, historical and political status of Judaism, which insistently trouble Voltaire's assertion of the prowess of Enlightenment rationalism. Far from being a quirk of his personal biography or temperament, Voltaire's persistent hostility towards Judaism in a sense draws into unique focus the problems underlying the general Enlightenment stance towards a minority that appeared profoundly unassimilable to its logic.

VOLTAIRE'S BIBLICAL CONTRADICTIONS

Voltaire repeatedly asserted that he found the Jews a distasteful subject. 'It is with regret that I discuss the Jews: this nation is, in many respects, the most detestable ever to have sullied the earth', he writes in the article on 'Tolerance' in his *Dictionnaire Philosophique*.[9] In this essay, however, he repeatedly returns to Jewish themes; as he does in the volume as a whole, almost a third of which consists of sustained attacks on the Pentateuch.[10] Despite his professed desire to dismiss the Jews as a historical irrelevance and a cultural embarrassment, Jews populate his writings more ubiquitously than any other people. This structural contradiction arches over a cluster of fundamental intellectual paradoxes that mark Voltaire's approach to Judaism, the Jewish Bible and Jewish history.

Voltaire's vast historical work, the *Essai sur les moeurs* (1756) has been widely recognised as a landmark in historiography. In this majestic, sprawling survey of Islamic, Chinese and Indian history, as well as of Europe since Charlemagne, Voltaire advanced a pioneering vision of 'universal history',

---

[8] Norman L. Torrey, *Voltaire and the English Deists* (1930); Haydn Mason, *Pierre Bayle and Voltaire* (1963); Spink, *French Free-Thought*, 280–324.
[9] Voltaire, *Dictionnaire Philosophique* (1764) M.xx.517–18.
[10] David Levy, 'Voltaire et son exégèse du Pentateuque', *SVEC* 130 (1975) 223.

based not on events, but on the distillation of the cultural 'spirit' of nations and past eras.[11] This project was overtly polemical: the message of the *Essai*, and of its emphasis on the moral sophistication of non-Christian societies, was to highlight the detrimental influence of priesthoods in general, and the Christian priesthood in particular.[12] Voltaire's most explicit target was Bossuet's *Discours sur l'Histoire Universelle*. Bossuet's incorporation of all history into the framework of the Bible was not in fact universal at all, Voltaire argued, but merely an account of 'four or five peoples, and mostly of the small Jewish nation, which has either been ignored or justly despised by the rest of the world'.[13] In the *Essai* he pointedly almost ignored the Jews, giving them only a brief mention subsumed within his lengthy section on the Arabs. Jewish history, as recounted in the Old Testament, was for Voltaire anti-history, in deliberate contrast to which he forged his own historical narratives.

In the introduction to the *Essai* (first published separately in 1765 as *La Philosophie de l'Histoire*) Voltaire defended his marginalisation of the Jewish past. His priority, he writes, is 'always to adhere to the historical', of which there is very little to be said concerning the Jews, because of the unreliability and absurdity of the Bible.[14] He then ridicules the Old Testament at some length, ironically feigning surprise that the dramatic escape of the Jews from Egypt – 'surely the greatest event in the history of the world' – was not mentioned by Herodotus, the Egyptian annalists, or indeed anywhere other than in the Bible.[15] In the *Essai* itself a silent Jewish presence nonetheless hovers over much of the text: Voltaire's high praise for the purity and simplicity of Indian and Chinese religion carries a clear condemnatory overtone of the contrasting corruption of Christianity, and above all of Jewish rigidity and legalism. In his later *Dieu et les hommes* (1769) he deploys this strategy more explicitly. Voltaire's discussion of Indian, Babylonian, Phoenician and Persian religion is here seeded with passing references to much later Jewish imitations.[16]

Voltaire's unfavourable comparison of Judaism to the superior cultural achievements of other civilisations draws on the long-standing tradition, through Spencer and Toland, of emphasis on the sophistication of ancient Egypt. He also closely echoes the arguments of Boulainvilliers' clandestine historical works, which juxtapose both Egyptian wisdom and Chinese

[11] See J. H. Brumfitt, *Voltaire Historian* (1958) esp. 61–70.
[12] This point was first made by Carl Becker, in *The Heavenly City of the Eighteenth-Century Philosophers* (1932) 111.
[13] *Le Pyrrhonisme de l'histoire* (1769) M.xxvii.237.   [14] *Essai sur les moeurs* (1765) M.xi.110.
[15] *Ibid.*, 62.   [16] *Dieu et les hommes* (1769) M.xxviii.138, 147, 149 and elsewhere.

simplicity to the primitivism of the ancient Hebrews.[17] The bitingly satirical tone of Voltaire's belittling of Jewish history is much bolder than Boulainvilliers' playfully subversive irony, but the substance of their arguments is very similar.

However, Voltaire's repeated portrayal of the ancient Jews as inveterate imitators stands at odds with his professed historiographical aim to demonstrate the general principles of cultural influence between civilisations. 'All nations...often imitate the cults and ceremonies of others', he writes in the introduction to the *Essai*.[18] He follows this observation with a long excursus highlighting the foreign origins of many Jewish traditions: the principle of cultural transmission that he has just presented as universal is immediately applied to the Jews in the very different spirit of a hostile exposé of hypocrisy. History, for Voltaire, is constitutively and irreducibly oppositional to the Bible. He thus applies his historical methodology not in order to reinterpret the Jewish past, but solely to discredit its leading source. This leads him, like so many of his intellectual antecedents, into a classic Enlightenment paradox. While demanding that the Jews renounce their claim to a privileged place in history, Voltaire simultaneously refuses, or is unable, to evaluate them according to normal historical standards.

Voltaire's treatment of Jewish history intermittently appears to extend beyond biblical critique. Discussing the origins of the Jews, he dismisses the biblical account as utterly incredible, insisting that before the time of Saul the Hebrews 'were nothing but a horde of desert Arabs'.[19] Echoing a long-standing association of Jews with lepers, derived ultimately from Manetho and reiterated in Mirabaud's clandestine *Opinions des Anciens sur les Juifs*,[20] Voltaire notes that more than one ancient authority records that the Jews were expelled from Egypt simply because they were ridden with leprosy.[21] However, he does not attempt to accord any stable authority to this theory, which he casually conflates with a similarly scurrilous but distinct thesis, from Diodorus Siculus, that the Jews were originally a band of robbers who infested Egypt from Ethiopia.[22] Voltaire makes no serious attempt to assess any of these sources. Despite his professed commitment to objective historical inquiry, it is clear that his forays into the Jewish past are exclusively motivated by a polemical desire to ridicule and discredit the traditional biblical narrative.

A similar suppressed tension suffuses Voltaire's attacks on the Jewish Bible. The Old Testament, as we have seen, is in his eyes simply a collection

---

[17] See Benítez, 'L'ailleurs dans la littérature clandestine'.   [18] *Essai sur les moeurs*, M.xi.13.
[19] *Ibid.*, M.xi.110.   [20] Assmann, *Moses the Egyptian*, 29–44; *Opinions des Anciens sur les Juifs*, 173.
[21] *Dieu et les hommes*, M.xxviii.158.   [22] *Ibid.*, 158–9.

of confused, absurd stories that are utterly worthless as historical evidence. However, he nonetheless uses this same text as the basis for his allegations of the exceptional barbarism, immorality and primitiveness of the ancient Jews. He ridicules the biblical account of the slaughter of the Midianites as impossibly exaggerated, but also cites the biblical figure of 23,000 massacred victims as evidence of the Jews' appalling bloodthirstiness.[23] He calculates from the Bible that precisely 239,020 Jews were exterminated by other Jews, many of them on God's express orders: while mocking the reductive and implausible exactitude of the Bible, he also shudders at the horrific barbarism suggested by these same statistics.[24] Voltaire repeatedly decries Scripture on two incompatible grounds, as both utterly discredited and uniquely scandalous. These twin accusations are frequently elided together, masking the incoherence of simultaneously rejecting the authority of the Jewish Bible and using it as a source for anti-Jewish polemics. Despite his apparent aspiration to treat the Bible simply as 'a book similar to other books',[25] Voltaire's underlying approach to the Old Testament is both exceptionalist and profoundly internally inconsistent.

Voltaire's rejection of the Bible is based on many arguments aired in earlier decades. Drawing on Spinoza, and also on the work of English Deists such as Collins and Woolston, he repeatedly ridicules the belief that Moses was the author of the Pentateuch.[26] Extending Toland's inversion of Pierre-Daniel Huet's attempt to establish the Mosaic narrative as the basis for all religions, Voltaire questions whether Moses even existed: given the far more widespread fame of other very similar ancient figures, such as Bacchus, was it not far more probable that the Jews copied their Mosaic fables from the Greeks?[27] Unlike Spinoza or Toland, however, Voltaire makes no serious attempt to develop an alternative interpretation of the biblical text. Toland's reading of Scripture, despite its eclecticism, nonetheless has an underlying coherence: his *Origines Judaicae* reinterprets the Pentateuch as the product of the human wisdom of Moses, inspired by his Egyptian priestly training. Voltaire intermittently echoes the essence of Toland's argument, but he does not commit himself to this or any other account of the sources of

---

[23] *Dictionnaire Philosophique*, M.xix.526–7; *Un chrétien contre six juifs* (1776) M.xxix.510–11; *Dieu et les hommes*, M.xxviii.172.

[24] *Essai sur les moeurs*, M.xi.117–8.

[25] Pierre Aubery, 'Voltaire and Antisemitism – a Reply to Hertzberg', *SVEC* 217 (1983) 177. See also Bertram Eugene Schwarzbach, *Voltaire's Old Testament Criticism* (1971); Arnold Ages, 'Voltaire, Calmet and the Old Testament', *Studies on Voltaire and the Eighteenth Century* 41 (1966).

[26] *Dieu et les hommes*, M.xxviii.175ff; *Dictionnaire Philosophique*, M.xx.95ff; *Examen important de milord Bolingbroke* (1767) M.xxvi.201. On Voltaire's sources see Levy, 'Voltaire', 123–8.

[27] *Dieu et les hommes*, M.xxviii.184–5.

the Hebrew Bible. While relentlessly mocking conventional opinions, he flaunts his professed disinterest in the subject. If Moses conceivably had been the true author of the Pentateuch, Voltaire facetiously comments that he must have been mad;[28] but he asserts that the question is in any case trivial, concerning merely the history of 'the forgotten chiefs of an unfortunate, barbarous land'.[29]

Voltaire's treatment of the subject of miracles highlights the difference between his approach and that of Spinoza. In the *Tractatus Theologico-Politicus* Spinoza gives a simple explanation of the abundance of miracles in the Jewish Bible: because of their scientific ignorance, the ancient Hebrews routinely misunderstood ordinary natural phenomena as instances of miraculous divine intervention.[30] Voltaire, while emphatically sharing Spinoza's repudiation of the concept of miracles, does not avail himself of this straightforward but polemically undramatic argument. Spinoza normalises early Jewish ignorance: all people, he writes at the opening of his treatment of miracles, naturally ascribe to the Divine whatever they cannot understand.[31] Voltaire's biting critique of the Old Testament, however, would be banalised by this explanatory argument. Rather than following Spinoza, he instead combs the Old Testament for miracles that seem to him particularly absurd. Why, he wonders through the mock-innocent voice of 'Zapata', a Spanish theological scholar, was a miracle necessary to enable the Jews to cross the River Jordan, which is nowhere more than forty-five feet wide, and can easily be crossed in the most simple raft?[32] Unlike Spinoza, Voltaire is ultimately not interested in a historically contextualised interpretation of Scripture. The title of his most systematic biblical commentary, *La Bible enfin expliquée* (1776) is pointedly ironic: the Bible, in his opinion, is too ridiculous to be explained, and can only be exposed in its full absurdity.

The immorality of the Jews, as reported in the Old Testament, had already been abundantly highlighted in Bayle's *Dictionnaire*. However, whereas for Bayle the incommensurability of the Ancient Jews' moral standards and their divine election was a key manifestation of the inscrutably mysterious relationship between reason and faith, for Voltaire the same biblical passages simply provide a springboard for piercing and scurrilous satire. Abraham was forced to introduce circumcision, he suggests, in order to impede the Jews' rampant masturbation: it would be understandable, he comments, had the practice simply been invented to prevent 'the abuses of puberty', but why had Abraham himself needed to be circumcised at the

---

[28] *Examen important de milord Bolingbroke*, M.xxvi.206.   [29] *Dictionnaire Philosophique*, M.xix.242.
[30] Spinoza, *TTP*, 81–97.   [31] *Ibid.*, 81.   [32] *Les questions de Zapata* (1767) M.xxvi.173.

age of almost a hundred?[33] Using a similarly strained logic, he half-jokingly claims that Jews must have been particularly susceptible to bestiality, because they were the only ancient people to have needed expressly to forbid the practice in their holy laws.[34]

Voltaire's writings on the Jews are not uniformly hostile. Although he at times specifically associates Judaism with intolerance,[35] he more than once asserts that the Ancient Jews, unlike modern Christians, were notably tolerant of religious diversity: 'The Jews venerated their God, but they were never surprised that other peoples worshipped their own.'[36] He vigorously condemns both the popular and royal persecution of Jews in medieval Europe.[37] Writing ventriloquistically through the voice of the second-century Rabbi Akiba, Voltaire puts forward one of his most passionate pleas for tolerance, highlighting the absurdity of Christians' persecution of the religion that Jesus himself practised throughout his life: 'he lived as a Jew and died a Jew, and you burn us because we are Jewish'.[38] Voltaire was not a blindly prejudiced anti-Jewish polemicist: he was capable of an empathetic understanding of Jewish oppression, and was sincerely and powerfully opposed to the ignorant Christian prejudices that he believed were its cause.

Voltaire's anti-Judaic rhetoric was also highly opportunistic: he seized on all chances to topple Judaism from its historical and theological pedestal. He was untroubled by the incompatibility of his various arguments, because his overriding aspiration, famously, was not to construct a new intellectual order, but to destroy the worst of the old: 'ecrasez l'infâme'. His attacks on Judaism, as his defenders have pointed out, were intended primarily as a strategic component of a wider political campaign directed against institutional Christianity.[39] However, the ubiquity and intensity of Voltaire's onslaughts against Judaism overflow beyond this ancillary purpose, while their logical slipperiness betrays their deeper significance. Judaism as a living eighteenth-century tradition unquestionably aggravated Voltaire far less than Christianity. As a conceptual presence, however, Judaism was uniquely troubling, disrupting the order of his thought like a stubbornly ineradicable particle of intellectual grit.

Judaism preoccupies Voltaire because it encapsulates the residuum of myth and tradition that is impervious to his Enlightenment critique. Attempting to demolish biblical myth with logical reason, Voltaire's attacks slide off their target, unable to find an effective grip. His use of internal

---

[33] *Dictionnaire Philosophique*, M.xvii.44.   [34] *Ibid.*, M.xix.535; *Un chrétien contre six juifs*, M.xxix.514.
[35] *Un chrétien contre six juifs*, M.xxix.522.   [36] *Dictionnaire Philosophique*, M.xx.520.
[37] *Ibid.*, M.xx.524–5.   [38] *Sermon du Rabbin Akib* (1761) M.xxiv.282.
[39] See, e.g., Peter Gay, *The Party of Humanity: Studies in the French Enlightenment* (1964) 103.

textual evidence to expose the logical contradictions of Scripture cannot undermine the authority of the Bible as myth. His circular argument is dependent on precisely what it aims to destroy. It is therefore inevitably inconclusive, and dependent for its impact not on its logic but on its rhetorical power. It is this that drives Voltaire's relentless repetition, with increasing ferocity as his writing career progressed, of the barbarism, immorality and insignificance of the Jews.

MYTH, ORIGINS, IDENTITY

Voltaire wrote from an assurance that his basic values of rationalism, tolerance and freedom of thought were pre-eminently simple. He knew what he was opposed to, and considered his positive principles to be the straightforward antithesis of the fanatical barbarism of religious intolerance and the insular sophistry of literalist biblical scholarship. Roland Barthes very aptly characterised Voltaire as 'The Last Happy Writer', contrasting his witty pamphleteering against 'l'infâme' in all its guises with the need for later writers to offer a more considered response to cruelty and intolerance than simple Voltairean astonishment. We have since witnessed the Holocaust, Barthes writes, but 'we have not had a single pamphlet against that'.[40]

Only twice during his lifetime, in his *Traité de Metaphysique* (1734–7) and *Le Philosophe Ignorant* (1766), did Voltaire write a positive exposition of his philosophy. Elsewhere, he propounded his beliefs essentially through negative argument: we are left to extrapolate our sense of Voltaire's positive beliefs from the many examples he presents of what he is against. His project was in large measure a destructive one, holding in its sights not only the overtly non-rational realm of religion and mythology, but also ill-founded certainties of all kinds. The happy confidence and assumed self-evidence of his rhetoric, while undoubtedly reflecting Voltaire's prevalent conscious attitude, also nimbly mask the violence and the indirectness of his method. Despite the titular claim of such essays as his *Traité sur la Tolérance* (1763), he scarcely even attempted to provide a considered definition of reason, justice or tolerance. Unable to define the meaning of these concepts in positive terms, Voltaire instead asserts their discursive power through the gesture of destructive polemic directed against their designated antitheses.

Judaism was the ideal target for this destructive energy, because it was centrally associated with a cluster of the most troublesome issues in Enlightenment thought: the nature of myth, the problem of origins and

[40] Roland Barthes., 'The Last Happy Writer', *Critical Essays* (1972) 83–4.

the formation of group identity. In the first two of these cases, Judaism represents that which Voltaire wishes to deny and destroy: the persistence and power of myth, and the rootedness of European Christian culture in the Judaic originary myth of the Bible. The Jewish relation to identity, however, was less a target for destruction than an intellectual provocation. The endurance and cohesiveness of Jewish peoplehood, founded on biblical myth, highlighted the great difficulty of constructing any alternative form of group identity that was both truly different and equally compelling.

The Jewish Bible, for Voltaire, consists of nothing other than a collection of ridiculous stories and arbitrary laws, which the Jews absurdly persist in believing and obeying. He denies any distinction between faith and superstition, or between ritual and magic, thus reducing Jewish religiosity to the level of everyday stupidity. He habitually refers to the Old Testament narratives as 'contes' (fairy-stories) or 'rêveries' (daydreams), and dismisses prophecy as straightforward lies and imposture: 'the first prophet was the first rogue to meet an imbecile'.[41] However, in asserting the meaninglessness of biblical myth, Voltaire is inevitably led into generating a new mythology of rationalism. In opposition to the biblical narrative, Voltaire produces a counter-narrative of negation, which itself does not escape from the subjectivity of myth. Moses, who did not write the Pentateuch, is re-cast (if he even existed) as an incompetent and barbarous tribal chief; the Jews, emphatically not the chosen people, become an insignificant horde of Arab thieves; and circumcision becomes a marker not of their pact with God, but of their immorality. Determined to destroy the error and deception of religious myth, Voltaire's contrary readings and interpretations of the Bible are themselves no more firmly grounded.

Voltaire treats Jewish legalism as a sub-category of Jewish superstition. Rejoicing in the absurdity of the Mosaic Law, he blurs the distinction between the content of the laws and the inflexible psychology of legalism that for him they embody. One of his favourite examples is the biblical injunction not to eat the meat of the hare, because it ruminates and does not have a cleft foot, whereas in truth the opposite is the case on both counts.[42] In ridiculing this legal pronouncement Voltaire gestures that he is highlighting its specific illogicality, compounded by its inaccuracy. His wider intent, however, is to expose the entire basis of Jewish dietary law as absurd. These attacks are subsumed within a broader characterisation of the mentality of Judaism as one of arbitrary and unthinking legalism.

---

[41] *Examen Important de milord Bolingbroke*, M.xxvi.217.
[42] *Dieu et les hommes*, M.xxviii.210; *Dictionnaire Philosophique*, M.xx.523; *Questions de Zapata*, M.xxvi.178. Biblical reference: Deuteronomy 14:7.

Voltaire's sweeping repudiation of revealed law is problematised, however, by the question of the derivation of his own ethical first principles. The essence of reason and justice must also, after all, be traceable to some originary source. Much of Voltaire's historical writing, in groping towards a secular understanding of cultural transmission, attempts indirectly to address this question. However, the positive dimension of Voltaire's thought on this subject is inevitably extremely speculative and inconclusive, and is largely drowned out by his negative assertion of the falsity of the Judaic narrative of revelation. Voltaire's rejection of the Mosaic Law is a focus of anger and frustration because it represents his attempt to extirpate the final, inextinguishable trace of revelation from his own thought. Lacking any conclusively authoritative alternative basis for his own philosophy, he can only challenge Judaic myth and law with an unacknowledged counter-myth of rationalist transparency.

Voltaire's repudiation of myth is thus intimately related to his attempt to address the question of historical origins. Within Judaism and Jewish mythology lie the origins of Christianity, and therefore also, according to traditional understanding, the essential ethical roots of European culture. It is this traditional genealogy of Western civilisation that Voltaire is determined to displace, asserting instead a vague alternative genealogy derived largely from the Ancient Romans and Greeks. He examines the Greek and Roman religions extremely closely, arguing that they acknowledged a single supreme God, and, unlike Judaism, recognised the immortality of the soul.[43] For Voltaire, cultural interaction between the Greeks and the Jews flowed only in one direction: 'the Greeks had nothing to learn from the Hebrews',[44] while they should be credited even with the naming of the city of Jerusalem, replacing the 'barbarous' Jewish name that 'grated in the throat of any Athenian'.[45] In his determination to deny any Jewish contribution to later European civilisation, Voltaire severely distorts the principles of his theory of history. He notes the resemblances between different peoples, and the cultural interchange amongst them, but excludes the Jews from this process, insisting that they alone greedily copied from their neighbours, and taught them nothing.

The problems of myth and of origins are both closely associated with that of identity, and, in particular, national identity. As Homi Bhabha has observed, 'Nations, like narratives, lose their origins in the myths of time.'[46] Voltaire's texts oscillate between contradictory opposing impulses towards

[43] *Dieu et les hommes*, M.xxviii.152–3; *Essai sur les moeurs*, M.xi.147.
[44] *Essai sur les moeurs*, M.xi.145   [45] *Ibid.*, M.xi.73.
[46] Homi K. Bhabha, 'Narrating the Nation', in Bhabha, ed., *Nation and Narration* (1990) 1.

philosophical universalism and national particularism. In his fictional *contes*, as Roland Barthes has noted, 'we are always travelling':[47] this is particularly so in *Candide*, in the course of which we are taken on a whirlwind tour of most of Europe and South America. Through his exposure of the meaningless reciprocal violence of the war between the Bulgars (Prussians) and the Abars (French), Voltaire exhorts the reader of *Candide* to transcend the pettiness of national distinctions.[48] Similarly, in his famous celebration of the London Stock Exchange he sees a vision of rational, tolerant interaction that dissolves all barriers of difference: 'Enter into the London Stock Exchange, this place more respectable than many courts, and you will see representatives of all nations gathered for the utility of mankind; there, the Jew, the Mohammedan and the Christian behave towards each other as if they were of the same religion, and reserve the word "infidel" for those who go bankrupt.'[49] Voltaire's cosmopolitan vision, while suffused with a consciousness of cultural difference, is nonetheless predicated on the erasure, or at least the reduction to irrelevance, of these same differences that sustain his fascination.

However, in much of his writing Voltaire was proudly and bombastically French. His early epic poem, *La Henriade*, was dedicated to the glorification of Henri IV, and he worked for more than twenty years on his historical *Le Siècle de Louis XIV*, in which he proudly asserted that of all the nations 'there is none that has shined as brilliantly, in every sense, for the last century, than the nation formed, in some sense, by Louis XIV'.[50] In contrast to this image of France as a glorious seventeenth-century invention, Voltaire elsewhere evokes a timeless Frenchness, created not by the transient influences of government, religion and education, but by the indelible stamp of 'climate and soil': 'The people of Gascony and of Normandy differ greatly; nonetheless, we can recognize in them the genius of the French.'[51] In his patriotic mode Voltaire searches for a notion of nationhood that is in some sense both historical and fixed. This ideal is not only internally fissured, but also stands in marked tension with the inclusive politics of his utopian cosmopolitanism.

The Jews, as a starkly anomalous 'non-national nation', exposed the tenuousness of eighteenth-century (and later) notions of national identity.[52] Blurring national frontiers and patriotisms, the Jewish diasporic presence highlighted their arbitrariness. However, while frustrating the neat national partitioning of Europe, Jews simultaneously stood as the nation *par*

---

[47] Barthes, 'Last Happy Writer', 87.   [48] *Candide* (1759) M.xxi.191–3.
[49] *Lettres philosophiques* (1734) M.xxii.99.
[50] *Le Siècle de Louis XIV* (1751) M.xiv.518; Haydn Mason, *Voltaire* (1975) 32.
[51] *Dictionnaire Philosophique* M.xix.179.   [52] See Bauman, *Modernity and the Holocaust*, 52–53.

excellence. Through the biblical narrative, and its almost explicit invocation of myth, the Jews had come as close as possible to resolving the tension between voluntarist and determinist notions of national identity. Jewish origins are not *lost* in the myths of time, but found there; while the performative rituals of national memory, awkwardly invented and contested in the case of modern nations,[53] stand at the heart of Jewish rituals of remembrance. Voltaire's hostility towards the Jews is suffused with a resentment towards the preposterous arrogance of the Jews' confidence that they are God's chosen people. Despite his repeated derision of Jews as wanderers and vagabonds, he is much more profoundly troubled by their extremely tight sense of national identity than by their non-nationhood in a geographical sense. His vehement decrial of Jewish history and memory is fuelled by a need to repress acknowledgement that no nation can exist without a similarly mythic element to its identity, the forging of which in a sense necessitates seeking to emulate the very aspects of Judaism that he most vigorously derides.

Although Voltaire makes no distinction between Judaism as philosophical construct and as social reality, this does not lead to an immediate, total dismissal of the Jewish people. Voltaire's judaeophobia is repeatedly offset by his commitment to universal tolerance – and vice versa. Individual Jews, as Jews, are hopelessly immersed in a culture of absurdity, but, as individuals, they are both entitled to toleration and deserving of sympathy for their suffering. This separation is, however, extremely precarious. Even as he specifically highlights the participation of Jews in the harmonious trading of the London Stock Exchange, he undercuts this celebration with a hostile barb towards Judaism: 'On leaving these peaceable and free assemblies, some go to synagogue, and others for a drink...and everybody is happy.'[54]

This juxtaposition of the straightforward pleasures of alcohol with the implied arcane futility of synagogue worship undermines from within Voltaire's affirmation of the Jews' straightforward right to toleration. Voltaire conceived of his twin battles against intolerance and irrationality as mutually supportive: only the intolerance of the Church prevents the triumph of our innate rational capacities over the ignorance fostered by religious dogmatism. The case of the Jews, however, sets these two causes against each other. Judaism represents the most heightened form of blinkered prejudice and irrationality, and yet the Jews are one of the leading

---

[53] See Homi K. Bhabha, 'DissemiNation', in Bhabha, ed., *Nation and Narration*, 291–322; Linda Colley, *Britons: Forging the Nation 1707–1837* (1992) esp. 217–36; Benedict Anderson, *Imagined Communities* (1983).

[54] *Lettres philosophiques* M.xxii.99.

victims of Christian religious bigotry. Voltaire more than once powerfully condemns Christian persecution and exploitation of Jews, and at times contrasts Judaism favourably against the most fanatical elements of Christianity.[55] However, while noting that Judaism, unlike Christianity, espouses the tolerance of other faiths, he observes that this is a strange contradiction in the light of the barbarism of Judaism itself.[56] Even as he argues for the toleration of Jews, Voltaire implies that any genuine acceptance of Judaism is essentially impossible.

Voltaire neither acknowledges nor denies the paradox of the Jews' position as the intolerable that must nonetheless be tolerated. This unspoken contradiction is lodged at too deep a level in his thought for it to surface easily, and his restless, fitful writing style is ideally suited to preventing its doing so. It is this enduring ambiguity that keeps at bay the collapse of Voltaire's anti-Jewish polemics into unrestrained verbal violence. The tolerant and the intolerant strands in his thought each hold the other in check, precluding any definitive closure of his stance on Judaism. A final assessment of Voltaire's innermost prejudices is not only impossible to establish, but also of little ultimate significance. Of much greater interest is the tight web of antinomies and tensions that define the significance of Judaism and the Jews in his writing. These contradictions are left open in his texts, for us to continue to grapple with.[57]

The tension between Voltaire's general politics of toleration and his particular hostility towards Jews did not go unnoticed during his lifetime. Isaac de Pinto, a Sephardic financier and would-be *philosophe* from Amsterdam, wrote to Voltaire in 1762 objecting to and refuting his 'calumnies' against Judaism.[58] Voltaire's letter of response was deftly ambiguous, its superficially respectful tone laced with an undercurrent of patronising contempt. Voltaire first concedes that he has been 'cruel and unjust', and promises to correct his errors in a future edition: 'When a person is in the wrong they should make amends, and I was wrong in attributing to a whole nation the vices of some individuals.'[59] However, he then issues an abrupt and impossible challenge to de Pinto:

---

[55] See Allan Arkush, 'Voltaire on Judaism and Christianity', *AJS Review* 18 (2) (1993) 223–43.

[56] *Traité sur la Tolérance* (1763) M.xxv.83.

[57] For an elaboration of this argument see Adam Sutcliffe, 'Myth, Origins, Identity: Voltaire, the Jews and the Enlightenment Notion of Toleration', *The Eighteenth Century: Theory and Interpretation* 38 (1998) 67–87.

[58] Isaac de Pinto, *Apologie pour la nation juive: Réflexions critiques sur le premier chapitre du VIIe tome des oeuvres de M. Voltaire* (1762), in Antoine Guénée, ed., *Letters of Certain Jews to Monsieur Voltaire* (1795) 21.

[59] Voltaire to De Pinto, 21 July 1762, in Theodore Besterman, ed., *Voltaire's Correspondence*, vol. XLIX (1959) 131–2.

I shall tell you as frankly that there are many who cannot endure your laws, your books, or your superstitions. They say that your nation has done, in every age, much hurt to itself and to the human race. If you are a philosopher, as you seem to be, you will think as those gentlemen do, but you will not say it.[60]

Voltaire here demands that de Pinto repudiate Judaism, and yet insistently binds him to it: '*your* laws, *your* books, *your* superstitions'. He thus simultaneously asserts and denies the possibility of de Pinto, as a Jew, also being a philosopher: to be accepted as such de Pinto must transcend and disavow an identity that Voltaire himself seems determined to pin back on to him. This exchange, which foreshadows the mass encounter of nineteenth-century Jewry with the shifting and ambiguous cultural tribunals that sought to police Jewish assimilation, highlights the immediate interpersonal impact and significance of Voltaire's contradictory rhetoric.[61]

The same tensions that marked Voltaire's attitude towards Jews also suffused the lengthy deliberations of the revolutionary Constituent Assembly on the subject. Despite the immensely crowded agenda facing the revolutionaries between 1789 and 1791, they repeatedly and vociferously debated the appropriate status of the approximately 40,000 Jews of France, while utterly ignoring, for example, the question of the rights of women.[62] The position of Jews was politically insignificant in itself, but as an abstract principle it crucially demarcated the limits and inflected the nature of citizenship in general. The universalism of the revolutionary principles of liberty and fraternity was immediately problematised by the anomalous case of Jewish religious and cultural difference. This tension was first expressed in terms of doubts among many deputies concerning the Jews' own desire and ability to integrate into French society. During the Terror, however, radical Jacobins actively sought to erase all markers of Jewish difference: the institution of the ten-day week made the observance of the Sabbath illegal, and even secular customs, such as the wearing of beards and sidelocks by men and wigs by married women, were regarded as unacceptable.[63] As with Voltaire's earlier literary challenge to the biblical roots of European civilisation, the Jacobin attempt to impose a new cultural order jarred

---

[60] *Ibid.*

[61] See Adam Sutcliffe, 'Can a Jew be a *Philosophe*? Isaac de Pinto, Voltaire and Jewish Participation in the European Enlightenment', *Jewish Social Studies* 6:3 (2000) 31–51. On Voltaire, Judaism and slavery see Pierre Pluchon, *Nègres et juifs au XVIII e siècle* (1984) 274–5.

[62] Gary Kates, 'Jews into Frenchmen: Nationality and Representation in Revolutionary France', in Ferenc Fehér, ed., *The French Revolution and the Birth of Modernity* (1990) 108–9.

[63] Paula E. Hyman, *The Jews of Modern France* (1998) 32–3; Jacques Godechot, 'La Revolution française et les juifs', in Bernhard Blumenkranz and Albert Soboul, eds., *Les Juifs et la révolution française* (1976) 47–70.

most insistently against the unique endurability and mythic power of Judaism.

In 1942, the propaganda wing of the Nazi administration of Occupied France published a book by a history teacher from the Gironde, Henri Labroue, entitled *Voltaire antijuif*. Consisting largely of thematically classified extracts from Voltaire's writings on Jews and Judaism, Labroue proudly enlisted the *philosophe* to the antisemitic cause. Were he alive today, Labroue claimed, Voltaire would undoubtedly concur that 'either [the Jews] will subjugate everybody, or they must be crushed'.[64] This Nazi appropriation of Voltaire was swiftly and forcefully rebutted in the clandestine resistance press. An article in *J'accuse*, an 'organ of struggle against racism and antisemitism', angrily asserted the absurdity of Labroue's argument, offering citations from Voltaire's *Dictionnaire Philosophique* to show that the 'great French philosopher' was firmly opposed to all forms of intolerance and persecution.[65] The symbolic power of the Enlightenment, and of its leading French figurehead, was important enough to merit vigorous contestation at this calamitous moment, and still today this tussle has not lost its political significance. An acknowledgement of the pervasiveness and vigour of Voltaire's anti-Jewish animus, however, in no sense cedes his legacy to fascism. This recognition ought on the contrary to facilitate a richer understanding of the complexity and precariousness of precisely the values on which opposition to intolerance must be based.

[64] Henri Labroue, *Voltaire antijuif* (1942) 244.
[65] 'Voltaire était-il anti-juif? Un faux grossier d'un schibouillard National Socialiste', anon. article in *J'accuse*, 'Organe de lutte contre le racisme et le antisémitisme', Bibliothèque National: Rés.G.1470, numéro spécial (May-June 1942) 186–187. I am grateful to Karen Adler for this reference.

Conclusion: reason versus myth?

Over the course of the Enlightenment the role of Judaic themes in European thought was radically transformed. Rabbinic and other religious texts were intensively studied by mid seventeenth-century Christians of a wide range of hues, eagerly scouring the Jewish tradition for guiding insights into fundamental questions of history, theology, hermeneutics and politics. A century later the prevalent tone of references to Judaism in dominant intellectual discourse was almost diametrically in contrast. Traditional theology now fought a rearguard battle on all fronts, and Judaism, widely derided as the epitome of irrational legalism and superstition, was dismissed by most Enlightenment thinkers more swiftly and intensively than any other contemporary religion. Seventeenth-century Christian interest in Judaism was seldom disinterested and often heavily coloured by an assumption of the older faith's obsolescence. Nonetheless, in the Dutch Republic in particular, attempts were made to overcome ignorance, and Jewish scholars such as Simone Luzzatto and Menasseh ben Israel were taken seriously as contributors to public debate. After Orobio de Castro's debate with Phillip van Limborch, however, no other individual was respectfully and publicly acknowledged both as an observant Jew and as a serious thinker until Moses Mendelssohn more than two generations later. And the case of Mendelssohn is an exception that confirms the general late eighteenth-century disdain for Judaism: his celebrity was in large measure due to the widely assumed paradoxicality – and for some, such as the Swiss pastor Johann Caspar Lavater, impossibility – of his status as an enlightened Jew.[1]

Christian biblical scholarship by no means ceased in the eighteenth century. In the latter half of the century there was a significant revival in the subject, spearheaded by Benjamin Kennicott and Robert Lowth in England and Johann David Michaelis in Germany. All three scholars were formidable Hebraists, and, deeply influenced by Enlightenment critical values, were

---

[1] See Alexander Altmann, *Moses Mendelssohn: A Biographical Study* (1973) 194–263.

committed to the rigorous philological revision of the Masoretic text. This project not only challenged the authority of the Hebrew Bible but also rean- imated old accusations that the Masoretic scribes and subsequent rabbinic interpreters were guilty of carelessness and distortion. In both England and Germany Jewish intellectuals advanced a defence against these arguments, and Moses Mendelssohn's own biblical scholarship was in large measure a response to the challenge of Christian theological rationalism.[2] These debates were highly significant in shaping the later development both of Protestant scholarship and of the Jewish *Haskalah*. However, they were so far from the cutting edge of Enlightenment thought that they can scarcely be encompassed under that rubric. Kennicott's critical project, and the ripostes of his Christian fundamentalist critics, the Hutchinsonians, echoed and in essence reiterated the squabble between Cappel and the younger Buxtorf in the 1630s and 1640s. However, whereas these scholars were among the most respected of their generation, biblical scholarship was by the later eighteenth century relegated to the distant margins of intellectual life, and derided in fashionable life as irredeemably dull and irrelevant.

Few eighteenth-century thinkers were as vocally preoccupied with Jewish matters as was Voltaire. Jean Jacques Rousseau, most notably, wrote vir- tually nothing on Judaism. However, a brief discussion of Moses in his *Considerations on the Government of Poland* (1772) reveals that he too had absorbed the prevalent anti-Jewish assumptions of late eighteenth-century philosophical culture. Moses' 'astonishing' achievement, he writes, had been to forge a nation out of 'a swarm of wretched fugitives, without arts, arms, talents, virtues or courage', who to this day remain 'fanatical' in their ob- servance of the burdensome laws he created for them.[3] Denis Diderot also pungently denigrated the superstition and arrogance of the ancient Jews.[4] However, the hostility of both these *philosophes* is undercut by a contrary strain of fascination and admiration. Rousseau is awed by Moses' skill as a lawgiver, while Diderot dwells extensively on the poetic power of the Jewish Bible.[5] These tensions stem from the same structural ambivalence towards Judaism that suffuses Enlightenment writings on the topic. While differ- ences of tone and emphasis between writers are of course worthy of note, what is most striking is the communality and the interconnectedness of the

---

[2] Ruderman, *Jewish Enlightenment*, 23–88; Edward Breuer, *The Limits of Enlightenment: Jews, Germans and the Eighteenth-Century Study of Scripture* (1995) 77–143.
[3] Jean Jacques Rousseau, *Considerations on the Government of Poland* (1986 (1772)) 163–4.
[4] See Leon Schwartz, *Diderot and the Jews* (1981) 26–48.
[5] *Ibid.*, 100–23. See also Dominique Bourel, 'Les Rasés et les barbus: Diderot et le judaïsme', *Revue philosophique* 3 (1984) 275–85.

twists and contradictions that recur in so many Enlightenment discussions of Jewish themes.

The central aim of this study has been to develop an understanding of the underlying ambivalence that characterised Enlightenment responses to Judaism. Attempts to split this tradition into two – the putatively opposing genealogies of Jewish emancipation and of the emergence of modern antisemitism – are futile, because, as we have seen, positive and negative attitudes are frequently intertwined in the same text and even in the same sentence. Rather than focusing on the evaluation of the superficial tenor of seventeenth- and eighteenth-century writings on Jews, it is far more intellectually illuminating to explore these texts' inner paradoxes. The shift towards more trenchant denigration of Judaism over the course of the Enlightenment can only be understood in relation to the philosophical dilemmas that animated this rhetoric. Despite the bombastic confidence of polemicists such as Voltaire (though very much in alignment with the insights of Pierre Bayle), the principles of the Enlightenment were far from straightforward; and no group was a more troublesome reminder of this than the Jews. The many and varied attempts over the course of this period to account for Jewish history and identity within a rationalist framework, however construed, constitute some of the earliest and most revealing attempts to wrestle with the constitutive dilemmas of reason itself.

These engagements with Judaism thus reveal a great deal about the Enlightenment's own limits and dynamics. Before the 1780s, however, non-Jews hardly ever thought seriously about Jewish matters in practical terms. Explicitly political interventions, such as Toland's plea in 1714 for Jewish naturalisation, are notably rare, and, as we have noted in relation to both this text and the later furore over the 'Jew Bill' in 1753, party-political polemics and fanciful stereotyping easily overpowered any consideration of the actual needs and entitlements of English Jewry. Jewish stereotypes were deeply lodged in the European cultural and intellectual imagination. As Jews became increasingly visible participants in urban society, their presence in contexts such as London theatre audiences encountered resistance precisely because this social reality contaminated and confused the reassuringly familiar Jewish caricatures presented on the stage.[6] It would be anachronistic to expect from writers of Voltaire's generation and earlier any sustained pressure for the reform of Jews' political status: this idea did not seriously emerge until the closing decades of the century. The symbolic

---

[6] Michael Ragussis, 'Jews and Other "Outlandish Englishmen": Ethnic Performance and the Invention of British Identity under the Georges', *Critical Inquiry* 26 (2000) 773–97.

significances of Jews were so multi-valenced and deeply rooted that Enlightenment thinkers were generally very slow to absorb the discomfiting realities of actual Jewish existence.

These realities, however, could not be evaded indefinitely. The question of the appropriate status of the Jews of Europe dramatically emerged in the 1780s as a pressing political issue in France, Germany and the Habsburg Empire. To some extent this wave of administrative interest in Jews was given impetus by the first partition of Poland in 1772, which significantly enlarged the Jewish populations under the jurisdiction of Prussia, Austria and Russia. More profoundly, though, the new reformist rhetoric of the 1780s reflected a significant intellectual watershed: it was now suddenly possible to envisage a future in which the status of Jews was to be profoundly transformed. While Emperor Joseph II's 'Edict of Tolerance' (1782) sought, in a spirit of reformist enlightened absolutism, to unleash the economic potential of the Jews of Austria, Christian Wilhelm von Dohm's essay *On the Civic Improvement of the Jews* (1781) much more boldly heralded a new era. 'The Jew is more human than Jewish', Dohm confidently asserted, arguing that they would therefore loyally and unreservedly love a state where they were not discriminated against and could rise to positions of honour and esteem.[7] Gotthold Ephraim Lessing's theatrical parable *Nathan the Wise* (1779), and in France the Abbé Grégoire's promotion of the ideal of Jewish 'regeneration', were other leading voices in this public debate, which culminated in the birth of Jewish emancipation in the wake of the French Revolution.[8]

This newly practical orientation in western European thinking concerning Jews was inseparable from a wider transformation in the understanding of history itself. Several historically minded *Aufklärer* of the 1760s and 1770s, such as Johann Georg Sulzer, Isaak Iselin and Johann Christoph Gatterer, began to enunciate a view of the past that was explicitly oriented towards progress: these intellectuals saw their historical investigations as preparatory to the overcoming of inherited problems in the present and the implementation of change in the future.[9] According to Reinhart Koselleck,

---

[7] Christian Wilhelm von Dohm, *Über die bürgerliche Verbesserung der Juden* (1781) 28.
[8] See Katz, *Out of the Ghetto*, 57–79; Pierre Birnbaum and Ira Katznelson, eds., *Paths of Emancipation: Jews, States and Citizenship* (1995); Ritchie Robertson, ' "Dies Hohe Lied der Duldung"? The Ambiguities of Toleration in Lessing's *Die Juden* and *Nathan der Weise*', *Modern Language Review* 93 (1998) 105–20; Benjamin W. Redekop, *Enlightenment and Community: Lessing, Abbt, Herder, and the Quest for a German Public* (2000) 58–122; Alyssa Goldstein Sepinwall, 'Strategic Friendships: Jewish Intellectuals, the Abbé Grégoire and the French Revolution', in Ross Brann and Adam Sutcliffe, eds., *Pasts Present: Reconfiguring Jewish Culture c.1100–c.1850* (forthcoming).
[9] Peter Hanns Reill, *The German Enlightenment and the Rise of Historicism* (1975) 48–74.

however, the crucial shift in Enlightenment historical consciousness occurred around 1780. It was only at this time that history was understood
as a universal singular. What had hitherto been seen as a plurality of local
histories (*Geschichten*) to be recounted and remembered was now eclipsed
by a sense of 'history in general' – *Geschichte* – that could be 'made' by
human actions.[10] This analysis matches exactly with the chronology of re-
formism in Enlightenment attitudes towards Jews. Until the 1770s scholars
of Jewish themes overwhelmingly focused their energies on projects of description, interpretation, classification or argument. Only in the early 1780s
did prominent minds seriously contemplate the transformation of Jewish
status. Within less than a decade history was unprecedentedly made by the
people of Paris, and these hypothetical reformist projects already abruptly
lurched towards realisation.

Dohm and Lessing were sincerely committed to the amelioration of
Jewish lives. However, their attitudes were also inflected with familiar
Enlightenment ambiguities. Both writers emphasised the potential virtue
and nobility of Jews, and argued for the irrelevance of religious difference in
social affairs. They thus moved beyond the residuum of Jewish exceptionalism that characterised Early Enlightenment arguments for toleration. However, this immediately gave rise to a new problem: their non-recognition
of any significance in the distinctive features of Judaism effectively erased,
or sought to erase, the cultural differences that gave rise to the need for
a more ample social toleration in the first place.[11] The 'Jewish Question',
as it soon came to be known, coalesced around these fundamental uncertainties concerning the existence, significance and fate of Jewish difference.
Johann Gottlieb Fichte posed this post-revolutionary tension starkly, and
with much anti-Jewish animus, in 1793. The Jews, Fichte claimed, were
already citizens of a uniquely sturdy and powerful 'state within a state', a
marker of their particularism and separateness, all traces of which would
have to be erased if they were safely to be granted civil rights.[12]

Judaism itself was of course also radically reshaped by the impact of the
Enlightenment. This process was already underway long before the French

[10] Reinhart Koselleck, 'On the Disposability of History', *Futures Past: On the Semantics of Historical
Time* (1985) 198–212. See also the multi-authored article 'Geschichte, Historie' in Otto Brunner,
Werner Conze and Reinhart Koselleck, eds., *Geschichtliche Grundbegriffe* II (1975) 593–718.

[11] See Sorkin, *Transformation of German Jewry*, 23–8; Peter R. Erspamer, *The Elusiveness of Tolerance: The
'Jewish Question' from Lessing to the Napoleonic Wars* (1997) 32–63; Ritchie Robertson, 'Freedom and
Pragmatism: Aspects of Religious Toleration in Eighteenth-Century Germany', *Patterns of Prejudice*
32 (1998) 69–80.

[12] Johann Gottlieb Fichte, *Beitrag zur Berichtigung der Urtheile des Publicums über die französische
Revolution* (1793 (1845)) 149–50. See also Hans-Joachim Becker, *Fichtes Idee der Nation und das
Judentum* (2000) esp. 33–8.

Revolution. Lay criticism of rabbis and Jewish communal leadership rose to a new level of insistency across Europe in the eighteenth century, while members of the Sephardic elites of north-west Europe in particular drifted towards an increasingly secular, assimilated lifestyle.[13] While straightforward material and cultural temptations were clearly the primary inducement of this trend, the questions raised by the Enlightenment also played an important role. Intellectual contact between Jews and Christians was a crucial catalyst of cultural change in the seventeenth-century Sephardic community of Amsterdam; and at the very beginning of the eighteenth century, rabbis such as David Nieto in London were very aware of and eager to respond to the threat to religion posed by Newtonian science.[14] The tension between Enlightenment universalism and religious particularism posed a particularly stark challenge to philosophically minded Jews, because it threw into question the entire basis of their social identity. Spinoza's rejection of Judaism in the 1650s and the elaboration of a theology of Jewish reform over 150 years later are unified by a common determination to address this problem directly.

The most explicit conduit of Enlightenment ideas in a Jewish context, however, was the 'Jewish Enlightenment', or *Haskalah*, the unfolding of which in many respects echoed its wider parent. Taking its early shape in Berlin in the 1770s around the cultural and educational ideals of Moses Mendelssohn, this period of crystallization was anticipated from the 1720s onwards by numerous initiatives of intellectual religious renewal, which both paralleled and drew inspiration from similar attempts by German Protestant and Catholic thinkers to respond to Enlightenment rationalism.[15] However, the spread of Enlightenment ideas among Jews did not follow a single vector. Sephardic Amsterdam in the seventeenth century was, as we have seen, a centre of intellectual ferment that was both unique and influential beyond the Jewish sphere. In other prosperous ports, such as London or the Habsburg city of Trieste, Enlightenment ideals required no external impetus to take root among the Jewish elite, and were fostered by pragmatic commercially oriented policies and relatively open

---

[13] Chimen Abramsky, 'The Crisis of Authority within European Jewry in the Eighteenth Century', in Siegfried Stein and Raphael Loewe, eds., *Studies in Jewish Religious and Intellectual History* (1979) 13–28; Todd M. Endelman, *Radical Assimilation in English Jewish History, 1656–1945* (1990) 9–33; Israel, *European Jewry*, 254–7.

[14] Yosef Kaplan, *An Alternative Path to Modernity: The Sephardi Diaspora in Western Europe* (2000) 22–6; Ruderman, *Jewish Thought*, 310–31.

[15] David Sorkin, *The Berlin Haskalah and German Religious Thought* (2000); 'The Early Haskalah', in Shmuel Feiner and David Sorkin, eds., *New Perspectives on the Haskalah* (2001) 9–26; Moshe Pelli, *The Age of Haskalah* (1979) 7–47.

social and intellectual climates that were sharply distinct from those of Paris or Berlin.[16] In Russia and Eastern Europe, where the *Haskalah* was a powerful force into the final quarter of the nineteenth century, the *maskilim* who were the movement's proponents were motivated, unlike their non-Jewish Enlightenment forerunners before the 1780s, less by an anticlerical spirit or a pure desire for truth than by a reformist pragmatism that was unmistakably characteristic of their later era, and was shaped in response to local circumstances. History, for the *maskilim*, was a key cultural resource, which they used explicitly to promote their own regenerated visions of the Jewish future.[17]

Modernity thus impacted on Jewish life very differently in diverse economic and political contexts.[18] Nonetheless, as the cultural forces of secularism and ethnically based patriotism advanced over the course of the nineteenth century, Jews across Europe grappled with a common and inescapable dilemma, inherited from the abstract debates of the eighteenth-century Enlightenment but now dramatically staged as the daily paradox of bourgeois Jewish life. How could Jews reconcile a positive sense of Jewish being with comfortably belonging also in the wider non-Jewish world, despite its deep-seated and volatile unease towards all traces of Jewish difference? There was no easy answer.[19]

Jean-François Lyotard has argued that we should draw a clear separation between 'the jews' – an abstract category representative of whatever is irreducibly alien and unassimilable to the totalising impulses of western thought – and the actual, embodied Jews of past and present. ' "The jews" ', he writes, 'are the object of a dismissal with which Jews, in particular, are afflicted in reality.'[20] This stark severance problematically side-steps the complex and fraught relationship between non-Jewish notions of Jewishness and the lives and actions of real Jews. Although the application of Enlightenment emancipatory politics to the Jewish case was somewhat belated, it nonetheless eventually had sweeping consequences, which although double-edged were in no sense merely an affliction. Jews were also not passive bystanders to the Enlightenment: they repeatedly intervened in

---

[16] Lois C. Dubin, *The Port Jews of Habsburg Trieste: Absolutist Politics and Enlightenment Culture* (1999); David B. Ruderman, 'Was There a "Haskalah" in England? Reconsidering an Old Question', in Feiner and Sorkin, eds., *New Perspectives*, 64–85.

[17] Shmuel Feiner, *Haskalah and History: The Emergence of a Modern Jewish Historical Consciousness* (2002).

[18] For a comparative study see Jacob Katz, ed., *Toward Modernity: The European Jewish Model* (1987).

[19] See Mendes-Flohr, *Divided Passions*, esp. 54–63.

[20] Jean-François Lyotard, *Heidegger and 'the jews'* (1990) 3.

debates, and in the case of Spinoza powerfully fashioned them. Nonetheless, Lyotard's argument that Judaism is freighted in European thought with associations that overflow beyond its own identity is borne out by the heavy overdetermination of Judaism in the Enlightenment. The Jews did indeed represent the Enlightenment's primary 'unassimilable Other'.[21] This produced not only a desire to dismiss or eradicate Judaism, as Lyotard suggests, but also counterbalancing impulses towards co-option, idealisation and confused fascination.

The Enlightenment response to Judaism, this study has argued, was fundamentally split. Judaism was frequently cast as the essence of unenlightened thought, and even held responsible for the elements of western culture that seemed to obstruct the authority of reason. However, as a system of belief and memory of uniquely venerable status, Judaism retained an aura of mystery, and many Enlightenment thinkers located the kernel of their own positive ideals in strands of the Jewish tradition, such as the pure theocracy of the Mosaic Republic, the mystical *prisca theologica* of the Kabbalah, or the hazily utopian national vision of proto-Zionism. Such transvaluation is eclipsed in the writings of vociferous Enlightenment polemicists such as Voltaire and most of the authors and compilers of the radical clandestine manuscripts. However, these writers' aggression concealed a submerged ambivalence. Their hostility was in large measure animated by an unacknowledged fear that Judaism perhaps was not irredeemably inferior to the Enlightenment, but, because of its myth-based self-sufficiency, cultural power and secure sense of identity, in some sense ahead of it.

This schizophrenic view of Judaism as both beneath and beyond reason has, since its emergence with the Enlightenment, remained an extremely resilient and potent trope of western thought. Immanuel Kant, in the evolutionary scale of religions he delineates in *Religion Within the Boundaries of Reason Alone* (1793), excludes Judaism entirely from his hierarchy, on the grounds that it is not a religion at all, but merely a legal and political system. This exclusion introduces an unexplained anomaly into Kant's argument: how, then, is the survival of Judaism to be accounted for historically? It also leaves the implied status of Judaism strikingly ambiguous. Kant's own comments on this subject are overwhelmingly negative, but he does not conclusively foreclose the earlier argument of his friend Moses Mendelssohn, for whom Judaism, precisely because of its practical basis, was free from the irrational elements that blighted other religions.[22]

---

[21] *Ibid.*, 25.   [22] See Yirmiyahu Yovel, *Dark Riddle: Hegel, Nietzsche and the Jews* (1998) 10–20.

Hegel's view of Judaism was more overtly ambivalent and mobile. The 'spirit of Judaism', he wrote as a young man, was one of slavery and alien- ation: the Jews' fearful dependency on sterile laws disposed them to fanati- cism and hatred of others.[23] However, in later texts he revised his arguments, ascribing to Judaism a crucial historical position as the first religion to break with nature and introduce the consciousness of 'Spirit' that from then on defined the superior civilisation of the West.[24] Hegel's struggle to distil a ra- tional kernel from the distorting irrationalities of religion repeatedly drew him back to Judaism, the unique historical significance and endurance of which powerfully resisted accommodation within his own dialectical systems of thought. The recalcitrant anomalousness of Judaism ensnared both Hegel and Kant within essentially the same structural paradoxes that had prevented so many earlier Enlightenment thinkers from arriving at a stable and coherent account of the relationship of this ancient religion to their overall philosophical outlook.

The impossibility of comfortably integrating Judaism within the post- Enlightenment framework of nation-state government and semi-Christian, semi-universalist public culture continued to haunt European thought throughout the nineteenth and early twentieth centuries. The structural precariousness of the modern acceptance of Jews and Judaism was already starkly evident in the acrimonious 'Spinoza Quarrel' of the 1780s between Mendelssohn and Friedrich Jacobi. For Jacobi Enlightenment rationalism *in toto* was at root nothing but a sterile 'Spinozist' atheism. He implied that Mendelssohn, as a Jew, was, despite his protestations to the contrary, inescapably tainted with this pernicious godlessness, which Jacobi viewed as the ineluctable essence of both philosophy and Judaism.[25] Jeffrey Librett has incisively analysed the successive reconfigurations of these underlying tensions in German cultural dialogue during the nineteenth and twentieth centuries. Since the Reformation, he argues, Judaism, Catholicism and Protestantism have been locked in an intrinsically unstable rhetorical triad of the literal, the prefigural and the fulfilled, within which the three traditions have repeatedly shuffled their associated positions. Romanti- cism thus emerged, Librett shows, as a Catholic rejection of the 'Jewish' Enlightenment, which was in turn overcome by a Germanic/Protestant neopagan post-Romanticism. This in its turn gave way to modernism, the

---

[23] Georg W. F. Hegel, *The Spirit of Christianity and its Fate* (1971 (1799)) 182–205.
[24] See Yovel, *Dark Riddle*, 59–63.
[25] See Gérard Vallée, ed., *The Spinoza Conversations Between Lessing and Jacobi* (1988); Adam Sutcliffe, 'Quarreling over Spinoza: Moses Mendelssohn and the Fashioning of Jewish Philosophical Heroism', in Brann and Sutcliffe, eds., *Pasts Perfect*.

putative Jewishness of which was violently repudiated by anti-modernist antisemitism, with which certain contemporary anti-modern intellectual currents continue to share unspoken similarities.[26]

It is not surprising, therefore, that the most penetrating exploration of the deep structures of modern ambivalence towards Judaism was written by Sigmund Freud: the Jewish intellectual who pushed the neo-Enlightenment potential of modernism to its furthest possible extent. In *Moses and Monotheism* (1939) Freud famously and spectacularly revived the Enlightenment hypothesis, expounded by Spencer, Toland and Warburton, that Moses' ethnic origins and intellectual inspiration were not Hebraic but Egyptian. The religion Moses devised for the post-exilic Hebrews, Freud speculates, was based on the incipient monotheism of the Pharaoh Akhenaten, whose heretical Aten religion was vigorously erased by his successors.[27]

Freud merges this historical theory into a much broader psychohistorical interpretation of western culture. Moses, he alleges, was murdered by his fractious followers, who later fused elements of his Egyptian religion with embellishments absorbed from neighbouring cults, and especially the Midianites' worship of the volcanic deity Yahweh.[28] The identity of Moses himself was fused with that of a Midianite priest of the same name, and all memory of his murder was repressed. Freud identifies this process with the originary murder of the Father by the primal horde. This parricide, which stands as the cultural equivalent of the resolution of the Oedipus complex, enabled the mass renunciation of instinct and the development of civilisation, but also created a heavy burden of repressed guilt.[29] Inevitably, the repressed returned to haunt the Jews, leading to the emergence of the doctrine of the Passion of Christ, in which the murder of the Father is symbolically re-enacted and atoned for.[30] Only a minority of Jews refused to accept this new mythology of ritualised atonement, and, in doing so, they and their successors became the inevitable and eternal targets of the animosity of the Christian majority:

In full, this reproach would run as follows: 'They will not accept it as true that they have murdered God, whereas we admit it and have been cleansed of that guilt' ... A special inquiry would be called for to discover why it has been impossible for the

---

[26] Jeffrey S. Librett, *The Rhetoric of Cultural Dialogue: Jews and Germans from Moses Mendelssohn to Richard Wagner and Beyond* (2000) esp. 9–40, 259–85.

[27] Sigmund Freud, *Moses and Monotheism* (1985 (1939)) 254–62. See also Assmann, *Moses the Egyptian*, 144–67; Geoffrey Bennington, 'Mosaic Fragment: If Derrida Were an Egyptian . . .', in David Wood, ed., *Derrida: A Critical Reader* (1992) 97–119.

[28] Freud, *Moses*, 275–81.   [29] *Ibid.*, 323–6. See also Freud, *Totem and Taboo* (1985 (1913)) 202–17.

[30] Freud, *Moses*, 372–80.

Jews to join in this forward step which was implied, in spite of all its distortions, by the admission of having murdered God. In a certain sense they have in that way taken a tragic load of guilt on themselves; they have been made to pay heavy penance for it.[31]

Freud was profoundly committed to the values of the Enlightenment: he has been admiringly described as 'the last of the philosophes'.[32] In keeping with this image of his intellectual approach, Freud's response to antisemitic hysteria – which in 1938, while he was still working on *Moses and Monotheism*, forced him to flee Vienna for London – was to seek to explain the underlying roots of the phenomenon dispassionately and with analytic boldness. His attempt to do this simultaneously deprivileges and privileges Judaism, casting it as imitative and outdated, and yet nonetheless mysteriously unique and historically crucial. The strain between these two faces of his argument essentially replicates the contradictions that, as we have seen, pervaded so many earlier Enlightenment responses to Judaism.

Freud's claim that Christian and post-Christian hostility towards Judaism most fundamentally stems from the repressed trauma of a primal murder could very neatly be reinterpreted to apply to the antagonisms of the Enlightenment. The originary status and mythic power of Judaism were precisely what many Enlightenment rationalists sought to annul; the enduring presence of Jews provoked frustration because they stood as an embodied reminder of the incompleteness of this project. However, rather than placing the Enlightenment on the couch, Freud's argument more explicitly reproduces its philosophical logic of exclusion. It is striking that Freud notes that in some respects Christianity was a 'cultural regression': it 'did not maintain the high level in things of the mind to which Judaism had soared'.[33] However, historically and psychologically the new religion was unambiguously a 'forward step', leaving the surviving remnant of Judaism from then on an anachronistic 'fossil', frozen in time and impervious to the forces of progress.[34]

The endurance of Judaism, and the reasons why so many Jews have not succumbed to the comforts of Christianity, remain unexplained: Freud makes no attempt to initiate the 'special inquiry' that he states would be necessary to answer this question. His evasion of this problem, however, leaves a striking lacuna at the heart of his argument. Freud at times appears to adhere to a loosely Lamarckian assumption that inherited cultural characteristics bind Jews to their cultural roots.[35] However, while stating in

[31] *Ibid.*, 386.
[32] Peter Gay, *A Godless Jew: Freud, Atheism and the Making of Psychoanalysis* (1987) 41.
[33] Freud, *Moses*, 332.   [34] *Ibid.*, 333.
[35] Yosef Hayim Yerushalmi, *Freud's Moses: Judaism Terminable and Interminable* (1991) 29–33.

Moses that he is strongly attracted to the 'alluring task' of investigating the nature and power of tradition in Jewish history in particular, he acknowledges at the end of the work that he has cast little light on the 'riddle' of how the Jewish people has retained its distinctiveness in the modern era.[36] Even at the end of this text, which itself stands at the end of his intellectual career, Freud leaves the core essence of Jewish identity essentially as an enigma. Paradoxically, and like so many of his Enlightenment predecessors, he concludes his attempt to illuminate the roots of Judaism without dislodging a sense of mystery surrounding the subject.

Moses and Monotheism clearly reflects Freud's profoundly conflicted attitudes towards his own Jewishness, to which, in the face of fascism in particular, he felt a strong loyalty despite his absolute disdain for Judaism.[37] Like Spinoza, who was one of his favourite philosophers,[38] he projected his admiration for Judaism into the archaic past, where he located the purest moment of (Egyptian) Mosaic monotheism. However, in terms of psychological health – the value to which he devoted his professional life – Freud casts Judaism as not only, like all religions, intrinsically infantile, but also uniquely outdated and masochistic. His penetrating critique of Judaism was nonetheless tempered and offset by an unwavering sense of connection to a culture of which he inescapably and unapologetically formed a part. This sense of connection crucially marked both Freud and Spinoza apart from the many non-Jews who grappled with the relationship of Enlightenment universalism to Jewish particularism. However, as thinkers writing under the sign of Enlightenment, both men addressed the same dilemmas as did these non-Jews, and their arguments skirted the same paradoxes and tensions. While individual loyalties and perspectives of course powerfully inflected all approaches to this problem, its underlying philosophical quandaries posed themselves equally insistently to all.

Despite Freud's determined commitment to the rational and scientific explanatory power of psychoanalysis, *Moses and Monotheism* in some senses leads us beyond the perspective of the Enlightenment. Freud described this text as 'my novel', and in its fanciful shifts and psychically dramatic narrative it invites being read not only as history but also as fiction.[39] In recent decades, as postmodern modes of interpretation avowedly sceptical of Enlightenment totalities have risen to prominence, Judaism has not ceased to be a central point of reference in western critical thought. Athens, the city

---

[36] Freud, *Moses*, 293–4, 386.
[37] See Yerushalmi, *Freud's Moses*; Ritchie Robertson, 'Freud's Testament: Moses and Monotheism', in Edward Timms and Naomi Segal, eds., *Freud in Exile: Psychoanalysis and its Vicissitudes* (1988) 80–9.
[38] Gay, *Godless Jew*, 46.   [39] See Michel de Certeau, *The Writing of History* (1988 (1975)) 308–54.

of Enlightenment reason and justice, is now unprecedentedly challenged for supremacy by the more ineffable, open-ended authority of Jerusalem.[40] This development has opened up many new and exciting strategies for acknowledging and thinking beyond the antinomies of rationalism. However, the advent of postmodernism can in no sense herald the dissolution of the inescapable tensions between universalism and particularism, and between Enlightenment and Judaism. We cannot abandon the indispensable intellectual tools for the furtherance of a politics of democracy and justice that are the Enlightenment's key legacy. Instead, we must continue to forge our understandings of the world from the difficult but honest philosophical terrain where sameness and difference, knowledge and instinct, and reason and myth perpetually clash, overlap and intertwine with each other.[41]

The limits of enlightened modernity as highlighted by the Jewish case are closely related to, and should certainly not overshadow, the conceptualisation and treatment of other subaltern groups. In particular, the dependency of eighteenth-century commodity capitalism on slavery, and the emergence of a doctrine of 'race' that legitimised this terror and oppression and occluded its flagrant incompatability with contemporary ideals of rational civility, established a profound and dark paradox at the heart of the Enlightenment.[42] If the supposed dogmatic legalism of Judaism provided the primary defining counterpoint against which reason was defined, then the enslavement of blacks, in Europe more discreetly and in America explicitly, constituted the definitional inverse of the ideal of freedom.[43] In the aftermath of the French Revolution the disjuncture between the status of Jews and the Enlightenment's emancipatory principles leapt to the top of the political agenda. The problem of slavery was far more widely evaded for much longer, but many Europeans closely followed the unfolding of the slave revolution in Saint-Domingue, and understood its philosophical significance as an inexorable corollary of the principle of liberty.[44]

---

[40] See, for example, Emmanuel Levinas, 'The Strings and the Wood: On the Jewish Reading of the Bible', *Outside the Subject* (1993) 126–34; Jacques Derrida, 'Violence and Metaphysics: An Essay on the Thought of Emmanuel Levinas', *Writing and Difference* (1978) 79–153.

[41] For the development of similar arguments see Leszek Kolakowski, *Modernity on Endless Trial* (1990) esp. 63–74; 'The Myth of Reason', *The Presence of Myth* (1989) 69–82; Gillian Rose, *Judaism and Modernity* (1993) esp. 37–51.

[42] See Paul Gilroy, *The Black Atlantic: Modernity and Double Consciousness* (1993) 41–71. On the tension between slavery and Enlightenment democracy in the antebellum United States, see Stephen J. Hartnett, *Democratic Dissent and the Cultural Fictions of Antebellum America* (2002) 11–92.

[43] Edmund S. Morgan, *American Slavery, American Freedom: The Ordeal of Colonial Virginia* (1975) 363–87.

[44] For an illuminating comparison of Hegel's response to these two issues of practical politics, see, on Jews, Yovel, *Dark Riddle*, 90–4; on slavery, Susan Buck-Morss, 'Hegel and Haiti', *Critical Inquiry* 26 (2000) 821–65.

Parallels between the positions of Jews and blacks in the nineteenth and early twentieth centuries were widely noted, and black diaspora consciousness and the politics of pan-Africanism were in large measure inspired by similar debates among Jews in relation to Zionism.[45] In recent decades the positioning of Judaism or Jews as quintessentially alien and unenlightened has diminished immensely in western public discourse, although it has certainly not disappeared. Other 'Others' – non-whites, above all, of almost any sub-category – are today much more likely to be caught within the sights of the exclusionary logic of Enlightenment absolutism. This pattern of non-recognition, however, was first and most extensively elaborated in the attempts of seventeenth- and eighteenth-century thinkers to make sense of Judaism within their own structures of rationalist thought. An understanding of these specific intellectual dynamics also offers an insight into the broader problematics of Enlightenment responses to difference, and into strategies for thinking beyond them. Non-western cultures, like Judaism, cannot conclusively displace the Eurocentric hubris of Enlightenment thought: intellectual renewal is rather to be found in the sometimes dissonant interplay between these traditions.[46]

Judaism, however, retains a particular power to decentre the too-easy assumptions of western categorical thought. The Jewish Bible, even in this secular age, has not lost its confusingly foundational resonance, and the knotty intertwinement of Jewish and non-Jewish history potently disrupts nation-based readings of the past. Above all, the elusive nature of Jewish identity still uniquely refuses to fit any of the boxes: not-quite race, not-quite nation, not-quite religion and not-quite culture. Contrary to the hopes of its early prophets, the realisation of the Zionist project has not comfortably normalised the status of Jewishness in the world, not only because of the injustices that have been and are being wrought in Zionism's name, but because the intellectual complexities that cling to Judaism cannot be shaken off so easily.[47] The disruptive impact of these complexities, however, carries much positive potential. In stark contrast to Zionism, the intricately multiple axes of Jewish diasporic identity destabilise the assumptions on

---

[45] Gilroy, *Black Atlantic*, 205–12. On the converse echo of the experience of the colonised in Herzlian Zionism, see Daniel Boyarin, *Unheroic Conduct: The Rise of Heterosexuality and the Invention of the Jewish Man* (1997) 304–10.

[46] See Dipesh Chakrabarty, *Provincialising Europe: Postcolonial Thought and Historical Difference* (2000) esp. 237–55.

[47] On the complicated relationship of Zionism to Jewish history and to the Enlightenment, see Shmuel Almog, *Zionism and History: The Rise of a New Jewish Consciousness* (1987); George L. Mosse, *Confronting the Nation: Jewish and Western Nationalism* (1993) 121–92; David N. Myers, *Re-inventing the Jewish Past: European Jewish Intellectuals and the Zionist Return to History* (1995).

which crude and violent nationalism is based.[48] More generally, the mythic depth of Judaism, and the historic legacy of its conflicted relationship with a sequence of European hegemonic ideologies up to and including the Enlightenment, endows this tradition with a particular resistive strength. The relationship between Judaism and Enlightenment rationality can never be straightforwardly easy – but this need not be a cause for lament. The mythic resilience of Judaism holds within it a unique power to call attention to the limits of Enlightenment, and to provide a bulwark against univocal rationalist arrogance and authoritarianism.

[48] See Daniel Boyarin and Jonathan Boyarin, 'Diaspora: Generation and the Ground of Jewish Identity', *Critical Inquiry* 19 (1993) 721–3.

Bibliography

MANUSCRIPT SOURCES

Aix-en-Provence: Bibliothèque Méjanes

MS 10: *Dissertation sur les 70 Semaines de Daniel; Objections contre les livres St des Juifs et des Chretiens; Objections raisonnable de la manière dont le soleil s'arresta du tems de Josue; Objections sur l'histoire du patriarche joseph; Extrait de Zinzendorf sur le Bible; La nouvelle Moysade.*

MS 62: *Doutes sur la religion.*

MS 63: *Analyse de la Religion Chrétienne.*

MS 814: *L'Idée d'un Philosophe.*

MS 816: *L'Exposition des Sentiments d'Espinosa; Examen d'une nouvelle réfutation du système de Spinoza par un Moine bénédictin; Que le Monde est éternel.*

MS 818: *Apologie de Spinoza, sur Dieu et la nature.*

MS 820: *Réflexions sur l'origine des americains.*

MS 828: *Dissertation sur Elie et sur Enoch.*

MS 1905: [Benoît de Maillet], *Système du Monde de Telliamed, Philosophe Indien.*

MS 1906: *Opinions des anciens sur le monde, et sur la nature de l'âme; Doutes sur la religion, dont on cherche de bonne foy les Eclaircissements; Lettre à M. * * * * sur l'origine des Juifs et l'aversion qu'avoient pour eux les autres nations ...*

Amsterdam: Bibliotheca Rosenthaliana

HS 76: Eliahu Montalto, *Tractado de Doctor Montalto Sobre o Principio do Capitulo 53 de Jesaias.*

HS 127: Saul Levi Morteira, *Preguntas que se hezieron de un clerigo de Ruan a Amsterdam.*

HS 494: Isaac Troki, *Hisuk Emuna* (in Dutch).

HS 542: Saul Levi Morteira, *Providencia de Dios con Ysrael y Verdad de la Ley de Moseh.*

HS 631:   Isaac Orobio de Castro, *Prevenciones Divinas contra la vana ydolotria de las Gentes; Invectiva contra un philosopho medico sobre la verdad de la divina ley; Tratado o respuesta aun cavallero Frances reformado doctismo y estudioso…; Respuesta a una persona que dudava si el libro de Reymundo* LULLIO… *ero yntelligible.*

The Hague: Museum Meermano-Westreenianum/Museum van het Boek

7D1, 7D2:   Adriaan Koerbagh, *Een Ligt schijnende in duystere plaatsen* (both copies part printed, part manuscript).

London: British Library

Harley 3430:   Orobio de Castro, *Prevenciones Divinas Contra la Vana Idolotria de las gentes; Respuesta a un Predicante Francés; Epístola Invectiva contra Prado.*

Add. MS 4257,
    fos. 74–81:   Pierre DesMaizeaux's notes on Orobio, *Prevenciones Divinas.*

Los Angeles: William Andrews Clark Memorial Library, University of California, Los Angeles

MS A527M3.P839
    1634:   *Porta Veritatis.*

Paris: Bibliothèque de l'Arsenal

MS 2091:   *Examen de la Religion.*
MS 2557:   *De l'Examen de la Religion; Réflexion sur l'existence de l'âme et sur l'existence de Dieu; Traité de la liberté; Sentimens des Philosophes sur la nature de l'âme.*
MS 2558:   *Recherches de la Vérité.*

Paris: Bibliothèque Mazarine

MS 3558:   *Métaphysique de Mr de B***.*
MS 1176:   Pierre Cuppé, *Le ciel ouvert à tous les hommes.*
MS 1178:   *Préface d'Orobius Médecin Juif sur La Réfutation qu'il a fait des Explications que les Chrétiens ont Inventées au Sujet du chapitre 53 d'Isäÿë le Prophète.*
MS 1190:   *La Divinité de Jésus Christ Détruite; Système sur l'universalité du Déluge, et sur l'origine des Nègres, des amériquains, des Caffres…; Méditations Philosophiques sur Dieu, le Monde et l'homme.*
MS 1191:   *Dialogues sur l'âme.*

MS 1192:   *Système de Religion purement naturelle.*
MS 1193:   *Traité des Trois Imposteurs.*
MS 1194:   *Preuves de l'Eternité du Monde; Dissertation sur Moyse; De la Conduite qu'un honnête homme doit garder pendant sa vie.*
MS 1197:   *Le Rabbinisme renversé, ou Dissertation Historique et critique sur le prophète Elie et sur le patriarche Enoch.*
MS 1198:   *Histoire critique du Christianisme; Dissertation sur l'Ecriture Sainte, et les Prophetes, Par Mr de Boulainvilliers.*

Paris: Bibliothèque Nationale

FF 6337:   [Jean Meslier], *Pensées sur la Religion.*
FF 6363:   *Abregé de l'Histoire Universelle Jusqu'à l'Exode.*
FF 6364:   *Abregé de l'Histoire Universelle Jusqu'à l'Exode, II Partie.*
FF 12242: *La Vie, Essay de Metaphysique, et l'Esprit de Spinoza, par Monsieur le comte de Boulainvilliers.*
FF 13351: *Dissertation sur le Messie.*
FF 14696: *Opinion des anciens sur le monde; Traité de l'immortalité de l'âme; Opinions des Anciens sur la nature de l'âme; Lettre a Monsieur * * * * sur les Juifs.*
FF 14928: *La Divinité de Jésus-Christ détruite; l'Explication du cinquante-troisième chapitre d'Isaïe; Dissertation sur le messie où l'on prouve qu'il n'est pas encore venu.*
FF 15288: *Lettre de Thrasybule à Leucippe.*
FF 22920: *Conference d'un Juif avec un Chrétien.*
FF 25290: *Traité des Trois Imposteurs.*
NAF 4369: *Opinions des Anciens sur la nature de l'Ame; Opinions des Anciens sur les Juifs.*

PRIMARY TEXTS (WRITTEN BEFORE 1850)

Anon., *L'Ame Matérielle*, c. 1720, ed. Alain Niderst, Rouen, Publications de l'Université de Rouen, 1969.
Anon., *Pieces on the 'Jew Bill'*, 1753, ed. Roy S. Wolper, Los Angeles, Augustan Reprint Society, 1983.
Anon., *Thérèse philosophe* (c. 1748), ed. Robert Darnton, *The Forbidden Best-Sellers of Pre-Revolutionary France*, New York, W. W. Norton, 1995.
Anon., *Traité des Trois Imposteurs*, The Hague, 1719, ed. Silvia Berti, Turin, Einaudi, 1994.
Argens, Jean Baptiste de Boyer, marquis d', *Lettres juives, ou correspondance philosophique, historique et critique*, 5 vols., The Hague, 1736–7.
Lettres cabalistiques, The Hague, 1737.
Arnold, Gottfried, *Unparteyische Kirchen und Ketzerhistorie*, 4 vols., Frankfurt, 1699–1700.

Augustine of Hippo, *City of God*, trans. William Chasse Green, London, Heinemann, 1960.

Banier, Antoine, *La Mythologie et les Fables Expliqués par l'Histoire*, 3 vols., Paris, 1738–40.

Bartolocci, Giulio, *Bibliotheca Magna Rabbinica, de Scriptoribus et Scriptis Hebraicis, Ordine Alphabetica Hebraicè, & Latinè digestis*, 4 vols., Rome, 1675–93.

Basnage de Beauval, Henri, ed., *Histoire des Ouvrages des Savans*, Rotterdam, 1687–1709.

    Tolérance des Religions, Rotterdam, 1684; repr., ed. Elizabeth Labrousse, New York and London, Johnson Reprint Company, 1970.

Basnage, Jacques, *Antiquitez Judaïques*, Amsterdam, 1713.

    Histoire des Juifs, depuis Jésus-Christ jusqu'à present, pour servir de supplément et de continuation de l'histoire de Joseph, 9 vols., The Hague, 1716.

    'Préface' to Petrus Cunaeus, *La République des Hebreux*, Amsterdam, 1705.

[Bayle, Pierre], *Avis Important aux Réfugiez sur leur prochain retour en France*, 1690, 'Paris' (Amsterdam), 1692.

Bayle, Pierre, *Ce que c'est que la France toute Catholique...*, 1686, ed. Elizabeth Labrousse, Paris, J. Vrin, 1973.

    Commentaire Philosophique sur ces paroles de Jésus-Christ, Contrain-les d'entrer, Amsterdam, 1686, ed. and trans. Amie Godman Tannenbaum, *Philosophical Commentary*, New York, Peter Lang, 1987.

    Dictionnaire Historique et Critique, Rotterdam, 1697, ed. and trans. Richard H. Popkin, *Historical and Critical Dictionary: Selections*, Indianapolis, Hackett, 1991.

    Pensées Diverses sur la Comète, 1683, ed. A. Prat, 2 vols., Paris, Droz, 1939.

Bayle, Pierre, ed., *Nouvelles de la République des Lettres*, Amsterdam, 1684–9.

Bekker, Balthasar, *De Betoverde Weereld*, Leeuwarden, 1691, trans. *Le Monde Enchanté, ou Examen des communs sentiments touchant les Esprits, leur nature, leur pouvoir, leur administration, et leurs opérations*, 4 vols., Amsterdam, 1694.

Bellarmine, Robert, *Institutiones linguae Hebraicae*, Rome, 1578.

Bodenschatz, Johann C. G., *Kirchliche Verfassung der heutigen deutschen Juden*, Frankfurt and Leipzig, 1748–9.

Bossuet, Jacques-Bénigne, *Discours sur l'Histoire Universelle*, Paris, 1681, trans. Elborg Foster, *Discourse on Universal History*, Chicago and London, University of Chicago Press, 1976.

Bredenburg, Johannes, *Enervatio Tractatus Theologico-Politici; Una cum Demonstratione, Geometrico ordine disposita, Naturam non Esse Deum*, Rotterdam, 1675.

    Mathematica Demonstratio, quod omnia entia, rationis capacia, necessario operantur, 1684, in Lenglet Dufresnoy, ed., *Réfutations des erreurs de Benoit de Spinosa*, Brussels, 1731.

Buddeus, J. F., 'Defensio Cabbalae Ebraeorum Contra Auctores Quosdam Modernos', in *Observatorium selectarum ad. rem. litterariim spectantium*, 1, Halle, 1700, 207–31.

Exercitatio Historico-Philosophica de Spinozismo ante Spinozam, Halle, 1701, *Analecta Historiae Philosophicae*, vol. XI, Halle, 1724, 307–59.

Introductio ad Historiam Philosophae Ebraeorum, Halle, 1702.

Prudentiae Civilis Rabbinicae, Specimen sive R. Isaaci Abrabanelis, Jena, 1694.

Theses theologicae de atheismo et superstitione variis…, Jena, 1717, 3rd edn, Utrecht, 1737, trans. Louis Philon, *Traité de l'athéisme et de la superstition*, Amsterdam, 1740.

Burigny, Jean Lévesque de, *Histoire de la Philosophie Payenne*, The Hague, 1724.

Burnet, Thomas, *Telluris Theoria Sacra*, London, 1680, trans. *The Sacred History of the Earth*, London, 1684, ed. Basil Wiley, Carbondale, Southern Illinois University Press, 1965.

Buxtorf, Johannes, the Elder, *Synagoga Judaica, das ist der Jüden Schul*, Basel, 1603, trans. *The Jewish Synagogue*, London, 1663.

Cappel, Louis, *Critica Sacra*, Paris, 1650.

Cardoso, Isaac, *Las Excelencias de los Hebreos*, Amsterdam, 1679.

Colerus, Johann, *The Life of Benedict de Spinoza*, London, 1706, repr. The Hague, Martinus Nijhoff, 1906.

Collins, Anthony, *A Discourse of Freethinking, occasioned by the rise and growth of a Sect called Freethinkers*, London, 1713.

Discourse of the Grounds and Reasons of the Christian Religion, London, 1724.

A Philosophical Inquiry Concerning Human Liberty, London, 1717.

A Scheme of Literal Prophecy Considered, London, 1727.

Cordovero, Moses, *Or Ne'erav* ['A Pleasant Light'], *c.* 1550, ed. and trans. Ira Robinson, New York, Yeshiva University Press, 1994.

Costa, Uriel da, *Exame das Tradições Phariseas*, Amsterdam, 1623, trans. H. P. Salomon and I. S. D. Sassoon, *Examination of Pharisaic Traditions*, Leiden, E. J. Brill, 1993.

Exemplar Humanae Vitae, in Phillip van Limborch, *De Veritate religionis Christianae. Amica Collatio cum Erudito Judaeo*, Gouda, 1687; trans. *The Remarkable life of Uriel Acosta, an eminent Freethinker, with his Reasons for rejecting all revealed religion, to which is added Mr Limborch's Defence of Christianity, in answer to Acosta's objections*, London, 1740.

Crequinière, M. de la, *Conformité des Coutumes des Indiens Orientaux avec celles des Juifs et des autres Peuples de l'Antiquité*, Brussels, 1704.

Crousaz, Jean Pierre de, *Cinq Sermons sur la Vérité de la Religion Chrétienne*, Amsterdam, 1722.

Cudworth, Ralph, *True Intellectual System of the Universe*, London, 1678, 3 vols., London, 1845.

Cunaeus, Petrus, *De republica Hebraeorum*, 1617, trans. Jacques Basnage, *La République des Hébreux*, Amsterdam, 1705.

Dale, Anton van, *De Oraculis ethnicorum*, Amsterdam, 1683.

Diderot, Denis, 'Intolérance', *Encyclopédie*, vol. VIII, Paris, 1765, trans. in J. H. Mason and R. Wokler, eds., *Diderot: Political Writings*, Cambridge, Cambridge University Press, 1992.

Dohm, Christian Wilhelm von, *Über die bürgerliche Verbesserung der Juden*, Berlin, 1781.

Duijkerius, Johannes, *Het Leven van Philopater, opgewiegt in Voetieansche Talmeryen, en groot gemaeckt in de Verborgentheden der Coccejanen: en waare Historie*, 'Groningen' (Amsterdam), 1691, ed. Geraldine Maréchal, Rodopi, Amsterdam and Atlanta, GA, 1991.

    Vervolg van 't leven van Philopater, 'Groningen' (Amsterdam), 1697, ed. Geraldine Maréchal, Rodopi, Amsterdam and Atlanta, GA, 1991.

Edelmann, Johann Christian, *Moses mit Aufgedeckten Angesicht*, n.p. (Freiburg?), 1740.

Eisenmenger, Johann Andreas, *Entdecktes Judenthum*, Frankfurt, 1700.

Enden, Franciscus van den, *Vrije Politijke Stellingen en Consideratien van Staat*, 1665, Amsterdam, Wereldbibliotheek, 1992.

Fichte, Johann Gottlieb, *Beitrag zur Berichtigung der Urtheile des Publicums über die französische Revolution*, 1793, in J. H. Fichte, ed., *Sämtliche Werke*, vol. VI, Berlin, 1845.

Fleury, Claude, *les Moeurs des Israélites, ou l'on voit le modèle d'une Politique simple et sincère pour le Gouvernement des Etats et la reforme des moeurs*, 1681, 4th edn, The Hague, 1683.

Fontenelle, Bernard le Bovier de, *De l'Origine des Fables*, Paris, 1724; repr. Geneva, Slatkine, 1968.

    Histoire des Oracles, Paris, 1686.

Giannone, Pietro, *Il Triregno*, *c*. 1730, ed. Sergio Bertelli and Giuseppe Ricuperati, Turin, Einaudi, 1977.

Gill, John, *The Prophecies of the Old Testament, respecting the Messiah, consider'd, and prov'd to be literally fulfill'd in Jesus*, London, 1728.

Harrington, James, *The Art of Lawgiving*, London, 1659, in J. G. A. Pocock, ed., *The Political Works of James Harrington*, Cambridge, Cambridge University Press, 1977, 599–704.

    The Commonwealth of Oceana, London, 1656, ed. J. G. A. Pocock, Cambridge, Cambridge University Press, 1992.

    The Prerogative of Popular Government, London, 1658, in J. G. A. Pocock, ed., *The Political Works of James Harrington*, Cambridge, Cambridge University Press, 1977, 389–566.

Hegel, Georg W. F., *The Spirit of Christianity and its Fate*, 1799, in T. M. Knox, trans., *G. W. F. Hegel: Early Theological Writings*, University of Pennsylvania Press, Philadelphia, 1971, 182–301.

Helmont, F. M. van, *Alphabeti veré Naturalis Hebraici brevissima delineato*, Sulzbach, 1667.

    The Paradoxical Discourses of F.M. van Helmont, concerning the Macrocosm and the Microcosm of the Greater and the Lesser World, and their Union, London, 1685.

Herrera, Abraham Cohen, *Puerta del Cielo*, *c*. 1630, ed. and trans. Friedrich Haußermann, 'Das Buch Sha'ar Hashamayim, oder Pforte des Himmels', Frankfurt, Suhrkamp, 1974.

Hobbes, Thomas, *Leviathan*, London, 1651.

Houtteville, Claude François, *La Vérité du Christianisme Prouvée par les Faits*, Paris, 1722, Paris, Migne, 1873.

Huet, Pierre-Daniel, *Demonstratio Evangelica*, Paris, 1679.

Dissertations sur diverses matières de Religion et de Philologie, 2 vols., Paris, 1712.

Imbonati, Carlo, *Bibliotheca Latino-Hebraica*, Rome, 1694.

Jenkin, Robert, *Remarks on Some Books Lately Published*, London, 1709.

Jurieu, Pierre, *L'Accomplissement des prophéties, ou la délivrance prochaine de l'Eglise*, Rotterdam, 1686.

Kettner, F. E., *De Duobus Impostoribus, Benedicto Spinoza et Balthasare Bekkero*, Leipzig, 1694.

Kidder, Richard, *Demonstratio Messiae*, 3 vols., London, 1684–1700, trans. *A Demonstration of the Messias*, 3 vols. in 1, London, 1726.

Kirchner, Paul Christian, *Jüdisches Ceremoniel*, Nuremberg, 1724.

Knorr von Rosenroth, Christian, *Kabbala Denudata*, 2 vols., I, Sulzbach, 1677; II, Frankfurt, 1684.

Koerbagh, Adriaan, *Een Bloemhof van allerley lieflijkheyd*, Amsterdam, 1668.

Een Ligt schijnende in duystere plaatsen, 1669, ed. H. Vandenbossche, Brussels, Vlaamse Vereniging voor Wijsbegeerte, 1974.

l'Estrange, Hamon, *Americans no Jews, or, Improbabilities that the Americans are of that Race*, London, 1651.

La Peyrère, Isaac, *Prae-Adamitae*, Amsterdam, 1655, trans. Moses Wall, *Men Before Adam*, London, 1655–6.

Lafitau, J. F., *Moeurs des sauvages amériquains*, 2 vols., Paris, 1724, ed. and trans. William N. Fenton and Elizabeth L. Moore, Toronto, The Champlain Society, 2 vols., 1974 and 1977.

Le Clerc, Jean, *Ars Critica*, London, 1698.

De L'Incrédulité, Amsterdam, 1696, trans. *A Treatise on the Causes of Incredulity*, London, 1697.

Défense des Sentiments de Quelques Théologiens de Hollande sur l'Histoire Critique du Vieux Testament, Contre la Réponse du Prieur de Bolleville, Amsterdam, 1686.

A Funeral Oration upon the Death of Mr Philip Limborch, Professor of Divinity among the remonstrants of Amsterdam, who died April 30, 1712, trans. from Latin, London, 1713.

Jean, *Sentiments de Quelques Théologiens de Hollande sur l'Histoire Critique du Vieux Testament*, Amsterdam, 1685.

Leenhof, Frederik van, *Den Hemel op Aarden*, Amsterdam, 1703, 2nd edn 1704.

Het Leven van den Wijzen en Magtigen Konink Salomon, Zwolle and Amsterdam, 1700.

De Prediker van den Wijzen en magtigen Konink Salomon, Zwolle and Amsterdam, 1700.

Leibniz, G. W., 'Animadversiones', ed. A. Foucher de Careil, *Réfutation Inédite de Spinoza par Leibniz*, Paris, 1854, repr., ed. Winfried Schröder, Stuttgart and Bad Cannstatt, Frommann-Holzboog, 1995.

Lightfoot, John, *Works*, 2 vols., London, 1684.

Limborch, Phillip van, and Bredenburg, Johannes, *Schriftelyke Onderhandeling tusschen Phillipus van Limborg, Proffifesor de Remonstranten, ende Johannes Bredenburg, Rekende't gebruyk der Reden in der Religie*, Rotterdam, 1686.

Limborch, Phillip van, *De Veritate religionis Christianae: Amica Collatio cum Erudito Judaeo*, Gouda, 1687.

Locke, John, *Epistola de Tolerantia*, trans. William Popple, *Letter Concerning Toleration*, London, 1689, in J. Horton and S. Mendus, eds., *John Locke – A Letter Concerning Toleration in Focus*, London, Routledge, 1991.

['Philanthropus'], *A Second Letter Concerning Toleration*, London, 1690.

Lucas, Jean Maximilien, 'The Life of the Late Mr de Spinosa', *c*. 1677, ed. and trans. A. Wolf, *The Oldest Biography of Spinoza*, London, George Allen and Unwin, 1927.

Luzzatto, Simone, *Discorso circa il stato de gl'Hebrei et in particolar dimoranti nell'inclita Città di Venetia*, Venice, 1638.

Maimon, Solomon, *Lebensgeschichte*, 1792, trans. J. Clark Murray, *Autobiography*, ed. Moses Hadas, New York, Schocken, 1947.

Maimonides, Moses, *The Guide of the Perplexed*, ed. and trans. Shlomo Pines, Chicago and London, University of Chicago Press, 1963.

Mandeville, Bernard, *Free Thoughts on Religion, The Church, and Natural Happiness*, London, 1720.

Marana, Giovanni Paolo, *Letters Writ by a Turkish Spy*, 1st English edn, London, 1694, ed. Arthur J. Weitzman, New York, Columbia University Press, 1970.

Marsham, John, *Canon Chronicus Aegyptius, Ebraicus, Graecus et Disquisitiones*, London, 1672, 2nd [?] edn, Leipzig, 1676.

Mayr, Giorgius, *Institutiones linguae Hebraicae*, Lyon, 1622.

Menasseh ben Israel, *Mekveh Israel: esto es, Esperança de Israel*, Amsterdam, 1650, trans. Moses Wall, *The Hope of Israel*, 1652, ed. H. Méchoulan and Gérard Nahon, Oxford, Oxford University Press, 1987.

Meyer, Lodowijk, *Philosophia S. Scripturae Interpres*, 1666, ed. and trans. Jacqueline Langrée and Pierre-François Moreau, *La Philosophie Interprète de l'Ecriture Sainte*, Paris, Intertextes, 1988.

Modena, Leone, *Historia di gli riti hebraici*, Paris, 1637.

Montesquieu, Charles de Secondat, Baron de, *Lettres Persanes*, Amsterdam, 1721, trans. C. J. Betts, *Persian Letters*, London, 1993.

More, Henry, *Fudamenta Philosophiae Sive Cabbalae Aeto-Paedo-Melissaeae*, in Christian Knorr von Rosenroth, ed., *Kabbala Denudata*, 1, Sulzbach, 1677, 293–312.

Nachmanides, *Vikuach*, ed. and trans. in Hyam Maccoby, *Judaism on Trial: Jewish–Christian Disputations in the Middle Ages*, London, Littman, 1982, 102–46.

Orobio de Castro, Isaac, *Certamen Philosophicum, Propugnatae Veritatis Divinae ac Naturalis, adversus Joh. Bredenburg*, Amsterdam, 1684; trans. in Lenglet Dufresnoy, ed., *Réfutations des Erreurs de Benoit de Spinosa*, Brusssels, 1731.

Israel Vengé, ou – Exposition naturelle des Prophéties Hebraïques que les Chrétiens appliquent à Jésus, leur prétendu Messie..., 'London', 1770.

Pascal, Blaise, *Pensées*, 1670, trans. Honor Levi, Oxford, Oxford University Press, 1995.

Pellison, M., 'Réponse aux objections envoyées d'Allemagne', in G. W. Leibniz, *De La Tolérance des Religions*, Paris, 1692, 23–91.

Pereyra, Abraham, *La Certeza del Camino*, Amsterdam, 1666, ed. Henry Méchoulan, Salamanca, Ediciones Universidad de Salamanca, 1987.

Pezron, Paul, *L'Antiquité du Tems Rétablie et Defendue*, Paris, 1687.
   Défense de l'Antiquité des Tems, Paris, 1691.

Picart, Bernard, *The Ceremonies and Religious Customs of the various Nations of the known world*, 7 vols., London, 1733–9 (Amsterdam, 1723), ed. Odile Faliu, Paris, Herscher, 1988.

Pinto, Isaac de, *Apologie pour la nation juive: Réflexions critiques sur le premier chapitre du VII e tome des oeuvres de M. Voltaire*, Amsterdam, 1762, trans. Rev. Philip Lafanu, 'Critical Reflexions…', in Antoine Guénée, ed., *Letters of Certain Jews to Monsieur Voltaire*, Philadelphia, 1795, 19–36.

Proast, Jonas, *Argument of the Letter Concerning Toleration, Briefly Consider'd and Answer'd*, London, 1690.

Raey, Johannes de, *Cogitata de Interpretatione*, 1666, Amsterdam, 1692.

Reimmann, Jacob Friedrich, *Historia Atheismi et Atheorum falso & merito suspectorum*, Hildesheim, 1725.

Reuchlin, Johannes, *De Arte Kabbalistica*, Hagenau, 1517, trans. Martin and Sarah Goodman, *On The Art of the Kabbalah*, Lincoln, NB and London, University of Nebraska Press, 1993.

Rossi, Giovanni Bernardo di, *Dizionario storico degli autori Ebrei, e dalle loro opere*, Parma, 1802.

Rousseau, Jean Jacques, *Considerations on the Government of Poland*, 1772, in Frederick Watkins, trans. and ed., *Jean Jacques Rousseau: Political Writings*, Madison, WI, University of Wisconsin Press, 1986, 159–274.

Schudt, Johann Jacob, *Jüdische Merkwürdigkeiten*, 4 vols., Frankfurt, 1714–18.

Selden, John, *The History of Tithes*, London, 1618.
   De Jure Naturali & Gentium juxta Disciplinam Ebraeorum, London, 1640.
   De Synedriis et Praefecturis Juridicis Veterum Ebraeorum, 3 vols., Amsterdam, 1679 (London, 1650–3).
   Table-Talk, Edinburgh, 1819 (London, 1777).
   Uxor Hebraica, London, 1646, ed. and trans. Jonathan R. Ziskind, Leiden, E. J. Brill, 1991.

Shaftesbury, Anthony Ashley Cooper, *Characteristicks of Men, Manners, Opinions, Times*, London, 1711, ed. Philip Ayres, 2 vols., Oxford, Clarendon Press, 1999.

Silva, Samuel da, *Tratado da Immortalidade da Alma*, Amsterdam, 1624, trans. H. P. Salomon and I. S. D. Sassoon, *Treatise on the Immortality of the Soul*, Leiden, E. J. Brill, 1993.

Simon, Richard ['le Sieur de Simonville'], *Comparaison des Cérémonies des Juifs, et de la Discipline de l'Eglise*, Paris, 1681.

Simon, Richard, *Histoire Critique du Vieux Testament*, Rotterdam, 1685 (Paris, 1678), repr. Geneva, Slatkine Reprints, 1971.

Réponse au livre intitulé 'Sentiments de Quelques Théologiens de Hollande sur l'Histoire Critique du Vieux Testament', par le Prieur de Bolleville, Rotterdam, 1686.

Spencer, John, *De Legibus Hebraeorum Ritualibus et Earum Rationibus*, London, 1685.

Spinoza, Benedict de, *The Correspondence of Spinoza*, ed. A. Wolf, London, George Allen and Unwin, 1928.

    Ethics, 1677, ed. and trans. G. H. R. Parkinson, London, Dent, 1989.

    Tractatus Politicus, 1677, trans. R. H. M. Elwes, New York, Dover Publications, 1951.

    Tractatus Theologico-Politicus, 1670, trans. R. H. M. Elwes, New York, Dover Publications, 1951.

Staalkopf, M. Iacobus, *Ab Impiis Detorsionibus Thomae Hobbesii et Benedicti de Spinoza Oraculum Paulinum*, Griefswald, 1707.

Stillingfleet, Edward, *Origines Sacrae, or a rational account of the Grounds of Christian Faith*, London, 1662.

Stosch, F. W., *Concordia Rationis et Fidei, sive Harmonia Philosophiae Moralis & Religionis Christianae*, 'Amsterdam' (Berlin), 1692.

Thorowgood, Thomas, *Jewes in America, or, Probabilities that the Americans are of that Race*, London, 1650.

Tindal, Matthew, *Christianity as Old as Creation*, London, 1730, repr., ed. Günter Gawlich, Friedrich Frommann, Stuttgart and Bad Cannstatt, 1967.

Toland, John, *Christianity not Mysterious*, London, 1696, repr. Stuttgart and Bad Cannstatt, Friedrich Frommann, 1964.

    Hodegus, or the Pillar of Cloud and Fire, in *Tetradymus*, London, 1720.

    Letters to Serena, London, 1704, repr. Stuttgart and Bad Cannstatt, Friedrich Frommann, 1964.

    Nazarenus, Or Jewish, Gentile and Mahometan Christianity, London, 1718, ed. Justin Champion, Oxford, Voltaire Foundation, 1999.

    Origines Judaicae, sive, Strabonis de Moyse et Religione Judaica breviter illustrata, The Hague, 1709.

    Reasons for Naturalizing the Jews in Great Britain and Ireland, London, 1714.

    Two Problems Concerning the Jewish Nation and Religion, London, 1709, ed. Justin Champion, in Toland, *Nazarenus*, Oxford, Voltaire Foundation, 1999, 235–40.

Tschirnhaus, E. W. von, *Medicina Mentis, sive artis invenierdi praecepta generalia*, Amsterdam, 1687; 2nd edn, Leipzig, 1695, repr., ed. Wilhelm Risse, Hildesheim, Georg Olms, 1964.

Tyssot de Patot, Simon, *Voyages et Avantures de Jacques Massé*, 'Bordeaux, 1710' (Amsterdam, 1714–17).

Ugolini, Biagio, *Thesaurus antiquitatum sacrarum*, 34 vols., Venice, 1744–69.

Vico, Giambattista, *Scienza Nuova*, 1725, 3rd edn 1744, trans. Thomas Goddard Bergin and Max Harold Fisch, *New Science*, Ithaca, NY, Cornell University Press, 1968.

Voltaire, *Oeuvres complètes*, ed. Louis Moland, 52 vols., Paris, Garnier, 1877–85.

Voltaire's Correspondence, vol. XLIX (June–August 1762), ed. Theodore Besterman, Geneva, Institut et Musée Voltaire, 1959.

Wachter, Georg, *De primordiis Christianae religionis*, 1717, ed. Winfried Schröder, Stuttgart and Bad Cannstatt, Frommann-Holzboog, 1995.

   Elucidarius Cabalisticus, sive Reconditae Hebraeorum Philosophiae Brevis & Succincta Recensio, 'Rome', 1706, ed. Winfried Schröder, Stuttgart and Bad Cannstatt, Frommann-Holzboog, 1995.

   Der Spinozismus in Judenthumb, Amsterdam, 1699, ed. Winfried Schröder, Stuttgart and Bad Cannstatt, Frommann-Holzboog, 1994.

Wagenseil, Johann Christoph, *Der Jüden Glaube und Aberglaube*, Leipzig, 1705.

   Tela Ignea Satanae – Hoc Est: Arcani et Horribiles Judaeorum adversus Christum Deum et Christianam Religionem Libri, Altdorf, 1681.

Warburton, William, *The Divine Legation of Moses Demonstrated*, 3 vols., London, 1846 (1738–41).

Wittich, Christopher, *Anti-Spinoza, sive Examen Ethices Benedicti de Spinoza*, Amsterdam, 1690.

Wolff, Johann Christoph, *Bibliotheca Hebraea*, Hamburg and Leipzig, 1715.

SECONDARY TEXTS (WRITTEN/PUBLISHED AFTER 1850)

Abramsky, Chimen, 'The Crisis of Authority within European Jewry in the Eighteenth Century', in Siegfried Stein and Raphael Loewe, eds., *Studies in Jewish Religious and Intellectual History*, University, AL, University of Alabama Press, 1979, 13–28.

Adorno, Theodor and Max Horkheimer, *Dialectic of Enlightenment*, 1944, trans. John Cumming, New York, Continuum, 1989.

Adorno, Theodor *et al.*, *The Authoritarian Personality*, New York, Harper, 1950.

Ages, Arnold, 'Voltaire, Calmet and the Old Testament', *Studies on Voltaire and the Eighteenth Century* 41 (1966).

Almog, Shmuel, *Zionism and History: The Rise of a New Jewish Consciousness*, New York, St Martin's Press, 1987.

Altkirch, Ernst, *Spinoza im Porträt*, Jena, Eugen Diederichs Verlag, 1913.

Altmann, Alexander, 'Eternality of Punishment: A Theological Controversy within the Amsterdam Rabbinate in the Thirties of the Seventeenth Century', *Proceedings of the American Academy for Jewish Research* 40 (1972) 1–88.

   'Lurianic Kabbalah in a Platonic Key: Abraham Cohen Herrera's *Puerta del Cielo*', in Isadore Twersky and Bernard Septimus, eds., *Jewish Thought in the Seventeenth Century*, Cambridge, MA and London, Harvard University Press, 1979, 1–38.

   Moses Mendelssohn: A Biographical Study, University, AL, University of Alabama Press, 1973.

Amaru, Betsy Halpern, 'Martin Luther and Jewish Mirrors', *Jewish Social Studies* 46 (1984) 95–102.

Anderson, Benedict, *Imagined Communities*, London, Verso, 1983.

Arendt, Hannah, *The Burden of Our Time: The Origins of Totalitarianism*, London, Secker and Warburg, 1951.

The Jew as Pariah: Jewish Identity and Politics in the Modern Age, New York, Grove Press, 1978.

Arkush, Allan, *Moses Mendelssohn and the Enlightenment*, Albany, State University of New York Press, 1994.

'Voltaire on Judaism and Christianity', *AJS Review* 18 (1993) 223–43.

Armogathe, J. R., *Theologia Cartesiana: l'explication de l'eucharistie chez Descartes et dans Desgabets*, The Hague, Martinus Nijhoff, 1977.

Assmann, Jan, *Moses the Egyptian: The Memory of Egypt in Western Monotheism*, Harvard University Press, Cambridge, MA and London, 1997.

Aubery, Pierre, 'Voltaire and Antisemitism – a Reply to Hertzberg', *SVEC* 217 (1983) 177–82.

'Voltaire et les juifs: ironie et démystification', *SVEC* 24 (1963) 69–78.

Baldi, Marialuisa, 'Il "Vero Sistema" dell'universo e il conflitto delle tradizioni in Cudworth', in Guido Canziani and Yves Charles Zarka, eds., *L'interpretazione nei secoli XVI e XVII*, Milan, FrancoAngeli, 1993, 185–208.

Balibar, Etienne, *Spinoza and Politics*, London and New York, Verso, 1998.

Baron, Salo Wittmayer, 'John Calvin and the Jews', *Ancient and Medieval Jewish History*, New Brunswick, NJ, Rutgers University Press, 1972, 338–52.

'The Council of Trent and Rabbinic Literature', *Ancient and Medieval Jewish History*, New Brunswick, NJ, Rutgers University Press, 1972, 353–71.

Barthes, Roland, 'The Last Happy Writer', *Critical Essays*, trans. R. Howard, Evanston, IL, Northwestern University Press, 1972.

Barzilay, I. E., 'John Toland's borrowings from Simone Luzzatto', *Jewish Social Studies* 31 (1969) 75–81.

Bauman, Zygmunt, 'Allosemitism: Premodern, Modern, Postmodern', in Brian Cheyette and Laura Marcus, eds., *Modernity, Culture and 'the Jew'*, Stanford, CA, Stanford University Press, 1998.

Modernity and Ambivalence, Cambridge, Polity, 1991.

Modernity and the Holocaust, Cambridge, Polity, 1989.

Becker, Carl, *The Heavenly City of the Eighteenth-Century Philosophers*, New Haven, Yale University Press, 1932.

Becker, Hans-Joachim, *Fichtes Idee der Nation und das Judentum*, Amsterdam and Atlanta, Rodopi, 2000.

Beiser, Frederick C., *The Fate of Reason: German Philosophy from Kant to Fichte*, Cambridge, MA, and London, Harvard University Press, 1987.

The Sovereignty of Reason: The Defence of Rationality in the Early English Enlightenment, Princeton, Princeton University Press, 1996.

Bell, David, *Spinoza in Germany from 1670 to the Age of Goethe*, London, Institute of Germanic Studies, 1984.

Benítez, Miguel, 'L'ailleurs dans le littérature clandestine: la Chine comme argument', *La Face cachée des lumières: recherches sur les manuscrits clandestins de l'âge classique*, Paris, Universitas, 1996, 403–20.

'Une histoire interminable: origines et développement du Traité des Trois Imposteurs', in Silvia Berti, Françoise Charles-Daubert and Richard H. Popkin, eds., *Heterodoxy, Spinozism and Free Thought in Early Eighteenth Century Europe: Studies on the 'Traité des Trois Imposteurs'*, Dordrecht, Kluwer, 1996, 53–74.

'Lumières et élitisme dans les manuscrits clandestins', *La Face cachée des lumières: recherches sur les manuscrits clandestins de l'âge classique*, Paris, Universitas, 1996, 199–211.

'Materiaux pour un inventaire des manuscrits philosophiques clandestins des XVIIe et XVIIIe siècles', *Rivista di Storia della Filosofia* 3 (1988) 501–31.

'Orobio de Castro et la littérature clandestine', *La Face cachée des lumières: recherches sur les manuscrits clandestins de l'âge classique*, Paris, Universitas, 1996, 147–54.

'Sociétés secrètes philosophiques à l'aube des lumières: pantheistes et naturalistes', *La Face cachée des lumières: recherches sur les manuscrits clandestins de l'âge classique*, Paris, Universitas, 1996, 191–8.

Bennington, Geoffrey, 'Mosaic Fragment: If Derrida Were an Egyptian...', in David Wood, ed., *Derrida: A Critical Reader*, Oxford, Blackwell, 1992, 97–119.

'Postal Politics and the Institution of the Nation', in Homi K. Bhabha, ed., *Nation and Narration*, London and New York, Routledge, 1990, 121–37.

Berg, J. van den, 'Priestley, the Jews and the Millennium', in David S. Katz and J. I. Israel, eds., *Sceptics, Millenarians and Jews*, Leiden, E. J. Brill, 1990, 256–74.

Berlin, Isaiah, *Vico and Herder: Two Studies in the History of Ideas*, London, The Hogarth Press, 1976.

Berman, David, 'Introduction' to *Atheism in Britain*, 5 vols., Thoemmes Press, Bristol, 1996, vol. 1, v–xxxix.

Berti, Silvia, 'At the Roots of Unbelief', *JHI* 56 (1995) 555–75.

'L'Esprit de Spinosa: ses origines et sa première édition dans leur contexte Spinozien', in Silvia Berti, Françoise Charles-Daubert and Richard H. Popkin, eds., *Heterodoxy, Spinozism and Free Thought in Early Eighteenth Century Europe: Studies on the 'Traité des Trois Imposteurs'*, Dordrecht, Kluwer, 1996, 3–50.

'Introduzione' to *Trattato dei Tre Impostori*, Turin, Einaudi, 1994.

'Jan Vroesen, áutore del *Traité des Trois Imposteurs?*', *Rivista storica italiana* 103 (1991) 528–43.

'*La Vie et l'Esprit de Spinosa* e la prima traduzione francese dell'*Ethica*', *Rivista storica italiana* 98 (1986) 5–46.

Besterman, Theodore, *Voltaire*, Oxford, Basil Blackwell, 1969.

Bhabha, Homi K., 'DissemiNation', in Homi K. Bhabha, ed., *Nation and Narration*, London and New York, Routledge, 1990, 291–322.

'Narrating the Nation', Homi K. Bhabha, ed., *Nation and Narration*, London and New York, Routledge, 1990, 1–7.

Bird, Stephen, *Reinventing Voltaire: The Politics of Commemoration in Nineteenth Century France*, Oxford, Voltaire Foundation, 2000.

Birnbaum, Pierre and Ira Katznelson, eds., *Paths of Emancipation: Jews, States and Citizenship*, Princeton, Princeton University Press, 1995.

Bléchet, Françoise, ed., *Voltaire et l'Europe*, Brussels, Complexe, 1994.

Bochinger, Christoph, 'J. H. Callenbergs Institutum Judaicum et Muhammedicum und seine Ausstrahlung nach Osteuropa', in Johannes Wallman and Udo

Sträter, eds., *Halle und Osteuropa: Zur europäischen Ausstrahlung des hallischen Pietismus*, Tübingen, Max Niemeyer, 1988, 331–48.

Bodian, Miriam, *Hebrews of the Portuguese Nation: Conversos and Community in Early Modern Amsterdam*, Bloomington and Indianapolis, Indiana University Press, 1997.

' "Men of the Nation": The Shaping of *Converso* Identity in Early Modern Europe', *Past and Present* 143 (1994) 48–76.

Bollacher, Martin, *Der Junge Goethe und Spinoza*, Tübingen, Max Niemeyer Verlag, 1969.

Borghero, Carlo, *La certezza e la storia: cartesianismo, pirronismo e conoscenza storica*, Milan, FrancoAngeli, 1983.

Bost, Hubert, *Un 'intellectuel' avant la lettre: le journaliste Pierre Bayle*, Amsterdam and Maarssen, APA Holland University Press, 1994.

Pierre Bayle et la religion, Paris, Presses universitaires de France, 1994.

Bots, Hans, 'La rôle des périodiques néerlandais pour la diffusion du livre, 1684–1747', in *Le Magasin de l'Univers: The Dutch Republic as the Centre of the European Book Trade*, Leiden, E. J. Brill, 1992, 49–70.

Bots, Hans and Lenie van Liesholt, *Henri Basnage de Beauval et sa correspondance à propos de l'Histoire des Ouvrages des Savans*, Amsterdam and Maarssen, APA Holland University Press, 1984.

Botwinick, Aryeh, *Skepticism, Belief and the Modern: Maimonides to Nietzsche*, Ithaca, NY and London, Cornell University Press, 1997.

Bourel, Dominique, 'Les Rasés et les barbus: Diderot et le judaïsme', *Revue philosophique* 3 (1984) 275–85.

Boyarin, Daniel, *A Radical Jew: Paul and the Politics of Identity*, Berkeley, Los Angeles and London, University of California Press, 1994.

Unheroic Conduct: The Rise of Heterosexuality and the Invention of the Jewish Man, Berkeley, Los Angeles and London, University of California Press, 1997.

Boyarin, Daniel and Jonathan Boyarin, 'Diaspora: Generation and the Ground of Jewish Identity', *Critical Inquiry* 19 (1993) 693–725.

Bracken, Harry M., 'Bayle's Attack on Natural Theology: The Case of Christian Pyrrhonism', in R. H. Popkin and Arjo Vanderjagt, eds., *Scepticism and Irreligion in the Seventeenth and Eighteenth Centuries*, Leiden, E. J. Brill, 1993, 254–66.

'Pierre Jurieu: The Politics of Prophecy', in John Christian Laursen and Richard H. Popkin, eds., *Continental Millenarians: Protestants, Catholics, Heretics*, Dordrecht, Kluwer, 2001, 85–94.

Braude, Morris, *Conscience on Trial: Three Public Disputations Between Christians and Jews in the Thirteenth and Fifteenth Centuries*, New York, Exposition Press, 1952.

Breuer, Edward, *The Limits of Enlightenment: Jews, Germans and the Eighteenth-Century Study of Scripture*, Cambridge, MA and London, Harvard University Press, 1995.

Brumfitt, J. H., *Voltaire Historian*, Oxford, Oxford University Press, 1958.

Brunner, Otto, Werner Conze and Reinhart Koselleck, eds, *Geschichtliche Grund-begriffe: Historisches Lexicon zur politisch-sozialen Sprache in Deutschland*, vol. 11, Stuttgart, Ernst Klett Verlag, 1975.

Brykman, Geneviève, *La Judéité de Spinoza*, Paris, Vrin, 1972.

'La "Réfutation" de Spinoza dans le *Dictionnaire* de Bayle', in Olivier Bloch, ed., *Spinoza au XVIIIe siècle*, Paris, Méridiens Klincksieck, 1990, 17–25.

Buck-Morss, Susan, 'Hegel and Haiti', *Critical Inquiry* 26 (2000) 821–65.

Bunge, Wiep van, 'Balthasar Bekker's Cartesian Hermeneutics and the Challenge of Spinozism', *British Journal for the History of Philosophy* 1 (1993) 55–79.

'Einleitung' to Balthasar Bekker, *Die Bezauberte Welt*, 1693, Stuttgart and Bad Cannstatt, Frommann-Holzboog, 1997, 7–78.

'Eric Walten (1663–1697): An Early Enlightenment Radical in the Dutch Republic', in Wiep van Bunge and Wim Klever, eds., *Disguised and Overt Spinozism Around 1700*, Leiden, E. J. Brill, 1996, 41–54.

'On the Early Dutch Reception of the *Tractatus Theologico-Politicus*', *Studia Spinozana* 5 (1989) 225–51.

'Van Velthuysen, Batelier and Bredenburg on Spinoza's Interpretation of the Scriptures', in Paolo Cristofolini, ed., *The Spinozistic Heresy: The Debate on the Tractatus Theologico-Politicus, 1670–1677, and the Immediate Reception of Spinozism*, Amsterdam and Maarssen, APA-Holland Press, 1995, 49–65.

Bunge, Wiep van, and Wim Klever, 'Introduction' to *Disguised and Overt Spinozism Around 1700*, Leiden, E. J. Brill, 1996.

Burke, Peter, *The Renaissance Sense of the Past*, London, Edward Arnold, 1969.

Burnett, Stephen G., 'Distorted Mirrors: Antonius Margaritha, Johann Buxtorf and Christian Ethnographies of the Jews', *Sixteenth Century Journal* 25 (1994).

From Christian Hebraism to Jewish Studies: Johannes Buxtorf (1564–1629) and Hebrew Learning in the Seventeenth Century, Leiden, E. J. Brill, 1996.

'Johannes Buxtorf I and the Circumcision Incident of 1619', *Basler Zeitschrift für Geschichte und Altertumskunde* 89 (1989) 135–44.

Butterfield, Herbert, 'Toleration in Early Modern Times', *JHI* 38 (1977) 573–84.

Campbell, Mary Baine, *Wonder and Science: Imagining Worlds in Early Modern Europe*, Ithaca, NY and London, Cornell University Press, 1999.

Cantelli, Gianfranco, *Teologia e ateismo: saggio sul pensiero filosofico e religioso di Pierre Bayle*, Florence, La Nuova Italia, 1969.

Vico e Bayle: premesse per un confronto, Naples, Guida, 1971.

Carayol, Elizabeth, *Thémiseul de Saint-Hyacinthe, 1684–1746*, Oxford, Voltaire Foundation, 1984.

Carlebach, Elisheva, *Divided Souls: Converts from Judaism in Germany, 1500–1750*, New Haven and London, Yale University Press, 2001.

Carpanetto, Dino and Giuseppe Ricuperati, *Italy in the Age of Reason 1685–1789*, London and New York, Longman, 1987.

Cassirer, Ernst, *The Philosophy of the Enlightenment*, 1932, trans. F. Koelln and J. Pettegrove, Princeton, Princeton University Press, 1951.

Censer, Jack, 'The History of the Book in Early Modern France: Directions and Challenges', *Eighteenth Century Life* 19 (1995) 84–95.

Cerny, Gerald, *Theology, Politics and Letters at the Crossroads of European Civilization: Jacques Basnage and the Baylean Huguenot Refugees in the Dutch Republic*, Dordrecht, Martinus Nijhoff, 1987.

Chakrabarty, Dipesh, *Provincialising Europe: Postcolonial Thought and Historical Difference*, Princeton and Oxford, Princeton University Press, 2000.

Champion, Justin, 'Introduction' to John Toland, *Nazarenus*, Voltaire Foundation, Oxford, 1999, 1–106.

    'John Toland: The Politics of Pantheism', *Revue de synthèse* 116 (1995) 259–80.

    The Pillars of Priestcraft Shaken: The Church of England and its Enemies, 1660–1730, Cambridge, Cambridge University Press, 1992.

    'Toleration and Citizenship in Enlightenment England: John Toland and the Naturalization of the Jews, 1714–1753', in Ole Peter Grell and Roy Porter, eds., *Toleration in Enlightenment Europe*, Cambridge, Cambridge University Press, 2000, 133–56.

Charles-Daubert, Françoise, '*L'Esprit de Spinosa et les Traités des Trois imposteurs*: rappel des différentes familles et de leurs principales Caractéristiques", in Silvia Berti, Françoise Charles-Daubert and Richard H. Popkin, eds, *Heterodoxy, Spinozism and Free Thought in Early Eighteenth Century Europe: Studies on the 'Traité des Trois Imposteurs'*, Dordrecht, Kluwer, 1996, 131–89.

    'L'Image de Spinoza dans la littérature clandestine et l'*Esprit de Spinoza*', in Olivier Bloch, ed., *Spinoza au XVIII e siècle*, Paris, Méridiens Klincksieck, 1990, 51–74.

    'Les Traités des Trois Imposteurs et l'*Esprit de Spinosa*, *Nouvelles de la république des lettres* 1 (1988) 21–50.

Chartier, Roger, *Cultural History: Between Practices and Representations*, trans. Lydia G. Cochrane, Cambridge, Polity, 1988.

    The Cultural Origins of the French Revolution, trans. Lydia G. Cochrane, Durham, NC, Duke University Press, 1991.

    The Order of Books: Readers, Authors and Libraries in Europe between the Fourteenth and the Eighteenth Centuries, Cambridge, Polity, 1994.

Chazan, Robert, *Daggers of Faith*, Berkeley and Los Angeles, University of California Press, 1989.

    'The Deteriorating Image of the Jews: Twelfth and Thirteenth centuries', in Scott L. Waugh and Peter D. Diehl, eds., *Christendom and its Discontents: Exclusion, Persecution and Rebellion, 1000–1500*, Cambridge, Cambridge University Press, 1996, 220–33.

    Medieval Stereotypes and Modern Antisemitism, Berkeley, Los Angeles and London, University of California Press, 1997.

Christianson, Paul, *Discourse on History, Law and Governance in the Public Career of John Selden (1610–1635)*, Toronto, Buffalo and London, University of Toronto Press, 1996.

Clark, Christopher, *The Politics of Conversion: Missionary Protestantism and the Jews in Prussia 1728–1941*, Oxford, Clarendon, 1995.

Cohen, Carl, 'Martin Luther and his Jewish Contemporaries', *Jewish Social Studies* 25 (1963) 195–204.

Cohen, Claudine, 'La Communication manuscrite et la genèse du Telliamed', in François Moureau, ed., *De bonne main: la communication manuscrite au XVIIIe siècle*, Paris, Universitas, 1993, 59–69.

Cohen, Jeremy, *The Friars and the Jews: the Evolution of Medieval Anti-Judaism*, London and Ithaca, NY, Cornell University Press, 1982.

Living Letters of the Law: Ideas of the Jew in Medieval Christianity, Berkeley, Los Angeles and London, 1999.

Cohen, Mark, *Under Crescent and Cross: The Jews in the Middle Ages*, Princeton, Princeton University Press, 1994.

Cohen, Richard A., 'Levinas on Spinoza's Misunderstanding of Judaism', in Melvyn New, ed., *In Proximity: Emmanuel Levinas and the Eighteenth Century*, Lubbock, Texas Tech University Press, 2001, 23–51.

Cohen, Richard I., *Jewish Icons: Art and Society in Modern Europe*, Berkeley, Los Angeles and London, University of California Press, 1998.

Colley, Linda, *Britons: Forging the Nation 1707–1837*, New Haven and London, Yale University Press, 1992.

Cooperman, Bernard, 'Eliahu Montalto's "Suitable and Incontrovertible Propositions": A Seventeenth-century Anti-Christian Polemic', in Isadore Twersky and Bernard Septimus, eds., *Jewish Thought in the Seventeenth Century*, Cambridge, MA and London, Harvard University Press, 1979, 469–97.

Corsano, Antonio, *Bayle, Leibniz e la storia*, Naples, Guida, 1971.

Coudert, Allison P., 'A Cambridge Platonist's Kabbalist Nightmare', *JHI* 35 (1975) 633–52.

'Henry More, the Kabbalah and the Quakers', in Richard Kroll, Richard Ashcraft and Perez Zagorin, eds., *Philosophy, Science and Religion in England, 1640–1700*, Cambridge, Cambridge University Press, 1992, 31–67.

The Impact of the Kabbalah in the Seventeenth Century: The Life and Thought of Francis Mercury van Helmont (1614–1698), Leiden, Brill, 1999.

'*The Kabbalah Denudata*: Converting Jews or Seducing Christians?', in R. H. Popkin and G. M. Weiner, eds., *Jewish Christians and Christian Jews: From the Renaissance to the Enlightenment*, Dordrecht, Kluwer, 1994, 73–96.

Leibniz and the Kabbalah, Dordrecht, Kluwer, 1995.

Coudert, Allison P., Richard H. Popkin and Gordon M. Weiner, eds, *Leibniz, Mysticism and Religion*, Dordrecht, Kluwer, 1998.

Cuddihy, John Murray, *The Ordeal of Civility: Freud, Marx, Lévi-Strauss and the Jewish Struggle with Modernity*, 2nd edn, Boston, Beacon Press, 1987.

Curley, Edwin, *Behind the Geometrical Method: A Reading of Spinoza's 'Ethics'*, Princeton, Princeton University Press, 1988.

Dan, Joseph, 'Menasseh ben Israel's *Nishmat Hayyim* and the Concept of Evil in Seventeenth-Century Jewish Thought', in Isadore Twersky and Bernard Septimus, eds., *Jewish Thought in the Seventeenth Century*, Cambridge, MA and London, Harvard University Press, 1979, 63–75.

Dán, Robert, 'Isaac Troky and his "Antitrinitarian" Sources', in Robert Dán, ed., *Occident and Orient: A Tribute to the Memory of Alexander Scheiber*, Leiden, E. J. Brill, 1988, 69–82.

Daniel, Stephen H., *John Toland: His Method, Manners and Mind*, Kingston and Montreal, McGill-Queens University Press, 1984.

'Toland's Semantic Pantheism', in Phillip McGuinness, Alan Harrison and Richard Kearney, eds., *John Toland's 'Christianity not Mysterious': Text, Associated Works and Critical Essays*, Dublin, Lilliput Press, 1997, 303–12.

Darnton, Robert, *The Forbidden Best-Sellers of Pre-Revolutionary France*, New York, W. W. Norton, 1995.

'George Washington's False Teeth', *New York Review of Books*, 27 March 1997.

The Literary Underground of the Old Regime, Cambridge, MA, Harvard University Press, 1982.

De Certeau, Michel, *The Writing of History*, trans. Tom Conley, New York, Columbia University Press, 1988 (1975).

DeJean, Joan, *Ancients Against Moderns: Culture Wars and the Making of a Fin de Siècle*, Chicago, University of Chicago Press, 1997.

Deleuze, Gilles, *Expressionism in Philosophy: Spinoza*, New York, Zone Books, 1992.

Derrida, Jacques, *Specters of Marx*, trans. Peggy Kamuf, New York, Routledge, 1994.

'Violence and Metaphysics: An Essay on the Thought of Emmanuel Levinas', *Writing and Difference*, trans. Alan Bass, London, Routledge, 1978, 79–153.

Dodge, Guy, *The Political Theory of the Huguenots of the Dispersion: With Special Reference to the Thought and Influence of Pierre Jurieu*, New York, Columbia University Press, 1947.

Donagan, Alan, 'Spinoza's Theology', in Don Garrett, ed., *The Cambridge Companion to Spinoza*, Cambridge, Cambridge University Press, 1996, 343–82.

Droixhe, Daniel, 'La Crise de l'hébreu langue-mère au XVIIe siècle', in Chantal Grell and François Laplanche, eds., *La République des Lettres et l'histoire du judaïsme antique, XVIe–XVIIIe siècles*, Paris, Presses de l'Université de Paris-Sorbonne, 1992, 65–99.

La Linguistique et l'appel de l'histoire (1600–1800), Geneva, Droz, 1978.

Dubin, Lois C., *The Port Jews of Habsburg Trieste: Absolutist Politics and Enlightenment Culture*, Stanford, CA, Stanford University Press, 1999.

Dunn, John, *The Political Thought of John Locke*, Cambridge, Cambridge University Press, 1969.

Eco, Umberto, *The Search for the Perfect Language*, trans. James Fentress, Blackwell, Oxford, 1995.

Elukin, Jonathan, 'Jacques Basnage and the *History of the Jews*: Anti-Catholic Polemic and Historical Allegory in the Republic of Letters', *JHI* 53 (1992) 603–30.

Endelman, Todd, *The Jews of Georgian England 1714–1830: Tradition and Change in a Liberal Society*, Philadelphia, Jewish Publication Society of America, 1979.

Radical Assimilation in English Jewish History, 1656–1945, Bloomington and Indianapolis, Indiana University Press, 1990.

Erspamer, Peter R., *The Elusiveness of Tolerance: The 'Jewish Question' from Lessing to the Napoleonic Wars*, Chapel Hill and London, University of North Carolina Press, 1997.

Ettinger, Shmuel, 'The Beginnings of the Change in the Attitude of European Society Towards the Jews', *Scripta Hierosolymitana* 7 (1961) 193–219.

Evans, Robert Rees, *Pantheisticon: The Career of John Toland*, New York, Peter Lang, 1991.

Farge, Arlette, *Subversive Words: Public Opinion in Eighteenth-Century France*, University Park, PA, Pennsylvania State University Press, 1994.

Faur, José, *In the Shadow of History: Jews and Conversos at the Dawn of Modernity*, Albany, State University of New York Press, 1992.

Feiner, Shmuel, *Haskalah and History: The Emergence of a Modern Jewish Historical Consciousness*, London and Portland, OR, Littman, 2002.

Feld, Edward, 'Spinoza the Jew', *Modern Judaism* 9 (1989) 101–19.

Felsenstein, Frank, *Anti-Semitic Stereotypes: A Paradigm of Otherness in English Popular Culture, 1660–1830*, Baltimore and London, Johns Hopkins University Press, 1995.

Fisch, Harold, 'The Messianic Politics of Menasseh ben Israel', in Yosef Kaplan, Henry Méchoulan and Richard H. Popkin, eds., *Menasseh ben Israel and his World*, Leiden, E. J. Brill, 1989, 228–39.

Fitzpatrick, Martin, 'Toleration and the Enlightenment Movement', in Ole Peter Grell and Roy Porter, eds., *Toleration in Enlightenment Europe*, Cambridge, Cambridge University Press, 2000, 23–68.

Fix, Andrew, 'Bekker and Spinoza', in Wiep van Bunge and Wim Klever, eds., *Disguised and Overt Spinozism Around 1700*, Leiden, E. J. Brill, 1996, 23–40.

Prophecy and Reason: The Dutch Collegiants in the Early Enlightenment, Princeton, Princeton University Press, 1994.

Foucher de Careil, A., *Réfutation inédite de Spinoza par Leibniz, précédée d'un mémoire par A. Foucher de Careil*, Paris, 1854, repr., ed. Winfried Schröder, Stuttgart and Bad Cannstatt, Frommann-Holzboog, 1995.

Freud, Sigmund, *Moses and Monetheism*, 1939, in Angela Richards and Albert Dickson, eds., *Pelican Freud Library* vol. XIII, London, Penguin, 1985, 237–386.

Totem and Taboo, 1913, in Angela Richards and Albert Dickson, eds., *Pelican Freud Library* vol. XIII, London, Penguin, 1985, 43–224.

Friedman, Jerome, *The Most Ancient Testimony: Sixteenth-Century Christian-Hebraica in the Age of Renaissance Nostalgia*, Athens, OH, Ohio University Press, 1983.

Friedmann, Georges, *Leibniz et Spinoza*, Paris, Gallimard, 1962.

Fuks, Lajb, 'Sebastianisme in Amsterdam in het begin van de 18e eeuw', *Studia Rosenthaliana* 14 (1980) 20–8.

Fuks, L, and R. G. Fuks-Mansfeld, *Hebrew and Judaic Manuscripts in Amsterdam Public Collections*, 2 vols., Leiden, E. J. Brill, 1975.

Funkenstein, Amos, *Perceptions of Jewish History*, Berkeley and Los Angeles, University of California Press, 1993.

Theology and the Scientific Imagination from the Middle Ages to the Seventeenth Century, Princeton, NJ, Princeton University Press, 1986.

Gargallo, Gioacchino, *Boulainvilliers e la storiografia dell'illuminismo francese*, Naples, Giannini, 1954.

Gatens, Moira and Genevieve Lloyd, *Collective Imaginings: Spinoza, Past and Present*, London, Routledge, 1999.

Gay, Peter, *The Enlightenment – An Interpretation: The Science of Freedom*, London and New York, W. W. Norton, 1977.

  A Godless Jew: Freud, Atheism and the Making of Psychoanalysis, New Haven and London, Yale University Press, 1987.

  The Party of Humanity: Studies in the French Enlightenment, New York, Knopf, 1964.

  Voltaire's Politics, Princeton, Princeton University Press, 1959.

Gibbs, Graham, 'The Radical Enlightenment', *British Journal for the History of Science* 17 (1984) 67–81.

  'The Role of the Dutch Republic as the Intellectual Entrepôt of Europe in the Seventeenth and Eighteenth Centuries', *BMBGN* 86 (1971) 323–49.

  'Some Intellectual and Political Influences of the Huguenot Emigrés in the United Provinces, 1680–1730', *BMBGN* 90 (1975) 255–87.

Gilroy, Paul, *The Black Atlantic: Modernity and Double Consciousness*, Cambridge, MA, Harvard University Press, 1993.

Giuntini, Chiara, *Panteismo e ideologia repubblicana: John Toland (1670–1722)*, Bologna, Mulino, 1979.

Glaser, Eliane, 'Hebrew as Myth and Reality in Renaissance England', in Robert Rabinowitz, ed., *New Voices in Jewish Thought*, London, Limmud Publications, 1998, 4–19.

Godechot, Jacques, 'La Revolution française et les juifs', in Bernhard Blumenkranz and Albert Soboul, eds., *Les Juifs et la révolution française*, Toulouse, Privat, 1976, 47–70.

Goldgar, Anne, *Impolite Learning: Culture and Community in the Republic of Letters 1680–1750*, New Haven and London, Yale University Press, 1995.

Goldie, Mark, 'Priestcraft and the Birth of Whiggism', in Nicholas Phillipson and Quentin Skinner, eds., *Political Discourse in Early Modern Britain*, Cambridge, Cambridge University Press, 1993, 209–31.

Goodman, David G. and Masanori Miyazawa, *The Jews in the Japanese Mind: The History and Uses of a Cultural Stereotype*, New York, Free Press, 1995.

Goodman, Dena, *The Republic of Letters: A Cultural History of the French Enlightenment*, Ithaca, NY and London, Cornell University Press, 1994.

Gordon, Daniel, 'On the Supposed Obsolescence of the French Enlightenment', in Daniel Gordon, ed., *Postmodernism and the Enlightenment: New Perspectives in Eighteenth-Century French Intellectual History*, New York and London, Routledge, 2001, 201–21.

Graetz, Michael, 'Court Jews in Economics and Politics', in Vivian B. Mann and Richard I. Cohen, eds., *From Court Jews to the Rothschilds: Art, Patronage and Power 1600–1800*, Munich and New York, Prestel, 1996, 27–43.

Grafton, Anthony, *Defenders of the Text: The Traditions of Scholarship in an Age of Science, 1450–1800*, Cambridge, MA and London, Harvard University Press, 1991.

'Joseph Scaliger and Historical Chronology: The Rise and Fall of a Discipline', *History and Theory* 14 (1975) 156–85.

Joseph Scaliger: A Study in the History of Classical Scholarship, vol. 11, Oxford, Clarendon Press, 1993.

Gray, John, *Enlightenment's Wake: Politics and Culture at the Close of the Modern Age*, London and New York, Routledge, 1995.

Grell, Chantal, *L'Histoire entre érudition et philosophie: étude sur la connaissance historique à l'age des lumières*, Paris, Presses universitaires de France, 1994.

Gritsch, Eric W., 'The Jews in Reformation Theology', in Marvin Perry and Frederick M. Schweitzer, eds., *Jewish–Christian Encounters Over the Centuries: Symbiosis, Prejudice, Holocaust, Dialogue*, New York, Peter Lang Publishing, 1994, 197–213.

Grossman, Walter, *Johann Christian Edelmann: From Orthodoxy to Enlightenment*, The Hague and Paris, Mouton, 1976.

Gullan-Whur, Margaret, *Within Reason: A Life of Spinoza*, London, Jonathan Cape, 1998.

Habermas, Jürgen, *The Philosophical Discourse of Modernity*, 1985, trans. Frederick Lawrence, Cambridge, Polity, 1987.

The Structural Transformation of the Public Sphere, 1962, trans. Thomas Burger, Cambridge, Polity, 1989.

Hacking, Ian, *The Emergence of Probability: A Philosophical Study of Early Ideas About Probability, Induction and Statistical Inference*, Cambridge, Cambridge University Press, 1975.

Hadas-Lebel, Mireille, 'La Lecture du Flavius Josèphe aux XVIIe et XVIIIe siècles', in Chantal Grell and François Laplanche, eds., *La République des lettres et l'histoire du judaïsme antique*, Paris, Presses de l'Université de Paris-Sorbonne, 1992, 101–13.

Hall, A. Rupert, *Henry More: Magic, Religion and Experiment*, Oxford, Basil Blackwell, 1990.

Haller, William, *Foxe's Book of Martyrs and the Elect Nation*, London, Jonathan Cape, 1963.

Harrison, Peter, *The Bible, Protestantism and the Rise of Natural Science*, Cambridge, Cambridge University Press, 1998.

'Religion' and the Religions in the English Enlightenment, Cambridge, Cambridge University Press, 1990.

Hartnett, Stephen J., *Democratic Dissent and the Cultural Fictions of Antebellum America*, Urbana and Chicago, University of Illinois Press, 2002.

Harvey, Zev Warren, 'Maimonides and Spinoza on the Knowledge of Good and Evil', in Joseph Dan, ed., *Binah: Studies in Jewish Thought* vol. 11, New York, Praeger, 1989, 131–46.

'A Portrait of Spinoza as a Maimonidean', *Journal of the History of Philosophy* 19 (1981) 151–72.

Häseler, Jens, 'Réfugiés français à Berlin – Lecteurs de manuscrits clandestins', in Guido Canziani, ed., *Filosofia e religione nella letteratura clandestina, secoli XVII e XVIII*, Milan, FrancoAngeli, 1994, 373–85.

Hatin, Eugène, *Bibliographie historique et critique de la presse périodique française*, Paris, 1866.

Haynes, Stephen R., *Jews and the Christian Imagination*, Basingstoke, Macmillan, 1995.

Hazard, Paul, *The European Mind 1680–1715*, 1935, trans. J. Lewis May, London, Hollis and Carter, 1953.

Herrick, James A., *The Radical Rhetoric of the English Deists*, Columbia, University of South Carolina Press, 1997.

Hertzberg, Arthur, *The French Enlightenment and the Jews: The Origins of Modern Anti-Semitism*, New York, Colombia University Press, 1968.

Heyd, Michael, *'Be Sober and Reasonable': The Critique of Enthusiasm in the Seventeenth and Early Eighteenth Centuries*, Leiden, E. J. Brill, 1995.

    Between Orthodoxy and Enlightenment: Jean-Robert Chouet and the Introduction of Cartesian Science in the Academy of Geneva, Jerusalem, The Magnes Press, 1982.

    'A Disguised Atheist or a Sincere Christian? The Enigma of Pierre Bayle', *Bibliothèque d'humanisme et Renaissance: travaux et documents* 39 (1977) 157–65.

Hill, Christopher, *The English Bible and the Seventeenth-Century Revolution*, London, Allen Lane, 1993.

    'Till the Conversion of the Jews', *The Collected Essays of Christopher Hill*, Brighton, Harvester Press, 1986, vol. II, 269–300.

Hillesum, J. M., 'De *Porta Veritatis* van Jacob van Amram', *Het Boek* 17 (1928) 335–46.

Hodgen, Margaret, *Early Anthropology in the Sixteenth and Seventeenth Centuries*, Philadelphia, University of Pennsylvania Press, 1964.

Hundert, E. G., *The Enlightenment's Fable: Bernard Mandeville and the Discovery of Society*, Cambridge, Cambridge University Press, 1994.

Huppert, George, *The Idea of Perfect History: Historical Erudition and Historical Philosophy in Renaissance France*, Urbana, Chicago and London, University of Illinois Press, 1970.

Hutton, Sarah, 'Edward Stillingfleet, Henry More, and the Decline of *Moses Atticus*: a Note on Seventeenth-century Anglican Apologetics', in Richard Kroll, Richard Ashcraft and Perez Zagorin, eds., *Philosophy, Science and Religion in England, 1640–1700*, Cambridge, Cambridge University Press, 1992, 68–84.

    'Henry More, Anne Conway and the Kabbalah: A Cure for the Kabbalist Nightmare?' in Alison P. Coudert, Sarah Hutton, Richard H. Popkin and Gordon M. Weiner, eds., *Judaeo-Christian Intellectual Culture in the Seventeenth Century: A Celebration of the Library of Narcissus Marsh (1638–1713)*, Dordrecht, Kluwer, 1999, 27–42.

    'Henry Oldenburg and Spinoza', in Paolo Cristofolini, ed., *The Spinozistic Heresy: The Debate on the Tractatus Theologico-Politicus, 1670–1677, and the Immediate Reception of Spinozism*, Amsterdam and Maarssen, APA-Holland Press, 1995, 106–119.

    'Reason and Revelation in the Cambridge Platonists, and their Reception of Spinoza', in Karlfried Gründer and Wilhelm Schmidt-Biggemann, eds.,

Spinoza in der Frühzeit seiner religiösen Wirkung, Lambert Schneider, Heidelberg, 1984, 181–200.

Hyman, Paula E., *The Jews of Modern France*, Berkeley, Los Angeles and London, University of California Press, 1998.

Idel, Moshe, 'Differing Conceptions of Kabbalah in the Early Seventeenth Century', in Isadore Twersky and Bernard Septimus, eds., *Jewish Thought in the Seventeenth Century*, Cambridge, MA and London, Harvard University Press, 1979, 137–200.

'Jewish Kabbalah and Platonism in the Middle Ages and Renaissance', in Lenn E. Goodman, ed., *Neoplatonism and Jewish Thought*, Albany, State University of New York Press, 1992, 319–51.

Kabbalah: New Perspectives, New Haven and London, Yale University Press, 1988.

Iofrida, Manlio, 'Linguaggio e verità in Lodiwijk Meyer', in Paolo Cristofolini, ed., *The Spinozistic Heresy: The Debate on the Tractatus Theologico-Politicus, 1670–1677, and the Immediate Reception of Spinozism*, Amsterdam and Maarssen, APA-Holland Press, 1995, 25–35.

Israel, Jonathan I., 'The Banning of Spinoza's Works in the Dutch Republic', in Wiep van Bunge and Wim Klever, eds., *Disguised and Overt Spinozism Around 1700*, Leiden, E. J. Brill, 1996, 3–14.

'The Bekker Controversies as a Turning Point in the History of Dutch Culture and Thought', *Dutch Crossing* 20 (1996) 5–21.

'Les controverses pamphlétaires dans la vie intellectuelle hollandaise et allemande à l'époque de Bekker et Van Leenhof', *Dix-huitième siècle* 195 (1997) 253–64.

The Dutch Republic: Its Rise, Greatness and Fall, 1477–1806, Oxford, Oxford University Press, 1995.

'Dutch Sephardi Jewry, Millenarian Politics and the Struggle for Brazil', in David S. Katz and Jonathan I. Israel, eds., *Sceptics, Millenarians and Jews*, Leiden, E. J. Brill, 1990, 76–97.

European Jewry in the Age of Mercantilism 1550–1750, 1985, 2nd edn, Oxford, Oxford University Press, 1989.

'Gregorio Leti (1631–1701) and the Dutch Sephardi Elite at the Close of the Seventeenth Century', in Ada Rapaport-Albert and Steven J. Zipperstein, eds., *Jewish History: Essays in Honour of Chimen Abramsky*, London, Peter Halban, 1988, 267–84.

'The Intellectual Debate about Toleration in the Dutch Republic', in C. Berkvens-Stevelinck, J. I. Israel and G. H. M. Posthumus Meyjes, eds., *The Emergence of Tolerance in the Dutch Republic*, Leiden, E. J. Brill, 1997, 3–36.

Radical Enlightenment: Philosophy and the Making of Modernity, 1650–1750, Oxford, Oxford University Press, 2001.

'De Republiek der Verenigde Nederlanden tot omstreeks 1750: Demographie en economische activiteit', in J. C. H. Blom, R. G. Fuks-Mansfeld and I Schöffer, eds., *Geschiedenis van de Joden in Nederland*, Amsterdam, Balans, 1995, 97–126.

'Spinoza, King Solomon, and Frederik van Leenhof's Spinozistic Republican-ism', *Studia Spinozana* 6 (1995) 303–17.

'Spinoza, Locke and the Enlightenment Battle for Toleration', in Ole Peter Grell and Roy Porter, eds., *Toleration in Enlightenment Europe*, Cambridge, Cambridge University Press, 2000, 102–13.

'Toleration in Seventeenth-Century Dutch and English Thought', in Simon Groenveld and Michael White, eds., *The Exchange of Ideas: Religion, Scholar-ship and Art in Anglo-Dutch Relations in the Seventeenth Century*, Walburg Instituut, Zutphen, 1994, 13–30.

Ivry, Alfred L., 'Maimonides and Neoplatonism: Challenge and Response', in Lenn E. Goodman, eds., *Neoplatonism and Jewish Thought*, Albany, State University of New York Press, 1992, 137–56.

Jacob, Margaret C., 'The Crisis of the European Mind: Hazard Revisited', in Margaret C. Jacob and Phyllis Mack, eds, *Politics and Culture in Early Mod-ern Europe: Essays in Honor of H. G. Koenigsburger*, Cambridge, Cambridge University Press, 1987, 251–7.

Living the Enlightenment: Freemasonry and Politics in Eighteenth-Century Europe, New York, Oxford University Press, 1991.

'The Materialist World of Pornography', in Lynn Hunt, ed., *The Invention of Pornography: Obscenity and the Origins of Modernity, 1500–1800*, New York, Zone Books, 1993, 157–202.

The Radical Enlightenment: Pantheists, Freemasons and Republicans, London, George Allen and Unwin, 1981.

Scientific Culture and the Making of the Industrial West, Oxford and New York, Oxford University Press, 1997.

James, Susan, *Passion and Action: The Emotions in Seventeenth-Century Philosophy*, Oxford, Clarendon Press, 1997.

Jay, Martin, *The Dialectical Imagination: A History of the Frankfurt School and the Institute of Social Research, 1923–1950*, Berkeley, Los Angeles and London, University of California Press, 1973.

Jenkinson, Sally, 'Two Concepts of Tolerance: Or Why Bayle is Not Locke', *Journal of Political Philosophy* 4 (1996) 302–22.

Jongeneelen, Gerrit H., 'La philosophie politique d'Adrien Koerbagh', *Cahiers Spinoza* 6 (1991) 247–67.

Jossua, Jean-Pierre, *Pierre Bayle, ou l'obsession du mal*, Paris, Aubier-Montaigne, 1977.

Jowett, Claire, 'Racial Identities? Native Americans, Jews and the English Com-monwealth', in Siân Jones, Tony Kushner and Sarah Pearce, eds., *Cultures of Ambivalence and Contempt: Studies in Jewish–Non-Jewish Relations*, Valentine Mitchell, London and Portland OR, 1998, 153–80.

Kamen, Henry, *The Rise of Toleration*, London, Weidenfeld and Nicholson, 1967.

The Spanish Inquisition: A Historical Revision, New Haven and London, Yale University Press, 1998.

Kaplan, Yosef, *An Alternative Path to Modernity: The Sephardi Diaspora in Western Europe*, Leiden, Brill, 2000.

'From Apostasy to Return to Judaism: The Portuguese Jews in Amsterdam', in Joseph Dan, ed., *Binah: Studies in Jewish Thought, vol. 1*, New York, Praeger, 1989, 99–117.

'Deviance and Community in the Eighteenth Century: A Chapter in the Social History of the Sephardi Community of Amsterdam', in Jozeph Michman, ed., *Dutch Jewish History*, vol. v, Assen and Maastricht, Van Gorcum, 1993, 103–15.

From Christianity to Judaism: The Story of Isaac Orobio de Castro, Oxford, Oxford University Press, 1989.

'De joden in de Republiek tot omstreeks 1750: Religieus, cultureel, en sociaal leven', in J. C. H. Blom, R. G. Fuks-Mansfeld and I Schöffer, eds., *Geschiedenis van de Joden in Nederland*, Amsterdam, Balans, 1995, 129–73.

Judíos nuevos en Amsterdam: estudio sobre la historia social e intelectual del judaísmo sefardí en el siglo XVII, Barcelona, Gedisa, 1996.

' "Karaites" in Early Eighteenth-Century Amsterdam', in David S. Katz and Jonathan I. Israel, eds., *Sceptics, Millenarians and Jews*, Leiden, E. J. Brill, 1990, 196–236.

'The Self-Definition of the Sephardic Jews of Western Europe and Their Relation to the Alien and the Stranger', in Benjamin R. Gampel, ed., *Crisis and Creativity in the Sephardic World, 1391–1648*, New York, Columbia University Press, 1997, 121–45.

'The Social Functions of the *Herem* in the Portuguese Jewish Community of Amsterdam in the Seventeenth Century', in Jozeph Michman, ed., *Dutch Jewish History*, vol. 1, Tel Aviv University/Hebrew University of Jerusalem, 1984, 111–56.

'Spinoza Scholarship in Israel', in C. de Deugd, ed., *Spinoza's Political and Theological Thought*, Amsterdam, North-Holland Publishing Company, 1984, 19–22.

'The Travels of Portuguese Jews from Amsterdam to the "Lands of Idolatry" ', in Yosef Kaplan, ed., *Jews and Conversos: Studies in Society and the Inquisition*, Jerusalem, The Magnes Press, 1985, 197–224.

Kasher, Asa and Shlomo Bideman, 'Why Was Baruch de Spinoza Excommunicated?', in David S. Katz and J. I. Israel, eds, *Sceptics, Millenarians and Jews*, Leiden, E. J. Brill, 1990, 98–141.

Katchen, Aaron, *Christian Hebraists and Dutch Rabbis: Seventeenth Century Apologetics and the Study of Maimonides' 'Mishneh Torah'*, London and Cambridge, MA, Harvard University Press, 1984.

Kates, Gary, 'Jews into Frenchmen: Nationality and Representation in Revolutionary France', in Ferenc Fehér, ed., *The French Revolution and the Birth of Modernity*, Berkeley and Los Angeles, University of California Press, 1990, 103–16.

Katz, David S., 'The Hutchinsonians and Hebraic Fundamentalism in Eighteenth-Century England', in David S. Katz and J. I. Israel, eds., *Sceptics, Millenarians and Jews*, Leiden, E. J. Brill, 1990, 327–55.

'Isaac Vossius and the English Biblical Critics, 1670–1689', in Richard H. Popkin and A. Vanderjagt, eds., *Scepticism and Irreligion in the Seventeenth and Eighteenth Centuries*, Leiden, E. J. Brill, 1993, 141–84.

The Jews in the History of England, 1485–1850, Oxford, Clarendon Press, 1982.

'Menasseh ben Israel's Christian Connection: Henry Jessey and the Jews', in Yosef Kaplan, Henry Méchoulan and Richard H. Popkin, eds., *Menasseh ben Israel and his World*, Leiden, E. J. Brill, 1989, 117–38.

'The Phenomenon of Philo-Semitism', in *Christianity and Judaism: Papers Read at the 1991 Summer Meeting and the 1992 Winter Meeting of the Ecclesiastical History Society*, Oxford, Blackwell, 1992, 327–61.

Philo-Semitism and the Readmission of the Jews to England, 1603–1655, Oxford, Clarendon Press, 1982.

Sabbath and Sectarianism in Seventeenth-Century England, Leiden, E. J. Brill, 1988.

Katz, David S. and Richard H. Popkin, *Messianic Revolution: Radical Religious Politics to the End of the Second Millennium*, Penguin, London, 1999.

Katz, Jacob, *Exclusiveness and Tolerance: Studies in Jewish–Gentile Relations in Medieval and Modern Times*, Oxford, Oxford University Press, 1961.

Jews and Freemasons in Europe, 1723–1939, trans. Leonard Oschry, Cambridge, MA, Harvard University Press, 1970.

Out of the Ghetto: The Social Background of Jewish Emancipation, 1770–1870, Cambridge, MA, Harvard University Press, 1973.

From Prejudice to Destruction: Anti-Semitism, 1700–1933, Cambridge, MA, Harvard University Press, 1980.

Tradition and Crisis: Jewish Society at the End of the Middle Ages, Syracuse, NY, Syracuse University Press, 2000 (1957).

Katz, Jacob, ed., *Toward Modernity: The European Jewish Model*, New Brunswick, NJ and Oxford, Transaction Books, 1987.

Katz, Steven T., 'Utterance and Ineffability in Jewish Neoplatonism', in Lenn E. Goodman, ed., *Neoplatonism and Jewish Thought*, Albany, State University of New York Press, 1992, 279–98.

Kelley, Donald R., 'Faces in Clio's Mirror: Mistress, Muse, Missionary', *Journal of Modern History* 47 (1975) 679–90.

Foundations of Modern Historical Scholarship: Language, Law and History in the French Renaissance, New York and London, Columbia University Press, 1970.

Kenshur, Oscar, 'Pierre Bayle and the Structures of Doubt', *Eighteenth-Century Studies* 21 (1988) 297–315.

Kilcullen, John, *Sincerity and Truth: Essays on Arnauld, Bayle and Toleration*, Oxford, Clarendon Press, 1988.

Klein, Lawrence E., *Shaftesbury and the Culture of Politeness: Moral Discourse and Cultural Politics in Early Eighteenth-Century England*, Cambridge, Cambridge University Press, 1994.

Klever, W. N. A., 'Inleiding' to Franciscus van den Enden, *Vrije Politijke Stellingen en Consideratien van Staat*, Amsterdam, Wereldbibliotheek, 1992, 11–119.

'Spinoza's Life and Works', in Don Garrett, ed., *The Cambridge Companion to Spinoza*, Cambridge, Cambridge University Press, 1996, 13–60.

Kochan, Lionel, *Jews, Idols and Messiahs: the Challenge from History*, Oxford, Basil Blackwell, 1990.

Kolakowski, Leszek, *Chrétiens sans église: la conscience religieuse et le lien confessionnel au XVII e siècle*, 1965, trans. Anna Posner, Paris, Gallimard, 1969.

Modernity on Endless Trial, Chicago and London, University of Chicago Press, 1990.

'The Myth of Reason', *The Presence of Myth*, Chicago and London, University of Chicago Press, 1989, 69–82.

Kors, Alan Charles, *Atheism in France, 1650–1729: Volume I – The Orthodox Sources of Disbelief*, Princeton, Princeton University Press, 1990.

'Skepticism and the Problem of Atheism in Early Modern France', in R. H. Popkin and A. Vanderjagt, eds., *Scepticism and Irreligion in the Seventeenth and Eighteenth Centuries*, Leiden, E. J. Brill, 1993, 185–215.

Koselleck, Reinhart, 'On the Disposability of History', *Futures Past: On the Semantics of Historical Time*, trans. Keith Tribe, Cambridge, MA and London, MIT Press, 1985, 198–212.

Krabbenhoft, Kenneth, 'Kabbalah and Expulsion: The Case of Abraham Cohen de Herrera', in Raymond B. Waddington and Arthur H. Williamson, eds., *The Expulsion of the Jews: 1492 and After*, New York and London, Garland, 1994, 127–46.

'Syncretism and Millennium in Herrera's Kabbalah', in Matt D. Goldish and Richard H. Popkin, eds., *Jewish Messianism in the Early Modern World*, Dordrecht, Kluwer, 2001, 65–76.

Krauss, Samuel and William Horbury, *The Jewish–Christian Controversy: Volume I – History*, J. C. B. Mohr, Tübingen, 1995.

Kreimendahl, Lothar, 'Das Theodizeeproblem und Bayle's fideistischer Lösungsversuch', in R. H. Popkin and A. Vanderjagt, eds., *Scepticism and Irreligion in the Seventeenth and Eighteenth Centuries*, Leiden, E. J. Brill, 1993, 267–81.

Kuhn, Thomas, *The Structure of Scientific Revolutions*, Chicago and London, Chicago University Press, 1962.

Labroue, Henri, *Voltaire antijuif*, Paris, Les Documents contemporains, 1942.

Labrousse, Elizabeth, 'Note sur la théorie de la tolérance chez Pierre Bayle', *Notes sur Bayle*, Paris, J. Vrin, 1987, 173–6.

Pierre Bayle – I: du pays de Foix à la cité d'Erasme, The Hague, Martinus Nijhoff, 1963.

Pierre Bayle – II: hétérodoxie et rigorisme, The Hague, Martinus Nijhoff, 1964.

'Reading Pierre Bayle in Paris', in Alan Charles Kors and Paul J. Korshin, eds., *Anticipations of the Enlightenment in England, France and Germany*, Philadelphia, University of Pennsylvania Press, 1987, 7–16.

Lamont, William M., *Godly Rule: Politics and Religion, 1603–60*, London, Macmillan, 1969.

Langmuir, Gavin, 'The Faith of Christians and Hostility to Jews', in *Christianity and Judaism: Papers Read at the 1991 Summer Meeting and the 1992 Winter Meeting of the Ecclesiastical History Society*, Oxford, Blackwell, 1992, 77–92.

History, Religion and Antisemitism, Berkeley, Los Angeles and Oxford, University of California Press, 1990.

Toward a Definition of Antisemitism, Berkeley, Los Angeles and Oxford, University of California Press, 1990.

Langrée, Jacqueline and Pierre-François Moreau, 'Louis Meyer et Spinoza', introduction to Lodowijk Meyer, *La Philosophie interprète de l'ecriture sainte*, Paris, Intertextes, 1988.

Laplanche, François, *La Bible en France: entre mythe et critique, XVI e–XIX e siècles*, Paris, Albin Michel, 1994.

L'Ecriture, le sacré et l'histoire: érudits et politiques protestants devant la Bible en France au XVII e siècle, Amsterdam and Maarssen, APA Holland University Press, 1986.

'L'Érudition chrétienne aux XVIe et XVIIe siècles et l'état des hébreux', in *L'Ecriture sainte au temps de Spinoza et dans le système Spinoziste*, Paris, Presses de l'Université de Paris Sorbonne, 1992, 133–47.

Laursen, John Christian, 'Baylean Liberalism: Tolerance Requires Nontolerance', in John Christian Laursen and Cary J. Nederman, eds., *Beyond the Persecuting Society: Religious Toleration Before the Enlightenment*, Philadelphia, University of Pennsylvania Press, 1998, 197–215.

'The Politics of a Publishing Event: The Marchand Millieu and *The Life and Spirit of Spinoza* of 1719', in Silvia Berti, Françoise Charles-Daubert and Richard H. Popkin, eds., *Heterodoxy, Spinozism and Free Thought in Early Eighteenth Century Europe: Studies on the 'Traité des Trois Imposteurs'*, Dordrecht, Kluwer, 1996, 273–96.

Laursen, John Christian and Cary J. Nederman, eds., *Beyond the Persecuting Society: Religious Toleration Before the Enlightenment*, Philadelphia, University of Pennsylvania Press, 1998.

Lennon, Thomas M., *Reading Bayle*, Toronto, Buffalo and London, University of Toronto Press, 1999.

Levinas, Emmanuel, 'Spinoza's Background', *Beyond the Verse: Talmudic Readings and Lectures*, trans. Gary D. Mole, London, The Athlone Press, 1994, 168–76.

'The Strings and the Wood: On the Jewish Reading of the Bible', *Outside the Subject*, trans, Michael B. Smith, London, Athlone, 1993, 126–34.

Levine, Joseph M., *The Battle of the Books: History and Literature in the Augustan Age*, Ithaca, NY and London, Cornell University Press, 1991.

Levy, David, 'Voltaire et son exégèse du Pentateuque', *SVEC* 130 (1975).

Liberles, Robert, 'From Toleration to *Verbesserung*: German and English Debates on the Jews in the Eighteenth Century', *Central European History* 21:1 (1989) 1–31.

Librett, Jeffrey S., *The Rhetoric of Cultural Dialogue: Jews and Germans from Moses Mendelssohn to Richard Wagner and Beyond*, Stanford, CA, Stanford University Press, 2000.

Liebersohn, Harry, *Aristocratic Encounters: European Travelers and North American Indians*, Cambridge, Cambridge University Press, 1998.

Ligota, C. R., 'Histoire à fondement théologique: la république des hébreux', in *L'Ecriture sainte au temps de Spinoza et dans le système Spinoziste*, Paris, Presses de l'Université de Paris Sorbonne, 1992, 149–67.

Liljegren, S. B. 'Harrington and the Jews', *Humanistiska Vetenskapssamfundets*, Lund, 1932, 65–92.

Lloyd Jones, Gareth, *The Discovery of Hebrew in Tudor England: a Third Language*, Manchester, Manchester University Press, 1983.

Loewe, Raphael, 'Hebraists, Christian', in *Encyclopaedia Judaica*, Jerusalem, Keter, 1971, vol. VIII, 10–71.

Lurbe, Pierre, 'John Toland et l'utilisation de l'histoire juive: entre l'histoire et le mythe', in Chantal Grell and François Laplanche, eds., *La République des lettres et l'histoire du judaïsme antique*, Paris, Presses de l'Université de Paris-Sorbonne, 1992, 149–62.

'Le Spinozisme de John Toland', in Olivier Bloch, ed., *Spinoza au XVIIIe siècle*, Paris, Méridiens Klincksieck, 1990, 32–47.

Lyotard, Jean-François, *Heidegger and 'the jews'*, trans. A. Michel and M. S. Roberts, Minneapolis, University of Minnesota Press, 1990.

Maccoby, Hyam, *Judaism on Trial: Jewish–Christian Disputations in the Middle Ages*, London, Littman, 1982.

A Pariah People: The Anthropology of Antisemitism, London, Constable, 1996.

Malino, Frances, *A Jew in the French Revolution: The Life of Zalkind Hourwitz*, Oxford and Cambridge, MA, Blackwell, 1996.

Mandelbrote, Scott, 'Isaac Newton and Thomas Burnet: Biblical Criticism and the Crisis of Late Seventeenth-Century England', in James E. Force and Richard H. Popkin, eds., *The Books of Nature and Scripture: Recent Essays on Natural Philosophy, Theology, and Biblical Criticism in the Netherlands of Spinoza's Time and the British Isles of Newton's Time*, Dordrecht, Kluwer Academic Publishers, 1994, 149–78.

Manuel, Frank, *The Broken Staff: Judaism Through Christian Eyes*, Cambridge, MA., Harvard University Press, 1992.

'Israel in the Christian Enlightenment', *The Changing of the Gods*, Hanover, NH and London, University Press of New England, 1983, 105–34.

Maréchal, Geraldine, 'Inleiding' to Johannes Duijkerius, *Het leven van Philopater, en Vervolg van't leven van Philopater*, 1691/1697, Rodopi, Amsterdam and Atlanta, GA, 1991, 11–38.

Marius, Richard, *Martin Luther: The Christian Between God and Death*, Cambridge, MA and London, Harvard University Press, 1999.

Markish, Shimon, *Erasmus and the Jews*, Chicago and London, University of Chicago Press, 1986.

Marshall, David, *The Surprising Effects of Sympathy: Marivaux, Diderot, Rousseau and Mary Shelley*, Chicago and London, University of Chicago Press, 1988.

Marshall, John, *John Locke: Resistance, Religion and Responsibility*, Cambridge, Cambridge University Press, 1994.

Martin, Henri-Jean, *Print, Power and People in 17th-Century France*, trans. D. Gerard, Metuchen, NJ and London, 1993.

Mason, Haydn, *Pierre Bayle and Voltaire*, Oxford, Oxford University Press, 1963. *Voltaire*, London, Hutchinson, 1975.

Matar, N. I., 'The Controversy over the Restoration of the Jews in English Protestant Thought', *Durham University Journal* 49 (1987–8) 241–56.

'John Locke and the Jews', *Journal of Ecclesiastical History* 44 (1993) 45–62.

McGinn, Bernard, 'Cabalists and Christians: Reflections on Cabala in Medieval and Renaissance Thought', in R. H. Popkin and G. M. Weiner eds., *Jewish Christians and Christian Jews: From the Renaissance to the Enlightenment*, Dordrecht, Kluwer, 1994, 11–34.

McKee, David Rice, *Simon Tyssot de Patot and the Seventeenth Century Background of Critical Deism*, Baltimore, Johns Hopkins Press, 1941.

McKenna, Anthony, *De Pascal à Voltaire*, 2 vols., Oxford, Voltaire Foundation, 1990.

'Les Manuscrits clandestins dans la bibliothèque du marquis de Méjanes', in *Treize études sur Aix et la Provence au XVIII e siècle*, Aix-en-Provence, Université de Provence, 1995, 19–40.

'Les *Pensées* de Pascal dans les manuscrits clandestins du XVIII e siècle', in Olivier Bloch, ed., *Le Matérialisme du XVIII siècle et la littérature clandestine*, Paris, J. Vrin, 1982, 131–42.

'Réflexions sur un receuil de manuscrits philosophiques clandestins', in François Moureau, ed., *De bonne main: la communication manuscrite au XVIII e siècle*, Paris, Universitas, 1993, 51–7.

'Sur l'hérésie dans la littérature clandestine', *Dix-huitième siècle* 22 (1990) 301–13.

Méchoulan, Henry, *Etre juif à Amsterdam au temps de Spinoza*, Paris, Albin Michel, 1991.

Hispanidad y Judaismo en tiempos de Espinoza: edición de 'La Certeza del Camino' de Abraham Pereyra, Salamanca, Ediciones Universidad de Salamanca, 1987.

'Menasseh ben Israel and the World of the Non-Jew', in Yosef Kaplan, Henry Méchoulan and Richard H. Popkin, eds., *Menasseh ben Israel and His World*, Leiden, E. J. Brill, 1989, 83–97.

'Morteira et Spinoza au carrefour du socinianisme', *Revue des études juives* 135 (1976) 51–65.

Meinsma, K. O., *Spinoza et son cercle: étude critique historique sur les hétérodoxes hollandais*, 1896, trans. S. Roosenburg, Paris, J. Vrin, 1983.

Melamed, Abraham, 'English Travellers and Venetian Jewish Scholars: The Case of Simone Luzzatto and James Harrington', in Gaetano Cozzi, ed., *Gli ebrei e Venezia: secoli XIV –XVIII*, Milan, Comunità, 1987, 507–26.

'Simone Luzzatto on Tacitus: Apologetica and Ragione Di Stato', in Isodore Twersky, ed., *Studies in Medieval Jewish History and Literature*, vol. II, Cambridge MA and London, Harvard University Press, 1984, 143–70.

Melnick, Ralph, *From Polemics to Apologetics: Jewish–Christian Rapprochement in Seventeenth Century Amsterdam*, Assen, Van Gorcum, 1981.

Mendes-Flohr, Paul, *Divided Passions: Jewish Intellectuals and the Experience of Modernity*, Detroit, Wayne State University Press, 1991.

German Jews: A Dual Identity, New Haven and London, Yale University Press, 1999.

Meyer, Michael A., 'The Emergence of Jewish Historiography', *Essays in Jewish Historiography* (*History and Theory* Beiheft 27), Middletown CN, Wesleyan University Press, 1988, 160–75.

Meyer, Paul H., 'The Attitude of the Enlightenment towards the Jew', *SVEC* 26 (1963) 1161–205.

Micale, Mark S., and Robert L. Dietle, eds., *Enlightenment, Passion, Modernity: Historical Essays in European Thought and Culture*, Stanford, CA, Stanford University Press, 2000.

Millner, Simon L., *The Face of Benedictus Spinoza*, New York, Machmadim Art Editions, 1946.

Moerkerken, P. H. van, *Adriaan Koerbagh (1633–1699): Een Strijder voor het Vrije Denken*, Amsterdam, Van Oorschot, 1948.

Moreau, Pierre-François, 'Spinoza's Reception and Influence', in Don Garrett, ed., *The Cambridge Companion to Spinoza*, Cambridge, Cambridge University Press, 1996, 408–34.

Morgan, Edmund S., *American Slavery, American Freedom: The Ordeal of Colonial Virginia*, New York and London, W. W. Norton, 1975.

Mosse, George L., *Confronting the Nation: Jewish and Western Nationalism*, Hanover, NH, and London, University Press of New England, 1993.

German Jews Beyond Judaism, Bloomington, IN, Indiana University Press, 1985.

Moureau, François, 'La Plume et le plomb', in François Moureau, ed., *De bonne main: la communication manuscrite au XVIII e siècle*, Paris, Universitas, 1993, 5–16.

Mowbray, Malcolm de, '*Libertas Philosophandi*. Wijsbegeerte in Groningen rond 1650', in H. A. Krop, J. A. van Ruler and A. J. Vanderjagt, eds., *Zeer kundige professoren. Beofening van de filosofie in Groningen van 1614 tot 1996*, Hilversum, 1997, 33–46.

Munck, Thomas, *The Enlightenment: A Comparative Social History 1721–1794*, London, Arnold, 2000.

Myers, David N., *Re-inventing the Jewish Past: European Jewish Intellectuals and the Zionist Return to History*, New York, Oxford University Press, 1995.

Nadler, Steven, *Spinoza: A Life*, Cambridge, Cambridge University Press, 1999.

'Spinoza in the Garden of Good and Evil', in Elmar J. Kremer and Michael J. Latzer, eds., *The Problem of Evil in Early Modern Philosophy*, Toronto, Buffalo and London, University of Toronto Press, 2001, 66–80.

Nahon, Gérard, 'Amsterdam, metropole occidentale des séfarades au XVII e siècle', *Cahiers Spinoza* 3 (1980) 15–50.

Negri, Antonio, *The Savage Anomaly: The Power of Spinoza's Metaphysics and Politics*, Minneapolis and Oxford, University of Minnesota Press, 1991.

Netanyahu, Benzion, *The Origins of the Inquisition in Fifteenth Century Spain*, New York, Random House, 1995.

Niderst, Alain, 'Fontenelle et la littérature clandestine', in Guido Canziani, ed., *Filosofia e religione nella letteratura clandestina, secoli XVII e XVIII*, Milan, FrancoAngeli, 1994, 161–73.

Nisbet, H. S., '*De Tribus Impostoribus*: On the Genesis of Lessing's *Nathan the Wise*', *Euphorion* 73 (1979) 365–87.

Niżnik, Józef and John T. Sanders, eds, *Debating the State of Philosophy: Habermas, Rorty and Kolakowski*, Westport, CT and London, Praeger, 1996.

Norris, Christopher, *Spinoza and the Origins of Modern Critical Theory*, Oxford, Basil Blackwell, 1991.

O'Cathasaigh, Sean, 'Skepticism and Belief in Pierre Bayle's *Nouvelles Lettres Critiques*', *JHI* 45 (1984) 421–33.

O'Higgins, James, *Anthony Collins: The Man and his Works*, The Hague, Martinus Nijhoff, 1970.

Offenberg, A. K., 'Jacob Jehuda Leon (1602–1675) and his Model of the Temple', in J. van den Berg and Ernestine G. E. van der Wall, eds., *Jewish–Christian Relations in the Seventeenth Century: Studies and Documents*, Kluwer, Dordrecht, 1988, 95–115.

Otto, Rüdiger, 'Johann Christian Edelmann's Criticism of the Bible and its Relation to Spinoza', in Wiep van Bunge and Wim Klever, eds., *Disguised and Overt Spinozism Around 1700*, Leiden, E. J. Brill, 1996, 171–88.

Studien zur Spinozarezeption in Deutschland im 18 Jahrhundert, Frankfurt am Main, Peter Lang, 1994.

Parkes, James, *The Conflict of the Church and the Synagogue*, London, The Soncino Press, 1934.

The Jew and his Neighbour: A Study of the Causes of Antisemitism, London, SCM Press, 1930.

Passmore, J. A., *Ralph Cudworth: An Interpretation*, Cambridge, Cambridge University Press, 1951, 79–89.

Pearson, Samuel C., Jr, 'The Religion of John Locke and the Character of his Thought', in Richard Ashcraft, ed., *John Locke: Critical Assessments*, London, Routledge, 1991, vol. II, 133–50.

Pelli, Moshe, *The Age of Haskalah: Studies in Hebrew Literature of the Enlightenment in Germany*, Leiden, E. J. Brill, 1979.

Perry, Norma, 'City Life in the 1720s: The Example of Four of Voltaire's Acquaintances', in T. D. Hemming, E. Freeman and D. Meakin, eds., *The Secular City: Studies in the Enlightenment*, Exeter, University of Exeter Press, 1994, 42–56.

Perry, Thomas W., *Public Opinion, Propaganda and Politics in Eighteenth-Century England: A Study of the Jew Bill of 1753*, Cambridge, MA, Harvard University Press, 1962.

Pflug, Günter, 'The Development of Historical Method in the Eighteenth Century', in *Enlightenment Historiography: Three German Studies* (*History and Theory* Beiheft 11), Middletown, CN, Wesleyan University Press, 1971, 1–30.

Pines, Shlomo, 'Spinoza's *Tractatus Theologico-Politicus* and the Jewish Philosophical Tradition', in Isadore Twersky and Bernard Septimus, eds., *Jewish Thought in the Seventeenth Century*, Cambridge, MA and London, Harvard University Press, 1979, 499–521.

Pitassi, Maria Cristina, *Entre croire et savoir: le probème de la méthode critique chez Jean le Clerc*, Leiden, E. J. Brill, 1987.

Pluchon, Pierre, *Nègres et juifs au xviii e siècle*, Paris, Tallandier, 1984.

Pocock, J. G. A., *The Ancient Constitution and the Feudal Law: A Study in English Historical Thought in the Seventeenth Century*, 2nd edn, Cambridge, Cambridge University Press, 1987.

    Barbarism and Religion 1: The Enlightenments of Edward Gibbon, 1734–1764, Cambridge, Cambridge University Press, 1999.

    Barbarism and Religion ii: Narratives of Civil Government, Cambridge, Cambridge University Press, 1999.

    'Historical Intoduction' to Pocock, ed., *The Political Works of James Harrington*, Cambridge, Cambridge University Press, 1977, 1–152.

    'Introduction' to James Harrington, *The Commonwealth of Oceana*, Cambridge, Cambridge University Press, 1992, vii–xxv.

    'Machiavelli, Harrington and English Political Ideologies', *Politics, Language and Time: Essays on Political Thought and History*, New York, Atheneum, 1971, 104–47.

    The Machiavellian Moment: Florentine Political Thought and the Atlantic Republican Tradition, Princeton, Princeton University Press, 1975.

    'Post-Puritan England and the Problem of the Enlightenment', in Perez Zagorin, ed., *Culture and Politics from Puritanism to the Enlightenment*, Berkeley and Los Angeles, University of California Press, 1980, 91–112.

    'Time, History and Eschatology in the Thought of Thomas Hobbes', *Politics, Language and Time: Essays on Political Thought and History*, New York, Atheneum, 1971, 148–201.

Poliakov, Léon, *The History of Anti-Semitism*, 4 vols., trans. R. Howard *et al.*, London, Routledge and Kegan Paul, 1965–85.

Pomeau, René, *Politique de Voltaire*, Paris, Armand Colin, 1963.

    La Religion de Voltaire. Paris, Nizet, 1969.

Popkin, Richard H., 'The Convertible Jew', in Paolo Cristofolini, ed., *The Spinozistic Heresy: The Debate on the Tractatus Theologico-Politicus, 1670–1677, and the Immediate Reception of Spinozism*, Amsterdam and Maarssen, APA-Holland Press, 1995, 119–22.

    'The First Published Reaction to Spinoza's *Tractatus*: Col. J. B. Stouppe, the Condé Circle, and the Rev. Jean Lebrun', in Paolo Cristofolini, ed., *The Spinozistic Heresy: The Debate on the Tractatus Theologico-Politicus, 1670–1677, and the Immediate Reception of Spinozism*, Amsterdam and Maarssen, APA-Holland Press, 1995, 6–12.

    The History of Scepticism from Erasmus to Spinoza, Berkeley and Los Angeles, University of California Press, 1979.

    'The Image of the Jew in Clandestine Literature circa 1700', in Guido Canziani, ed., *Filosofia e religione nella letteratura clandestina*, Milan, FrancoAngeli, 1994, 13–34.

'Introduction' to *Pierre Bayle – Historical and Critical Dictionary: Selections*, Indianapolis, IN, Hackett, 1991.

Isaac La Peyrère (1596–1676): His Life, Work and Influence, Leiden, E. J. Brill, 1987.

'Jacques Basnage's *Histoire des Juifs* and the Biblioteca Sarraziana', *Studia Rosenthaliana* 21 (1987) 154–62.

'Jewish Anti-Christian Arguments as a Source of Irreligion from the Seventeenth to the Early Nineteenth Century', in Michael Hunter and David Wootton, eds., *Atheism from the Reformation to the Enlightenment*, Oxford, Oxford University Press, 1992, 159–81.

'The Jews of the Netherlands in the Early Modern Period', in R. Po-Chia Hsia and Harmut Lehmann, eds., *In and Out of the Ghetto: Jewish–Gentile Relations in Late Medieval and Early Modern Europe*, Cambridge, Cambridge University Press, 1995, 311–16.

'The Marranos of Amsterdam', *The Third Force in Seventeenth-Century Thought*, Leiden, E. J. Brill, 1992, 156–78.

'Medicine, Racism, Anti-Semitism: A Dimension of Enlightenment Culture', in G. S. Rousseau, ed., *The Languages of Psyche: Mind and Body in Enlightenment Thought*, Berkeley, Los Angeles and London, University of California Press, 1990, 405–42.

'Millenarianism and Nationalism – A Case Study: Isaac La Peyrère', in John Christian Laursen and Richard H. Popkin, eds., *Continental Millenarians: Protestants, Catholics, Heretics*, Dordrecht, Kluwer, 2001, 77–84.

'The Rise and Fall of the Jewish Indian Theory', in Yosef Kaplan, Henry Méchoulan and Richard H. Popkin, eds., *Menasseh ben Israel and his World*, Leiden, E. J. Brill, 1989, 63–82.

'Some Aspects of Jewish–Christian Theological Interchanges in Holland and England, 1640–1700', in J. van den Berg and Ernestine G. E. van der Wall, eds., *Jewish–Christian Relations in the Seventeenth Century: Studies and Documents*, Dordrecht, Kluwer, 1988, 3–32.

'Spinoza and Bible Scholarship', in James E. Force and Richard H. Popkin, eds., *The Books of Nature and Scripture: Recent Essays on Natural Philosophy, Theology, and Biblical Criticism in the Netherlands of Spinoza's Time and the British Isles of Newton's Time*, Dordrecht, Kluwer Academic Publishers, 1994, 1–20.

'Spinoza and the Conversion of the Jews', in C. De Deugd, ed., *Spinoza's Political and Theological Thought*, Amsterdam, North-Holland Publishing Company, 1984, 171–83.

'Spinoza and the Three Impostors', in Edwin Curley and P-F. Moreau, eds., *Spinoza: Issues and Directions*, Leiden, E. J. Brill, 1990, 347–58.

'Spinoza and La Peyrère', *The Southwestern Journal of Philosophy* 8 (1977) 177–95.

'Spinoza and Samuel Fisher', *Philosophia* 15 (1985) 219–36.

'Spinoza, Neoplatonic Kabbalist?', in Lenn E. Goodman, ed., *Neoplatonism and Jewish Thought*, Albany, State University of New York Press, 1992, 387–409.

'Spinoza's Relations with the Quakers in Amsterdam', *Quaker History* 37 (1984) 14–28.

'Two Treasures of Marsh's Library', in Alison P. Coudert, Sarah Hutton, Richard H. Popkin and Gordon M. Weiner, eds., *Judaeo-Christian Intellectual Culture in the Seventeenth Century: A Celebration of the Library of Narcissus Marsh (1638–1713)*, Dordrecht, Kluwer, 1999, 1–12.

Popkin, Richard H., ed., *Millenarianism and Messianism in English Literature and Thought, 1650–1800*, Leiden, E. J. Brill, 1988.

Porter, Roy and Teich, Mikuláš, eds., *The Enlightenment in National Context*, Cambridge, Cambridge University Press, 1981.

Porter, Roy, *The Creation of the Modern World: The Untold Story of the British Enlightenment*, New York and London, W. W. Norton, 2000.

Pratt, Mary Louise, *Imperial Eyes: Travel Writing and Transculturation*, Routledge, London and New York, 1992.

Pulzer, Peter, *The Rise of Political Anti-Semitism in Germany and Austria*, London, Peter Halban, 1988.

Ragussis, Michael, 'Jews and Other "Outlandish Englishmen": Ethnic Performance and the Invention of British Identity under the Georges', *Critical Inquiry* 26 (2000) 773–97.

Ravid, Benjamin C. I., *Economics and Toleration in Seventeenth Century Venice: The Background and Context of the 'Discorso' of Simone Luzzatto*, Jerusalem, American Academy for Jewish Research, 1978.

Reale, Mario, 'Vico e il problema della storia ebraica in una recente interpretazione', *La cultura* 8 (1970) 81–107.

Redekop, Benjamin W., *Enlightenment and Community: Lessing, Abbt, Herder, and the Quest for a German Public*, Montreal, Kingston, London and Ithaca, McGill-Queens University Press, 2000.

Rée, Jonathan, 'Cosmopolitanism and the Experience of Nationality', in Pheng Cheah and Bruce Robbins, eds., *Cosmopolitics: Thinking and Feeling Beyond the Nation*, Minneapolis and London, University of Minnesota Press, 1998, 77–90.

Reill, Peter Hanns, *The German Enlightenment and the Rise of Historicism*, Berkeley, Los Angeles and London, University of California Press, 1975.

Rengger, N. J., *Political Theory, Modernity and Postmodernity*, Oxford, Blackwell, 1995.

Rétat, Pierre, *Le Dictionnaire de Bayle et la lutte philosophique au XVIII e siècle*, Paris, Audin, 1971.

Révah, I. S., 'La Religion d'Uriel da Costa, Marrane de Porto', *Revue de l'histoire des religions* 161 (1962), 45–76.

Spinoza et le Dr Juan de Prado, Paris and The Hague, Mouton, 1959.

Rex, Walter, *Essays on Pierre Bayle and Religious Controversy*, The Hague, Martinus Nijhoff, 1965.

Ricuperati, Giuseppe, *L'esperienza civile e religiosa di Pietro Giannone*, Milan and Naples, Riccardo Ricciardi, 1970.

'Libertismo e deismo a Vienna: Spinoza, Toland e *Il Triregno*', *Rivista storica italiana* 79 (1967) 628–95.

Robertson, Ritchie, ' "Dies Hohe Lied der Duldung"? The Ambiguities of Toleration in Lessing's *Die Juden* and *Nathan der Weise*', *Modern Language Review* 93 (1998) 105–20.

'Freedom and Pragmatism: Aspects of Religious Toleration in Eighteenth-Century Germany', *Patterns of Prejudice* 32 (1998) 69–80.

'Freud's Testament: Moses and Monotheism', in Edward Timms and Naomi Segal, eds., *Freud in Exile: Psychoanalysis and its Vicissitudes*, New Haven and London, Yale University Press, 1988, 80–9.

Rooden, Peter van, 'The Amsterdam Translation of the Mishnah', in William Horbury, ed., *Hebrew Study from Ezra to Ben-Yehuda*, Edinburgh, T.&T. Clark, 1999, 257–67.

'Constantijn l'Empereur's Contacts with the Amsterdam Jews and his Confutation of Judaism', in J. van den Berg and Ernestine G. E. van der Wall, eds., *Jewish–Christian Relations in the Seventeenth Century: Studies and Documents*, Kluwer, Dordrecht, 1988, 51–72.

'A Dutch Adaptation of Elias Montalto's *Tractado Sobre o Principio do Capitulo 53 de Jesaias*', *LIAS* 16 (1989) 189–204.

Theology, Biblical Scholarship and Rabbinical Studies in the Seventeenth Century: Constantijn l'Empereur (1591–1648), Professor of Hebrew and Theology at Leiden, Leiden, E. J. Brill, 1989.

Rooden, Peter van, and J. W. Wesselius, 'The Early Enlightenment and Judaism: the "Civil Dispute" between Philippus van Limborch and Isaac Orobio de Castro (1687)', *Studia Rosenthaliana* 21 (1987) 140–53.

Rose, Gillian, *Judaism and Modernity: Philosophical Essays*, Oxford and Cambridge, MA, Blackwell, 1993.

Rose, Paul Lawrence, *Revolutionary Antisemitism in Germany from Kant to Wagner*, Princeton, Princeton University Press, 1990.

Rosenberg, Audrey, *Tyssot de Patot and his Work, 1655–1738*, The Hague, Martinus Nijhoff, 1972.

Rossi, Paulo, *The Dark Abyss of Time: The History of the Earth and the History of Nations from Hooke to Vico*, Chicago, Chicago University Press, 1984.

Le sterminate antichità: studi vichiani, Pisa, Nistri-Lischi, 1969.

Roth, Cecil, *A History of the Marranos*, Philadelphia, Jewish Publication Society of America, 1941.

Roth, Leon, *Spinoza, Descartes and Maimonides*, Oxford, Oxford University Press, 1924.

Rubinstein, Hilary L. and William D. Rubinstein, *Philosemitism: Admiration and Support in the English-Speaking World for Jews, 1840–1939*, New York and London, Palgrave, 1999.

Ruderman, David B., *Jewish Enlightenment in an English Key: Anglo-Jewry's Construction of Modern Jewish Thought*, Princeton, NJ and Oxford, Princeton University Press, 2000.

Jewish Thought and Scientific Discovery in Early Modern Europe, New Haven and London, Yale University Press, 1995.

'Was There a "Haskalah" in England? Reconsidering an Old Question', in Shmuel Feiner and David Sorkin, eds., *New Perspectives on the Haskalah*, London and Portland, OR, 2001, 64–85.

Ruler, J. A. van, *The Crisis of Causality: Voetius and Descartes on God, Nature and Change*, Leiden, E. J. Brill, 1995.

Said, Edward, *Orientalism*, New York, Random House, 1978.

Salecker, Kurt, *Christian Knorr von Rosenroth (1632–1689)*, Leipzig, Mayer & Müller, 1931.

Salomon, H. P., 'A Copy of Uriel da Costa's *Exame das Tradições Phariseas* Located in the Royal Library of Copenhagen', *Studia Rosenthaliana* 24 (1990) 153–68.

'Saul Levi Mortera en zijn Traktaat Betreffende de Waarheid van der Wet van Mozes', Braga, Portugal, Barbosa-Xavier, 1988.

Salomon, H. P. and I. S. D. Sassoon, 'Introduction' to Uriel da Costa, *Examination of Pharisaic Traditions*, Leiden, E. J. Brill, 1993.

Saperstein, Marc, 'History as Homiletics: The Use of Historical Memory in the Sermons of Saul Levi Morteira', in Elisheva Carlebach, John M. Efron and David N. Meyers, eds., *Jewish History and Jewish Memory: Essays in Honor of Yosef Hayim Yerushalmi*, Hanover and London, Brandeis University Press, 1998, 113–33.

'Saul Levi Morteira's Treatise on the Immortality of the Soul', *Studia Rosenthaliana* 25 (1991) 131–48.

'Your Voice Like a Ram's Horn': Themes and Texts in Traditional Jewish Preaching, Cincinnati, Hebrew Union College Press, 1996.

Sartre, Jean-Paul, *Anti-Semite and Jew*, New York, Schoken Books, 1948.

Schäfer, Peter, and Joseph Dan, eds., *Gershom Scholem's 'Major Trends in Jewish Mysticism': 50 Years After*, Tübingen, J. C. B. Mohr, 1993.

Schäfer, Peter, *Judeophobia: Attitudes Toward the Jews in the Ancient World*, Cambridge, MA and London, Harvard University Press, 1997.

Schama, Simon, *The Embarrassment of Riches: An Interpretation of Dutch Culture in the Golden Age*, New York, Vintage, 1997 (1987).

Schechter, Ronald, 'Rationalizing the Enlightenment: Postmodernism and Theories of Anti-Semitism', in Daniel Gordon, ed., *Postmodernism and the Enlightenment: New Perspectives in Eighteenth-Century French Intellectual History*, New York and London, Routledge, 2001, 93–116.

Schlobach, Jochen, 'Secrètes correspondences: la fonction du secret dans les correspondences littéraires', in François Moureau, ed., *De bonne main: la communication manuscrite au XVIIIe siècle*, Paris, Universitas, 1993 29–42.

Schmidt, James, ed., *What is Enlightenment? Eighteenth-Century Answers and Twentieth-Century Questions*, Berkeley and Los Angeles, University of California Press, 1996.

Schnedermann, Georg, *Die Controverse des Ludovicus Cappelus mit den Buxtorfen über das Alter der Hebräischen Punctation*, Leipzig, 1879.

Schoeps, Hans Joachim, *Barocke Juden, Christen, Judenchristen*, Bern, Francke Verlag, 1965.

 The Jewish–Christian Argument: A History of Theologies in Conflict, trans. David Green, London, Faber and Faber, 1965.

 Philosemitismus im Barock, Tübingen, J. C. B. Mohr, 1952.

Scholem, Gershom, 'Abraham Cohen Herrera: Leben, Werk und Wirkung', in Abraham Cohen Herrera, *Sha'ar Hashamayim, oder Pforte des Himmels*, ed. and trans. Friedrich Haußermann, Frankfurt, Suhrkampf, 1974, 7–67.

 Kabbalah, Jerusalem, Keter Publishing House, 1974.

 Major Trends in Jewish Mysticism, London, Thames and Hudson, 1955.

 On Jews and Judaism in Crisis: Selected Essays, New York, Schocken Books, 1976.

 Origins of the Kabbalah, Princeton, Princeton University Press, 1987.

 Sabbatai Sevi: The Mystical Messiah (1626–1676), London, Routledge and Kegan Paul, 1973.

 'Die Wachtersche Kontroverse über den Spinozismus und ihre Folgen', in Karlfried Gründer und Wilhelm Schmidt-Biggemann, eds., *Spinoza in der Frühzeit seiner religiösen Wirkung*, Lambert Schneider, Heidelberg, 1984, 15–25.

Schröder, Winfried, 'Einleitung' to Georg Wachter, *Elucidarius Cabalisticus*, Stuttgart and Bad Cannstatt, Frommann-Holzboog, 1995, 7–29.

 'Einleitung' to Georg Wachter, *Spinozismus in Judenthumb*, Stuttgart and Bad Cannstatt, Frommann-Holzboog, 1994, 7–34.

 Spinoza in der Deutschen Aufklärung, Würzburg, Königshausen & Neumann, 1987.

 ' "... Spinozam Tota Armenta in Belgio Sequi Ducem": The Reception of the Early Dutch Spinozists in Germany', in Wiep van Bunge and Wim Klever, eds., *Disguised and Overt Spinozism Around 1700*, Leiden, E. J. Brill, 1996, 157–70.

 Ursprünge des Atheismus: Untersuchungen zur Metaphysik- und Religionskritik des 17. und 18. Jahrhunderts, Stuttgart and Bad Cannstatt, Frommann-Holzboog, 1998.

Schur, Nathan, *History of the Karaites*, Frankfurt am Main, Peter Lang, 1992.

Schwartz, Leon, *Diderot and the Jews*, London and Toronto, Associated University Presses, 1981.

Schwarzbach, B. E., and W. Fairbairn, 'History and Structure of our *Traité des Trois Imposteurs*', in Silvia Berti, Françoise Charles-Daubert and Richard H. Popkin, eds., *Heterodoxy, Spinozism and Free Thought in Early-Eighteenth-Century Europe: Studies on the 'Traité des Trois Imposteurs'*, Dordrecht, Kluwer, 1996, 75–129.

 'Sur les rapports entre les éditions du *Traité des Trois Imposteurs* et la tradition manuscrite de cette ouvrage', *Nouvelles de la république des lettres* (1987) 111–36.

Schwarzbach, Bertram Eugene, 'Voltaire et les Juifs: bilan et plaidoyer', *Studies on Voltaire and the Eighteenth Century* 358 (1998) 27–91.

 Voltaire's Old Testament Criticism, Geneva, Droz, 1971.

Schwarzfuchs, Simon, *Napoleon, the Jews and the Sanhedrin*, London, Routledge and Kegan Paul, 1979.

Scibilia, Antonello, 'Balthasar Bekker: articulazioni e limiti di una lotta', in Sergio Bertelli, ed., *Il libertinismo in Europa*, Milan and Naples, Riccardo e Ricciardi, 1980, 271–304.

Scott, Jonathan, 'The Rapture of Motion: James Harrington's Republicanism', in Nicholas Phillipson and Quentin Skinner, eds., *Political Discourse in Early Modern Britain*, Cambridge, Cambridge University Press, 1993, 139–63.

Scribano, Maria Emanuela, *Da Descartes a Spinoza: percorsi della teologia rationale nel seicento*, Milano, FrancoAngeli, 1988.

'Johannes Bredenburg (1643–1691) confutatore di Spinoza?', in Paolo Cristofolini, ed., *The Spinozistic Heresy: The Debate on the Tractatus Theologico-Politicus, 1670–1677, and the Immediate Reception of Spinozism*, Amsterdam and Maarssen, APA-Holland Press, 1995, 66–76.

Secret, François, *Le Zôhar chez les kabbalistes chrétiens de la Renaissance*, Paris, Mouton, 1958.

Segal, Lester, 'Jacques Basnage de Beauval's *Histoire des Juifs*: Christian Historiographical Perception of Jewry and Judaism on the Eve of the Enlightenment', *Hebrew Union College Annual* 54 (1983) 303–24.

Sepinwall, Alyssa Goldstein, 'Strategic Friendships: Jewish Intellectuals, the Abbé Grégoire and the French Revolution', in Ross Brann and Adam Sutcliffe, eds., *Pasts Perfect: Reconfiguring Jewish Culture c.1100–c.1850*, Philadelphia, University of Pennsylvania Press, forthcoming.

Septimus, Bernard, 'Biblical Religion and Political Rationality in Simone Luzzatto, Maimonides and Spinoza', in Isadore Twersky and Bernard Septimus, eds., *Jewish Thought in the Seventeenth Century*, Cambridge, MA and London, Harvard University Press, 1979, 399–433.

Shachar, Isaiah, 'The Emergence of the Modern Pictorial Stereotype of "The Jews" in England', in Dov Noy and Issachar Ben-Ami, eds., *Studies in the Cultural Life of the Jews in England*, Magnes Press, Jerusalem, 1975, 331–66.

Shackleton, Robert, *Montesquieu: A Critical Biography*, Oxford, Oxford University Press, 1961.

Shapin, Steven, *A Social History of Truth: Civility and Science in Seventeenth-Century England*, Chicago and London, University of Chicago Press, 1994.

Shapiro, James, *Shakespeare and the Jews*, Columbia University Press, New York, 1996.

Shmueli, Efraim, 'The Geometrical Method, Personal Caution, and the Idea of Tolerance', in R. W. Shahan and J. I. Biro, eds., *Spinoza: New Perspectives*, Norman, University of Oklahoma Press, 1978, 197–234.

Siebrand, H. J., *Spinoza and the Netherlanders: An Inquiry into the Early Reception of his Philosophy of Religion*, Assen and Wolfeboro, NH, Van Gorcum, 1988.

Silvera, Miriam, 'L'ebreo in Jacques Basnage: apologia del cristianesimo e difesa della tolleranza', *Nouvelles de la république des lettres* 1 (1987) 103–15.

'Il *Tratado de Verdade da Ley de Moisés* di Saul Levi Mortera e i "miracoli nascosti" nella natura e nella storia', in Paolo Cristofolini, ed., *The Spinozistic Heresy: The Debate on the Tractatus Theologico-Politicus, 1670–1677, and the Immediate*

Reception of Spinozism, Amsterdam and Maarssen, APA Holland University Press, 1995, 13–24.

Simon, Renée, *Henri de Boulainvilliers: historien, politique, philosophe, astrologue, 1658–1722*, Paris, 1941.

Simonutti, Luisa, *Arminianesimo e tolleranza nel seicento olandese: il carteggio Ph. van Limborch/J. le Clerc*, Florence, Olschi, 1984.

Skinner, Quentin, *The Foundations of Modern Political Thought*, 2 vols., Cambridge, Cambridge University Press, 1978.

Liberty Before Liberalism, Cambridge, Cambridge University Press, 1998.

Smith, Steven B., *Spinoza, Liberalism and the Question of Jewish Identity*, New Haven and London, Yale University Press, 1997.

Somerville, J. P., 'John Selden, The Law of Nature, and the Origins of Government', *Historical Journal* 27 (1984) 437–47.

Sorkin, David, *The Berlin Haskalah and German Religious Thought*, London and Portland, OR, Vallentine Mitchell, 2000.

'The Case for Comparison: Moses Mendelssohn and the Religious Enlightenment', *Modern Judaism* 14:2 (1994) 121–38.

'The Early Haskalah', in Shmuel Feiner and David Sorkin, eds., *New Perspectives on the Haskalah*, London and Portland, OR, Littman, 2001, 9–26.

'Jews, the Enlightenment and Religious Toleration: Some Reflections', *Leo Baeck Institute Yearbook* (1992) 3–16.

Moses Mendelssohn and the Religious Enlightenment, Berkeley and Los Angeles, University of California Press, 1996.

The Transformation of German Jewry 1780–1840, Detroit, Wayne State University Press, 1999 (1987).

Spink, J. S., *French Free-Thought from Gassendi to Voltaire*, London, The Athlone Press, 1960.

Stankiewicz, W. J., *Politics and Religion in Seventeenth-Century France*, Berkeley and Los Angeles, University of California Press, 1960.

Steinsieck, Wolf, *Die Funktion der Reise- und Briefliteratur in der Aufklärung untersucht am Beispiel der 'Lettres Chinoises' des Marquis d'Argens*, I. A. Mayer, Aachen, 1975.

Stern, Selma, *The Court Jew*, Philadelphia, Jewish Publication Society of America, 1950.

Strauss, Leo, *Persecution and the Art of Writing*, London and Chicago, University of Chicago Press, 1988 (1952).

Spinoza's Critique of Religion, trans. and ed. E. M. Sinclair, New York, Schocken Books, 1965 (1930).

Sullivan, Robert E., *John Toland and the Deist Controversy: a Study in Adaptations*, Cambridge, MA, Harvard University Press, 1982.

Sutcliffe, Adam, 'Can a Jew be a *Philosophe*? Isaac de Pinto, Voltaire and Jewish Participation in the European Enlightenment', *Jewish Social Studies* 6: 3 (2000) 31–51.

'Judaism and Jewish Arguments in the Clandestine Radical Enlightenment', in Gianni Paganini, Miguel Benítez and James Dybikowski, eds., *Scepticisme, clandestinité et libre pensée*, Paris, Champion, 2002, 97–113.

'Myth, Origins, Identity: Voltaire, the Jews and the Enlightenment Notion of Toleration', *The Eighteenth Century: Theory and Interpretation* 38 (1998) 67–87.

'Quarreling over Spinoza: Moses Mendelssohn and the Fashioning of Jewish Philosophical Heroism', in Ross Brann and Adam Sutcliffe, eds., *Pasts Perfect: Reconfiguring Jewish Culture c.1100–c.1850*, Philadelphia, University of Pennsylvania Press, forthcoming.

Swetschinski, Daniel M., *Reluctant Cosmopolitans: The Portuguese Jews of Seventeenth-Century Amsterdam*, London and Portland, OR, Littman, 2000.

Szyszman, Simon, *Le Karaïsme*, Lausanne, Editions l'âge d'homme, 1980.

Tannenbaum, Amie Godman, 'Introduction' to *Pierre Bayle's 'Philosophical Commentary': A Modern Translation and Critical Interpretation*, New York, Peter Lang, 1987.

Taylor, Charles, *Sources of the Self: The Making of Modern Identity*, Cambridge, MA, Harvard University Press, 1989.

Thomson, Ann, 'Qu'est-ce qu'un manuscrit clandestin?', in Olivier Bloch, ed., *Le Matérialisme du XVIII siècle et la littérature clandestine*, Paris, J. Vrin, 1982, 13–16.

Torrey, Norman L., *The Spirit of Voltaire*, Oxford, Marston Press, 1963.

Voltaire and the English Deists, New Haven, Yale University Press, 1930.

Trachtenberg, Joshua, *The Devil and the Jews: the Medieval Conception of the Jew and its Relation to Modern Antisemitism*, New York, Harper and Row, 1966.

Tuck, Richard, 'The Civil Religion of Thomas Hobbes', in Nicholas Phillipson and Quentin Skinner, eds., *Political Discourse in Early Modern Britain*, Cambridge, Cambridge University Press, 1993, 120–38.

Natural Rights Theories: Their Origins and Development, Cambridge, Cambridge University Press, 1979.

'Scepticism and Toleration in the Seventeenth Century', in Susan Mendus, ed., *Justifying Toleration*, Cambridge, Cambridge University Press, 1988, 21–35.

Vallée, Gérard, ed., *The Spinoza Conversations Between Lessing and Jacobi*, Lanham, MD, New York and London, 1988.

Vandenbossche, Hubert, *Adriaan Koerbagh en Spinoza*, Mededelingen vanwege het Spinozahuis 39, Leiden, E. J. Brill, 1978.

Vartanian, Aram, 'Quelques réflexions sur le concept d'âme dans la littérature clandestine', in Olivier Bloch, ed., *Le Matérialisme du XVIII siècle et la littérature clandestine*, Paris, J. Vrin, 1982, 149–63.

Venturi, Franco, *Utopia and Reform in the Enlightenment*, Cambridge, Cambridge University Press, 1971.

Verbeek, Theo, 'Les Cartésiens face à Spinoza: l'exemple de Johannes de Raey', in Paolo Cristofolini, ed., *The Spinozistic Heresy: The Debate on the Tractatus Theologico-Politicus, 1670–1677, and the Immediate Reception of Spinozism*, Amsterdam and Maarssen, APA Holland University Press, 1995, 77–88.

'Spinoza and Cartesianism', in Alison P. Coudert, Sarah Hutton, Richard H. Popkin and Gordon M. Weiner, eds., *Judaeo-Christian Intellectual Culture in the Seventeenth Century: A Celebration of the Library of Narcissus Marsh (1638–1713)*, Dordrecht, Kluwer, 1999, 173–84.

'Tradition and Novelty: Descartes and Some Cartesians', in Tom Sorell, ed., *The Rise of Modern Philosophy: The Tension between the New and Traditional Philosophies from Machiavelli to Leibniz*, Oxford, Clarendon Press, 1993, 167–96.

De Vrijheid van de Filosofie: Reflecties over een Cartesiaans Thema, Utrecht, Universiteit Utrecht Faculteit der Wijsbegeerte, 1994.

Vercruysse, Jeroom, 'Les Trois Langages du Rabbin de Woolston', in Guido Canziani, ed., *Filosofia e religione nella letteratura clandestina, secoli XVII e XVIII*, Milan, FrancoAngeli, 1994, 337–53.

Vermij, Rienk, 'Matter and Motion: Toland and Spinoza', in Wiep van Bunge and Wim Klever, eds., *Disguised and Overt Spinozism Around 1700*, Leiden, E. J. Brill, 1996, 275–88.

Vernière, Paul, *Spinoza et la pensée française avant la révolution*, Paris, Presses universitaires de France, 1954.

Vienne, Jean-Michel, 'De la Bible à la science: l'interprétation du singulier chez Locke', in Guido Canziani and Yves Charles Zarka, eds., *L'interpretazione nei secoli XVI e XVII*, Milan, FrancoAngeli, 1993, 771–88.

Vivian, Angelo, 'Biagio Ugolini et son *Thesaurus antiquitatum sacrarum*: bilan des études juives au milieu du XVIIIe siècle', in Chantal Grell and François Laplanche, eds., *La République des lettres et l'histoire du judaïsme antique, XVIe–XVIIIe siècles*, Paris, Presses de l'Université de Paris-Sorbonne, 1992, 115–45.

Volkov, Shulamit, 'Exploring the Other: The Enlightenment's Search for the Boundaries of Humanity', in Robert S. Wistrich, ed., *Demonizing the Other: Antisemitism, Racism and Xenophobia*, Amsterdam, Harwood, 1999, 148–67.

Wade, Ira O., *The Clandestine Organization and Diffusion of Philosophic Ideas in France from 1700 to 1750*, Princeton, Princeton University Press, 1938.

The Intellectual Development of Voltaire, Princeton, Princeton University Press, 1969.

The Intellectual Origins of the French Enlightenment, Princeton, Princeton University Press, 1971.

Wall, Ernestine G. E. van der, 'The Amsterdam Millenarian Petrus Serrarius (1600–1669) and the Anglo-Dutch Circle of Philo-Judaists', in J. van den Berg and Ernestine G. E. van der Wall, eds., *Jewish–Christian Relations in the Seventeenth Century: Studies and Documents*, Kluwer, Dordrecht, 1988, 73–94.

'The Dutch Hebraist Adam Boreel and the Mishnah Project', *LIAS* 16 (1989) 239–63.

'Petrus Serrarius and Menasseh ben Israel: Christian Millenarianism and Jewish Messianism in Seventeenth-Century Amsterdam', in Yosef Kaplan, Henry Méchoulan and Richard H. Popkin, eds., *Menasseh ben Israel and His World*, Leiden, E. J. Brill, 1989, 164–90.

Walther, Manfred, '*Machina Civilis oder Von Deutscher Freiheit*: Formen, Inhalte und Trägerschichten der Reaktion auf den Politiktheoretischen Gehalt von Spinoza's *Tractatus Theologico-Politicus* in Deutschland, bis 1700', in Paolo Cristofolini, ed., *The Spinozistic Heresy: The Debate on the Tractatus Theologico-Politicus, 1670–1677, and the Immediate Reception of Spinozism*, Amsterdam and Maarssen, APA-Holland Press, 1995, 184–221.

Walzer, Michael, *Exodus and Revolution*, New York, Basic Books, 1985.

On Toleration, New Haven and London, Yale University Press, 1997.

Warnock, Mary, 'The Limits of Toleration', in Susan Mendus and David Edwards, eds., *On Toleration*, Oxford, Oxford University Press, 1987, 123–39.

Weibel, Luc, *Le Savoir et le corps: essai sur P. Bayle*, Paris, Editions l'âge d'homme, 1975.

Weil, Françoise, 'La fonction du manuscrit par rapport à l'imprimé', in François Moureau, ed., *De bonne main: la communication manuscrite au XVIIIe siècle*, Paris, Universitas, 1993, 17–27.

Weinbrot, Howard D., *Britannia's Issue: The Rise of British Literature from Dryden to Ossian*, Cambridge, Cambridge University Press, 1993.

Weiner, Gordon M., 'Sephardic Philo- and Anti-Semitism in the Early Modern Era: The Jewish Adoption of Christian Attitudes', in G. M. Weiner and R. H. Popkin, eds., *Jewish Christians and Christian Jews: From the Renaissance to the Enlightenment*, Dordrecht, Kluwer, 1994, 189–209.

Whaley, Joachim, *Religious Toleration and Social Change in Hamburg, 1529–1819*, Cambridge, Cambridge University Press, 1985.

Whelan, Ruth, 'The Anatomy of Superstition: a Study of the Historical Theory and Practice of Pierre Bayle', *SVEC* 259 (1989).

Wielema, Michiel, 'Spinoza in Zeeland: The Growth and Suppression of Popular Spinozism', in Wiep van Bunge and Wim Klever, eds., *Disguised and Overt Spinozism Around 1700*, Leiden, E. J. Brill, 1996, 103–15.

Wistrich, Robert S., *Antisemitism: The Longest Hatred*, London, Methuen, 1991.

Wittmann, Reinhard, 'Was There a Reading Revolution at the End of the Eighteenth Century?', in Guglielmo Cavallo and Roger Chartier, eds., *A History of Reading in the West*, trans. Lydia G. Cochrane, Amherst, MA, University of Massachusetts Press, 1999, 284–312.

Wolf, A., 'Introduction' to Benedict de Spinoza, *Correspondence*, London, George Allen and Unwin, 1928.

Wolper, Roy S., 'Circumcision and Polemic in the Jew Bill of 1753: The Cutter Cut?', *Eighteenth-Century Life* 8 (1982) 28–36.

Wolper, Roy S., ed., *Pieces on the 'Jew Bill'*, 1753, Los Angeles, Augustan Reprint Society, 1983.

Woolf, D. R., 'Erudition and the Idea of History in Renaissance England', *Renaissance Quarterly* 40 (1987) 11–48.

Wootton, David, 'Introduction: The Republican Tradition: From Commonwealth to Common Sense', in David Wootton, ed., *Republicanism, Liberty and Commercial Society*, Stanford, CA, Stanford University Press, 1994, 1–44.

'New Histories of Atheism', in Michael Hunter and David Wootton, eds., *Atheism from the Reformation to the Enlightenment*, Oxford, Clarendon Press, 1992, 13–53.

'Pierre Bayle, libertine?', in M. A. Stewart, ed., *Studies in Seventeenth-Century European Philosophy*, Oxford, Clarendon Press, 1997, 197–226.

Worden, Blair, 'James Harrington and *The Commonwealth of Oceana, 1656*', in David Wootton, ed., *Republicanism, Liberty and Commercial Society*, Stanford, CA, Stanford University Press, 1994, 82–110.

Yaffe, Martin D., ' "The Histories and Successes of the Hebrews": The Demise of the Biblical Polity in Spinoza's *Theologico-Political Treatise*', *Jewish Political Studies Review* 7 (1995) 57–75.

Yardeni, Miriam, *Anti-Jewish Mentalities in Early Modern Europe*, Washington DC, University Press of America, 1990.

'French Calvinist Political Thought, 1534–1715', in Menna Prestwich, ed., *International Calvinism, 1534–1715*, Oxford, Clarendon Press, 1985, 315–36.

'New Concepts of Post-Commonwealth Jewish History in the Early Enlightenment: Bayle and Basnage', *European Studies Review* 7 (1977) 245–58.

Le refuge protestant, Paris, Presses universitaires de France, 1985.

'La Vision des juifs et du judaïsme dans l'oeuvre de Pierre Bayle', in M. Yardeni, ed., *Les Juifs dans l'histoire de France*, Leiden, E. J. Brill, 1980, 86–95.

Yates, Frances A., *Giordano Bruno and the Hermetic Tradition*, Chicago, University of Chicago Press, 1964.

The Rosicrucian Enlightenment, London and New York, Routledge, 1972.

Yerushalmi, Yosef Hayim, *Freud's Moses: Judaism Terminable and Interminable*, New Haven and London, Yale University Press, 1991.

From Spanish Court to Italian Ghetto – Isaac Cardoso: A Study in Seventeenth-Century Marranism and Jewish Apologetics, Seattle and London, University of Washington Press, 1981.

'The Re-Education of Marranos in the Seventeenth Century', *The Third Annual Rabbi Louis Feinberg Memorial Lecture in Judaic Studies*, Cincinnati, 1980.

Zakhor: Jewish History and Jewish Memory, Seattle and London, University of Washington Press, 1982.

Yolton, John W., *Locke and French Materialism*, Oxford, Oxford University Press, 1991.

Thinking Matter: Materialism in Eighteenth-Century Britain, Minneapolis, University of Minnesota Press, 1983.

Yosha, Nissim, 'Abraham Cohen de Herrera: An Outstanding Exponent of Prisca Theologica in Early Seventeenth-Century Amsterdam', in Jozeph Michman, ed., *Dutch Jewish History*, V, Assen and Maastricht, Van Gorcum, 1993, 117–26.

Myth and Metaphor: Abraham Cohen Herrera's Philosophic Interpretation of Lurianic Kabbalah (in Hebrew, with English summary), Jerusalem, The Magnes Press, 1994.

Young, B. W., *Religion and Enlightenment in Eighteenth-Century England: Theological Debate from Locke to Burke*, Oxford, Clarendon Press, 1998.

Yovel, Yirmiyahu, *Dark Riddle: Hegel, Nietzsche and the Jews*, University Park, PA, Pennsylvania State University Press, 1998.

Spinoza and Other Heretics – volume 1: The Marrano of Reason, Princeton, Princeton University Press, 1989.

Spinoza and Other Heretics – volume II: The Adventures of Immanence, Princeton, Princeton University Press, 1989.

Zac, Sylvain, *Spinoza et l'interprétation de l'écriture*, Paris, Presses universitaires de France, 1965.

'Spinoza et ses rapports avec Maïmonide et Mosé Mendelssohn', in Renée Bouveresse, ed., *Spinoza, science et religion: de la méthode géométrique à l'interpétation de l'écriture sainte*, Paris, Vrin, 1988, 3–9.

Zinguer, Ilana, ed., *L'Hébreu au temps de la Renaissance*, Leiden, E. J. Brill, 1992.

Ziskind, Jonathan R., 'Introduction' to John Selden, *Uxor Hebraica*, Leiden, Brill, 1991, 1–30.

Index

IDEAS IN CONTEXT

Edited by QUENTIN SKINNER (*General Editor*),
LORRAINE DASTON, DOROTHY ROSS and JAMES TULLY

Made in United States
North Haven, CT
10 May 2024

52339560R00202